ARABIA AND THE ARABS

Long before Muhammad preached the religion of Islam, the inhabitants of his native Arabia had played an important role in world history as both merchants and warriors.

Arabia and the Arabs provides the only up-to-date, one-volume survey of the region and its peoples from prehistory to the coming of Islam.

Using a wide range of sources – inscriptions, poetry, histories and archaeological evidence – Robert Hoyland explores the main cultural areas of Arabia, from ancient Sheba in the south to the deserts and oases of the north. He then examines the major themes of:

- the economy
- society
- religion
- art, architecture and artefacts
- language and literature
- Arabhood and Arabisation.

The volume is illustrated with more than fifty photographs, drawings and maps.

Robert G. Hoyland has been a research fellow of St John's College, Oxford since 1994. He is the author of *Seeing Islam As Others Saw It* and several articles on the history of the Middle East. He regularly conducts fieldwork in the region.

ARABIA AND THE ARABS

From the Bronze Age to the coming of Islam

Robert G. Hoyland

London and New York

First published 2001
by Routledge
11 New Fetter Lane, London EC4P 4EE

Simultaneously published in the USA and Canada
by Routledge
29 West 35th Street, New York, NY 10001

Routledge is an imprint of the Taylor & Francis Group

Typeset in Garamond 3 by Keystroke,
Jacaranda Lodge, Wolverhampton.
Printed and bound in Great Britain by
TJ International Ltd, Padstow, Cornwall.

British Library Cataloguing in Publication Data
A catalogue record for this book is available from the British Library.

Library of Congress Cataloging in Publication Data
Hoyland, Robert G.
Arabia and the Arabs : from the Bronze Age to the coming of Islam /
Robert G. Hoyland.
p. cm.
Includes bibliographical references and index.
1. Arabian Peninsula—History. I. Title.
DS231.H69 2001
953—dc21   2001019298

ISBN 0–415–19535–7 (pbk)
ISBN 0–415–19534–9 (hbk)

To A.F.L.B.

How many a night, mild of air and sweet in laughter
and revelry,
I have passed chatting away the dark hours
(Labid, *Mu'allaqa*, tr. A.F.L.B.,
Journal of Arabic Literature 7, 1976, 3)

CONTENTS

LIST OF PLATES

LIST OF MAPS AND
FIGURES

Maps

Figures

ACKNOWLEDGEMENTS

In writing this book I have drawn upon two main wellsprings of inspiration. The first is the fieldwork that I have undertaken over the last decade or so in the Middle East, which has led me to appreciate the topographic and cultural diversity of this ancient land. Particularly memorable have been the seasons spent in the company of the erstwhile bedouin of Homeh in the far north of the Syrian desert while participating in the Oxford–Heidelberg excavations at Andarin (directed by Drs Marlia Mango and Christine Strube). And in the summer of 1999 I was fortunate enough to be able to visit archaeological sites in Yemen, aided by Professor Dr Yusuf Abdallah, Director of Antiquities, and a grant from the Leigh Douglas Memorial Fund, and also to undertake an epigraphic survey of Jabal Says in the Syrian Harra with the help of Ms Muna Muezzin of the Damascus Museum and funding from the British Academy. The success of the latter trip was in no small measure due to my learned and amiable companions: Felix Ng (photographer), David Hopkins (archaeological illustrator) and Michael Decker (agricultural historian).

My second inspiration has been the many experts in their field who have graciously and unstintingly availed me of their time and advice. Venetia Porter, Julia Bray, Dan Potts and Walter Müller all made many suggestions and gave much needed encouragement, and Professor Müller also took the trouble to check all the south Arabian texts that I cite. Laila Nehmé, Patricia Crone and Michael Macdonald provided very thorough critiques of earlier drafts and this book, despite its many remaining failings, has been immeasurably improved by their incisive comments and great learning. Though he was no longer with us during the gestation of this work, I would also like to record my gratitude to Freddie Beeston. He lived in the flat below me at St John's in the last few months of his life and both there and at dinner we had many discussions about the history of pre-Islamic Arabia, a subject that he knew and loved so well.

But books are not written on inspiration alone. For material sustenance I have been able to count on St. John's College to furnish good company and fine food (its provision adroitly managed by Mr Tim Webber). I am also very grateful to the British Academy for supporting me financially for the past three years. Then there are the many libraries and institutions that have freely made their resources available to me, especially Oxford's Bodleian library and Oriental Institute (its smooth running ensured by the labours and charms of Ms. Eira Spinetti). For allowing me to use their illustrations I have to thank the British Museum and the Louvre (thanks particularly to John Hurst in the former and Patricia Kalensky in the latter for all their assistance), the Walters Art Gallery, the Brooklyn Museum of Art, the Bahrain National Museum, and a number of friends and colleagues, most notably Michael Macdonald, who has always responded so help- fully and stoically to my constant stream of demands. Merilyn Hodgson, president of the American Foundation for the Study of Man, which is currently excavating the Awwam temple (Mahram Bilqis) in Marib, was kind enough to let me use a number of the AFSM's photographs, including one taken by herself at the Awwam temple in spring 2000. To Drs. Sultan Muheisin, Abdarrahman al-Ansary, Fawwaz Khraysheh, and Yusuf Abdallah, the director of antiquities of Syria, Saudi Arabia, Jordan, and of Yemen respectively, I am most grateful for granting me their permission to present here a few of the treasures of their great countries. And finally I have to thank Dr. Amrita Narlikar who bore with so much love and patience the many irascible outbursts and long nights.

INTRODUCTION

Only a small proportion of the lore of the Arabs has come
down to you. Had it reached you in its entirety, much
scientific and literary knowledge would have been yours.
(Ibn Sallam al-Jumahi, *Ṭabaqât fuḥûl al-shuʿarâ'* 25, citing
the famous Muslim philologist Abu ʿAmr ibn al-ʿAla',
d. AH 154 /AD 770)

Many books are published every year in the West on Arabia and
on the Arabs, but their concern is with Islamic (and especially oil-
producing) Arabia and with the Muslim Arabs, descendants of those
who emigrated *en masse* from Arabia in the seventh century to conquer
and colonise the whole Middle East. Such books will devote at most
a few pages to Arabia and its inhabitants before this exodus, and even
then will usually only treat the lifetime of Islam's founder, the Prophet
Muhammad (*c*. AD 570–632). The many centuries of Arabian history
that precede the death of Muhammad are little studied and little
known in the West. It might be thought that this neglect reflects
Arabia's insignificance in world history before the emergence of Islam,
but this would be an unfair judgement. Though the inhabitants of
Arabia lived on the periphery of the great empires, they were of great
importance to them. Firstly their homeland occupies a central position
between India, Africa, Mesopotamia and the Mediterranean world,
which meant that people or goods passing from one to the other would
often be obliged to have dealings with them. It was, for example, only
with the help of Arab tribes that the Assyrian king Esarhaddon in 671
BC ('camels of all the kings of the Arabs I gathered and water-skins I
loaded on them', IA 112), and the Persian rulers Cambyses in 525 BC
('the Arab . . . filled skins with water and loaded all his camels with
these', Herodotus 3.9) and Artaxerxes in 343 BC were able to cross

1

north Arabia in order to march on Egypt. Secondly the existence in south Arabia of frankincense, myrrh and other aromatics – all much in demand in the civilisations of the Mediterranean and Mesopotamia – brought wealth and renown to its Arabian cultivators and expeditors. And thirdly Arabia provided a reservoir of military manpower, one experienced in travel in the desert, and they played an important role both as allies on behalf of various powers and as foes against them.

However, the would-be student of ancient Arabian history is confronted with a Herculean task. Greco-Roman authors penned a number of treatises on Arabia and matters Arab, but these are all now lost except for a few fragments and scattered citations by later writers. Muslim scholars produced numerous monographs on this theme, but they chiefly focused on tribal and prophetic traditions from the Arabia of Muhammad rather than on its more remote past. Finally modern Westerners have composed learned discourses, enthusiastic travel accounts and most recently glossy art publications, but they have very rarely attempted to produce a narrative history that would be intelligible to a non-expert audience. The only two that spring to mind are De Lacy O'Leary's *Arabia before Muhammad* (London, Trubner, 1927) and Adolf Grohmann's *Arabien* (Munich, C.H. Beck, 1963), both of which have been rendered all but obsolete by recent archaeological discoveries.[1] Certainly there are understandable reasons for this dearth, particularly the problems posed by the source material and the great diversity of the cultural traditions of the region. It is also true that a tremendous amount more spadework (literally and figuratively) needs to be done before anything like a comprehensive exposition on Arabia before Islam can be written. And yet without some accessible account of the state of the field it will always be difficult to attract students to participate in this task and to shed the image of this subject as marginal and obscure.[2] Since this will be something of a rough ride for the reader in somewhat difficult territory, it would seem wise to begin with an outline of the terrain to be covered and of the manner of proceeding.

THE LAND OF ARABIA

In our earliest sources Arabia signifies the steppe and desert wastes bordering on the territories of the states and principalities of Egypt and the Fertile Crescent. For Herodotus (d. *c.*430 BC) Arabia chiefly designates parts of eastern Egypt, Sinai and the Negev (2.8, 11–12,

75, 158; 3.5, 9), which accords with the note of Pliny the Elder
(d. AD 79) that 'beyond the Pelusiac [easternmost] mouth of the Nile
is Arabia, extending to the Red Sea' (5.65). In Persian administrative
lists, mostly from the reign of Darius (521–486 BC), a district called
Arabâya is usually included between Assyria and Egypt, which is
probably Herodotus' Arabia plus parts of the Syrian desert. The latter
corresponds to Pliny's 'Arabia of the nomads', lying to the east of the
Dead Sea (5.72). In order to seize the Persian throne from his brother,
the young Cyrus led his army of ten thousand Greeks on an epic
journey from Sardis to Babylon in 401 BC. On the way 'he marched
through Arabia, keeping the Euphrates on the right' (Xenophon,
An. 1.4.19), the reference here being to the province of Arabia in
central Mesopotamia. This is qualified by Pliny as 'the district of
Arabia called the country of the Orroei' to the east of the Euphrates
and south of the Taurus mountains (5.85).

Herodotus knew of south Arabia as well: 'Arabia is the most
distant to the south of all inhabited countries and this is the only
country which yields frankincense and myrrh' (3.107). He had little
information about it, however, and it remained for him a land of
mystery and legend, abounding with aromatics, 'vipers and winged
serpents'. This was to change after the voyage of Scylax of Caryanda
commissioned by Darius (Herodotus 4.44) and particularly after
the journeys of exploration dispatched by Alexander the Great (d. 323
BC), which made the Arabian peninsula much better known to the
outside world. Theophrastus of Eresus (d. 287), interested in botanical
matters, gives it only a passing mention (9.4.2), but Eratosthenes
of Cyrene (d. *c.*202 BC), chief librarian to the Ptolemies of Egypt,
furnishes a proper description. 'The northern side', he says, 'is formed
by the above-mentioned [Syrian] desert, the eastern by the Persian
Gulf, the western by the Arabian Gulf, and the southern by the great
sea that lies outside both gulfs' (cited in Strabo 16.3.1; cf. Pliny 6.143).

We shall likewise define Arabia in this book as the Arabian
peninsula together with its northern extension, the Syrian desert. The
borders of the latter are loosely demarcated by the 200 mm/year
rainfall line, the point at which agriculture can only be practised, if
at all, by means of various water catchment and distribution techniques (Map 1). This vast landmass amounts to almost one and a half
million square miles, slightly larger than India or Europe (West, East
and Scandinavia). It is mostly composed of a single uniform block
of ancient rocks, referred to as the Arabian shield, with an accu-
mulation of younger sedimentary rocks, particularly in the eastern
part. Accompanying this structural unity is a fairly uniform climatic

Map 1 Arabia: the peninsula and the Syrian desert (adapted by author from M.C.A. Macdonald, 'Reflections on the linguistic map of pre-Islamic Arabia', 39).

pattern: everywhere long, very hot summers; everywhere, except for the southwest (modern Yemen), receiving on average less than 200 mm (8 inches) of rainfall per year, and most parts less than 100 mm (4 inches). It may be divided into four principal geographical regions. There are the western highlands, which run the length of the Red Sea and reach as high as 3600 metres in the south. Then there is the vast interior, comprising the sandy and stony wastes of the Rub' al-Khali ('Empty Quarter') in the south, of the Nafud and Dahna deserts in the centre, and of the Hisma, Hamad and Syrian deserts in the north. The third region and the most famous in antiquity was the southwest, a land of towering mountains, beautiful coastal plains and plunging valleys, which is endowed with the double blessing of monsoon rains and aromatic plants. Lastly there are the hot and humid eastern coastlands of the Persian Gulf, the harsh climate mitigated by the existence of abundant groundwater. It is the unrelenting harshness and grandiose monotony of the Arabian landscape that has fascinated Western adventurers, and yet at the micro-level there is much variety and diversity. There are palm-laden oases, mudflats and dried salt marshes, extinct volcanoes with their expansive ebony lava beds, uplands such as those of Najd and Oman, rock formations wind-weathered into strange patterns and shapes; and when the seasonal rains arrive, they spawn unexpected water pools and pasture for sheep, goats and camels (Pls. 1a–d).

THE INHABITANTS OF ARABIA

The Greco-Roman and Persian terms for Arabia derive from the word 'Arab', which is the name of a people. 'Arabia' is thus equivalent to the Assyrian expression 'land of the Arabs' (*mât Aribi*). It must be borne in mind, however, that the Arabs did not initially inhabit all the huge territory designated as Arabia, and this landmass certainly contained many other peoples. Because of the varied topography and climate of Arabia these other peoples were often quite distinctive and had distinctive histories. The deserts of the interior, especially the Empty Quarter, to some degree isolated east Arabia and southwest Arabia from each other and from north and west Arabia, and so the populations of each region originally evolved fairly independently of each other. This became less true in the course of the first millennium BC, especially when circumnavigation of Arabia became possible and strengthening demand from the Mediterranean and Mesopotamian powers for the aromatics of south Arabia induced the latter to increase its contacts with the rest of Arabia and with the outside world. And it became even less true in the Byzantine/Sasanian period (*c.* AD 240–630) when competition between the two superpowers of the day intensified and obliged the peoples of Arabia to play a part in world politics. Thus we witness a gradual opening up of Arabia to the outside world over the course of its history and also an increase in traffic in goods and ideas within Arabia itself.

Yet, though Arabia was a country of diverse peoples and traditions, it is the Arabs whom we hear of most and who rise to increasing prominence in the course of Arabian history. They are first mentioned in Biblical and Assyrian texts of the ninth to fifth centuries BC where

(a)

(b)

Plate 1 Arabian landscapes: (a) the Harra (Jabal Says, southeast Syria, by Felix Ng); (b) the Hisma (near Ramm, southwest Jordan, by the author, 1.1.2000); (c) the Du'an valley of Hadramawt at the time of the summer rains (by the author); (d) a view over the mountains of central Oman (note water channel and terracing; from Sir Donald Hawley, *Oman and its renaissance*, London, 1977, p. 131, courtesy of Stacey International).

(c)

(d)

they appear as nomadic pastoralists inhabiting the Syrian desert. The fact that the name begins to be used by both cultures during the same period suggests that 'Arab' was how these pastoralists designated themselves. What its original significance was we do not know,[3] but it came to be synonymous with desert-dweller and a nomadic way of life in the texts of settled peoples. 'You waited by the roadside for lovers like an Arab in the desert', says the prophet Jeremiah (3.2). 'Babylon . . . will be overthrown by God,' prophesies Isaiah (13.19–20), 'never again will the Arab pitch his tent there or the shepherds make their folds.' 'Do not show to an Arab the sea or to a Sidonian the desert, for their occupations are different', opined a seventh-century BC sage (Ahiqar 110). And the Assyrian king Sargon II (721–705 BC) speaks of 'the Arabs who live far away in the desert and who know neither overseers nor officials' (AR 2.17).

Arabs do feature in one very early south Arabian inscription, most probably of the seventh/sixth century BC (RES 3945), but in general they are rarely encountered in the texts of that region until the first century BC.[4] After that date they seem to impinge ever more on the lives of the south Arabians, and it is not long before we can trace the same process taking place in east Arabia. In other words there was an inexorable Arabisation of Arabia, though at the same time the Arabs were being shaped by the cultural traditions of south and east Arabia. This gradual transformation of the originally diverse peoples of Arabia into a single ethnic group is a major aspect of the region's history.[5] It is a process comprising many strands: linguistic, literary, historical, territorial, religious and so on. And it is an issue that has implications for our own day, since, still now, converts to Islam outside the Middle East will usually adopt an Arab name, will often have a desire to learn at least some Arabic so that they can read the Arabian scripture, and will feel impelled to visit at least once in their life the Arabian homeland of their Arab prophet.

SOURCES FOR THE HISTORY OF ARABIA

Almost the only texts that the inhabitants of Arabia themselves have left us are the inscriptions that are found in their tens of thousands all over the land. Most are brief and treat only a limited range of subjects, but they are precious for being testimonies of the people themselves. From the sixth and early seventh centuries AD there is also Arabic poetry, which is invaluable for the vivid scenes it paints and for the moral world it conjures up, though inevitably, given the nature of the genre, it does not provide a sustained narrative of events. Otherwise we are forced to rely upon the observations of non-Arabian peoples, such as Assyrians, Babylonians, Israelites, Greeks, Romans and Persians. These are very useful for giving us an outsider's view, but will for that very reason be potentially biased or misinformed. Then there are the findings of archaeologists, which are very often all that we have. Until recently excavations have been few and in limited areas, but this is now changing and we can certainly look forward to many new discoveries in the future that will greatly enhance our understanding and knowledge of Arabia. However, though I have made use of the insights offered by archaeology, this book is in the end a textual history and will not give detailed discussion of archaeological sites and their material yields.

These aforementioned resources all originate in the period before Islam and on this account they will form the basis of this book. The picture they present is, however, frequently unclear and incomplete, and so we will sometimes draw upon the vast compilations of early Muslim authors on pre-Islamic history in order to elucidate and supplement this picture. But for two reasons we will not use Muslim authors as our primary resource. Firstly, as noted above, they chiefly focus on the lifetime of Muhammad (c. AD 570–632). This is because they were mostly either storytellers wishing to instruct converts in the essentials of Islam or lawyers seeking to formulate Islamic law, and in both cases the Quran and the sayings and deeds of Muhammad were their two major concerns. Secondly they entertained a certain ambivalence towards the age preceding that of the Prophet, and some early Muslim scholars would perform expiation after studying pre-Islamic poetry just as medieval Christian monks might do penance after reading the classics. To them this literature smacked of a pagan era when impetuous passions (*jahl*) were, from a pious Muslim point of view, little tempered by wise forbearance (*hilm*). As an envoy from Muhammad's Mecca said to the ruler of Ethiopia: 'Previously we were a barbarous people who worshipped idols, ate carrion and committed shameful deeds. . . . Thus we were until God sent us an apostle whose glorious lineage, truth, trustworthiness and clemency is well known to us' (Ibn Hisham 219).[6] Consequently these Muslim histories of pre-Islamic Arabia offer us a presentation of the past that reflects the changes that Islam had wrought upon Arab society. Yet plenty of nuggets of information survived these processes, especially the traditions and genealogies preserved by and reported from tribes. Thus the Tha'laba ibn Salul who is mentioned as chief of the tribe of Iyad in a south Arabian inscription of AD 360 ('Abadan 1) is also recorded some four and a half centuries later by the tribal historian Hisham al-Kalbi (1.174).

It is clear from the above list of sources that our knowledge of ancient Arabian history rests on meagre foundations. There is no Arabian Tacitus or Josephus to furnish us with a grand narrative. Rather we have to piece a picture together from a snippet of verse here, a chance comment of a foreign observer there, perhaps a hint from an inscription or an object from a datable context, and so on. This makes source criticism difficult to practise, since one will often have only one reference for a particular event or phenomenon and so lack the means properly to assess its worth, or else two or three references but of such different natures that they are almost impossible to compare. Then there is the ever-present danger of generalisation over time and place. Pre-Islamic poetry, for example, is rich in allusions to the social and moral world of its authors and their tribesfolk, but it mostly derives from north and central Arabia of the sixth century AD, and it may well therefore be wrong to use it to elucidate earlier centuries or to characterise other regions of Arabia. But if the present situation looks somewhat bleak, the future seems definitely brighter, for as modern Arabia opens its doors wider more discoveries of inscriptions and archaeological treasures are certain.

PERIOD TO BE COVERED

Though Arabia now has no lakes or rivers, this was not always the case. The deep erosion channels of the main wadi systems, as well as the enormous gravel fans associated with them, indicate tremendous surface runoff and hence, at certain times at least, a high level of rainfall. Suggestive also of a one-time relatively lush environment is the abundance of floral and faunal remains, the latter including members of the giraffe, bovine, pig, crocodile and rhinoceros families. The most recent major wet period lasted approximately from 8000 to 4000 BC and this led to an explosion in the number of late prehistoric sites, with the activities of hunting, gathering, animal husbandry and rock art all well attested in Arabia during this time. The onset of arid conditions affected the north and centre dramatically, but had far less impact on south and east Arabia, the former having monsoon rains, the latter abundant groundwater. It was therefore in the south and east that the first civilisations of Arabia emerged. Contact with Mesopotamia stimulated two closely related but distinct cultures in east Arabia in the third millennium BC. Dilmun, based on modern Bahrain and the adjacent coastland, thrived as a result of the maritime trade passing between the Middle East and Iranian and Indian ports. Magan, the ancient name for the Oman peninsula, was important for the mining and smelting of the local copper ore as well as other minerals. Since there are Mesopotamian records detailing these activities, we will begin our discussion of east Arabia from this point. For the rest of Arabia, and especially in the south, there is evidence in the Bronze Age for irrigation, animal husbandry, manufacture of practical, ornamental and ritual objects from stone, clay and bronze, erection of funerary structures and so on. It is not, however, until the late second or early first millennium BC that we have any written information, and so it is only from this time that we can begin to write its history.

METHODOLOGY

The first three chapters present an outline of the history of Arabia from the time of its first documentation in written sources (c.2500 BC in east Arabia, c.900 BC in the north and south) until the lifetime of Muhammad. Since for a large part of this period Arabia was made up of quite distinctive peoples, this will be respected in the outline, which will be structured according to the three principal cultural areas. These are east Arabia (modern Kuwait, Bahrain, Qatar, the east coast of Saudi Arabia, the Emirates and Oman), south Arabia (approximately modern Yemen) and north and central Arabia (modern Saudi Arabia minus the east coast, the Sinai and Negev deserts, and parts of modern Jordan, Syria and Iraq). However, since these three areas came to interact more and more with one another as time progressed, the following five chapters (four to eight), concerning aspects of society and culture, will proceed thematically. This has its disadvantages; in particular it will be necessary sometimes to hop abruptly between different times and places. Yet it should serve to illustrate that there were similarities between the various peoples of Arabia as well as differences. The last chapter (nine) will be devoted to a subject that has been touched upon throughout the book, but which will now be presented more coherently: the history of the most successful people of Arabia, the Arabs, and their absorption of all other groups in the region.

It is common practice in present-day documentaries to let witnesses speak for themselves rather than to deploy an omnipotent narrator, thus allowing the viewers the chance to form their own opinions. The approach strikes me as particularly well suited to the topic of this book, since the materials for pre-Islamic Arabian history are little known and often difficult to interpret. A substantial selection of these materials is therefore quoted so that readers can see for themselves on what our knowledge of this land is founded and on that basis make their own judgements. This will serve as a corrective to the speculations in which I have often been obliged to indulge in order to eke out a narrative from frequently obdurate and disparate texts, the interpretation of many of which is hotly disputed by experts. The bibliography at the end is ordered by subject in order to guide those who might feel tempted to delve further into this as yet very young field.

A note on conventions

References to primary sources are given in brief in the text and in full in the bibliography, and the secondary literature on which each section relies is wholly relegated to the corresponding section in the bibliography. Except for Arabic we do not know how ancient Arabian languages were vocalised, so I will follow standard scholarly practice in this field and only write the consonants, including the glottal stop (pronounced as in Cockney English 'bu'er' for 'butter') and also the 'ayn (like the glottal stop, but voiced further down the throat). However, for ease of reading, all proper names will be vocalised, generally on the basis of classical Arabic and, for the same reason, they will be free of diacritical marks (these will be reserved for the transliteration of certain key words). I have used translations where they exist (listed in the bibliography), though sometimes with minor modifications, and otherwise provided my own rendering.

1

EAST ARABIA

THE BRONZE AGE (c.3200–1300 BC)

The Middle East in this period was dominated by two great centres of power, namely Mesopotamia and Egypt, with the area between and around them consisting of an ever-changing array of kingdoms, city-states, tribal confederations and the like. During this time we only hear about the eastern shores of Arabia and the islands nestling close by, which benefited from proximity to and contact with the ancient civilisations of Mesopotamia in Iraq, Elam in southwest Iran and Meluhha in the Indus valley (Map 2). The northern section (modern Kuwait, Bahrain, Qatar and the adjacent coast of Saudi Arabia), known as the land of Dilmun, achieved particular prominence. The geographical position of its capital on Bahrain, as well as its abundant underground water supplies and easy anchorages for ships, made it an ideal staging post in long-distance trade and through it were channelled all manner of commodities, many of an exotic character. For this reason the land of Dilmun is often portrayed in a legendary light in Mesopotamian literature. The creation myth known as 'Enki and Ninhursag' links Dilmun to the origins of the world. It is there that the gods settled Ziusudra, the Sumerian Noah, to live for eternity after the flood had destroyed mankind. It is extolled as being 'pure' and 'pristine', where:

> the lion did not slay, the wolf was not carrying off lambs.
> . . . No eye-diseases said there: 'I am the eye disease'. No
> headache said there: 'I am the headache'. No old woman
> belonging to it said there: 'I am an old woman'; no old man
> belonging to it said there: 'I am an old man'.

13

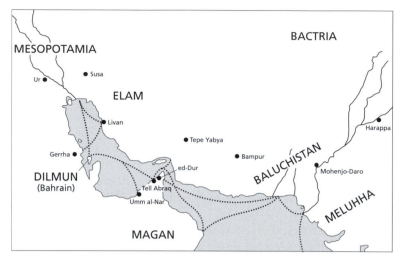

Map 2 East Arabia showing trade routes (adapted by author from D. Potts, *Ancient Magan*, 128).

It is a gift to the mother-goddess from the great god Enki, who promises her: 'fresh waters shall run out of the ground for you. . . . Your pools of salt water shall become pools of fresh water. . . . Dilmun shall become an emporium on the quay for the land' (CSL Enki 1.1.1.1–49). Also mentioned in the same myth is the southern section of east Arabia, the Oman peninsula (modern United Arab Emirates and Oman), which provided 'sissu and abba wood in large ships for you . . . strong powerful copper and various kinds of stones' (CSL Enki 1.1.1.49AP).[1]

Numerous excavations have shown that east Arabia enjoyed an economic boom in the period from 2500 to 1750 BC, and this is confirmed by literary evidence. Ur-Nanshe, king of the south Mesopotamian city-state of Lagash c.2520 BC, boasts that he had 'ships of Dilmun import timber from foreign lands' (La 1.2). And a few decades later two other kings of Lagash dispatched merchants with wool, silver, fat, salve and various milk and cereal products to exchange at Dilmun for copper. So already at this early date the Dilmunites were acting as import–export agents in international trade. Sargon (2334–2279 BC), founder of the Akkadian empire, 'moored the ships of Meluhha, Magan and Dilmun at the quay of Akkad', the north Mesopotamian capital of the Akkadians (RIM 28). And two of Sargon's successors, Manishtusu (2269–2255) and Naram-Sin (2254–2218), even deemed it worth making forays into Magan, seeking its submission: the former 'conquered their cities and struck down their rulers' and the latter 'conquered Magan and captured Manium, the ruler of Magan'. Both then 'quarried the black stone of the mountains . . . loaded it on ships and moored at the quay of Akkad' where they 'fashioned a statue . . . and dedicated it to the gods' (RIM 75–76, 97, 100, 117). Thereafter references to east Arabia in Mesopotamian texts become common, almost always on the subject of trade. Most are dry records of transactions, but by good fortune the personal correspondence of one Dilmun merchant, a certain Ea-Nasir, based in Ur, survived in the ruins of his house. He was a dealer in copper ingots from Magan and was active in business around the turn of the nineteenth century BC. He comes across as a somewhat unscrupulous character, or perhaps he just fell on hard times at one point in his career, for there are a number of angry letters from his backers in Ur while he is away in Dilmun complaining that he has not delivered the promised goods. Here is an example from one of his associates named Nanni, decrying Ea-Nasir's unbecoming conduct:

> Now when you had come you spoke saying thus: 'I will give good ingots to Gimil-Sin.' This you said to me when you had come, but you have not done it. You have offered bad ingots to my messenger, saying 'if you will take it take it, if you will not take it go away.' Who am I that you are treating me in this manner, treating me with such contempt, and that between gentlemen such as we are! I have written to you to receive my purse, but you have neglected it. Who is there among the Dilmun traders who have acted against me in this way?
>
> (UET 5.81)

Not long after the time of Ea-Nasir a combination of factors brought about the contraction of the economy of Dilmun and Magan. For reasons unknown the Indus Valley civilisation suffered a severe decline and southern Mesopotamia was adversely affected by the collapse of Hammurabi's kingdom in 1750 BC. Moreover there were now alternative sources of copper available in Anatolia and Cyprus, the latter first attested in Babylonia on a receipt dated 1745 BC for 'refined copper of Cyprus (*Alashiya*) and Dilmun'. East Arabia had thus lost its privileged position. The world of Ea-Nasir and his fellow merchants had begun to change and Dilmun would never again occupy the special place that it did for the Sumerians and their immediate successors. Now it was merely a distant province of whatever power ruled Mesopotamia.

The first such rulers were the Kassites, a people of unsure origin who assimilated to Babylonian culture and held southern Mesopotamia for some four centuries (1595–1158 BC). A few documents pertaining to their period of government in Bahrain have been found, including a stone bearing the obscure text 'palace of Rimum servant of [the deity] Inzak of Agarum' and the seal of a viceroy (*shakkanakku*) of Dilmun (Pl. 2). In addition two inscribed tablets of the Kassite period, found at Nippur in Mesopotamia, mention Dilmun. Both are from a certain Ili-ippashra, a high-ranking citizen of Nippur, who has been posted to serve as governor in Dilmun and is writing to his colleague Ililiya, perhaps governor of Nippur. He has evidently been having problems with a tribal people called the Ahlamu, who 'have carried away the dates' and who 'talk to me only of violence and plunder, of conciliation they do not talk to me'. And there is a general sense of anarchy and decay with old houses collapsing and needing repair and prophecies abounding about 'the destruction of the palace', but we can obtain no clear picture of the situation (Ni. 615, 641).

THE IRON AGE (*c.*1300–330 BC)[2]

In the early second millennium BC there was an escalation of inter-regional trade in the eastern Mediterranean and greater development of rural hinterlands by the city-states of Syria and Palestine. The resultant rise in prosperity attracted the attention of the Egyptians and the Hittites of Anatolia (in modern Turkey), both of whom intervened economically, politically and militarily in the southern and northern Levant respectively from the sixteenth century BC onwards. The intensification of competition between the two powers led to occasional armed confrontations (most famously the battle of Kadesh of 1286 BC) and increased economic exploitation. Some regional centres collapsed under the weight of imperial demands and this led to a period of international instability. But the loss of power by established centres also released dependent populations and allowed new configurations of economic activity, such as opportunistic trading (in contrast to the previous command-led style) by interstitial and peripheral groups, especially in small boats by coastal peoples and on camels by steppe peoples.

This already volatile situation was compounded by two further stimuli to flux and change, namely the spread of iron at the expense of bronze and the emergence of consonantal alphabets, which competed with the cumbersome and complex syllabic/pictorial writing

Plate 2 Kassite cylinder seal from Bahrain (with seal impression)
belonging to Ubalisu-Marduk, son of Arad-Ea, who bears the title 'viceroy
of Dilmun', *c*.15th century BC, length 4.2 cm (British Museum 122696).

systems of Egypt and Mesopotamia. Both items had been in existence much earlier, but only began to make gains towards the end of the second millennium. Both are seen as having a decentralising influence upon political and economic power. Iron, unlike copper or tin (from which bronze is made), is found practically everywhere on the globe, and so its mining could not practically be controlled by ruling elites as copper had been. And consonantal alphabets, unlike syllabic/ pictorial systems, do not require a lengthy training, and so literacy could escape the control of the state and become much more pervasive. The new scripts were particularly advantageous to merchants who could now make deals and contracts with greater ease, and it is perhaps no accident that the alphabets emanated from such trading centres as Palestine and Phoenicia.

The exact nature and significance of this transition from the late Bronze Age to the early Iron Age is still much disputed, but it is certainly true that the geopolitical scene in the Middle East was drastically altered during this time. The Hittite kingdom had disappeared completely by 1150 BC; Egypt contracted, losing control of Palestine, Sinai and Nubia. Several cities in the Levant, most noticeably Ugarit and Emar, were destroyed and their sites not reoccupied. By 1050 Assyria had lost control of its territories in Upper Mesopotamia. Historical sources become scarce, and when the picture clears again in the mid-tenth century the political landscape looks very different. In particular the old palace-centred city-states have been replaced by a number of tribal kingdoms drawn from the aforementioned interstitial and peripheral groups (Aramaeans,[3] Israelites, Ammonites, Moabites and Edomites) and commercial and manufacturing coastal colonies (Philistines and Phoenicians). It is also at the end of this tumultuous period that Arabs begin to crop up in our sources and states emerge in south Arabia.

Egypt never fully recovered its former greatness, and for the next six hundred years the balance of power shifted eastwards, to the land of the Assyrians. This people began as traders, operating out of their city of Assur in the north of modern Iraq. Then in the fourteenth century BC they embarked upon an aggressive policy of expansion which lasted, bar a few interruptions (especially that of the Aramaean incursions c.1100–930 BC), nearly 800 years. They extended westwards towards the Mediterranean and frequently threatened Egypt. By virtue of their defeat of the Kassites they became sovereigns of Dilmun, and the Assyrian king Tukulti-Ninurta I (1243–1207) accordingly took the title 'king of Dilmun and Meluhha'. This may not have reflected any real involvement in east Arabian affairs, however, since we find no other mention of Dilmun in Assyrian sources until much later. It reappears in the context of the campaign of Sargon II (721–705 BC) against the Babylonian monarch Merodach-Baladan. The victory of Sargon had many hastening to pay him homage: 'Uperi, king of Dilmun, who lives, like a fish, thirty double-hours away in the midst of the sea of the rising sun, heard of my lordly might and brought his gifts'. Similarly in the wake of Sennacherib's sack of the city of Babylon in 687 'the Dilmunites saw it and terror of the splendour of Assur fell upon them, and they brought their audience-gift'. And in the royal inscriptions of Assurbanipal (668–627) it is recorded that 'Hundaru, the king of Dilmun . . . with his rich tribute to Nineveh yearly without ceasing he came and besought my lordship'. Of Magan we learn nothing from Assyrian sources except that tribute was sent to Assurbanipal in 640 BC by a certain 'Pade, king of the land of Qade, who dwelt in the city of Iske', usually identified with modern Izki in the interior of Oman.[4]

Assyria fell to the combined forces of the Medes and Babylonians by 609 BC to the discontent of few ('Nineveh has been ruined; who will mourn for her?', Nahum 3.7). These two peoples held on to the Assyrian territories for a time, but were themselves swept away by the Persians coming from southwest Iran. Cyrus the Great conquered the Medes in 549, and in 539 Babylon submitted. At its height the empire he founded comprised parts of India and Egypt and all the land in between. The empire was Persian-led in its highest offices, loyal to the one great king, the governor on earth of the Persian god Ahuramazda, but it sat loosely on top of the cosmopolitan Middle East, respecting the traditions of the conquered peoples and taking from them whatever seemed useful. Aramaic became the lingua franca of the empire, the Phoenician navy was adopted whole, roads were built on the Assyrian pattern and coinage was based on that of Greece and Asia Minor. Their two centuries or so of rule (550–334) were therefore remembered by their subjects and neighbouring peoples as a time of tolerance and peace.

Babylonian influence in the Gulf is attested by a text dated to the eleventh year of the reign of Nabonidus (554 BC) which makes mention of the brother of an 'administrator of Dilmun', perhaps entrusted with the promotion or safeguarding of trade between Dilmun and Babylonia. And on the island of Ikaros (modern Failaka, off the coast of Kuwait) a large slab of dressed stone has been discovered engraved with the words 'palace of Nebuchadnezzar, king of Babylon'. Of the Persians' role in this region, however, we know very little. Their lists of subject provinces and peoples offer two possibilities, Arabia and

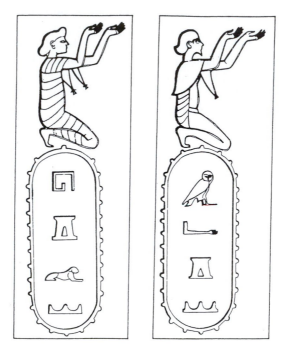

Fig. 1 Representation of an Arab (left, designated *Hagor*, the Arabs
of northwest Arabia in demotic Egyptian – confirmed to me by
Prof. J. Baines) and a Macian (right, designated *Maka*) from a statue of
Darius found in Susa, but made in and intended for Egypt (from Roaf,
'The subject peoples on the statue of Darius', 135, 144). As with other
Persian representations (see Schmidt, *Persepolis III*, figs. 47, 50), the Arab
wears a long gown and the Macian a short tunic.

Maka, whose inhabitants are represented very differently (Fig. 1). The
first probably refers only to the Sinai–Syrian desert region, the inhabitants of which had helped Cambyses attack Egypt in 525, and so 'did
not yield the obedience of slaves to the Persians, but were united
to them by friendship' (Herodotus 3.88). Perhaps for this reason
the Arab throne-bearer in one of the Persian royal tomb reliefs is
honoured, along with the Scythian, by a golden neck-chain. The
second possibility, the Macians and their country of Maka, is a more
likely contender for east Arabia. It is glossed in one list with the phrase
'the lands that are beyond the sea' (Persepolis E) and is described
by classical writers (Arrian, *Ind.* 32.7; Strabo 16.3.2; Pliny 6.98;
Ammianus 23.6.10) as the headland on the Arabian side of the straits
of Hormuz.

THE GRECO-ROMAN/PARTHIAN
PERIOD (*c*.330 BC–AD 240)

In this period the balance of power in the Middle East initially shifted westwards, the Persian empire being swept away by the conquests of the violent, drunken, emotionally unstable but brilliant Alexander, who is usually dubbed 'the Great'. With a mixed force of Macedonian and Greek soldiers, probably some 50,000 strong, he crossed the Hellespont in 334 BC, proceeded to take all the lands held by the Persians and even probed into India. He assumed eastern titles, gave Persians and Macedonians and Greeks equal rights, and maintained the Persian system of satrapies (territories over which a person called a satrap was given military and civil command by the Great King), thus securing the loyalty of the Persian nobility. But he imported Greek elements too: a smaller and more disciplined army, a unified fiscal system and monetary economy based on the Athenian silver coin, and the Greek language. The union of Greece and Persia was symbolised by a mass wedding ceremony when Alexander and 10,000 of his troops took Persian wives. No succession arrangements had been made with the result that after his death in Babylon in 323 his generals proceeded to carve out for themselves as much territory as they could. In 281, after many wars, three principal monarchies were secured: the Antigonid dynasty in Macedonia, the Seleucids in Asia Minor and the Middle East, and the Ptolemies in Egypt. They were loose Persian-style states, though the Greek rulers promoted Greek elites, institutions and thought, which blended with local traditions to produce what we call Hellenistic cultures. In the course of the second century BC the Seleucids were squeezed on both sides, by the Romans to the west and by the Parthians arriving from northeast Iran. By 140 BC the latter had made themselves masters of Babylonia. The Romans mainly contented themselves with destabilising tactics, supporting rival pretenders to the Seleucid throne and promoting secessionist regimes such as the Maccabaeans in Judaea. Only in 63 BC did they finally oust the Seleucid dynasty, annexing the latter's last stronghold, Syria, as a Roman province. Thereafter the Middle East returned to polarised politics, with Rome and Parthia eyeing each other warily across the Syrian desert for the next few centuries and neighbouring peoples often being forced to take sides:

> The Euphrates and the land beyond it constitute the boundary of the Parthian empire. But the parts this side of the river are held by the Romans and the chieftains (*phylarchs*) of the

21

Arabs as far as Babylonia, some of these chieftains preferring to give ear to the Parthians and others to the Romans.

(Strabo, 16.1.28)

East Arabia enjoyed something of an upturn in its fortunes in this period, the result of an increase in trade through the Gulf and in contacts with south Arabia and the Nabataeans. And we know from numismatic evidence that it supported a monarchy for a time, its seat being in the region of the modern Arab Emirates (Pl. 3).[5] At the outset, however, it only narrowly escaped being invaded by Alexander. Having returned safely to Babylon after a successful conclusion of his Indian campaign, he turned his attention to the Arabian peninsula:

Alexander was planning to colonise the coast along the Persian Gulf and the islands there, as he thought that it would become just as prosperous a country as Phoenicia. His naval preparations were directed at the greater number of the Arabs on the pretext that they alone of the barbarians in these parts had sent no envoys and had taken no other action reasonable or honorific to him. The truth in my own belief is that Alexander was always insatiate in winning possessions. . . . The prosperity of the country was also an incitement, since he heard that cassia grew in their marshes, that the trees produced myrrh and frankincense, that cinnamon was cut from the bushes and that spikenard grew self-sown in their meadows.

Plate 3 Silver coin from east Arabia, modelled on the Alexandrian tetradrachm: head of Heracles wearing the pelt of the Nemean lion on the obverse and modified Zeus figure on the reverse (see chapter 7 below); 'Abi'el daughter of . . . ' is written in Aramaic letters in place of the name of Alexander (British Museum 314284).

Then there was also the size of their territory, since he was informed that the seacoast of Arabia was nearly as long as that of India, and that there were many islands off-shore and harbours everywhere in the country, enough to give anchorages for his fleet and to permit cities to be built on them, which were likely to prosper.

(Arrian, *An.* 7.19–20)

Although he died before he was able to initiate any conquest or colonisation of Arabia, Alexander did dispatch three intelligence-gathering missions, which greatly enhanced contemporary knowledge of the Persian Gulf region:

He was informed of two islands out at sea near the mouth of the Euphrates. The first [Ikaros, modern Failaka] was not far from its outlet, about twelve miles from the shore and the river mouth. This one is smaller, thickly wooded with every kind of tree; it also contained a shrine of Artemis and the island's inhabitants spent their lives around the shrine. It pastured wild goats and deer, which were consecrated to Artemis and could range free, and no one was allowed to hunt them unless he desired to sacrifice one to the goddess; only on this condition was hunting not forbidden. . . . The other island was said to be about a day and night's sail distant from the mouth of the Euphrates for a ship running before the wind. It was called Tylos [ancient Dilmun, modern Bahrain] and was large and neither rough nor wooded for the most part, but of a kind to bear cultivated crops and all things in due season.

(Arrian, *An.* 7.20).

Alexander's Seleucid successors also took an interest in eastern Arabia. They stationed a small garrison for a time on the island of Ikaros. And Ikadion, a high-up official close to Seleucus II (246–226 BC) wrote a letter to its inhabitants and their representative about the transfer of a local sanctuary and reported that 'the king is concerned about the island of Ikaros'. In addition, according to Pliny (6.147), 'the coast from Charax onwards was explored for king [Antiochus] Epiphanes [175–164 BC]'. But, like Alexander before them, they established no permanent presence, and while the peoples and polities of the Gulf were in touch with the Greek world, exchanging goods and ideas, they nevertheless remained outside its boundaries.

What attracted the attention of Alexander and the Seleucids in the Gulf was the trade in luxury products. Without question the single most important trading entity in this region in Hellenistic times, functioning as a supplier of Arabian aromatics and goods from India, was the northeast Arabian city known to Greek authors as Gerrha, 'which measures five miles round and has towers made of squared blocks of salt' (Pliny 6.148):[6]

> After sailing along the [east] coast of Arabia [from the outlet of the Euphrates] for a distance of 2400 stadia [c.380 km] one comes to Gerrha, a city situated on a deep gulf. It is inhabited by Chaldaeans, exiles from Babylon. The soil contains salt and the people live in houses made of salt; and since flakes of salt continually scale off, owing to the scorching heat of the rays of the sun, and fall away, the people frequently sprinkle the houses with water and thus keep the walls firm. The city is 200 stadia [c.32 km] distant from the sea; and the Gerrhaeans traffic by land, for the most part, in the Arabian merchandise and aromatics. However Aristobulus says, on the contrary, that the Gerrhaeans import most of their cargoes on rafts to Babylonia, and thence sail up the Euphrates with them, and then convey them by land to all parts of the country.
>
> (Strabo 16.3.3, citing Eratosthenes and Aristobulus)

From this account it would seem that there was both a port of Gerrha ('situated on a deep gulf') and an inland town of Gerrha ('200 stadia distant from the sea'). Strabo's notice informs us that at some point there was a shift in the trajectory of Gerrha's foreign trade. In the lifetime of Aristobulus, who had participated in Alexander's campaigns, Gerrha shipped merchandise to Babylonia by sea. This is confirmed by a notice that the ships of Alexander 'anchored in the mouth of the Euphrates near a village of Babylonia called Diridotis; here the merchants gather together frankincense from the land of Gerrha and all the other sweet-smelling spices which Arabia produces' (Arrian, *Ind.* 41). But in the course of the third century, as is related by the great Greek scholar Eratosthenes of Cyrene, Gerrha began to export its goods by land. This probably meant towards Egypt and Syria, and certainly we hear of Gerrhaean incense in the Mediterranean world at that time. It was used, for example, as an ingredient in an antidote to poison in Greece (Nicander 100) and featured as an essential item on the shopping lists of the Egyptian elite (e.g. *Zenon papyri*

59536, dated 261 BC). The presence of individual Gerrhaeans in the west is also recorded, such as Taymallat of Gerrha, who made several offerings at shrines on the island of Delos in the Aegean (Delos 1439, 1442, 1444, 1449–50).

In 205 BC the Seleucid king Antiochus III sailed to Gerrha:

> The Gerrhaeans begged the king not to abolish the gifts the gods had bestowed on them, perpetual peace and freedom. The king, when the letter had been interpreted to him, said that he granted their request. . . . When their freedom had been established, the Gerrhaeans passed a decree honouring Antiochus with the gift of five hundred talents of silver, a thousand talents of frankincense, and two hundred talents of the so-called myrrh-oil.
>
> (Polybius 13.9.4–5)

His aim was probably to persuade its inhabitants, by show of force, to direct more of their trade towards Babylonia so that tax revenues would go to his realm rather than to his enemies, the Ptolemies, who held Palestine and Syria at that time. Following the Seleucid victory over their rivals in 200 BC, however, these provinces became a Seleucid domain, and the Gerrhaeans could resume trade with the Mediterranean via the more direct route up the Wadi Sirhan rather than via the Euphrates. According to Agatharchides (c.200–131 BC), author of a five-volume study of the Red Sea, they also seem to have begun trading with the Nabataeans. To Petra and Palestine, he reports, 'the Gerrhaeans, Minaeans and all the Arabs who live in the region convey, so it is said, incense from the highlands and cargoes of aromatic products' (in Photius 250). Presumably the Gerrhaeans were transporting Indian commodities to Petra, for south Arabian goods would have been conveyed along the west Arabian route or via the Red Sea. Later again, in the first century BC and first century AD, the Gerrhaeans supplied the Parthian empire:

> For these trades [with Iran] they [the Arabs] have opened up the city of Gerrha,[7] which is the market town of these parts. From Gerrha everybody used formerly to go on to Gabba, a journey of twenty days, and to Syria–Palestine. Afterwards, according to Juba, they began to make for the Characene and the Parthian kingdoms for the sake of the perfume trade.
>
> (Pliny 12.80)

Thereafter Gerrha's fortunes seem to decline, possibly because of Characene and Parthian usurpation of the Gulf trade route between India and the west. Certainly the presence of these two powers in the region is well attested. Coins of the little kingdom of Characene in southern Babylonia have been found at the extensive site of ed-Dur on the coast of the Emirates. In AD 131 Palmyrene merchants based in Characene commissioned the erection of a statue at Palmyra in honour of Iarhai son of Nebozabad, who is said to have served as governor of the inhabitants of Tylos (Bahrain) for the king of Characene (PAT 1374). And a first-century AD maritime manual states that after the Kuria Muria islands (off the coast of modern southeast Oman) 'stretches another country, inhabited by an indigenous people, which is no longer in the same kingdom [of south Arabia], but already in that of Persia' (*Periplus* 33), though this probably meant no more than that the principal ports of eastern Arabia were under the control of Parthia.

At about the same time as inland centres such as Gerrha decline we witness the encroachment of Arab tribes. This change is most clearly witnessed in the considerable difference in the names given to peoples of this region by Strabo and Pliny on the one hand (who completed their works in AD 23 and 77 respectively) and Ptolemy on the other (who completed his work *c.* AD 150). In the latter's account (6.7) many of the names are familiar to us from later Arabian history. In the 'Thanuitae', for example, we can recognise Tanukh,[8] an Arab tribal confederation said by Muslim sources to have left the Tihama and Najd and to have settled in northeast Arabia. Here they were joined by Ptolemy's 'Abucaei' and 'Ioleisitai', namely 'Abd al-Qays and the Banu 'Ulays. Migrations of Arabs to this region are also recorded by Muslim sources, though often recounted in terms of the heroic actions of individual leaders. 'Mazun son of al-Azd', for example, 'dispatched his brother Nasr son of the [tribe of] al-Azd to Shihr [in southeast Yemen] with horses and many men. . . . He marched to Shihr and then settled in it, and its people paid allegiance and their dues to him' (Asma'i 67). These movements, attributed by Muslim writers to a breaching of the Marib dam, must have occurred after Pliny and before Ptolemy, so in the late first or early second century AD (see chapter 9 below).

THE BYZANTINE/SASANIAN PERIOD
(*c*.240–630 AD)

Again we enter upon a period in which the Middle East underwent much transformation. The loose-knit territorial empires of the Romans and Parthians gave way to the integrated ecumenical empires of the Byzantines and Sasanians (an Iranian dynasty). Their close proximity, the result of Rome's shift to the east in the second century and the assertiveness of the Sasanians, compared to their complacent predecessors, led to confrontation. Inevitably such emulation between states of similar standing engendered large-scale political, social and cultural change. Both moved towards greater administrative centralisation and absolutist government, to the detriment of civic autonomy in the west and of the provincial nobility in the east. Byzantium would seem to have had the upper hand initially, at least in terms of wealth and centralisation, and so the Sasanian emperors embarked upon a vigorous campaign of Byzantinisation, actively setting out to acquire the money, skills and ideas of their rival. This they did by extortion as much as by imitation, using their formidable military capacity, or the threat of it, to extract material, human and intellectual resources. Furthermore both empires engaged in a scramble for influence, striving to win peripheral peoples over to their side. Thus the peoples of Ethiopia and Arabia were both actively courted for their allegiance and support. They benefited from this in that they could extract subsidies and power, but only at the price of compromising their independence and freedom of action. Finally, the ruling elites no longer remained indifferent to the beliefs of the masses. Indeed the emperors of both realms, now sharing their creed with the majority of their subjects, evinced an interest in the promotion of religious uniformity within their lands, achieving this via a hierarchically organised clergy. As religion and politics became ever more closely related, warfare assumed an increasingly religious character and religious difference frequently became equated with political dissidence, the result being persecutions. On the Arabian stage this was played out most dramatically in the south when a pro-Byzantine ruler of Ethiopia invaded Yemen to aid Christians suffering under a Jewish king and installed on the throne a Christian monarch (see chapter 2 below).

In east Arabia the Sasanians moved quickly to establish their sovereignty. No sooner had he wrested control of the principal regions from Parthian control than Ardashir (AD 224–42), the first Sasanian ruler, 'marched forward to Oman and Bahrain and Yamama. And

Sanatruq, the king of Bahrain, came forth against him and fought him, but Ardashir killed him and ordered his city to be destroyed' (Dinawari 44). This foray and the removal of Sanatruq, whose name suggests he was a Parthian, marked the beginning of roughly four centuries of Sasanian domination in the area. Its formal inauguration is recorded on the great inscription of Shapur I (AD 242–70) at Naqsh-i Rustam, in which he states that 'I rule over the following countries: Persia, Parthia . . . Arabia . . . and, on the other side of the sea [to Iran], Mazun [Oman].' As yet not many archaeological remains from the Sasanian period have been discovered, but a fourth-century source paints a prosperous scene: 'all along the coasts is a throng of cities and villages, and many ships sail to and fro' (Ammianus 23.6.10). Probably their rule was for the most part exercised through alliances with various Arab tribes and otherwise confined to a few key coastal sites such as Bahrain and Sohar. Thus a Muslim source maintains that before Islam the Sasanians were 'on the shores and strands of the sea' whereas the Arab tribes were in the mountains and deserts (Awtabi 271r). The primary aim of the Sasanians was evidently to control traffic through the Gulf, but they could exert their authority over the interior if need be. This is demonstrated by the campaign of Shapur II (AD 309–79), which he led in response to the incursions of indigent Arabs from eastern Arabia into southern Iran:

> He crossed the sea at the head of his troops and reached Khatt [in the present-day Emirates]. He marched through the land of Bahrain, killing its people, not letting himself be bought off by any kind of payment and not turning aside to take plunder. He went back on his tracks and reached Hajar, where there were nomads from the tribes of Tamim, Bakr ibn Wa'il and 'Abd al-Qays. He spread general slaughter among them and shed so much of their blood that it flowed like a torrent swollen by a rainstorm. Those who were able to flee realised that no cave in a mountain nor any island in the sea was going to save them. After this he turned aside to the lands of 'Abd al-Qays and destroyed all the people there except for those who fled into the desert sands. He passed on to Yamama where he made general slaughter like that of the previous occasion. He did not pass by any of the local Arabs' springs of water without blocking them up, nor any of their cisterns without filling them in.
>
> (Tabari 1.839)

At a later date the Sasanians tightened their hold on their Arabian possessions. In particular emperor Khosro I (AD 531–79) implemented a reorganisation of the realm and established more direct control from the centre, a move prompted by the escalation of the superpower struggle in the sixth century. Thus it is from his time that we begin to hear of centrally appointed governors in Arabia, some dispatched to areas where there had previously been no concrete Iranian presence. The renowned Arab poet Tarafa ibn al-'Abd (d. c.560s) is said to have died at the hands of the governor of Bahrain, and the existence of such an office is indicated in a number of anecdotes, such as the following:

> Once wealth and valuable specialities of Yemen were dispatched to Khosro. . . . Yarbu' [a subgroup of the tribe of Tamim] plundered the caravan. . . . The people of the caravan then went to Hawda ibn 'Ali al-Hanafi in Yamama, who provided them with clothing, food supplies, and mounts, and personally accompanied them until reaching Khosro's presence. . . . Khosro resolved to send a force of cavalry against Tamim. He was informed however that 'their land is a bad land, made up of deserts and wastes with tracks that cannot be followed. Their water comes from wells, and one cannot be sure that they will not block them up with the result that your troops will perish.' He was advised to write to his governor in Bahrain, Azadhfiruz son of Gushnas, whom the Arabs called 'the mutilator', because he used to cut off hands and feet [to punish criminals]. . . . Khosro followed this advice and sent an envoy to him, and told Hawda: 'Travel back with this envoy of mine and secure a satisfactory solution for both myself and yourself.' . . . Meanwhile Tamim had moved to Hajar in order to get provisions and gleanings. The governor's herald proclaimed: 'Let those of Tamim who are here come forward, for the ruler has decreed that provisions and food should be made available for them and divided out among them.' They came forward and he led them into Mushaqqar, which is a fortified place facing another fortress called Safa. . . . Once the governor had got Tamim within Mushaqqar, he massacred their menfolk and spared only the boys.
>
> (Tabari 1.984–86)

In southeast Arabia, as well as recognising a paramount clan among the Azd and according them the title of Julanda, the Sasanians installed a governor with military backing (Awtabi 271r). Later in the sixth century a similar system was implemented in Yemen. And at Hira in lower Iraq the Nasrids, the long-time allies of Iran, were cast off and replaced by the tribe of Tayyi' to whom was assigned a Persian commander by the name of Nakhirjan (Tabari 1.1038). This action would seem to have provoked some consternation among certain Arab tribes:

> When Khosro II [591–628] deceitfully poisoned Nu'man ibn Mundhir [d. c.602], king of the Arabs, and his son, the Arabs in the empires of the Persians and Romans broke off allegiance and dispersed, each acting according to their own whim. . . . So they became strong and caused much mischief in the provinces, and thus they remained until the emergence of the Muslim lawgiver.
>
> (*Chron. Siirt* 13.539–40)

And there were a number of confrontations between tribes allied to the Iranians and others hostile to them, some involving Iranian troops. The most famous such incident took place in southern Iraq at Dhu Qar in the first decade of the seventh century. Muslim storytellers singled it out as 'the first encounter in which the Arabs got even with the non-Arabs' (Tabari 1.1016) and fashioned it into a historical romance packed with stirring rhetoric and dramatic battle scenes.

The Sasanian period was also marked by the introduction and expansion of Christianity in east Arabia. From the biography of a monk named Jonah we learn that in the region of Qatar there existed a monastery in the 340s AD. Around 390 a certain 'Abdisho' left southern Iraq for 'an island of Yamama and Bahrain', where 'he lived an ascetic life, baptised its inhabitants and built a monastery' (*Chron. Siirt* 5.310). In the year 410 Batai, bishop of Mashmahig (modern Muharraq island next to Bahrain), was excommunicated and replaced by a certain Elias (*Synod Or.* 34, 36). And the acts of a synod of 424 record a John, bishop of Mazun (Oman), in attendance (*Synod Or.* 43). Though as yet scanty, there is also archaeological evidence for Christianity in this region. This consists of two monasteries on islands off the coast of Abu Dhabi, the remains of churches on the island of Failaka and at Jubayl and Thaj in northeast Arabia, sundry crosses and possibly a cemetery at Hinna near Thaj (six stones found bearing crosses).

Besides these brief isolated references we hear nothing about the activities of east Arabian Christians in the fourth to sixth centuries.

However, they suddenly come into the limelight in the early seventh century when they threw their lot in with the Christians of southwest Iran and attempted to secede from Iraqi control. The Iranian and Arabian Christian communities had always been reluctant to submit to Seleucia–Ctesiphon, where the head of the eastern church resided, but the arrival of the Muslims gave them the chance of winning outside backing. This drew an angry response from Isho'yahb III, the eastern prelate in the 640s and 650s, which he voiced in a letter to the Christians of Qatar:

> Not satisfied with their wickedness against the church of God, your so-called bishops extended the demonstration of their rebellion to the rulers there and to the chief ruler who is above the rulers of this time. They rose up against the primacy of the church of God, and they have now been scorned by the rulers as befits their insubordination.
>
> *(Epistulae* 266)[9]

He then appeals to the priests and deacons of Qatar to cast off their unruly bishops and to send to him persons more worthy of the episcopal office:

> You, my faithful, in whose salutary power are the islands and desert dwellers (*yotbay madbro*) – namely those of Dirin [modern Tarut], Mashmahig, Tilun [Dilmun/Bahrain], Khatt and Hajar – should be diligent now more than ever before in the assistance of your faith and in the lawful establishment of the priesthood that sanctifies you even more than in attending to worldly affairs. So pick out and send to us either those fallen bishops who are in your mind suitable once more to be restored to sacerdotal service, or others considered by you more suitable than them for the great task of the exalted service of God's church, so that thus they might be anointed, consecrated and perfected.
>
> *(Epistulae* 267–68)

By such entreaties and threats Isho'yahb managed to heal the division and achieve a secure arrangement, allowing the Qatar region more independence under its own metropolitan.

The last Christian notice about east Arabia before its Islamisation comes from a cleric writing in southwest Iran in the 650s AD, who pens a short piece on Arabian geography:

Hasor, which scripture calls 'head of the kingdoms' [Joshua 11.10], belongs to the Arabs, while Medina is named after Midian, Abraham's fourth son by Qetura; it is also called Yathrib. And Dumat al-Jandal [modern al-Jawf] belongs to them, and the territory of the people of Hajar, which is rich in water, palm trees and fortified buildings. The territory of Khatt [in the modern Emirates], situated by the sea in the vicinity of the islands of Qatar, is rich in the same way; it is also thickly vegetated with various kinds of plants. The region of Mazun [Oman] also resembles it, and it too lies by the sea, comprising an area of more than 100 parasangs. So [belongs to the Arabs] also the territory of Yamama, in the middle of the desert, and the territory of Tawf, and the city of Hira, which was the seat of king Mundhir, surnamed the 'warrior'.

(*Chron. Khuzistan* 38–39)

The author ends with the laconic observation that 'he [Mundhir] was sixth in the line of the Ishmaelite kings', implying that he regarded the Arab kings ruling in his own day to be a continuation of the rule of these pre-Islamic Arab monarchs. If so, he was very likely writing during the time of 'Ali ibn Abi Talib, son-in-law of the Prophet Muhammad and 'emir of Hira' (656–60).[10]

THE ARCHAEOLOGY OF EAST ARABIA

Reconstruction of the history of this region is severely hampered by a lack of written sources. There are almost no texts in an indigenous language and very few in foreign tongues. On the plus side, however, the archaeological investigation of east Arabia is considerably more advanced than that of the rest of the peninsula. In 1878 the first survey was carried out when a young British officer, Captain E.L. Durand, arrived in Bahrain to review the island's antiquities. In 1953 the first professional excavations were undertaken when a Danish expedition was granted permission to commence work in Bahrain. And in the intervening half century much progress has been made and exploration has spread to the rest of east Arabia, particularly the Emirates. The material exhumed may be difficult to interpret and may not take us in the direction that we had hoped to go, but it always conveys to us some sort of story about the region's past and permits us a glimpse of the everyday life of the region's inhabitants that is much more real than that offered by most literary texts.

The composition and style of a manufactured object often betray its date and place of origin, and from this we can learn when a site flourished and who were its trading partners. The large quantity of foreign-produced goods discovered in east Arabia from the late third/early second millennium BC and the Greco-Roman period demonstrates that it was particularly active in international trade at these times. And this involved not only its immediate neighbours, Mesopotamia and Iran, but also powers at much greater remove. Thus there have been found Bactrian combs at Tell Abraq (Pl. 4), south Arabian alabaster vases and Greek amphorae at Mleiha, Roman glass vessels and Indian red polished pottery at ed-Dur (all three being major sites in the Emirates) and Nabataean coins at Thaj and Qatif in northeast Arabia.

Of course the majority of objects used in east Arabia would have been locally made and a number of crafts are attested. Of these one

Plate 4 Bactrian bone comb from Tell Abraq with flower motif, *c*.1500 BC (Dan Potts).

reached the proportions of an industry, namely the smelting and working of copper in Magan, which also provided ingots and finished products for export. Numerous ancient mines have been located and some 150 smelting sites. Hammer stones for crushing ore, kilns for smelting and moulds for casting have all been uncovered and many concentrations of slag documented. Excavations have also yielded ample evidence for the use of copper/bronze items in daily life: pins, fish-hooks, needles, chisels, awls, knives, axes, spear points, arrowheads and various different kinds of bowls and personal ornaments.

Remains of flora (especially seeds) and fauna (especially bones) make up a large part of the finds of most excavations and furnish many insights into the local economy. On Bahrain, for example, such finds reveal that horticulture, notably date-palm gardening, was an important activity and that date honey was produced from the second millennium BC onwards. Wheat and barley were cultivated, and also cotton, which confirms the report of the Greek botanist Theophrastus (4.7.7) to that effect. Sheep and goats were herded on the island and on the adjacent mainland. Fishing and shellfish gathering were commonly practised, and pearls were already being harvested by the early second millennium BC. The existence of these marine gems in the waters of Bahrain came to the attention of outsiders, who deemed the region 'extremely famous for its numerous pearls' (Pliny 6.148). And it was related that 'round about the island there are rafts made of reeds, from which men dive into the sea to a depth of twenty fathoms and bring up double-shelled oysters' (Athenaeus 3.146).

Buildings can be particularly difficult to interpret, particularly when they belong to a people whose imaginary and symbolic world is almost totally unknown to us. For example circular mud-brick towers begin to crop up in third-millennium BC Magan. They will typically be 20–40 metres in diameter, originally standing some 7–8 metres in height and have a stone-lined well running straight through the centre of the building down to the water table. It has been suggested that they represent the strongholds of the likes of the 'rulers' of Magan who resisted the Akkadian sovereign Manishtusu when he campaigned there in the twenty-third century BC. In this case the tower would have been the residence of a lord and his family and probably also a place of refuge in time of crisis for the community, who otherwise would have lived round about the tower in palm-frond houses. But there are other possibilities, such as that these structures served as the centres of governance of settlements, where the elders would meet to decide matters for the community, or else that they had some cultic significance. Whatever the case they evidently formed the nucleus of the first agricultural communities of east Arabia. The best known site, Hili in the al-'Ain oasis, already had a highly diversified regime by 3000 BC. Analysis of soil samples from this period shows that cereals (wheat and barley), fruit (jujube and melon) and dates were cultivated. And tests on bones demonstrate domestication of sheep, goat and cattle, the last clearly having been used for traction, perhaps ploughing or operating a well. Thus the oasis way of life for which Arabia is celebrated began very early, some 5000 years ago.

2

SOUTH ARABIA

THE IRON AGE (c.1300–330 BC)

The history of south Arabia (modern Yemen) is easier to reconstruct than that of east Arabia in that we are equipped with some ten thousand inscriptions. Unfortunately, however, these are not dated according to an absolute era until the first century AD and they almost never allude to events outside south Arabia. Scholars have tried to arrange them in chronological order according to the style of their script, but with hardly any firmly dated examples to provide a fixed point this method can offer no more than a rough indication. It is therefore very difficult to produce a sequential narrative of early south Arabian history. The period after the conquests of Alexander the Great is elucidated to some degree by the accounts of adventurous foreign explorers and merchants, but the earliest centuries, which witnessed such momentous developments as the emergence of complex states and the inception of the aromatics trade, as yet remain obscure.

The very mountainous terrain impeded the formation of a single regime, and political power was in general fragmented among the various peoples of south Arabia (Map 3). Each would seem to have constituted a cult community, a human collective bound together by allegiance to a patron god and presided over by a ruler who took the title of 'king' (*mlk*) and sometimes 'unifier' (*mkrb*). There were probably many other ties, such as language for example, but it is the cult and its sanctuaries that seem to play the most important role in forging the identity of each community. Many such peoples feature in the inscriptions, some of whom seem to disappear as time goes on, presumably absorbed by others who sought to expand their sway over a greater expanse of territory. The first whose exploits we can track is Saba (Sheba), whose rulers are the most abundantly attested in the surviving records.

36

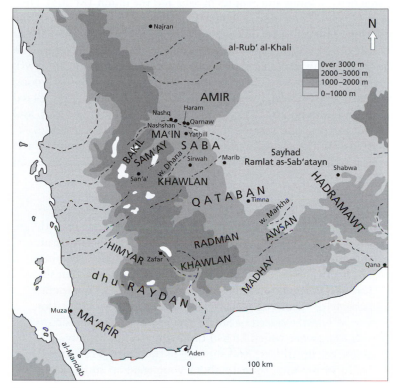

Map 3 South Arabia (adapted by author from Christian Robin, 'La Fin du royaume de Ma'in', 179).

The Sabaeans were principally defined by their allegiance to the god Almaqah. They were 'the progeny (*wld*) of Almaqah' (RES 3945, CIS 4.363), bound together by common sanctuaries, rituals, festivals and ruler. Their territory was probably limited initially to Marib and its environs, but the military exploits of various leaders added new lands and the latter's inhabitants were also expected to pay respects to Almaqah. Thus a monarch in the region of Jawf 'together with his tribe Kaminahu erected two towers [of the city walls of Nashq] for Almaqah and for [the kings of] Marib and for Saba' (CIS 4.377). And upon its defeat Nashshan was obliged 'to construct a temple of Almaqah in the centre of the city' (RES 3945). In addition we frequently encounter the expression 'Saba and the union (*gw*)' (e.g. CIS 4.967, Ja 2848), which refers to a much bigger entity. The author of one inscription includes in his dedication mention of 'all the gods,

37

patron deities, kings and peoples of Saba and the union' (M 203). Here we have something like a federation, of which Saba assumed the headship. The common link was allegiance to the high god 'Athtar and the union was regularly renewed at a ceremony in his temple on the ancient Kawran mountain (modern Jabal al-Lawdh in the Jawf). The union presumably served to maintain peace and security among its members, particularly respect for each others' holy places and sacred times, and possibly to facilitate mutual aid in times of hardship and cooperation in grand ventures (especially hydraulic construction).

Ostensibly the earliest reference to the Sabaeans is found in the Biblical narrative of the visit of the queen of Sheba to King Solomon (c.970–931 BC):

> The queen of Sheba heard of Solomon's fame and came to test him with difficult questions. She arrived in Jerusalem with a very large retinue, with camels laden with spices and an immense quantity of gold and precious stones. Having reached Solomon, she discussed with him everything that she had in mind, and Solomon had an answer for all her questions; not one of them was too obscure for the king to answer for her. When the queen of Sheba saw how very wise Solomon was, the palace which he had built, the food at his table . . . it left her breathless. And she said to the king: 'The report I heard in my own country about your wisdom in handling your affairs was true then. . . . Blessed be Yahweh your God who has shown you His favour by setting you on the throne of Israel.' . . . And she presented the king with a hundred and twenty talents of gold and great quantities of spices and precious stones; no such wealth of spices ever came again as those which the queen of Sheba gave to king Solomon.
>
> (1 Kings 10.1–10)

It used to be thought that states were not yet in existence in south Arabia at such an early date, and so this account was rejected as a fabrication or a retrojection of a later situation.[1] Recently, however, excavations at a number of sites (e.g. Hajar ibn Humayd and Yala) have yielded evidence of substantial settlement from the late second/early first millennium BC, including some very short south Arabian inscriptions on pottery. In addition an incense altar from Moab (modern central west Jordan) and a storage jar inscribed with south Arabian letters from Muweilah (in the modern Emirates) have been discovered in securely dated contexts of c.800 and c.700 BC respectively, suggesting that south Arabia already had trade contacts with the outside world by this time. Of course the Biblical passage above is intended to exalt Solomon and the god of Israel, and the exotic name of Saba may only have been slipped in at a later date to further that aim. Yet the assumption of the report, that relations between south Arabia and the Mediterranean had already been established in the tenth century BC, may have some basis in fact. However, we have to wait until the mid-eighth century before we have firm literary testimony. At this time a governor of Suhu in the area of the Middle Euphrates launched a punitive raid upon a caravan belonging to 'the people of Tayma and Saba whose own country is far away, whose messengers had never come to me and who had never travelled to meet me'. He clearly felt affronted, for, so he tells us, 'I captured one hundred of them alive; I captured their two hundred camels together with their loads . . . every kind of merchandise' (Suhu 346/351). A little later a certain 'Ita'amara the Sabaean' – mentioned alongside a king of Egypt and a queen of the Arabs, so likely himself to be a sovereign – sent aromatics and precious stones to Sargon II in 716 BC, as did 'Karib'il king of Saba' to Sennacherib some thirty years afterwards (AR 2.18, 440). These two names are commonly found among lists of Sabaean rulers, so we cannot be sure which are meant, but it is at least possible to say that Saba was already flourishing in the eighth century BC.

The Sabaean sovereign most frequently mentioned in inscriptions is a certain Karib'il Watar son of Dhamar'ali. He would seem to have been responsible for the rise of Saba to pre-eminence in southern Arabia, and his deeds are commemorated in two lengthy texts engraved on two massive blocks (RES 3945–46) in the grand temple of the Sabaean national god Almaqah at Sirwah (Pl. 5). The first details his military campaigns in which he won 'for Almaqah and Saba' control of the incense route, crushing the kingdoms of Awsan and Nashshan which lay to the southeast and northwest respectively, and extending Sabaean influence over the fertile agricultural lands of the highlands both to the north and to the south. With these great conquests completed, Karib'il set about consolidating his gains, as is recorded in the second inscription. He fortified towns, initiated irrigation works and installed Sabaean colonies in the vanquished areas.

Plate 5 The ancient city of Sirwah with the temple of Almaqah in the centre (Venetia Porter).

THE GRECO-ROMAN/PARTHIAN PERIOD (*c.*330 BC–AD 240)

The Assyrians and Persians tell us almost nothing about south Arabia, but the Greeks and Romans, beneficiaries of a number of exploratory expeditions to that part of the world, are much more informative, though it still remained for them a strange and exotic land. Two of our earliest Greek sources on south Arabia, Theophrastus of Eresus (372–287 BC) and Eratosthenes of Cyrene (*c.*284–202 BC), describe it as dominated by four major peoples (*ethnê*). In the words of the latter (cited by Strabo 16.4.2) these were 'the Minaeans, on the side towards the Red Sea, whose largest city is Qarnaw (*Karna*); next to these, the Sabaeans, whose metropolis is Marib (*Mariaba*); third, Qatabanians . . . whose royal seat is called Timna (*Tamna*); and farthest towards the east, the Hadramites, whose city is Shabwa (*Sabata*)'. These capital cities of theirs, along with those of a number of more minor peoples, were all located on the fringes of the desert known to medieval Arab geographers as the Sayhad (modern Ramlat al-Sab'atayn). A site in the cooler, more verdant highlands might seem a more sensible choice, but it was via the perimeter of the desert that aromatics passed on their long journey to the Mediterranean and Mesopotamia. Whoever

40

wished to participate in this trade was therefore obliged to take up a position near to this route.

The only south Arabian people to speak about trade in their inscriptions are the Minaeans, who established themselves as a thriving economic power in their own right. Unlike the other three major kingdoms they advanced no political pretensions – their rulers fought no wars and minted no coins – but instead concentrated on commerce. Though their territory was small, they traded far and wide, sending out caravans to Egypt, Gaza, Syria, Mesopotamia and Tyre. Their name was practically synonymous with aromatics in the eyes of consumers (cf. *Zenon papyri* 59536: 'Minaean frankincense', dated 261 BC). And in addition:

> through their territory the transit for the export of the frankincense is along one narrow track. It was these people who originated the trade and who chiefly practise it. . . . It is said that there are not more than 3000 families who retain the right of trading in it as a hereditary property. Consequently the members of these families are called sacred and are not allowed to be polluted by ever encountering women or funeral processions when they are engaged in making incisions in the trees in order to obtain the frankincense. In this way the price of the commodity is increased owing to scruples of religion.
>
> (Pliny 12.54)

The Minaeans are also the only people to have composed a text that refers to an event external to south Arabia. Its authors are the merchants 'Ammisadaq and Sa'd, who thank their gods for bringing them home safely from an expedition to Egypt despite 'the hostilities which Saba and Khawlan had engaged upon against their persons' and despite 'the conflict which took place between the Medes (i.e. Persians) and the Egyptians' (M 247). This latter incident could refer to the campaign of Artaxerxes in 343 BC or possibly to that of Cambyses in 525 BC, or else to some more minor skirmish that occurred between the two powers. In lists recording payment for foreign women to be admitted into Minaean society (M 392–98) there are thirty-two mentions of Gaza, a city that enjoyed great prosperity and fame during the Persian period (539–334 BC). One Minaean trader died in Egypt and inscribed on his sarcophagus that 'he imported myrrh and calamus for the temples of the gods of Egypt' (M 338). It is dated to the twenty-second year of Ptolemy son of Ptolemy, which allows us to

41

place it somewhere between 262 and 59 BC. Finally a Greek–Minaean bilingual inscription from the island of Delos conveys the dedication of an altar to 'Wadd and the Minaean gods', most likely executed shortly after Delos' transformation into a free port in 166 BC (M 349). Though precision is as yet impossible, we can at least deduce from all these texts that the Minaeans flourished between about 500 and 100 BC.

Qataban is mentioned for the first time in the aforementioned inscription of Karib'il Watar (RES 3945), where it appears as an ally of Saba. Some time later inscriptions speak of conflict between Saba and Qataban. One, for example, is dated to 'the time of the war which was led by . . . the kings of Saba, Saba itself, and their allied tribes . . . against Yada''ab [king of Qataban], Qataban and the progeny of 'Amm [i.e. the Qatabanians]' (RES 3858). It is also noticeable that at some point the rulers of Qataban claim sovereignty over places formerly under Sabaean influence, and indeed Qatabanian inscriptions have been discovered in these places. The implication is that Qataban was now, like Saba before it, pursuing an expansionist policy. Eratosthenes of Cyrene states that their 'territory extends down to the straits and the passage across the Arabian Gulf' (cited by Strabo 16.4.2), but says nothing about the Sabaean lands. Thus it would seem that by the third century BC Qataban was challenging Saba's dominant position in south Arabia. And it is presumably to this period of expansion that one should attribute many of the magnificent tombs found on the slopes of Mount Hayd ibn 'Aqil outside the capital Timna, housing the exquisitely fashioned memorials of the great and good of the city (Pl. 6). Our knowledge of Hadramawt is even scantier due to a dearth of inscriptions, but its career would seem to be similar to that of Qataban. It is likewise named as an ally of Saba in the time of Karib'il Watar, and excavations at its capital give the impression that it was prospering about the fourth to second centuries BC when substantial fortifications and many secular and religious buildings were constructed.

The first century BC seems to be a turning point in the history of south Arabia, since the peoples located around the Sayhad desert, who had dominated the region's affairs up until this point, were now gradually overtaken by the tribes of the highlands. One factor in this transition was the establishment of a regular maritime link between the Mediterranean world, Arabia and India. Frequent attempts had been made to sail from Egypt to India with mixed success, but the first to do it repeatedly and with the aid of, rather than in spite of, the monsoon winds, was Eudoxus of Cyzicus, who accomplished three

Plate 6 Alabaster female bust from the cemetery of Hayd ibn 'Aqil outside Timna, named Myriam by its discoverers, *c.*1st century AD, 36.5 × 18 cm (AFSM).

successful voyages between 117 and 109 BC. This traffic was greatly
boosted when Augustus incorporated Egypt into the Roman empire,
so that by the end of the first century BC Strabo could write:

> Since the merchants of Alexandria are already sailing with
> fleets by way of the Nile and of the Arabian Gulf as far as
> India, these regions have become far better known to us of
> today than to our predecessors. At any rate when Gallus was
> prefect of Egypt, I accompanied him and ascended the Nile
> as far as Syene and the frontiers of Ethiopia. I learned that as
> many as one hundred and twenty vessels were sailing from
> Myos Hormos [a Red Sea port on the Egyptian coast] to India,
> whereas formerly, under the Ptolemies, only a very few
> ventured to undertake the voyage and to carry on traffic in
> Indian merchandise.
>
> (2.5.12)

This meant that the future in south Arabia lay in ports, not in caravan
cities. Hadramawt realised this and established harbours at Qana (next
to modern Bir Ali) and Samhar (modern Khor Rori in south Oman).
A mid-first century AD author of a handbook on maritime trade gives
us the following information about the former harbour:

> After Eudaimon Arabia [modern Aden] . . . is another port
> of trade on the coast, Qana, belonging to the kingdom of
> Eleazos, the frankincense-bearing land. . . . Above it inland
> lies the metropolis of Shabwa, which is also the residence of
> the king. All the frankincense grown in the land is brought
> into Qana as if to a warehouse, by camel as well as by rafts
> of a local type made of leather bags, and by boats. It also
> carries on trade with the ports across the water [i.e. in India]
> . . . and with its neighbour Persia. Its imports from Egypt are
> wheat, a limited quantity, wine . . . Arab clothing . . . copper,
> tin, coral, storax. . . . Also, for the king, [there is imported]
> embossed silverware and money, rather large quantities, plus
> horses and statuary and fine-quality clothing with no
> adornment. It exports local wares, namely frankincense and
> aloe; the rest of its exports are through its connections with
> the other ports of trade.
>
> (Periplus 27–28)

A second possible factor in the decline of the old south Arabian
caravan cities was Rome's attempted invasion. The result of the battle

of Actium in 31 BC, with its defeat of Cleopatra, was that the emperor
Augustus was in possession of Egypt and its Red Sea coast. It then
occurred to him to extend Roman domination over the whole of the
Red Sea, giving the empire control of all trade coming from India and
Arabia. His personal motive was probably to better Alexander the
Great, who had long fascinated him and who had once boasted to his
tutor, in vain, that he would conquer the incense-producing lands. To
this end Augustus dispatched in 26 BC the commander Aelius Gallus:

> to explore the tribes and the places, not only in Arabia, but
> also in Ethiopia, since Caesar saw that the Troglodyte country
> which adjoins Egypt neighbours upon Arabia, and also that
> the Arabian Gulf, which separates the Arabs from the
> Troglodytes, is extremely narrow. Accordingly he conceived
> the purpose of winning over the Arabs as a client nation or
> of conquering them outright. Another consideration was the
> report, which had prevailed from all time, that they were very
> wealthy, and that they sold aromatics and the most valuable
> stones for gold and silver, but never expended with outsiders
> any part of what they received in exchange. For he hoped
> either to enjoy the Arabs as his rich friends or to subjugate
> them as his rich enemies.
>
> (Strabo 16.4.22)

However, the Nabataean administrator Syllaeus, who 'had promised
to be his guide on the march and to supply all needs and to cooperate
with him, acted treacherously in all things, and pointed out neither
a safe voyage along the coast nor a safe journey by land, misguiding
him through places that had no roads and by circuitous routes and
through regions destitute of everything'. This and the sickness of
many of his army meant that Gallus did not reach south Arabia until
24 BC. There he captured a number of cities and began the siege of
Marsiaba, 'but for want of water desisted' and was obliged to retrace
his steps. He nevertheless claimed a victory for Augustus, and on his
return was able to report a number of discoveries, namely:

> that the nomads live on milk and the flesh of wild animals;
> that the rest of the tribes extract wine out of palm trees, as
> the natives do in India, and get oil from sesame; that the
> Himyarites are the most numerous tribe; that the Minaeans
> have land that is fertile in palm groves and timber, and wealth
> in flocks; that the Cerbanians [Qatabanians?] and Agraeans,

and especially the Hadramites, excel as warriors; that the
Carraeans have the most extensive and most fertile agricultural land; that the Sabaeans are the most wealthy, owing
to the fertility of their forests in producing scents, their gold
mines, their irrigated agricultural land and their production
of honey and wax. . . . The Arabs wear turbans or else go
with their hair unshorn; they shave their beards but wear
a moustache; others, however, leave the beard also unshaven.
(Pliny 6.161–62)

The Himyarites, described above as 'the most numerous tribe', had
their capital at Zafar in the fertile southern highlands (Pl. 7), whence
led a road to the port of Muza (modern Mocha) at the northern end of
the straits of Bab al-Mandab, where Arabia almost touches Africa.
Already by the mid-first century AD they had achieved a prominent

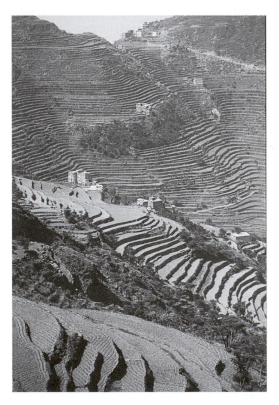

Plate 7 A typical view of the highlands of Yemen (J. Leslie).

position in the region, as is indicated by the aforementioned maritime manual:

> On the very last bay on the lefthand shore of this [the Red] sea is Muza. . . . The whole place teems with Arabs – shipowners or charterers and sailors – and is astir with commercial activity. For they share in the trade across the water [the African coast] and with Barygaza [on the Indian coast], using their own outfits. . . . Nine days further inland is Zafar, the metropolis, residence of Karib'il, legitimate king of the two nations, the Himyarites and the one lying next to it, called the Sabaean. He is a friend of the emperors thanks to continuous embassies and gifts. The port of trade of Muza, though without a harbour, offers a good roadstead for mooring because of the anchorages with sandy bottom all around.
>
> *(Periplus* 23–24)

The mention that Karib'il was king of two nations refers to the fact that Saba was obliged, through straitened circumstances, to seek a coalition with Himyar, forming the united monarchy of 'Saba and Dhu Raydan'. In the second century AD, however, the fortunes of the Sabaean people revived somewhat and they began to campaign vigorously against the Himyarites. During this period of renaissance, which lasted about a century and a half, the temple of Almaqah at Marib became once more an important religious centre and dedications were numerous, a new coinage was inaugurated, and the magnificent palace of Ghumdan was built at the highland town of San'a, which had been elevated to the status of capital city alongside Marib. But then at the end of the third century AD the Sabaean dynasty seems simply to die out and we hear no more of Saba as an independent power. The Minaeans had already lost their influence in the course of the first century BC. Himyar and Hadramawt appropriated and divided up Qataban's territories in the late second century AD. Finally, in the late third century, King Shammar Yuhar'ish of Himyar conquered Hadramawt, which subsequently ceased to be a major player on the political stage. The Himyarite era, an absolute system of dating, now became commonly used throughout south Arabia. And on an inscription dated 409 of the Himyarite era (AD 299) Shammar styled himself 'king of Saba and of Dhu Raydan and Hadramawt and Yamanat' (YMN 13), reflecting the fact that south Arabia had become a unified state for the first time.

The glorious days when the caravan cities of the Sayhad desert exercised a monopoly over the provisioning of aromatics had gone. And as these cities became poorer, they were less and less able to withstand the encroachments of Arab tribes to their north. From the first century BC onwards Arabs are mentioned with increasing frequency in inscriptions. Sometimes this will be in connection with raids against them. Thus the highland tribe of Hashid in northwest Yemen had once to make 'war against some of the Arabs on the borders of the tribe Hashid and in some of the lands of the Arabs, Arabs who had acted wrongfully toward their lords, the kings of Saba, and in some of the lands of the tribes of the king of Saba' (Ja 561 bis). At other times Arabs feature as auxiliaries in the armies of the settled kingdoms, as when the Sabaean kings confronted a coalition comprising 'Hadramawt and Qataban and Radman and Madhay and every person and the Arabs who were with them' (Ja 629). The settled states were obliged to develop a policy for dealing with these tribes: singling out certain chiefs for recognition as kings, taking hostages as guarantee of good behaviour, conducting punitive raids in cases of violation of agreements and so on. We see an example of Saba practising just such a policy in an inscription in which two Sabaean kings give thanks to the god Almaqah:

> because he enabled them successfully to exact from Malik, king of [the Arab tribe of] Kinda, the reparation which Malik was required to make to Almaqah and the kings of Saba, [namely the person of] Imru' al-Qays son of 'Awf, king of Khasasa, by holding that Malik and the leaders of Kinda in detention in Marib until they surrendered that young man Imru' al-Qays and gave as hostages from Kinda his [Malik's] child and the sons of the chiefs and leaders of Kinda, and made [further] reparation to Almaqah and the kings of Saba in horses, riding camels and transport camels.
>
> (Ja 576)

And we also have evidence of diplomatic exchanges, such as the mission of a personal assistant of the early third-century AD Sabaean king Ilsharah Yahdib 'to the kings of the north, namely al-Harith ibn Ka'b, king of Asad, and Malik ibn Badd, king of Kinda and Madhhij and some other Arabs' (CIAS 2.33; cf. ZI 75: mission of Ilsharah to 'kings of Ghassan, Nizar and Madhhij').

48

THE BYZANTINE/SASANIAN PERIOD
(c. AD 240–630)

The kings of Himyar, now masters of all south Arabia, followed the example of Saba and Hadramawt in extending their influence over the Arab tribes, though ranging much further to the north than their predecessors. An inscription dated to the year 470 (AD 360) enumerates the military campaigns of certain Himyarite kings, who advanced as far as Yabrin (an oasis in east Arabia), Jaww (modern Yamama in northeast Arabia) and Kharj (central Arabia), clashing with, among others, the tribes of Murad, Iyad, Ma'add and 'Abd al-Qays, the latter two defeated at Siyyan (northeast of Mecca) 'between the land of Nizar and the land of Ghassan' ('Abadan 1). An inscription of the first half of the fifth century from central Arabia relates how the ruler Abikarib As'ad and his son Hassan Yuha'min 'went and sojourned in the land of Ma'add on the occasion of the establishment of certain of their tribes' (Ry 509). Muslim sources also describe an expedition of Abikarib As'ad to the north, during which 'he placed Hujr al-Kindi over the tribe of Ma'add' (Ibn Habib, *Muh.* 368; Isfahani 16.354). Evidently Himyar had appointed Hujr's clan, from the tribe of Kinda, to act as their deputies in central Arabia, maintaining order among the Arab tribes in that area. This would explain why Himyarite rulers subsequently adopted the additional title of 'kings . . . of their Arabs of the highlands and of the coast' and why Hujr felt justified in styling himself 'king of Kinda' in a south Arabian graffito. The respective sons of these leaders then continued this arrangement:

> Among those who served the Himyarite king Hassan was 'Amr son of Hujr al-Kindi, the chief of Kinda during his time. When Hassan led an expedition against the Jadis [in Yamama], he appointed 'Amr as his deputy over certain affairs. . . . 'Amr son of Hujr was a man of sound judgement and sagacity.
>
> (Tabari 1.880–81)

And apparently their own sons after them followed suit: 'He [the son of Hassan Yuha'min] dispatched Harith son of 'Amr son of Hujr al-Kindi to Ma'add and set him over them' (Wahb ibn Munabbih 299). At this point the Byzantines began to woo the clan of Hujr, as is recounted by a certain Nonnosus, who belonged to a Byzantine diplomatic dynasty. He tells us that his grandfather had been sent to Harith son of 'Amr son of Hujr al-Kindi by the emperor Anastasius (491–518),[2] and both his father Abraham and himself were sent to Qays, 'a descendant of Harith', in the time of Justinian (527–65).

> Now Qays, to whom Nonnosus was sent, commanded two of the most notable Arab tribes, Kinda and Ma'add. Before Nonnosus' appointment his father, Abraham, had also been sent on Justinian's orders to this Qays and had made a peace treaty, under the terms of which he took Qays' son, called Mu'awiya (*Mauias*), as hostage and carried him off to Byzantium. Subsequently Nonnosus negotiated with two aims: to bring Qays, if possible, to the emperor, and to reach the king of the people of Axum [in Ethiopia], then Ella Asbeha, and in addition to reach the Himyarites. . . . When Abraham came on another legation to Qays, the latter went to Byzantium, dividing his own command between his brothers 'Amr and Yazid, while he personally received from the emperor command of Palestine.
>
> (Photius 3)

During their time as Himyar's client kings, and briefly as Rome's, the chiefs of Kinda based themselves at Qaryat Dhat Kahl (modern Qaryat al-Faw), 280 km northeast of Najran. This settlement lay on the trade route connecting south Arabia with east Arabia and Iraq, and it had already been used by the Minaeans around the third to second centuries BC. Thereafter it became the capital of the Arab tribes of Qahtan and Madhhij, as is indicated by the gravestone of Mu'awiya ibn Rabi'a, 'king of Qahtan and Madhhij'. During their time and that of Kinda it became an impressive town, comprising a market, palace, temple, tombs and houses, and its notables were wealthy enough to commission fine frescoes and grand statues and to import high-quality objects of glass, metal and ivory (Pl. 8). At the height of their influence Kinda felt confident enough to mint their own coins, stamping them with the name of their patron god Kahl.

Around AD 300 the Himyarite king Shammar Yuhar'ish sent an envoy 'to Malik son of Ka'b, king of [the tribe of] al-Azd, and from there he [the envoy] undertook two further journeys, to Ctesiphon and Seleucia, the two royal cities of Persia, and he reached the land of [the tribe of] Tanukh [in southern Iraq]' (Sharaf 31). A few decades later there was an exchange of ambassadors and establishment of peaceful relations between Himyar and Ethiopia (Ir 28). And about the

Plate 8 A nobleman of Qaryat al-Faw as portrayed on a fresco found in the city (A. al-Ansary; see his *Qaryat al-Faw*, 136–37).

same time the Byzantine emperor Constantius (337–61) dispatched ambassadors, accompanied by the missionary Theophilus the Indian, to the ruler of the Himyarites, seeking permission to build churches for the use of visiting Byzantine merchants and 'of any others who might incline towards Christianity' (Philostorgius 3.4). Already by this time, then, south Arabia was becoming involved in superpower politics. This was to intensify dramatically in the early sixth century when full-scale war broke out between Ethiopia and Himyar. Christian writers portray these events in terms of religious oppression and martyrdom. There is no suggestion in indigenous sources, however, of persecution of Christians solely for their faith. The objection seems rather to be bound up with politics, for extension of Christianity was perceived as extension of Byzantine political influence, which was opposed by pro-Persian parties and champions of Yemen's independence. A hint of future trouble came in the 470s when a priest named Azqir was executed for active proselytisation in Najran. Then the Byzantine merchant Cosmas Indicopleustes informs us that while he was in the vicinity of Ethiopia, 'at the beginning of the reign of Justin [518–27], emperor of the Romans, Ella Asbeha, then king of the Axumites, was on the point of going to war against the Himyarites' (2.56).

The reason why they waged war between themselves was that
. . . when the aforementioned Roman merchants crossed over
from the lands of the Himyarites to enter those of the Indians
to trade there as usual, the king of the Himyarites, Dimnos,
learned about it, seized them, killed them and plundered all
their merchandise, saying: 'this is because in the countries
of the Romans the Christians wickedly harass the Jews who
live in their countries and kill many of them. Therefore I
am putting these men to death.' In this way he used to kill
numerous merchants until many were seized by terror and
refused to come to the country, and the trade with the kingdom of the Ethiopians ceased. . . . Because of this they came
to great enmity and declared war on each other. . . . Then they
fought a battle with each other and the king of the Ethiopians
was victorious over the king of the Himyarites. He took him
captive, killed him and plundered his kingdom.

(Pseudo-Dionysius 54–56; cf. Malalas 18.15;
Theophanes 223)

Ella Asbeha then installed over the south Arabians a Christian king.
However:

after some time the Himyarite Jews grew stronger. When
the Christian king whom the king of the Ethiopians had
established there died, they chose a king from among themselves over the people of the Himyarites [named Yusuf, Dhu
Nuwas in Muslim sources]. And in bitter wrath they slew
and destroyed all the Christian people there, men, women,
young people and little children, poor and rich.

(Pseudo-Dionysius 56)

This is to some extent borne out by a number of other Syriac documents and also by three contemporary south Arabian inscriptions:

He [king Yusuf] destroyed the church and massacred the
Ethiopians in Zafar, and waged war on [the pro-Ethiopian
tribes of] Ash'ar, Rakb, Farasan and Mukha'. And he undertook the war and siege of Najran and the fortification of the
chain [across the harbour at the straits] of Mandab. So he
mustered troops under his own command, and sent them [the
chiefs loyal to him] with an independent detachment. And
what the king successfully took in spoils in this campaign

was 12,500 slain, 11,000 captives, and 290,000 camels, oxen and sheep. This inscription was written by the lord Sharah'il the Yazanid when he was taking precautionary measures against Najran with the Hamdanid tribesmen, both towns-folk and nomads (*hgr w'rb*), and a striking force of Yazanites and nomads of Kinda, Murad and Madhhij, while his brother lords were with the king for defence on the sea from the Ethiopians and were fortifying the chain of Mandab. All that they have recorded in this inscription in the way of killings, booty and precautionary measures was on a campaign, the termination of which, when they turned homeward, was in thirteen months [from its start].

(Ja 1028, July 633/AD 523)[3]

Then he [Yusuf] sent [an envoy] to Najran in order that hostages might be exacted from them, otherwise he would wage war against them [in earnest]. But there was no surrender of hostages; on the contrary they [the Najranites] committed criminal aggression on them [the Himyarites].

(Ry 507, July 633/AD 523; cf. Ry 508)

A moving account of these events from a Christian perspective (portrayed as a martyrdom of innocent believers) is given by a certain Harith (*Arethas*), who dates the calamity to November of the Seleucid year 835/AD 523 (though at the end a scribe wrote 830, forgetting the word 'five', unwittingly causing much debate among modern scholars about the date of these events). A response from the Ethiopians to this aggression was not long in coming:

He [Ella Asbeha] collected a fleet of ships and an army and came against them, and he conquered them in battle and slew both the king and many of the Himyarites. He then set up in his stead a Christian king, a Himyarite by birth, by name Esimiphaeus[4], and after ordaining that he should pay tribute to the Ethiopians every year he returned to his home. In this Ethiopian army many slaves and all who were readily disposed to crime were quite unwilling to follow the king back, but were left behind and remained there because of their desire for the land of the Himyarites, for it is an extremely good land. These fellows at a time not long after this, in company with certain others, rose against the king Esimiphaeus

and put him in confinement in one of the fortresses there, and
established another king over the Himyarites, Abraha by
name. Now this Abraha was a Christian, but a slave of a
Roman citizen who was engaged in the business of shipping
in the city of Adulis in Ethiopia.

(Procopius 1.20; cf. Pseudo-Dionysius 68)

That imperial politics and matters of trade lay behind these conflicts
is clear from the subsequent Byzantine response:

At that time, when Ella Asbeha was reigning over the
Ethiopians and Esimiphaeus over the Himyarites, the emperor
Justinian sent an ambassador, Julianus, demanding that both
nations on account of their community of religion should
make common cause with the Romans in the war against the
Persians. For he purposed that the Ethiopians, by purchasing
silk from India and selling it among the Romans, might
themselves gain much money, while causing the Romans
to profit in only one way, namely, that they be no longer
compelled to pay over their money to their enemy. . . . As for
the Himyarites it was desired that they should establish Qays,
the fugitive, as chief over Ma'add, and with a great army of
their own people and of the Ma'add Saracens[5] make an
invasion into the land of the Persians. This Qays was by birth
of chiefly rank and an exceptionally able warrior, but he had
killed one of the relatives of Esimiphaeus and was a fugitive
in a land utterly destitute of human habitation. So each king,
promising to put this demand into effect, dismissed the
ambassador, but neither one of them did the things agreed
upon by them. For it was impossible for the Ethiopians to
buy silk from the Indians, since the Persian merchants always
locate themselves at the very harbours where the Indian
ships first put in, as they inhabit the adjoining country and
are accustomed to buy the whole cargoes. And it seemed
to the Himyarites a difficult thing to cross a country which
was a desert and which extended so far that a long time was
required for the journey across it, and then to go against a
people much more warlike than themselves.

(Procopius 1.20)

Another source, apparently using a first-hand report, is more positive:

54

When the Roman ambassador was brought in he knelt and made obeisance, and the Ethiopian king ordered me [*sic*] to arise and approach him. When he received the letter from the Roman emperor he kissed the seal, and when he received the gifts the emperor sent him he was amazed. Opening the letter and reading it, through an interpreter, he discovered that its contents were that he should arm himself against Kawad [488–531], the emperor of the Persians, and destroy the territory bordering on his own. And in future he was no longer to engage in commerce with him, but to carry on trade through the country of the Himyarites he had subjugated, then by way of the Nile to Alexandria in Egypt. Immediately Ella Asbeha, the king of the Ethiopians, in the sight of the Roman ambassador, declared war on the Persians. He sent out ahead the Himyarite Saracens he had under him and attacked Persian territory on behalf of the Romans.

(Malalas 18.56; cf. Theophanes 244–45)

The Abraha brought to power by insurrectionaries proved to be an able ruler and was the last great monarch of south Arabia. He successfully fought off attempts by Ella Asbeha to oust him, though he continued to send tribute to Ella Asbeha's successor. By 658 (548 AD), however, he felt able to assume the title of king and, according to a lengthy inscription at the Marib dam (CIS 4.541), he received embassies from no less than five neighbouring powers: the Ethiopians, the Byzantines, the Persians, Mundhir of Lakhm, Harith ibn Jabala of Ghassan and his kinsman Abikarib ibn Jabala.[6] He also managed to quell a revolt by his appointee over Kinda, one Yazid ibn Kabasha, 'whom he had appointed as deputy (*khlft*) over Kinda at a time when it had no deputy' (CIS 4.541). And in 552 he launched two campaigns, one led by himself (often equated with the expedition of the elephant alluded to in Quran 105) and the other by his Arab allies, in order to assert his authority over central Arabia:

By the power of the Merciful One and His messiah, the king Abraha . . . wrote this inscription when he had raided Ma'add in the spring razzia in the month of April when all the Banu 'Amir had revolted. Now the king sent Abu Jabr with [the tribes of] Kinda and 'Ali and [he sent] Bishr son of Hisn with [the tribes of] Sa'd and Murad. Kinda and 'Ali were present in the vanguard of the army against the Banu 'Amir in the valley of Dhu Markh, and Murad and Sa'd in a valley on the

Turaba route. And they slew and made captive the enemy
and took satisfactory booty. The king, on the other hand,
did battle at Haliban [west of modern Riyad] and the troops
of Ma'add were defeated and forced to give hostages. After all
this 'Amr son of Mundhir [of Lakhm] negotiated with Abraha
and agreed to give hostages to Abraha, for Mundhir had
invested him ['Amr] with the governorship over Ma'add. So
Abraha returned from Haliban by the power of the Merciful
One . . . in the year 662.

(Ry 506)

With an inscription of 669 (AD 559), the last dated south Arabian
text known, a long era of history comes to an end. Thereafter, so Arabic
sources tell us, the Ethiopian presence grew stronger and more
tyrannical, prompting the heroic and semi-legendary Sayf ibn Dhi
Yazan to seek outside help:

When the people of Yemen had long endured oppression,
Sayf ibn Dhi Yazan the Himyarite went . . . to Nu'man ibn
Mundhir, who . . . took him with him and introduced him
to Khosro. . . . When Sayf ibn Dhi Yazan entered his presence
he fell to his knees and said: 'O king, ravens [meaning the
Ethiopians] have taken possession of our country . . . and
I have come to you for help and that you may assume the
kingship of my country.' . . . So Khosro sent [to fight the
Ethiopians] those who were confined in his prisons to
the number of 800 men. He put in command of them a
man called Wahriz who was of mature age and of excellent
family and lineage. They set out in eight ships, two of which
foundered, so that only six reached the shores of Aden. Sayf
met Wahriz with all the people that he could muster, saying:
'My foot is with your foot, we die or conquer together.'
'Right!' said Wahriz. Masruq ibn Abraha, the king of Yemen,
came out against him with his army. . . . Wahriz bent his bow
– the story goes that it was so tough that no one but he could
bend it – and ordered that his eyebrows be fastened back.
Then he shot Masruq and split the ruby in his forehead, and
the arrow pierced his head and came out at the back of his
neck. He fell off his mount and the Ethiopians gathered
round him. When the Persians fell upon them, they fled and
were killed as they bolted in all directions. Wahriz advanced

to enter San'a, and when he reached its gate he said that his standard should never be lowered.

> (Ibn Hisham 41–43; cf. Ibn Qutayba 1.149, from 'the
> books of the Persians')

Sayf was made king on the understanding that he would remit taxes to Khosro every year and Wahriz returned to Persia. However, Sayf was stabbed to death by a group of Ethiopian servants and Khosro dispatched Wahriz once more, this time to bring Yemen under direct Persian rule. And so it remained until the early Muslim state took charge.

3

NORTH AND CENTRAL ARABIA

THE IRON AGE (*c*.1300–330 BC)

There were not equal opportunities for advancement for all the inhabitants of Arabia. Monsoon rains in the south and abundant groundwater in the east allowed agriculture to flourish there, whereas in the north and centre this was only possible in a limited number of locations, chiefly scattered oases. Easy moorings in the south and east and a strategic setting favoured trade, whereas 'to set a course along the [west] coast of Arabia is altogether risky, since the region with its lack of harbours offers poor anchorage, is foul with rocky stretches, cannot be approached because of cliffs, and is fearsome in every respect' (*Periplus* 20). Moreover the peoples of north Arabia were more prey to the whims of the great powers than were those of the south and east. Thus the polities of the Nabataeans, Characenes, Hatrans and Palmyrenes were each in their turn abolished by Rome or Iran. This disparity in opportunities and in potential for state formation is reflected in the historical sources for Arabia. Whereas the kingdoms of Saba, Dilmun and Magan achieve semi-legendary status in the writings of outsiders, famed for their wealth and exoticism, the rest of Arabia is mostly dismissed by outsiders as a wilderness and its inhabitants disdained for their peripatetic and parasitic mode of existence:

> Whenever Israel sowed seed, the Midianites would march up with Amalek and the sons of the east. . . . They would pitch camp on their territory and destroy the produce of the country as far as Gaza. They left Israel nothing to live on, not a sheep or an ox or a donkey . . . They entered the country to pillage it.
>
> (Judges 6.3–5)

In Biblical texts this disparity is mapped genealogically. The sons of Yoqtan son of Abraham (Qeturah) are Saba and Dedan, directors of the incense trade, whereas the sons of Ishmael son of Abraham (by Hagar) are 'twelve princes according to their tribes' who, like their father, dwell in the desert. Isaiah (60.6–7) reports that 'everyone in Saba will come bringing gold and incense' at the same time as he speaks of 'the flocks of Qedar' and 'the rams of Nabayoth', the last two both sons of Ishmael. Likewise Ezekiel (27.20–21) notes that 'Arabia and all the princes of Qedar were your customers; they paid in lambs, rams and he-goats'. And in the same breath he states that 'the merchants of Saba and Raamah [Najran] traded with you; they supplied you with the finest spices, precious stones and gold for your merchandise'. In addition the disparity between the regions is illustrated archaeologically. Whereas the vestiges of grand cities, imposing temples, large funerary structures and finely crafted artefacts have been discovered in south and east Arabia, there is little evidence of substantial sedentary occupation in the north or centre before the sojourn of the Babylonian monarch Nabonidus in Tayma (c.552–543 BC), and it remains minimal until the establishment of the Nabataeans towards the end of the millennium.

It is, however, the nomadic pastoralists of northern and central Arabia who figure most in Israelite and Assyrian annals. This is because they impinged more directly on the lives of these peoples than did their distant cousins in the south and east of Arabia, and it is in these sources that we first encounter the term 'Arab'. The earliest reliable reference is given in an inscription dated 853 BC of the Assyrian king Shalmaneser III, who records a victory over a coalition of Syrian and Palestinian leaders, alongside of whom fought a certain 'Gindibu the Arab' with a thousand camels (AR 1.611). Ostensibly earlier, though edited much later, is the statement in the Bible that to King Solomon (c.970–931 BC) 'all the Arab kings and the provincial governors brought gold and silver' (2 Chronicles 9.14). Thereafter references to the Arabs in Assyrian and Biblical sources become more frequent, usually in that tone of superiority so commonly adopted by settled states towards the nomadic peoples on their borders. Most often they record their subjection of various tribes: for example the Israelite king Uzziah (781–740 BC) brings to submission 'the Arabs living at Gurbaal' (2 Chronicles 26.7), and the Assyrian monarch Tiglath-Pileser III (744–727 BC) paraded in word and image his trouncing of Shamsi (Pl. 9):

Plate 9 Assyrian relief showing Arab woman captured during
Tiglath-Pileser's campaign against Shamsi (British Museum 118901).

> As for Shamsi, queen of the Arabs, at mount Saqurri I
> defeated 9400 of her people. Her entire camp: 1000 people,
> 30,000 camels, 20,000 cattle . . . 5000 bags of all kinds of
> spices . . . pedestals of her gods, arms and staffs of her goddess
> and her property I seized. And she, in order to save her life,
> to the desert, an arid place, like a wild she-ass made off. The
> rest of her possessions and her tents, her people's safeguard,
> within her camp I set on fire. And she, startled by my mighty
> weapons, brought camels, she-camels with their young, to
> Assyria to my presence. I installed an inspector over her and
> 10,000 soldiers.
>
> (ITP 229)

The mention of aromatics in the list of booty taken by Tiglath-Pileser
gives us a clue as to why the Arabs suddenly enter upon the world
stage at this time. Evidently traffic in these products between south
Arabia and the Mediterranean world had begun and certain north
Arabian tribes were playing a major role in it. In turn this explains,
in part at least, the westward expansion of the Assyrian realm, a move
to control the northern termini of the trade routes, and also the
resistance of the Syrian and Palestinian principalities to this expansion.
The Assyrians proved too strong, however, and we hear of the kings
of Damascus, Samaria, Tyre and Zabibe, 'queen of the Arabs', paying
tribute to Tiglath-Pileser in 738 BC (ITP 69).

In his actions and those of Sargon II (721–705 BC) towards the Arabs we can discern the outlines of a policy of integrating nomad groups into the imperial system in border regions. This was important for maintaining peace and security in these areas and for providing a reserve of military manpower. Certain chiefs would be selected for official appointments, usually with titles and remuneration attached. For example one 'Idibi'ilu the Arab' was assigned to the 'wardenship of the entrance to Egypt', implying duties of supervision and checking. And a draft of a 'king's order' to an official states explicitly: 'give Badi'ilu an appointment before you and let him pasture in the midst of the land', and mentions in the same sentence 'these Arabs' and keeping 'checkpoints in the desert as before'. Nomads were sometimes settled in frontier areas, as was done by Sargon on the Palestine–Sinai border, both for security and to undertake the transport of goods between Assyria and Egypt. Both rulers also made attempts to bring more tribes within the imperial orbit, namely 'the distant Arabs dwelling in the desert, who knew neither overseers nor officials and had not brought their tribute to any king'.[1]

In the seventh century BC the Assyrians fought a long war against a rebellious faction of Babylonians, in which the Qedarite Arabs took the latter's side, incurring punitive raids by Sennacherib (704–681 BC) and Assurbanipal (668–627 BC), the latter's vengeance being particularly severe:

Uaite son of Haza'el, king of Arabia, threw off the yoke of my rule. . . . He incited the people of Arabia to revolt, raiding again and again the kings of the west, the subject vassals entrusted to me. Against him I sent my troops who were within his territory, and they defeated him. The people of Arabia (*mât aribî*), inasmuch as they had rebelled with Uaite, they overcame by force of arms. The steppe-houses, the tents in which they lived, they kindled and set on fire. People of both sexes, donkeys, camels, cattle and flocks without number I brought to Assur. The area of my whole land, in its entirety, they filled as far as it stretches. Camels like flocks I divided up and shared out to the people of Assur. Within my land one bought a camel at the market gate for a few pence. The alewife obtained for one portion, the brewer for one jar, the gardener for a bundle of cress, camels and people. The rest of Arabia, which had fled before my weapons, Erra the strong [god of plague and famine] overcame them. Famine broke out among them so that they ate the flesh of their children to keep from starving. . . . The people in Arabia asked each other: 'Why has such a disaster befallen Arabia? It is because we did not abide by the great oaths of Assur, we sinned against the kindness of Assurbanipal, the king who pleases the heart of Enlil.' To Uaite came misfortune so that he fled alone into the land of Nabayoth.

(VAT 5600)

Assyria crushed the insurrection only to become embroiled in a civil war which, together with incursions by the Medes, led to its own demise in 609 BC. Now the kingdom of Babylonia came to the fore once more. It produced two very famous monarchs in its brief renaissance. Best known to us is Nebuchadnezzar (605–562 BC), architect of the wondrous hanging gardens and conqueror of Jerusalem, who also sent military units 'to the desert, where they plundered extensively the possessions, animals and gods of the numerous Arabs' (ABC 101). More relevant to the history of Arabia, though, is Nabonidus, who 'took the road to [the north Arabian oasis towns of] Tayma, Dedan, Fadak, Khaybar, Yadi', and as far as Yathrib, where for ten years [c.552–543 BC] I went about among them and did not enter my city Babylon' (Harran inscription H2A 1.24–26). Documents concerned with this event relate that the king went there as a conqueror, vanquished the king of Dedan, slew the ruler of Tayma and erected a palace for himself in the latter oasis. They do not, however, make clear his reasons for his relocation. He is known to have been a fervent devotee of the moon god Sin, even demoting Marduk, the principal deity of Babylon, in Sin's favour, and may have gone to Tayma to escape opposition at home and to promote Sin abroad. Otherwise modern scholars look for more pragmatic explanations, such as control of the lucrative trade passing through north Arabia from the south or establishment of relations with polities near to Egypt, Babylon's main rival, like the confederation of Qedar.

From the ninth century onwards Assyrian rulers had on occasion to rein in these 'princes of Qedar', as also did Nebuchadnezzar in 598. Like the Midianites of the Bible these people were essentially nomadic pastoralists, who 'have no gates, no bars, who live in a remote place' (Jeremiah 49.31), who lived in 'tents' (Canticles 1.5, Psalms 120.5), who paid for their needs with 'lambs, rams and he-goats' (Ezekiel 27.21). And also like the Midianites certain Qedarite clans became wealthy from their involvement in trading activities. The advent of the Persians was propitious for Qedar and other Arab groups, since

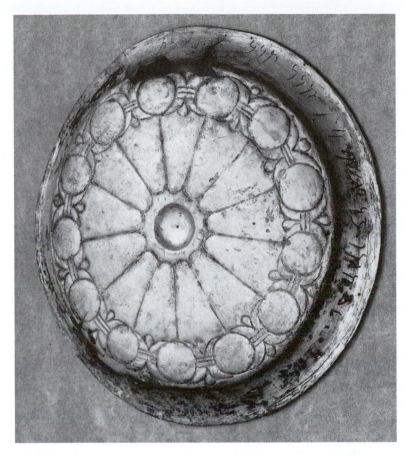

Plate 10 Silver bowl found at Tell el-Maskhuta near Ismailia in Egypt dedicated by a king of Qedar to the goddess Lat, diameter 16.7 cm (Brooklyn Museum of Art 545034).

'they did not yield the obedience of slaves to the Persians, but were united to them by friendship for having given Cambyses passage into Egypt, which the Persians could not enter without the consent of the Arabs' (Herodotus 3.88). And by 400 BC we detect Qedar's presence as far west as the borders of Egypt, as is illustrated by a silver bowl from that region bearing the Aramaic inscription: 'that which Qaynu son of Geshem, king of Qedar, brought in offering to the [goddess] Allat' (Pl. 10).[2]

THE GRECO-ROMAN/PARTHIAN
PERIOD (*c.*330 BC–AD 240)

Our documentation for Arabia, and for the north in particular, becomes much better in this period. In the first place the rise of Hellenistic and Roman rule was accompanied by the efflorescence of Hellenistic and Roman science, which provides us for the first time with detailed accounts of Arabia and its inhabitants. Imperialism and scholarship often went hand in hand, would-be conquerors launching fact-finding missions before embarking on their conquests. Three comprehensive works survive: Strabo's *Geography* (written and revised 25 BC–AD 23), Pliny the Elder's *Natural history* (completed AD 77) and Ptolemy's *Geography* (completed *c.*AD 150), all of which incorporate eyewitness observations of contemporaries as well as earlier reports. The first two follow the Hellenistic tradition of dividing Arabia into 'Felix' (the Arabian peninsula)[3] and 'Deserta' (mainly the Syrian desert). Ptolemy, however, subdivides the latter to make room for his 'Arabia Petraea' ('rocky Arabia'), which for him stretched from the lava-lands south of Damascus to the eastern delta of Egypt and was roughly coterminous with the former kingdom of the Nabataeans.

In the second place many indigenous groups of north and central Arabia began to find their own voice, making themselves known to the historical record by inscribing on stone. These texts are either in north Arabian dialects and various versions of the Arabian alphabet (see chapter 8 below), or they are written in the Aramaic language and script (often with Greek translation in the case of Palmyra). They are mostly graffiti, personal testimonies, noting private thoughts, feelings and daily activities, though a good number, especially the Aramaic texts, are formal statements commemorating commercial or military successes, the completion of a building or tomb, the dedication of a statue, and so on. Here we will give a brief account of the most important of these groups.

Writers of north Arabian texts

Tribes of the Harra

In the basalt desert (*ḥarra*) that stretches from southeast Syria across northeast Jordan and into northern Saudi Arabia, and also in the sandy deserts further east, there have been found some 20,000 graffiti written in a north Arabian dialect. Because the first texts discovered by Europeans were next to the Safa, the lava fields to the southeast of

Damascus, modern scholars usually refer to the language as Safaitic. Its users speak of their herding and pasturing of animals, particularly camels, their raiding and hunting, their prayers and their sacrifices, their sorrows and their loves, their hardships and their comforts, their genealogies and tribal affiliation, and their summer and winter migrations. Both the content and distribution of these texts make it clear that their writers were nomadic pastoralists. But though they lived apart from sedentary communities and chiefly concerned them-selves with their own activities, they were aware of events in the wider world. This might be via those who travelled abroad, for we have Safaitic graffiti from very diverse locations (Dura Europos, Palmyra, Hegra, Lebanon, Pompei), or from those who worked among settled peoples (one text, for example, mentions 'Aqrab son of Abgar, a horseman in the military unit of the Amrat tribe', MNA 64). If texts are dated, it will often be by reference to some external event: 'the year of the revolt of the Nabataeans against the Romans' (WH 2815), 'the year the Persians fought the Romans at Bosra' (CIS 5.4448), 'the year the troops of Germanicus were at Naq'at' (PAES 4C.653), 'the year Rabbel was made king' (ISB 57). Though it is rarely possible to assign a specific date to such references, they tell us that these tribes were active during the time of Nabataean and Roman rule, though how much before and after this is impossible to say.

Tribes of the Hisma

The sandy desert spanning modern southeast Jordan and northwest Saudi Arabia is known as the Hisma. Its ancient inhabitants are known only from the thousands of inscriptions they etched on the sandstone mountains and rocks of their desert. Their language was a north Arabian dialect, which we call Hismaic because of its provenance. Its users speak of their genealogical and tribal affiliation, call attention to their animal drawings, pray to be remembered, blessed, rewarded or heard by their deities, express their feelings of happiness, sickness, grief, love and desire, boast of their sexual conquests, record their building or ownership of animal enclosures and other structures, and describe hunting trips. Hismaic graffiti lack the dating formulae found in Safaitic, but there are good reasons for thinking that their owners were also contemporaries of Nabataean rule. Firstly Nabataean royal names often feature as part of their own names, such as 'Abd Haritat and 'Abd Obodat. Secondly they have recourse to much the same deities as the Nabataeans: Allat, Kutba and especially Dushara. And finally their writings occasionally exhibit features of Nabataean phonology and orthography. There is no evidence, however, for the length of time over which these texts were written.

Oasis-dwellers

Among the far-flung oases of this region there are three that receive attention from outsiders, namely Tayma, Dedan and Duma. Agriculture had long been practised at Tayma and it had been involved in trade since at least the mid-eighth century BC. Its script, a version of the Arabian type, may already have been in existence at this time, for an eighth-century BC prince regent of Carchemish in northern Syria claims knowledge of 'Taimani writing' (CHLI 1.131). Certainly many graffiti have been found in or around Tayma, written in a north Arabian dialect, but all are undated. One refers to 'Nabonidus, king of Babel' (Askubi 169), so it was penned in the mid-sixth century, but how much earlier or later the rest are we do not know. Most are brief and offer little more than names, though a few tell us about local gods and of conflicts with Dedan and neighbouring tribes, two of which – Nabayoth and Massa – are mentioned in the Bible as sons of Ishmael (WR T11, 13, 15–16; Genesis 25.13–14). In addition there have been found some thirty Aramaic inscriptions. Most simply convey names and dedications, but one, found in a sanctuary of Tayma along with offering tables, cultic implements and a decorated stone pedestal, is carved onto a stone tablet and records the installation in the oasis of a deity named Salm of Hagam. Though the exact dating of these texts is disputed, they probably belong to the Persian period when Aramaic became a lingua franca of the Middle East.

In the sixth century BC the oasis of Dedan receives mention from Biblical sources, which speak of its 'caravans' and merchandise of 'saddlecloths' (Isaiah 21.13; Ezekiel 27.20), and also from the account of Nabonidus' activities, which include the slaying of a 'king of Dedan'. Probably from the same period, if not the same person, is the epitaph of 'Kabir'il son of Mata''il, king of Dedan' (JS Lih138). Sometime later Dedan came under the domination of the 'kings of Lihyan', a number of whom are named in inscriptions of the town and its environs. We do not know precisely when this event occurred. An upper limit is given by an inscription (JS Lih349) recording a 'governor of Dedan' (rather than of Lihyan), which evidently belongs to the Persian period (539–334 BC), since the Persian term (*pḥt*) is used. A lower limit is set by the annexation of Dedan by the Nabataeans, which must have happened by 24 BC, when we know that they were in control of nearby Hegra, and probably a lot earlier.

Evidence of Ptolemaic influence on Lihyanite sculptural styles and the presence of the name Talmay among Lihyanite rulers may mean that the latter were contemporaries of the Ptolemies of Egypt (305–31 BC). Furthermore we know that the Lihyanite kingdom was contemporary with the Minaeans (*c*.500–100 BC), whose texts mention a trading colony at Dedan and also refer to Lihyan. All this together tells us that the kingdom of Lihyan flourished for at least a century and a half sometime between the fifth and first centuries BC.

As well as a few hundred graffiti, usually recording no more than the person's name, Lihyan left behind a good number of monumental inscriptions, commemorating the construction of tombs and agricultural installations and the dedication of stelae and statues (Pl. 11). The money to pay for this came from its involvement in the aromatics trade between south Arabia and the Mediterranean and Mesopotamian worlds. The exact nature of this involvement is not clear, since the main agents would seem to have been the Minaeans,

Plate 11 Head of a Lihyanite sandstone statue from Dedan (A. al-Ansary).

whose activities at Dedan are also attested by inscriptions. Possibly Lihyan was simply a powerful tribe that moved in to impose taxes in return for guaranteeing security. Otherwise it is possible that they acted as allies of Egypt against the Nabataeans, allowing aromatics to pass directly to Egypt via the Red Sea rather than going overland through Nabataean territory. The consequent loss of profits would then have been one of the reasons why the Nabataeans eventually decided to extend their sway southwards over the oasis towns of Tayma and Dedan and extirpate Lihyan. In any case the last disappear from the historical record at this time and are only heard of again in Muslim sources as a branch of the tribal confederation of Hudhayl, still in the Hijaz area.

Duma (early Islamic Dumat al-Jandal, modern al-Jawf) lies at the southern end of the Wadi Sirhan, which was an important route connecting northern Arabia and southern Syria. It is mentioned in Assyrian texts, under the name *Adummatu*, as the seat of the confederation of Qedar and the base of their cult. This receives confirmation from the inscriptions found in the vicinity, written in a similar language and script to those of Tayma, which offer prayers to a number of divinities. One requests 'help in the matter of my love' from Ruda, Nuha and Atarsamain, all three known to the Assyrians as gods of Qedar (WR J23; IA 53). None is dated, but they mostly likely belong to the period of Qedar's prosperity in the eighth to fifth centuries BC. Thereafter we hear nothing of Duma until it fell into the hands of the Nabataeans, whose presence there is known from a Nabataean inscription of AD 44 .

Thamud

This is the name of a tribe or tribal confederation of northwest Arabia. Sargon II (721–705 BC) boasts of having defeated them along with other tribes, 'the distant desert-dwelling Arabs', and of having resettled the survivors in Samaria (AR 2.17, 118). In classical times we find them recorded in texts such as Pliny's *Natural history* and Ptolemy's *Geography*, and some groups of them enrolled in the Roman army. One such group constructed a temple at Rawwafa in northwest Arabia and commemorated it with a bilingual Greek–Nabataean inscription:

For the wellbeing of the rulers of the whole world . . . Marcus Aurelius Anthoninus [AD 161–80] and Lucius Aurelius Verus, who are the conquerors of the Armenians. This is the temple that was built by the tribal unit[4] of Thamud, the leaders of their unit, so that it might be established by their hands and be their place of veneration for ever . . . with the support of Antistius Adventus the governor.

(BIA 10.55)

Later, in the fourth century AD, two military units drawn from Thamud are recorded as serving in the Byzantine army, one in Palestine and the other in Egypt (*Notitia dignitatum* Or. 28.17, 34.22).

According to Muslim historians Thamud was one of the ancient Arab tribes who had perished in remote antiquity. The Quran relates how they were destroyed by a 'shout', an earthquake or a thunderbolt, for having rejected the prophet Salih, who had been sent to them by God. And already Arab poets of the sixth century regarded Thamud as a people that had vanished in times past (see chapter 8 below). This then raises the question of whether we are talking about the same tribe over this very long period of time. Possibly the original tribe died out or dispersed at some point, but the name, on account of its antiquity, was subsequently adopted by some new grouping.

Writers of Aramaic/Greek texts

Around the fringes of the Syrian desert were found a number of polities that have often been described as Arab both by Greco-Roman writers and modern scholars. There are, for instance, the Nabataeans of Petra, the Idumaeans of southern Palestine, the Ituraeans around Mount Lebanon, the Emesenes of the Orontes valley, the Abgarids of Edessa, the Praetavi of Sinjar (Pliny 5.86), the Characenes of lower Iraq and the inhabitants of Hatra and Palmyra. In general there is not enough evidence to confirm or refute their Arab character. However, the position of these polities on the edge of the settled lands makes it likely that their populations, even if originally of Arab origin, soon became substantially assimilated to the prevailing Greco–Aramaean culture and fell to some extent under the sway of either Rome or Iran. Moreover, as urban societies, they would probably have perceived a marked contrast between themselves and the peoples of the steppe. Thus the inscriptions of Hatra distinguish between residents of Hatra and inhabitants of the outlying areas (IIH 336, 343). And a Palmyrene text honours Ogelos son of Makkaios in AD 199 'for his having served well in many campaigns against the nomads and having provided safety for the merchants and caravans' (PAT 1378). Lastly, many of these polities were centres of transit trade and so were open to a whole host of influences; the religious life of Hatra, for example, is a wonderfully eclectic mix of Mesopotamian, Syrian, Arab and Greco-Roman elements.

It is perhaps instructive to look at the career of the Emesenes. They are first referred to in a letter of Cicero of 51 BC where he notes that 'Iamblichus, a chief (*phylarch*) of the Arabs', was likely to be well disposed to Rome in the event of a Parthian invasion (*Ad familiares* 15.1.2). And with regard to the 40s BC Strabo speaks of Arethusa on the Orontes as 'belonging to Sampsikeramus and Iamblichus his son, chiefs of the people (*ethnos*) of the Emesenes' (15.2.10–11). By the first century AD this tribe seems to have settled down at its capital of Emesa (modern Homs), and its leading family has been recognised by Rome as kings (a 'king Shamashgeram' appears on a Palmyrene text, Sy 12.139). Furthermore it has acquired Roman citizenship, as is shown by the use of the name Julius in inscriptions (e.g. IGLS 5.2212: 'Julius Samsigeramus, son of Julius Alexio', dated AD 79). But we know next to nothing about the urban history of its capital or of the social structure or culture of its subjects. Indeed we know very little about any of these polities except for three – Petra, Palmyra and Hatra – which became very famous and so deserve a mention here.

Nabataeans

Eratosthenes of Cyrene (*c*.284–202 BC) records from his source, who had travelled the length of the incense route from south Arabia to Syria, that one passes in this journey through the lands 'of the Arab peoples' such as the Nabataeans and Hegraeans (cited in Strabo 16.4.2). Whether the Nabataeans thought themselves to be Arabs, however, we do not know for sure. They would seem to have moved into the area around Petra (modern south Jordan) in the wake of the demise of Qedar in the fourth century BC. Their nomadic roots are clear from the account of Diodorus Siculus (*c*.80–20 BC) whose chief source was the historian Hieronymus of Cardia, a high-ranking official in the court of Antigonus, one of the generals of Alexander the Great (d. 323):

> They live in the open air, claiming as native land a wilderness that has neither rivers nor abundant springs from which it is possible for a hostile army to obtain water. It is their custom neither to plant grain, set out any fruit-bearing tree, use wine, nor construct any house; and if anyone is found acting contrary to this, death is his penalty. They follow this custom

because they believe that those who possess these things are, in order to retain the use of them, easily compelled by the powerful to do their bidding. Some of them raise camels, others sheep, pasturing them in the desert. . . . They are exceptionally fond of freedom; and whenever a strong force of enemies comes near, they take refuge in the desert, using this as a fortress; for it lacks water and cannot be crossed by others. But to them alone, since they have prepared subterranean reservoirs lined with stucco, it furnishes safety.

(Diodorus 19.94)

In the pages of Strabo, writing three centuries after Hieronymus, a very different picture is painted. The Nabataeans have evidently now settled down: they have houses, a king, though aspects of tribal egalitarianism are still manifest in his behaviour, and they even practise agriculture:

The metropolis of the Nabataeans is Petra [rock], as it is called; for it lies on a site which is otherwise smooth and level, but it is fortified all round by a rock, the outside parts of the site being precipitous and sheer, and the inside parts having springs in abundance, both for domestic purposes and for watering gardens. Outside the circuit of the rock most of the territory is desert, in particular that towards Judaea. Here too is the shortest road to Jericho, a journey of three or four days, as also to the Palm Grove [the Tabuk region], a journey of five days. Petra is always ruled by some king from the royal family; and the king has as administrator one of his companions, who is called 'brother'. The Nabataeans are a sensible people, and are so much inclined to acquire possessions that they publicly fine anyone who has diminished his possessions and also confer honours on anyone who has increased them. Since they have but few slaves, they are served by their kinsfolk for the most part, or by one another, or by themselves; and the custom extends to their kings. . . . Their homes, through the use of stone, are costly; but, on account of peace, the cities are not walled. Most of the country is well supplied with fruits except the olive; they use sesame-oil instead. The sheep are white-fleeced and the oxen are large, but the country produces no horses. Camels afford the service they require instead of horses. They go out without

71

tunics, with girdles about their loins, and with slippers on their feet, even the kings, though in their case the colour is purple.

(Strabo 16.4.21, 26)

The nearby Dead Sea 'produces asphalt in abundance, and from it they derive not a little revenue' (Diodorus 2.48), but it was trade that made the Nabataeans famous, particularly in the luxury goods of southern Arabia:

> While there are many Arabian tribes who use the desert as pasture, the Nabataeans far surpass the others in wealth although they are not much more than ten thousand in number. For not a few of them are accustomed to bring down to the sea frankincense and myrrh and the most valuable kinds of spices, which they procure from those who convey them from what is called Arabia Felix.
>
> (Diodorus 19.94)

Their capital of Petra lay, as Pliny notes (6.144), where 'two roads meet, one leading from Syria via Palmyra, and the other coming from Gaza'. At the peak of their power the Nabataeans also controlled much territory around Petra: the Negev to the west, Transjordan and the Hawran to the north, and southwards and eastwards into Arabia as far as Hegra and Duma.

Inevitably such success did not come without a price and many ambitious leaders had their eye on Petra. The earliest encounter was with the aforementioned Antigonus, who dispatched two expeditions, one led by his commander Athenaeus, the second by his son Demetrius. The former was initially successful, for most of the citizens of Petra were away at a festival, and he was able to seize much 'frankincense and myrrh' and 'about five hundred talents of silver'. But the Nabataeans pursued them and came upon them asleep in their camp. 'Most of the hostile troops they slaughtered where they lay; the rest they slew with their javelins as they awoke and sprang to arms'. Demetrius at first set about besieging Petra, but an embassy from its citizens 'persuaded him to receive as gifts the most precious of their products and to make terms with them' (Diodorus 19.95–97). Yet in general the Nabataeans, as Strabo (16.4.18) notes, 'lived a peaceful life' and enjoyed quite good relations with the two empires on either side of them, the Ptolemies and the Seleucids. An emporium flourishes best under peaceful conditions and the Nabataeans are often reported to have made large payments and offered favourable terms to avoid conflicts that would damage their trading concerns. Their main enemy was the Jewish kingdom to their west, and throughout the first century BC the two bickered and intrigued, but here too confrontations were minor. With their annexation of Syria in 63 BC, the Romans drew near to the frontiers of the Nabataean realm. They were not, however, keen to govern this wild territory themselves, deciding instead to leave a local potentate in control as long as Roman suzerainty was at least nominally acknowledged. And this combination of close relations with Rome and local autonomy produced magnificent achievements in the domains of art, architecture and irrigation.

Yet this success was in a sense the Nabataeans' undoing, for they made their land into a worthwhile prize. In 106 AD it was annexed by Rome, as is recorded in the laconic notice of Cassius Dio: 'Palma, the governor of Syria, subjugated Arabia around Petra and made it subject to the Romans' (68.14.5). In typically efficient Roman manner auxiliary military units were immediately transferred to the new province, a road was built straight through it linking Syria to the Red Sea, dates were calculated according to years since the province's inauguration, and Greek quickly became the official language. Possibly there was even some social reorganisation: 'Recently the Romans have conquered Arabia and have done away with the old laws there used to be, particularly circumcision, which was a custom they practised' (Bardaisan 56). Thereafter Petra went into gentle decline, in part because Bosra became the principal city of the new province, but also because of changes in trade patterns which had begun long before. Improvements in navigational skills in the first century BC meant that the luxury goods of south Arabia no longer had to be transported overland to the Mediterranean, but could go by sea. Travel by land necessitated passing through Nabataean territory, but use of the sea offered an alternative passage via Egypt:

> The loads of aromatics are conveyed from Leuke Kome [a Red Sea port on the northwest Arabian coast] to Petra and thence to Rhinocoloura [modern al-Arish]. . . . But at the present time they are for the most part transported via the Nile to Alexandria. They are landed from Arabia and India at Myos Hormos [a Red Sea port on the Egyptian coast] and then they are conveyed by camels over to Coptus in Thebais, which is situated on a canal of the Nile, and then to Alexandria.
>
> (Strabo 16.4.24)

The competition for this lucrative trade seems to have driven the Nabataeans at times to attempt piracy: 'These Nabataeans formerly lived a peaceful life, but later by means of rafts took to plundering the vessels of people sailing from Egypt. But they paid the penalty when a fleet went over and ravaged their country' (Strabo 16.4.18).

Palmyrenes

It is in the context of trade that Palmyra (in modern Syria) first enters history. A tablet of the nineteenth century BC, deriving from an Assyrian commercial colony established in Asia Minor, mentions one Puzu-Ishtar 'the Tadmuraean' (Tadmur is the local name for Palmyra) as witness to a contract. There are, however, very few references to Tadmur in historical texts until the first century BC, when we also have archaeological evidence for its metamorphosis into a substantial settlement. Given its central location on the route between Mesopotamia and the Mediterranean, it was always in danger of falling prey to the whims of greater powers:

> Palmyra is a city famous for its situation, for the richness of its soil and for its agreeable springs. Its fields are surrounded on every side by a vast circuit of sand, and it is as it were isolated by nature from the world, having a destiny of its own between the two mighty empires of Rome and Parthia, and at the first moment of a quarrel between them always attracting the attention of both sides.
>
> (Pliny 5.88)

In 41 BC it caught the eye of Mark Antony, at a time when he was infatuated with Cleopatra and needed money:

> Antony sent a cavalry force to Palmyra, situated not far from the Euphrates, to plunder it, bringing the trifling accusation against its inhabitants that being on the frontier between the Romans and the Parthians, they had avoided taking sides between them. For being merchants they bring the products of India and Arabia from Persia and dispose of them in the Roman territory. But in fact Antony's intention was to enrich his horsemen. However, the Palmyrenes were forewarned and they transported their property across the river and, stationing themselves on the bank, prepared to shoot anybody who should attack them, for they are expert bowmen. The

74

cavalry found nothing in the city. They turned round and came back having met no foe and empty-handed.

(Appian 5.9)

But in these days of superpower conflict neutrality was not an option, and by AD 20 at the latest Rome had effectively annexed Palmyra. In the temple of Bel itself is a bronze statue of the emperor Tiberius (AD 14–37), its base bearing a dedication in Latin. Gradually Palmyra acquired all the trappings of a Greco-Roman city: senate, assembly of the people, magistrates, agora, theatre, baths, colonnaded streets, Roman garrison and so on. The Palmyrenes seem to have been content with their new lot and do not appear to have regarded the Roman troops in their city as an occupying force. When in AD 129 Hadrian came to pay them a visit, they took to calling themselves Hadrianopolitans, saying 'their city had been founded anew by the emperor' (Stephen of Byzantium, *s.v.* 'Palmyra'). Moreover we find detachments of Palmyrene archers deployed throughout the empire in places as far apart as Upper Dacia (in modern Romania) and Africa.

In the third century Rome was troubled by Germanic tribes in the west and by a new Iranian dynasty in the east, the Sasanians, who replaced the Parthians in AD 224. Their second ruler, Shapur (242–70), advanced into Roman territory and achieved sweeping victories, culminating in the capture of the emperor Valerian himself in 259. A leading citizen of Palmyra and a Roman senator, one Odenathus son of Hairan son of Wahballat son of Nasor – his genealogy indicating that he was of Arab ancestry – stepped into the power vacuum and took up Rome's cause. In the course of the 260s 'he collected a band of Syrian country folk and put up a spirited resistance. On a number of occasions he routed the Persians and not only defended our border, but even as the avenger of the Roman empire, marvellous to say, forced his way to Ctesiphon' (Festus 23). For this achievement he was named 'restorer of all the east' and effectively acted as the vicegerent of Rome in the east. Whether he had further ambitions we do not know. He may have witnessed the accession to the imperial office of Philip the Arab in 244 and the claim to the purple by an Arab potentate of Emesa in 253, both events occurring in response to a crisis posed by a Persian threat, and thought that he too should put himself forward for the supreme office. Any such dreams, however, were cut short by his and his son's assassination in 267.

The designs of his wife Zenobia, acting on behalf of her young son Wahballat, were more transparent. 'Boasting herself to be of the family

Plate 12 Silver tetradrachm, mint of Alexandria, showing bust of Zenobia and bearing the Greek legend *septim{ia} Zenobia seb{astê}*, Greek for 'Augusta', AD 271–73 (British Museum 314245).

of the Cleopatras and the Ptolemies, she proceeded upon the death of her husband to cast about her shoulders the imperial mantle' (*Scriptores historiae Augustae* 24.30.2). On a milestone and a statue-base she designated her husband posthumously as 'king of kings'. Her armies then set off to occupy Egypt and to advance across Asia Minor. The titles accorded Wahballat on milestones and coins suggest that she initially sought for her son joint rule with the successive emperors Claudius and Aurelian, far away in Europe. Only when Aurelian made it clear that he would have none of this and marched out to meet her did she adopt the titles 'Augusta' and 'Augustus' for herself and her son (Pl. 12). Aurelian brought his forces through Asia Minor, defeated the Palmyrene army near Antioch, then pursued Zenobia to her home city, capturing her and her city in AD 272. But though her reign was brief, Zenobia's fame was long-lived. Aurelian himself was supposed to have acknowledged that 'it was her doing that Odenathus defeated the Persians' and pointed out that 'such was the fear that this woman inspired in the peoples of the east and also the Egyptians that not Arabs nor Saracens nor Armenians ever moved against her'. And tales soon circulated of how 'her spirit was divinely great and her beauty incredible', 'she hunted with the eagerness of a Spaniard and often drank with her generals', 'at banquets she used vessels of gold and jewels', she spoke Greek, Latin and Egyptian, and was 'well versed in the history of Alexandria and the Orient' (*Scriptores historiae Augustae* 24.30.6–22). She was in short, as recorded on a milestone near Palmyra, a 'most illustrious queen' (CIS 2.3971).[5]

Hatrans

Hatra (in modern north Iraq) was a round-shaped city about 2 km in diameter, in its centre a great temple dedicated to the sun god Shamash. Of the four hundred or so Aramaic inscriptions discovered there some thirty are dated, ranging from AD 89 to 238, but how much before and after this period the city was settled is not yet certain. Two Roman emperors attempted to wrest it from its Parthian overlords, but its high, thick walls and arid hinterland saved it on both occasions:

> This city is neither large nor prosperous, and the surrounding country is mostly desert and has neither water, save a small amount and that poor in quality, nor timber nor fodder. These very disadvantages, however, afford it protection, making impossible a siege by a large multitude, as does also the sun god, to whom it is consecrated. For it was taken neither at this time by Trajan [AD 117] nor later by Severus [*c*.AD 198], although they both overthrew parts of the wall.
>
> (Cassius Dio 68.31)

Later, perhaps with the fall of the Parthians, it does seem to have gone over to the Romans, since Latin inscriptions attest to Roman troops stationed there in the 230s. But this incurred the wrath of the Sasanian emperor Ardashir, who, after a long siege, finally razed the city's bastions in AD 240, and by AD 363 it could be said by a casual observer to have been 'long since deserted' (Ammianus 25.8.5). Yet so strong was the belief in its invincibility that a rumour circulated that the king of Hatra's daughter, the fair Nadira, had fallen in love with Ardashir's son, the dashing young Shapur, and betrayed Hatra's Achilles' heel:

> She instructed him: 'Take a silver-coloured ring dove and write on its leg with the menstrual blood of a blue-eyed virgin girl. Then let it go and it will alight on the city wall and the latter will crumble away.' This was in fact the talisman of the city and only this could destroy it.
>
> (Tabari 1.829)

Since almost no historical writings have come down to us from the Parthians or Sasanians, we are obliged to rely upon the physical remains and inscriptions of Hatra for information about its past. Most of the inscribed texts are relatively brief, prayers for the author to be kept in mind or be blessed (*dkyr/bryk*) by the gods and dedications of statues, altars and the like, but interestingly occupations and offices are often given. Among the former we encounter stonemasons, sculptors, metalworkers, carpenters, scribes, tutors, priests, physicians, accountants, doorkeepers, merchants and winesellers. Of the offices many seem to have religious connections, such as 'accountant of the temple of [the deity] Ba'alshamin', 'standard-bearer of Shamash', 'steward of Allat' (IIH 49, 202, 384). The title of 'king' only appears around AD 160, perhaps reflecting that the city had acquired greater prominence or independence within the Parthian realm. The full title was 'king of *'Arab'* or 'king of *'Arabaye'*. These terms could signify the name of the region, or all its inhabitants, or just the nomadic part of the population. But since one would not expect a city-dwelling ruler to be called 'king of the nomads', the royal title most likely referred to the region and/or its population over which Hatra had authority.

BYZANTINE/SASANIAN PERIOD
(c.AD 240–630)

The various polities that flourished on the perimeter of the Syrian desert in the wake of the collapse of Seleucid power had established working relations with the nomadic pastoralists around them and performed the useful task of regulating the activities of these peoples on behalf of the empires of Rome and Persia. With their abolition of these polities in the course of the second and third centuries AD, the two empires were forced to deal directly with the nomads on their borders. In general they adopted the time-honoured methods of their imperial predecessors, handing out titles and subsidies to various Arab clans in exchange for desisting from attacking imperial citizens, maintaining order in the frontier regions and providing military aid when required. As the Persian emperor Khosro I reputedly said to Byzantine ambassadors suing for peace after his destruction of Antioch in AD 540: 'You give an annual payment of gold to some of the Huns and to the Saracens . . . in order that they may keep your land unplundered for all time' (Procopius 2.10). And the Persians did the same: 'They [the clan of Nasr ibn Rabi'a of the tribe of Lakhm] became rulers because the Persian kings employed them for this purpose, relying on them to keep the adjacent Arabs under control' (Tabari 1.769). The Persians chiefly depended upon these Nasrids, who had their base in Hira in southern Iraq; the Jafnids of Ghassan, based in the Golan, were the Byzantines' most famous Arab allies, though they also made use of chiefs of Salih, Tanukh and other tribes.

Our earliest literary source for such matters is the soldier and scholar Ammianus Marcellinus (d. *c*.395). With regard to AD 363 he describes a joint operation of the Persian prime minister and 'Malechus, known as Podosaces, chief of the Assanite Saracens, a notorious brigand, who with every kind of cruelty had long raided our territory' (24.2.4). In the same year, after the emperor Julian's victory at Callinicum, 'the princes of the Saracen nations, as supplicants on bended knees, presented him with a golden crown and did obeisance to him as lord of the world and its peoples. And they were gladly received since they were well suited to guerilla warfare' (23.3.8). In addition we have epigraphic evidence. A bilingual Persian–Parthian inscription (Paikuli 92) lists among the vassals of the Sasanian emperor Narseh (293–302) an "Amru king of the Lakhmids' (*'Amrw lhm'dyn mlk'*). His son Imru' al-Qays (d. 328) is described in Muslim sources as governor for the Persians 'over the frontier lands of the Arabs of Rabi'a, Mudar, and the rest of the tribes in the deserts of Iraq, Hijaz and Mesopotamia' (Tabari 1.833–34). His tomb lies in Byzantine territory, by the fort of Nemara in the basalt desert southeast of Damascus, possibly because 'he became a Christian' (Tabari 1.834) and went over to the Byzantines or maybe because he died while on a raiding expedition in enemy country. On it is inscribed the following epitaph (see Pl. 32a):

> This is the monument of Imru' al-Qays son of 'Amr, king of all the Arabs, who . . . ruled both sections of al-Azd and Nizar and their kings, and chastised Madhhij, so that he successfully smote, in the irrigated land of Najran, the realm of [the Himyarite king] Shammar. And he ruled Ma'add. . . . And no king had matched his achievements up to the time when he died, in prosperity, in the year 223, the seventh day of Kislul [AD 328].[6]

This is an extremely important document for charting the emergence of a sense of identity among Arabs, not only for its use of the expression 'king of all the Arabs', but also for its deployment of the Arabic language, albeit written in Nabataean script.

Providing subsidies to outlying tribes achieved two aims. Firstly it gave the chief on the receiving end some reason to adhere to a treaty for a number of years and not just to break it at the first opportunity. Secondly, by giving that chief wealth to redistribute within his own entourage, the empire could hope to build up the position of a leader who might otherwise be compromised by relations with a settled power. Diplomatic payments thus helped to create and support allies beyond the frontier who would have a stake in maintaining the status quo and supporting their paymasters. Given the benefits such an association could bring, there were many who actively sought to win the recognition of the authorities:

> Amongst the Persians was a certain Amorkesus of the tribe of Nomalius, who, whether because he did not receive honour in the land of Persia or because for some other reason he thought the Roman empire better, left Persia and travelled to that part of Arabia adjacent to Persia. Setting out from here he made forays and attacks not upon any Romans, but upon the Saracens whom he encountered. Building up his forces from these, he gradually advanced. He seized one of the islands belonging to the Romans [in the Gulf of Aqaba], which was named Iotabe, and, ejecting the Roman tax collectors, held the island himself and amassed considerable wealth through collecting taxes. When he had seized other villages nearby, Amorkesus wished to become an ally of the Romans and phylarch of the Saracens under Roman rule on the borders of Arabia Petraea. He therefore sent Peter, the bishop of his tribe, to Leo, the Roman emperor [457–74], to see if he could persuade Leo and arrange these things. When Peter arrived and spoke to the emperor, Leo accepted his proposals and immediately sent for Amorkesus to come to him.
>
> (Malchus, frag. 1)

If not by a display of force, a would-be leader might try to win recognition by gifts or by gaining a reputation for strength and efficacy:

> This [the Arabian] coast immediately beyond the boundaries of Palestine is held by Saracens, who have been settled from of old in the Palm Grove. These groves are in the interior, extending over a great tract of land, and there absolutely nothing else grows except palm trees. The emperor Justinian [527–65] had received these palm groves as a present from Abikarib,[7] the ruler of the Saracens there, and he was appointed by the emperor phylarch over the Saracens in Palestine. And he guarded the land from plunder constantly,

for both to the barbarians over whom he ruled and no less to the enemy Abikarib always seemed a man to be feared and an exceptionally energetic fellow.

(Procopius 1.19.7–11)

In the fourth and fifth centuries these Arab vassals were not of great significance to imperial politics, but as the cold war waxed hot in the sixth century they became ever more embroiled in this great conflict. To both empires there had been allied numerous minor Arab chiefs of equal standing; now super-chiefs were created. This was undertaken first by the Persian emperor Kawad (488–531), who appointed the Nasrid Mundhir ibn Nu'man (504–54) as sole overlord of the Arabs in Persian lands. To counter this man, 'the most difficult and dangerous enemy of all to the Romans', the various clans loyal to the Byzantines were brought together under one chief, the Jafnid Harith ibn Jabala (529–69), now granted the title of 'king' (previous Arab rulers had only claimed it for themselves):

Mundhir, holding the position of king, ruled alone over all the Saracens in Persia, and he was always able to make his inroad with the whole army wherever he wished in the Roman domain. Neither any commander of Roman troops, whom they call *duces*, nor any leader of the Saracens allied with the Romans, who are called *phylarchs*, was strong enough with his men to array himself against Mundhir, for the troops stationed in the different districts were not a match [individually] in battle for the enemy. For this reason the emperor Justinian [527–65] put in command of as many clans as possible Harith the son of Jabala, who ruled over the Saracens of Arabia, and bestowed upon him the dignity of king (*basileus*), a thing which among the Romans had never been done before.

(Procopius 1.17)

This meant that the clash between the two empires was often played out between these two vassals:

Khosro . . . conferred with Mundhir concerning this matter [violating the treaty with the Byzantines] and commanded him to provide causes for war. So Mundhir brought against Harith the charge that he, Harith, was doing him violence in a matter of boundary lines, and he entered into conflict with him in time of peace and began to overrun the land of the Romans on this pretext. And he declared that, as for himself, he was not breaking the treaty between the Persians and the Romans, for neither of them had included him in it. And this was true. For no mention of Saracens was ever made in treaties, on the ground that they were included under the names of Persians and Romans. Now this country which at that time was claimed by both tribes of Saracens is called Strata, and extends to the south of the city of Palmyra. Nowhere does it produce a single tree or any of the useful growth of corn-lands, for it is burned exceedingly dry by the sun, but from of old it has been devoted to the pasturage of some few flocks. Now Harith maintained that the place belonged to the Romans, proving his assertion by the name which has long been applied to it by all – for Strata signifies 'a paved road' in the Latin tongue – and he also adduced the testimonies of men of the oldest times. Mundhir, however, was by no means inclined to quarrel concerning the name, but he claimed that tribute had been given him from of old for the pasturage there by the owners of the flocks.

(Procopius 2.1)

These Arab chiefdoms of the fourth to sixth centuries were very different from the client states of the Nabataeans, Palmyrenes and Hatrans of former times. The latter peoples were in general sedentary, they were assimilated to Greco-Aramaean culture, and they had their own revenues, derived from trade and agriculture, with which they sponsored art and architecture. The Arab principalities, on the other hand, though they usually had a base, lived as nomads. Thus Tanukh 'dwelt in shelters and tents of hair and skins' at a certain distance from the town of Hira, while the Christian population resided in 'permanent houses' (Tabari 1.822). And in accounts of these client kings the talk is always of the paraphernalia of soldiers on campaign:

Mundhir ibn Harith [the Jafnid] entered and took possession of the tent of Qabus ibn Mundhir [the Nasrid] and his entire encampment, all his baggage and his herds of camels. Several also of his relatives he made prisoners and some of his nobles, but the rest he put to the sword. Next he crossed over the Euphrates and pitched his camp in the territories of Qabus, and marched inland to the distance of sixty leagues, and arrived at the place where the herds and all the riches of the

Persian Arabs were. There he pitched his camp for some time, and the hordes of Qabus, on seeing their master's well-known tent erected so far in their land, boldly came to it expecting to find their king there. But on entering they found themselves in Mundhir's camp, and were seized and put to death, except some of note who were kept as prisoners. And after staying there as long as he chose, Mundhir set out upon his return with much spoil, consisting of herds of horses and camels and armour and so forth.

(John of Ephesus 6.3)

In the verses of their poets and later Muslim literature there would seem to be none more powerful. 'Do you not see', asks rhetorically one court poet of his Jafnid patron, 'that God has granted you such a degree of power that you will observe every king trembling at your feet. For you are the sun, the [other] kings are stars; when the sun rises, no star will be seen' (Nabigha 28). And certainly they would seek to imitate their overlords, dedicating buildings (tombs, churches, etc.), setting up court and extending patronage to exponents of culture, in particular promoting the use of the Arabic language in poetry and prose. But for their revenue they were largely dependent on imperial handouts, and when these were withdrawn they disappeared leaving few traces.

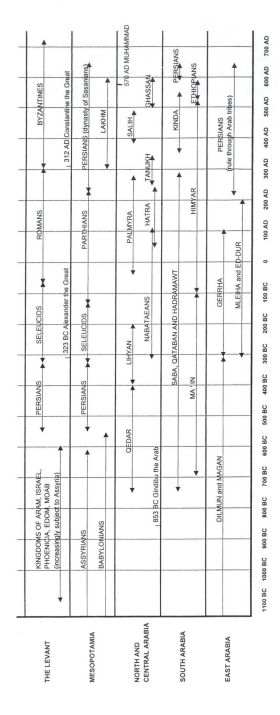

Fig. 2 Time chart showing approximate *floruit* of the principal polities mentioned in this book (Clare Hoyland).

4

ECONOMY

AGRICULTURE AND WATER MANAGEMENT

Arabia is more likely to conjure up images of desolate deserts than fertile fields, yet agriculture was, and still is, of great importance in certain parts (Pl. 13). However, since there are no permanent rivers or lakes in Arabia and rainfall is limited to certain times of the year (spring and summer in south Arabia, autumn/winter and spring elsewhere), careful management of water is everywhere necessary. Moreover high temperatures mean high evaporation rates, and when the rains do come they may be heavy but brief. Runoff is then immediate and often devastating. After a short time all the surface water has disappeared and the valleys become dry again. Methods had therefore to be devised for the effective catchment, distribution and storage of this precious resource. Terracing, the conversion of valley slopes into stone shelves, broke the pace of the floodwater, causing it to cascade gently down the step-like shelves, part of it sinking into the ground at each shelf, depositing in the process some of the soil and organic debris which it bore along (Pls. 1d, 7). Canals were cut to smooth out flooding irregularities, to circulate water evenly around fields and to convey it to areas lying beyond the reach of the floods. Small dams of compacted earth or loose stone were constructed at an angle to the banks of a valley to divert some of the floodwater to plots of land on either side. Across valleys more substantial dams would be built which served to calm the turbulence of the water, sometimes with the additional aid of stilling basins, and contain it until the desired level of water was reached, when it would be led off by canals to the awaiting fields. Finally, wells were dug and cisterns hollowed out in order to store water, chiefly for household consumption, but also to supplement irrigation sources in dry years.

Plate 13 Limestone Sabaean funerary stele showing the deceased engaged in ploughing, 1st–3rd century AD, 31.5 × 33.5 cm (Louvre AO20893).

There is good archaeological evidence for agriculture in east and south Arabia and in oases in the west and north, but textual references are more limited. The inhabitants of Dedan performed thanksgiving ceremonies to their god in gratitude for his blessings, such as 'abundant spring crops and abundant palm groves' (AH 150). The Nabataeans commemorated the building of dams in their inscriptions (e.g. NIA 7a, 7c, 10; NIN 8), and their construction of underground cisterns was remarked upon, a skill originally developed for crossing the desert, but which presumably stood them in good stead when they turned to agriculture:

> To them, since they have prepared subterranean reservoirs lined with stucco, it [the desert] furnishes safety. As the earth in some places is clayey and in others is of soft stone, they

make great excavations in it, the mouths of which they make very small. But by constantly increasing the width as they dig deeper, they finally make them of such size that each side has a length of one plethrum [*c*.30 metres]. After filling these reservoirs with rainwater, they close the openings, making them even with the rest of the ground, and they leave signs that are known to themselves but are unrecognisable by others.

(Diodorus 19.94)

But we hear most about agriculture from south Arabia where it features in a substantial proportion of all inscriptions, in odd contrast to commerce, which rarely receives a mention. The depth of silt deposits on some valley floors tells us that irrigation works began in this region as early as the mid-third millennium BC. The most prestigious project was the construction of a huge dam at Marib, which was possibly in operation as early as the mid-first millennium BC and which was maintained in use until the late sixth century AD (Pl. 14). The cultivated area that it watered attained some 9600 hectares (24,000 acres) or more, a vast patchwork of rectangular fields surrounded by earth walls and crisscrossed by an elaborate system of canals. Cereals were grown (wheat, barley and sorghum); also pulses, vegetables and other garden crops, dates, vines and fruits. Many times the dam was breached and had to be repaired, and its final destruction is recorded in the Quran:

> For the natives of Saba there was indeed a sign in their dwelling-place: a garden on their left and a garden on their right. We said to them: 'Eat of what your Lord has given you and render thanks to Him. Pleasant is your land and forgiving is your Lord.' But they gave no heed. So we unloosed upon them the waters of the dams and replaced their gardens by two others bearing bitter fruit, tamarisks, and a few nettle shrubs. Thus we punished them for their ingratitude.
>
> (34.15–17)

Offerings were frequently made to the gods in conjunction with requests for a good harvest. Typical is the prayer of a certain Lahay'at to the god 'Athtar for the protection 'of his family and their lands, in autumn and summer, and the vines that are in the fields' (RES 4230). Furthermore people would often record their contributions to the improvement of irrigation and cultivation, be they individuals, groups

Plate 14 Marib dam, ancient ruins of northern sluice system (AFSM).

or rulers. The most famous of such texts commemorates the repair of the Marib dam in 565 (AD 455), of which an extract is quoted here to give some impression of the scale of the undertaking:

> In 565 [of the Himyarite era] there was breached the diversion wall and the control wall and the settling basin and the dam and the canal from its foundations, the finished stone and the rough stone, while the dam was from its base a desolation. The king sent forth throughout Himyar and Hadramawt a summons among the tribes . . . and those who came were 20,000. Then they packed in the dam from its base up to its summit, packing in and facing with stone, and they made the face of its top six cubits. They built the diversion wall and the control wall with rough stone and polished stone and quoins of iron, while the settling basin they built with squared stones and rough stone, and then they cemented all . . . with lime. . . . That which they expended upon it, by estimation for the tribes who came to them and in actual expenditure for the craftsmen and the labourers, was 285,340 measures of fine flour, milled wheat, barley, corn and dates; 1363 slaughter camels, sheep and cattle; 1000 pairs of oxen and 670 camels carrying drink of different types of grapes and 42 loads of honey and butter.
>
> (CIS 4.540)

PASTORALISM

Whereas trees and plants are fixed assets, animals are mobile. Animal management (pastoralism) therefore allows greater flexibility of movement than crop management. At the sedentary end of the spectrum there is agropastoralism, which has been practised in the southern Levant and southern Arabia for thousands of years. This involves growing field crops such as wheat, barley and lentils on the arable plains, and raising sheep and goats on the stubble fields and on nearby mountain slopes and desert pastures. Further along the spectrum is transhumance, the seasonal movement of people and animals in search of grazing land. Typically transhumants specialise in sheep and goats which they move between winter pastures in the lowlands and summer pastures in the cooler highlands. In many cases they occupy permanent homes and villages in the winter seasons, moving into tents only in the spring and summer in order to follow their flocks. Finally, at the itinerant end of the spectrum and considered by outsiders most characteristic of Arabia, there is nomadic pastoralism. Its practitioners engage in horizontal rather than vertical movements and will often have to travel long distances in search of food and drink for their animals, following migratory routes that are determined by the availability of water and pasture. Even within this category there are distinctions, for some nomads will be moving around the arid enclaves located within settled lands, practising what anthropologists call enclosed nomadism. Others will traverse the 'sandy deserts spacious as the air in magnitude' and 'make their camps in plains of immeasurable extent' (Diodorus 2.54), practising what is called excluded or external nomadism.

Numerous variations on these models are possible, each representing an adaptation to local topographical, hydrological and ecological conditions as well as to social, political and economic circumstances. There may, for example, be specialised herding by members of a sedentary village to prevent overgrazing and to safeguard crops. Certain groups in the village will go off with the animals during the winter and spring seasons into the steppe and desert, only returning to the village in the dry summer months to make use of crop by-products and permanent water sources for their herds. Conversely pastoralists of all persuasions may sow if the weather permits. This is especially true of transhumants, who will often engage in the production of wheat and barley in the highlands and in the vicinity of springs and wadis, but also of nomads, who will seize the opportunity to cultivate in times of above average rainfall. And all groups are likely to indulge in complementary activities, such as the hunting of wild animals and birds and the gathering of wild herbs, roots and fruits. This particularly applies to nomads because of their wider movements, which enhance access, and because of the greater seasonal scarcity with which they have to cope.

From its earliest beginnings in the eighth millennium BC pastoralism has witnessed a number of developments. One was the realisation that animals could be exploited not just for their ultimate consumption as meat, but for a whole range of secondary products: milk, wool, hair, hide, labour, transport and so on. This was probably a long process, with some items, such as milk, being recognised fairly early on and others, such as transport, only capitalised on much later. A second development was the gradual emergence of an exchange-based economy, which inaugurated a shift in pastoralist interests from producing food solely for their own households to providing commodities for customers as well. This went hand in hand with the rise of cities and states, whose non-food-producing residents (craftsmen, bureaucrats, soldiers and managers) encouraged or compelled food-producers to think about generating products with the best market value. Examples are the selection for woolly and fat-tailed sheep and the enhancement through simple breeding programmes of milk yield from cattle, sheep and goats.

The most significant advance in pastoralism for Arabia was the domestication of the one-humped camel, a process that was probably begun in southeast Arabia in the third millennium BC. It was very likely exploited first for its dung, burnt as fuel, and its milk and flesh, consumed for sustenance. At the end of the process would have come its use for riding and transport. When this latter event occurred is a much debated question. It has been suggested that the emergence of a new larger type of storage jar (the collared-rim pithos) in the southern Levant during the thirteenth to twelfth centuries BC is linked to the camel, for its strength and endurance would have made it ideal for transporting these new containers, so heavy when laden (80–120 kg). The Egyptians were active in southern Palestine and northwest Arabia at this time, as is illustrated by pottery and inscribed Egyptian objects, and they may have used the local inhabitants as their agents in this trade. These locals are usually identified with the Midianites of the Bible, who were nomadic pastoralists ('they came . . . with their tents, and they and their camels were innumerable', Judges 6.5). And certainly some groups were involved in trade (note the 'Midianite merchants' who sell Joseph in Genesis 37.28 and 'the gold rings . . . and the purple garments worn by the Midianite kings' in Judges 8.26).

At Tell Jemmeh on the southern coast of Palestine bones of domesticated dromedaries have been found from the Egyptian period and then again, after a hiatus, in the Assyrian period. This same pattern obtains in northwest Arabia: Egypt's retreat from her imperial role is marked by a lacuna in the archaeological record, which is only filled once new trade routes have been established, enticing the Assyrians, in their turn, to take an interest in this region. In this latter phase aromatics are being transported, as is clear from the simultaneous increase in finds of camel bones from this time in both south Arabia and the southern Levant and also from the widespread appearance of small cuboid incense burners in the east Mediterranean and Mesopotamia. In the earlier period, however, it was probably the humbler commodities of grain, oil and wine that formed the camel's load.

In any case we have clear pictorial evidence of camels being ridden from Syria and Assyria from the ninth century BC (Pl. 15), and with this innovation camels now offered a full range of benefits to their owners:

> They [the Debae of west Arabia] are breeders of camels and make use of the services of this animal in connection with the most important needs of their life. For instance they fight against their enemies from their backs,[1] employ them for the conveyance of their wares and thus easily accomplish all their business, drink their milk and in this way get their food from them, and traverse their entire country riding upon their racing camels.
>
> (Agatharchides in Diodorus 3.45)

Moreover, because the camel can go without water for up to a month in the wintertime and for a number of days even in the height of summer, and can subsist on parched grass and desiccated shrubs, it is able to survive under the least favourable of watering and pasturing conditions. This allowed Arab pastoralists to penetrate much further into the interior of Arabia than before and made possible direct traffic between centres of civilisation separated by desert regions that had previously been regarded as impassable barriers.

HUNTING

As noted above, pastoralists will often supplement their diet by hunting game. This activity is very often commemorated in the

Plate 15 Limestone relief from Tell Halaf, Syria, showing camel-driver on box-like saddle, *c*.9th century BC (Walters Art Gallery).

inscriptions and rock drawings of the pastoralist inhabitants of central and northern Arabia. It need not, however, be regarded solely as a source of food and income, but might also be prized as a recreation, a physical exercise, a training in the arts of equitation and archery, and above all an opportunity to demonstrate skill and prowess. The methods of bagging game were numerous. The easiest was to use nets, snares and stone enclosures with guide walls (so-called desert kites). It would be the job of some of the hunt's participants to drive game towards these traps by shouting, beating on objects, gesticulating, waving torches and the like, while others would be manning the traps and overwhelming the animals (Pl. 16a). If the aim was chiefly sport, then more athletic modes were preferred, in particular the chase, usually on the back of a horse, in which the owner usually took a particular pride:

> Often I have gone out in the morning to hunt,
> my comrade a steed stout in the sides, a swift runner,
>   of mighty frame . . .
> Full of keenness when you let him go, throwing himself
>   forward,
> eager to run heat and heat whenever he is reined in . . .
> I trained him and expended on him all possible care,
> as much as a wealthy man gives to his dearest friend.
>
> (*Muf.* 9)

The hunter was armed with a bow and arrow and aided in the chase by the cheetah, the caracal lynx, or more commonly the hound:

> In his fright he [the oryx] turns to escape and finds the way
>   blocked by dogs well-trained,
> two with hanging ears, crop-eared the third
> With their teeth they grip him, but stoutly he thrusts them
>   away, sturdy of leg, his long sides streaked with brown.
> Sideways he turns to bring into play sharp-pointed horns,
> on them the blood shines red and bright as dye.
> Two spits they seem, fresh cut to skewer the feasters' meat,
> drawn off before ready [so still bloody]
> Till at last when all of the pack were checked, a good
> handful slain, and the rest dispersed, yelping with pain
> Stood forth the master, in his hand a sheaf of slender arrows
> with shining points, feathers cut close.
> Then he shot to save the fugitive hounds, the arrow sped
> and the shaft transfixed the oryx from side to side.
> Headlong he crashed, as a camel stallion falls outworn on the
>   soft ground, though the oryx was nobler by far.
>
> (*Muf.* 126: Abu Dhu'ayb)

93

Hunting could also bear cultic associations. On the island of Ikaros (modern Failaka) in the Persian Gulf:

> there is a temple of Artemis and quantities of wild goats and plump gazelles and hares also. If a man asks leave of the goddess to take them and then starts to hunt whatever is allowed, he does not fail in his object but succeeds and is glad of her gift. But should he fail to ask, he takes nothing and is punished.
>
> (Aelian 11.9)

Until very recently in Hadramawt it used to be said that 'if we did not hunt, the rain would not come to us; there would be drought in the country and scarcity of food'. And a number of pre-Islamic south Arabian inscriptions demonstrate this connection between hunting and divine blessings to be very ancient. Failure to perform the hunt at its appointed time could have dire consequences, and conversely its faithful execution could bring recompense:

> Thus commanded Shams, the lady of Mayfaʻa, for her servant Sharah'ilibn Bataʻ . . . that he should celebrate for her a hunt . . . for . . . days in each year. . . . And let the hunt on these days be performed by Sharah'il or his deputy, turn by turn in each year alternately over two years, in order that Shams may grant them, namely her servant Sharah'il and her servitors the Banu Bataʻ, bounty and booty.
>
> (CIS 4.571)

A wide variety of animals was hunted. For example 'Yada''il Bayan, king of Hadramawt . . . who founded and colonised the city of Shabwa, passed by this rock when they broke off the hunt after killing thirty oryx, eighty-two ibex, twenty-five gazelles and eight cheetahs' (RES 4192). And the whole affair might be fairly prolonged: 'Yada''il Bayan, king of Hadramawt . . . went out hunting in the wadi 'Irma; they hunted for twenty days and slew four panthers, two cheetahs and six hundred ibexes' (Ingrams 1). Monarchs crop up frequently in hunt inscriptions, which suggests that the activity formed a part of important royal ceremonies. In some cases 'title-giving' (*h-slqb*) is mentioned, and on one outing of Iliʻazz Yalut (*c*.AD 220s) there were present two Palmyrenes, two Chaldaeans and two Indians (Ja 931).[2] These were undoubtedly official delegations, and had been brought from nearby Shabwa to attend the accession of the king or some such

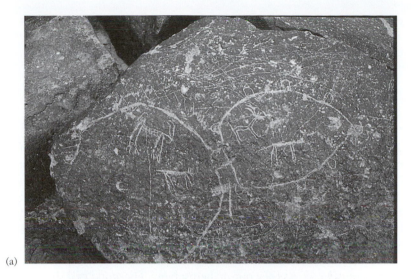

(a)

(b)

Plate 16 (a) Rock drawing from Wadi Hashad, northeast Jordan, showing a 'desert-kite' with guide walls, narrow entrance and hides (William Lancaster); (b) limestone funerary stele from the Jawf showing the deceased engaged in an ibex hunt, 1st–3rd century AD, 33 × 32 cm (National Museum of San'a).

event. The animal most sought after on these occasions was without a doubt the ibex, and its exalted status is emphasised by its very common appearance in south Arabian art and ornamentation (Pl. 16b).

ECONOMIC RELATIONS BETWEEN NOMADIC AND SETTLED PEOPLES

The basic premise of nomad life is autonomy and its corollary of equality. This was observed of Arab nomads by urban authors long ago: 'The distant Arabs dwelling in the desert . . . know neither overseers nor officials' (Sargon II, AR 2.17); 'the Arabs who inhabit this country, being difficult to overcome in war, remain always unenslaved; furthermore they never at any time accept a man of another country as their overlord and continue to maintain their liberty unimpaired' (Diodorus 2.48); 'the Saracens . . . all alike are warriors of equal rank' (Ammianus 14.4). As they put it themselves: 'The worst evil that can befall a people, and after which no good can come, is that their necks are bent.' Arab nomads were therefore, in their poetry at least, contemptuous of those who accepted to live as subjects of a state, for this was considered equivalent to servitude: 'The Himasi does not defend his honour, but is like the Mesopotamian peasant who patiently endures when one enslaves him' (Hassan ibn Thabit 189).

For their part sedentary folk were just as dismissive in their attitudes towards nomads. For example the 'Scenite Arabs' of Mesopotamia ('a wandering people, taking their name from their tents which they pitch wherever they fancy', Pliny 6.144) are portrayed by Strabo as 'a tribe of brigands and shepherds, who readily move from one place to another when pasture and booty fail them' (16.1.26). 'Whenever I mention Saracens, just consider, Persians,' exhorts the Roman ambassador Commentiolus in 566, 'the uncouthness and untrustworthiness of the nation' (Menander 9.1). 'There were many people between the Tigris and the Euphrates', comments a late sixth-century resident of Mesopotamia, 'who lived in tents and were barbarians and warlike; numerous were their superstitions and they were the most ignorant of all the peoples of the earth' (Ahudemmeh 21). 'The Saracen tribe', opines an early seventh-century historian, 'is known to be most unreliable and fickle, their mind is not steadfast and their judgement is not firmly grounded in prudence' (Theophylact 3.17.7). One reason for this prejudice is suggested by the church historian Eusebius (d. 339), who lists a number of nomadic peoples, including the Arabs, and notes that among them 'there is not a banker to be seen, nor modeller, nor painter, nor architect, nor geometer, nor singing-master, nor actor of dramatic poems' (6.10). In other words they were bereft of the virtues of civilisation and to the city-reared gentleman their lifestyle seemed so alien:

> The Saracens, whom we never found desirable either as friends or enemies, ranging up and down the country, in a brief space of time laid waste whatever they could find, like rapacious kites which, whenever they have caught sight of any prey from on high, seize it with swift swoop, and directly they have seized it make off. . . . Among those tribes whose original abode extends from the Assyrians to the cataracts of the Nile . . . all alike are warriors of equal rank, half-nude, clad in dyed cloaks as far as the loins, ranging widely with the help of swift horses and slender camels in times of peace or of disorder. No man ever grasps a plough-handle or cultivates a tree, none seeks a living by tilling the soil, but they rove continually over wide and extensive tracts without a home, without fixed abodes or laws. They cannot long endure the same sky, nor does the sun of a single district ever content them. Their life is always on the move. . . . Moreover they wander so widely as long as they live that a woman marries in one place, gives birth in another, and rears her children far away, without being allowed any opportunity for rest. They all feed upon game and an abundance of milk, which is their main sustenance, on a variety of plants, as well as such birds as they are able to take by fowling; and I have seen many of them who were wholly unacquainted with grain and wine. So much for this dangerous people.
>
> (Ammianus 14.4)

The hostility evinced by both sides in their rhetoric has beguiled many modern scholars into conceiving of nomad–sedentary relations as inherently antagonistic. There is, for example, the depiction of ancient Middle Eastern history as a long series of waves of tribal invaders rushing in from the Arabian deserts of the south or the Taurus–Zagros mountains of the north in times of ecological crisis or political weakness, ravishing civilisation and destroying all in their path. Then there are the various Roman desert frontier theories, which postulate the construction of a plethora of military installations and the maintenance of strict security by the Romans along their southeastern borders to counter the ever-present 'nomadic menace'. Related to this are the 'bedouinisation of Arabia' arguments, which regale us with images of a predatory expansionist elite of camel-mounted warriors who constantly harry and harass the settled populations.

The reality of nomad–sedentary relations is, however, much less clear cut than the rhetoric, for, despite all their fighting talk, Arab nomads were economically dependent on the settlements along their migratory routes. Often steppe and desert do not afford complete subsistence. In poor grazing seasons the migratory herder may be unable to supply his stock and he is forced into town by their needs, and perhaps into some arrangement with local farmers for access to the stubble or harvested fields. Nor is the mobile life compatible with developed craft specialisation, and a visit to the town will often be necessary for vital manufactures: metal utensils, weapons, clothing, and so on. In exchange pastoralists offer such products as milk, clarified butter, wool, hide, hair and meat, dung (for fertiliser) and draft and mount animals. They might also provide a range of other services. A renowned ascetic of Mount Sinai, when he lay dying in his cell, sent a Saracen to Aila (modern Aqaba) with a message to summon one of his spiritual brothers (Anastasius of Sinai 67). A steward of the monastery of Mar Sabas in the Judaean desert hired Saracen camels and a Saracen camel-driver to bring grain from Machaerus on the Dead Sea (Cyril of Scythopolis 186). A group of pilgrims paid the rather high sum of three and a half gold coins 'to the Saracen who took us to the Holy Mountain [in Sinai]', as well as paying along the way for a slave boy, camels and a donkey from other Saracens (*Nessana papyri* 89). The community of Pharan in Sinai had a treaty with a local chief named Ammanes, which guaranteed their security in return for a fee. When an outlaw band of his tribesmen killed some monks, the council of Pharan sent couriers to Ammanes complaining that the treaty had been breached:

> He confirmed the treaty and asked those who been wronged to come to him [for reparation], especially the kinsmen of the prisoners who were still alive. Further, if anyone wanted vengeance for those who had been murdered, he said he was prepared to punish the guilty. He also accepted to return the spoils to those people from whom it had been stolen. He was unwilling to violate the terms of the treaty, so he indicated, being satisfied with the agreement that he had reached with the Pharanites, because of the incentives that he received from

them. For their dealings with each other brought no small gain to those barbarians, who benefited from the resources of the Pharanites in the necessities which they lacked.

(Nilus 661–63)

Nomads might also serve in the military (e.g. PAES 3A.752: 'commander of the nomad units'). And in upper Mesopotamia 'the tent-dwellers are peaceful, and moderate towards travellers in the exaction of tribute, and on this account merchants avoid the land along the river and risk a journey through the desert, leaving the river on the right for approximately a three days' journey' (Strabo 16.1.27).

Yet it is true that, if trade were for some reason impossible or impracticable, nomads might turn to the alternative tactic of raid:

> Lying near the public highway from Beroea [modern Aleppo] to Edessa there is a desert through which nomad Saracens are always wandering back and forth. For this reason travellers along the way group together and by mutual aid decrease the danger of a surprise attack. There were in my company . . . about seventy. Suddenly Ishmaelites, riding upon horses and camels, descended upon us in a startling attack, with their long hair flying from under their headbands. They wore cloaks over their half-naked bodies, and broad boots. Quivers hung from their shoulders, their unstrung bows dangled at their sides; they carried long spears, for they had not come for battle but for plunder. We were seized, scattered and carried off in different directions. . . . We were led, borne aloft high on camels, and, always fearful of disaster, we hung rather than sat through the vast desert. Half-raw meat was our food, the milk of camels our drink. At length, after crossing a great river, we arrived at the solitude of the inner desert. Instructed to do obeisance to our mistress and the children, we bent our heads. Here, as though immured in prison, I changed my attire and learned to go naked. . . . The pasturing of sheep was entrusted to my care.

(Jerome, 'Vita Malchi' 55–56)

Persons snatched in this way would often be ransomed. Thus the eremite Theodoulos was kidnapped by Saracens in Sinai and put up for sale in the town of Sobata in southern Palestine, and 'when no one offered more than two pieces of gold, the barbarians threatened to kill him until someone paid the price' (Nilus 688). In exploiting sedentary folk by violence migratory peoples merely invert the ordinary course of relations. In peaceful trade the nomadic pastoralist is at a disadvantage. The exchange is more urgent to him than to the sedentary. And he cannot hold out indefinitely for favourable terms, for he must be off again, sooner rather than later, to new pastures. On the other hand, though economically inferior to the settled people, the nomads are 'well suited to stealth fighting' (Ammianus 23.3.8, 31.16.5). Born and bred to the saddle and to a career of hunting, raiding and feuding, the nomad can strike, steal and disappear into the great wastes before the alarm can even be raised. Sedentaries often have nothing to match these tactics beyond a wall or a fort. Thus the economic relation between nomads and sedentaries is inconsistent with the balance of force between them. Raid must often present itself to the nomads as a better choice than trade, especially when they have suffered stock losses due to weather, sickness or theft, and have in any case little to exchange.[3]

It is the numerous accounts of Arab pillagers in historical sources that have fuelled the arguments of the 'aggressive bedouin' lobby. What is wrong with their theories is not that tribes did not practise violence, but that they very seldom did so on a large scale. Raids both among themselves and against sedentaries tended to involve small numbers and to be of the hit and run type: at the first sign of any obstacle or trouble, the perpetrators would simply melt away into the desert. 'The Saracens are naturally incapable of storming a wall, and the weakest kind of barricade, put together with perhaps nothing but mud, is sufficient to check their assault . . . but they are the cleverest of all men at plundering' (Procopius 2.19, B2.9; cf. Ammianus 25.6.8). In fourth-century Sinai a band of Saracens attacked a group of monks, but then 'our armed guard appeared high on a hill and caused much confusion among the savages. As they made their presence known by shouting, none [of the Saracens] remained there; the whole area, which a short time ago had been full of people, became deserted' (Nilus 669). When large numbers of nomads did infiltrate settled areas, it was usually in response to some ecological disaster, and so they were economic migrants rather than warriors. Moreover, though they might cause much damage, they could usually be contained:

> For two successive years we have been afflicted by drought and a lack of basic necessities. There has been an influx of southern tribes and the numbers of them and their herds is such that they have destroyed and devastated the villages in

both plain and mountain. They have had the insolence to plunder and take captive men and beasts even in the territory of the Byzantines. The latter mustered a large army and came to the frontier accompanied by their tributary Arabs, and they demanded satisfaction for the damage done in their country by the Arab subjects of the Persians. The glorious and illustrious Persian governor . . . restrained them from this gently and wisely. He made an agreement with them to assemble the chiefs of the Persian Arabs and recover from them the booty and captives if the Byzantine Arabs would also restore the beasts and men which from time to time they had taken from Beth Garmai, Adiabene and Nineveh. Then these would be returned to the Byzantines and these to the Persians, and they would define the frontiers in a treaty so that these unfortunate events and their like would not recur.

(*Synodicon Or.* 526–27: letter of Bar Sauma, bishop of Nisibis, written in AD 484)[4]

A second problem with the 'nomadic menace' viewpoint is that it draws too rigid a line between nomads and sedentaries. The pastoral and farming peoples of a given area, whatever their degree of mobility, comprise complementary economic sectors of a single system; they are economically bound together, even if relations between them might often be tense. This is particularly true of enclosed nomadic tribes, which will commonly include a semi-sedentary urban elite who liaise between the townsfolk and the tribesmen. Moreover there is a good deal of fluidity in livelihood patterns in the Middle East. This is because between the fully desert and the fully sown there exist extensive swathes of semi-arid lands (150–300 mm/6–12 inches rainfall per year) which are ecologically fragile and therefore particularly prone to alternating movements in the direction of either greater stationary cultivation or increased migratory herding of animals. These movements are facilitated by the fact that, despite the negative stereotypes in terms of which farmers and herders view each other, they share certain techniques, beliefs and kinship organisation. The reasons for a shift towards one or the other end of the spectrum are many, and may involve a mixture of environmental, ecological, demographic, political and economic factors. Among nomadic pastoralists it tends to be the very poor and the very rich who turn sedentary. If a family's livestock holdings fall below the minimum required for subsistence, they will have to seek work either from a fellow tribesman or else in the town before they become a drag on the livestock-capital of their community. Big herds are difficult to manage, and the owner may be inclined to invest his surplus in land rather than risk loss by continuing to migrate, and then may be tempted to settle down for at least part of the year to oversee his holdings and enjoy the profits.

It is a much debated question how much pre-modern states ever directly promoted sedentarisation, whether by offering financial inducements, using compulsion or the like. They certainly had the motive, for sedentary people are easier and cheaper to control than nomads and there was always a need to increase food production (which could be done by farming more marginal areas). And there are occasional indications of such a policy in our sources:

> Alexander [the Great] pacified all these tribes [of north-western Iran], falling upon them in wintertime when they thought their country unapproachable. He also founded cities so that they should no longer be nomads but cultivators and tillers of the ground and, having a stake in the country, might be deterred from injuring one another.[5]
>
> (Arrian, *Ind.* 40)

In early Islamic times, too, Muslim leaders encouraged tribes to emigrate from Arabia and settle in the new garrison towns (*al-muhâjara*), and they issued stark warnings against returning to dwell in the desert (*al-ta'arrub*), equating it with apostasy. In any case it is at least true to say that the actions of the state had an impact upon these processes. Investment in roads, buildings and public safety boosted the local economy and the consequent demand for labour and opportunities for profit would draw in nomads, who might subsequently settle. Conversely predatory behaviour and over-taxation by the state could reverse this process and provoke flight from the land.

TRADE

Though it was agriculture and pastoralism that provided the inhabitants of Arabia with their basic livelihood, it was trade that brought them, or at least some of them, fame and fortune. Of course there was the mundane business of exchanging animal products for the goods of farming communities, but what fired the imagination of the writers of antiquity was that legendary trade in the 'spices of

Araby' which spurred many an emperor to dream of braving the desert wastes to wrest control of their cultivation, made 'many forget mortal pleasures and secretly suppose that they are partaking of ambrosia' (Agatharchides in Photius 250), and which kept many an imperial accountant awake at night worrying about balance of payments, 'because vast wealth from Rome and Parthia accumulates in their [Arab] hands, as they sell the produce they obtain from the sea or their forests and buy nothing in return' (Pliny 6.162).

Aromatics

These were Arabia's most famous export, particularly frankincense and myrrh, though Arabians themselves almost never mention them in their inscriptions. Both substances are gum resins, which exude from trees and contain a small quantity of volatile oil, the reason for their fragrance. They were either used on their own – usually burned and, in the case of myrrh, applied as an unguent – or blended with a variety of other ingredients to make ointments, perfumes, oils for embalming, medicines for all manner of ailments and of course incense (a compound usually sprinkled on lighted charcoal to produce scented smoke). Frankincense and myrrh were extremely efficacious in expelling bad odours and pestilential insects and so were much in demand in the home, about the person and in public places. From this function of physical purification it was a small step towards ceremonial purification, and these two aromatics became an integral part of religious rituals throughout much of the old world. Thus supplicants might beseech their deity: 'May my prayer be ever set as incense before you' (Psalms 141.2), and a poet could naturally link temples to 'altars fragrant with the smoke of incense' (Sappho, frag. 2). Moreover, as demand increased and the price rose, their consumption became a way of demonstrating wealth, magnanimity and kingship, the most notorious example of this being the Roman emperor Nero's dissipation of tens of kilograms of incense at the funeral of his favourite consort Poppaea. The trees from which these two aromatics were extracted grew only in southern Arabia and Somalia, and in the course of time a regular trade developed to meet the requirements of Egypt and Mesopotamia, Greece and Rome, India and even China. At the height of this trade, in the Seleucid and Roman periods, extensive camel caravans trudged the hundreds of miles up the length of the Arabian peninsula and fleets of ships plied the seas around it, transporting these precious commodities, together with other valuable spices, to their eager consumers.

Aromatics of various kinds had been in use in Egypt and Mesopotamia since the third millennium BC. There is, however, no firm evidence of traffic in specifically south Arabian products until the first millennium. This may have happened as early as the tenth century BC, if the Biblical account of the queen of Sheba is to be believed, and certainly by the eighth century, when Tiglath-Pileser III (744–727) seized '5000 bags of all kinds of spices' from 'Shamsi queen of the Arabs' and received 'all kinds of spices' in tribute from 'the people of Massa, Tayma and Saba' (ITP 229). In the course of the seventh century incense altars start to proliferate in Palestine and clear references to frankincense and myrrh begin to feature in Israelite and Greek sources. Thus the seventh-century poetess Sappho of Lesbos speaks of the celebration of the Trojans upon Hector's presentation of his bride Andromache, at which there was 'the sweet music of the flute . . . the sound of cymbals . . . myrrh and cassia and frankincense' (frag. 44). One can at least say, then, that by the seventh century BC use of south Arabian aromatics was becoming widespread in Mesopotamia and the eastern Mediterranean.

Yet firm information about the nature of these substances was still hard to come by and their harvesting a matter of legend and fantasy, as is evident from the account of Herodotus (d. c.430 BC):

When they [the Arabians] gather frankincense they burn storax – the gum of which is brought into Greece by the Phoenicians – in order to raise a smoke to drive off the flying snakes. These snakes . . . are small in size and of various colours, and great numbers of them keep guard over all the frankincense-bearing trees and the only way to get rid of them is by smoking them out with storax.

(3.107)

Only with the exploratory missions despatched by the Persian emperor Darius and Alexander the Great did more accurate reports begin to circulate, as is reflected in the botanical work of Theophrastus of Eresus (d. c.287 BC):

Frankincense and myrrh . . . are found in the Arabian peninsula about Saba, Hadramawt, Qataban and Ma'in (*Mamali*). The trees of frankincense and myrrh grow partly in the mountains, partly on private estates at the foot of the mountains, wherefore some are under cultivation, others not.

. . . The frankincense-tree, it is said, is not tall, about five cubits high, and it is much branched; it has a leaf like that of the pear, but much smaller and very grassy in colour, like rue; the bark is altogether smooth like that of a bay. The myrrh-tree is said to be still smaller in stature and more bushy; it is said to have a tough stem, which is contorted near the ground and is stouter than a man's leg, and to have a smooth bark like that of andrachne.

(9.4)

Eratosthenes of Cyrene (d. *c*.202 BC) is the first to refer to the transport of aromatic goods from south Arabia: 'Qataban produces myrrh and Hadramawt produces frankincense,[6] and both these and other aromatics they trade to merchants. The latter come to these parts from Aila [modern Aqaba] as far as Minaea in seventy days . . . and the Gabaioi arrive at Hadramawt in forty days' (cited in Strabo 16.4.4). Writing a century or so later, Artemidorus of Ephesus (wrote *c*.100 BC) tells us that 'those who live close to one another [in south Arabia] receive in constant succession the loads of aromatics and deliver them to their next neighbours as far as Syria and Mesopotamia' (cited in Strabo 16.4.19). But we have to wait until the time of Pliny the Elder (AD 23–79) to receive a more detailed account. He is able to describe the plants' cultivation and harvesting:

The chief products of Arabia are frankincense and myrrh. . . . It used to be the custom, when there were fewer opportunities of selling frankincense, to gather it only once a year, but the present-day demand introduces a second harvesting. The earlier and natural gathering takes place at about the rising of the Dogstar, when the summer heat is most intense. They make an incision where the bark appears to be fullest of juice and distended to its thinnest; and the bark is loosened with a blow, but not removed. From the incision a greasy foam spurts out, which coagulates and thickens, being received on a mat of palm-leaves where the nature of the ground requires this, but in other places on a space round the tree that has been rammed hard. . . . The myrrh-producing tree also is tapped twice a year at the same seasons as the frankincense-tree.

And he can also inform us about their transport and pricing:

Frankincense after being collected is conveyed to Shabwa on camels . . . and a tithe estimated by measure and not by weight is taken by the priests. . . . It can only be exported through the country of the Qatabanians (*Gebbanitae*), and accordingly a tax is paid on it to the king of that people as well. Their capital is Timna, which is 1487 miles[7] distant from the town of Gaza in Judaea on the Mediterranean coast; the journey is divided into sixty-five stages with halts for camels. Fixed portions of the frankincense are also given to the priests and the king's secretaries, but besides these the guards and their attendants and the gatekeepers and servants also have their pickings. Indeed all along the route they keep on paying, at one place for water, at another for fodder, or the charges for lodging at the halts, and the various tolls. Hence expenses mount up to 688 denarii per camel before the Mediterranean coast is reached, and then again payment is made to the customs officers of our empire. Consequently the price of the best frankincense is six, of the second best five, and of the third best three denarii a pound. . . . No tithes are given to a god from myrrh, as it also grows in other countries; however the growers have to pay a quarter of the yield to the king of the Qatabanians. For the rest it is bought up all over the district from the common people and packed into leather bags; and our perfumiers have no difficulty in distinguishing the different sorts by the evidence of the scent and consistency. . . . The prices vary with the supply of buyers; that of myrrh-oil ranges from three to fifty denarii a pound, whereas the top price for cultivated myrrh is eleven denarii.

(12.51–70)

The high prices fetched by the aromatics of south Arabia led many to suppose that 'from their trafficking both the Sabaeans and the Gerrhaeans have become richest of all' (Strabo 16.4.19). And indeed a considerable range of imports is mentioned by a first-century AD maritime manual at south Arabian ports such as Muza (modern Mocha):

Merchandise for which it offers a market are: purple cloth, fine and ordinary quality; Arab sleeved clothing . . . ; cloth; cloaks; blankets, in limited number, with no adornment as well as with traditional local adornment; girdles with shaded stripes; unguent, moderate amount; money, considerable amount; wine and grain, limited quantity because the region produces wheat in moderate quantity and wine in greater. To the king and the governor are given: horses and pack mules; gold ware; embossed silverware; expensive clothing and copperware.

(Periplus 24)

A concomitant of the spread of Christianity, however, was a reduction in the use of frankincense and myrrh. Christians wished to distance themselves from pagan and Jewish practices, and so emphasised that an incorporeal god had no need of corporeal substances. Aromatics certainly continued to be procured for sanitary and medical purposes and liturgical texts make clear that they were also important in church ceremony. Moreover in the sphere of private devotion incense would often be burned in homes and in churches by lay people and clerics alike to accompany their petitions to the saints. But it was now totally unacceptable to use incense for sacrifices and cremation, and its use for honorific purposes was more restricted. Thus Romans would honour not only gods and emperors with incense, but also dignitaries and even dancers, whereas the Byzantines tended to reserve honorific censing for the emperor by the patriarch. And in general the prodigality of Hellenistic and Roman incense consumption was never again to be matched in Christian times.

Transit trade

Its position between the Mediterranean world, Mesopotamia, Africa and India meant that a certain amount of commercial traffic was bound to pass through or round Arabia on its way to and from these regions. When political and economic conditions permitted, various peoples of Arabia would take advantage of their location to act as middlemen in this traffic, occasionally earning enough to pay for all the trappings of civilisation. Unfortunately for them conditions could just as quickly change again and reverse their fortunes, and the annals of pre-Islamic Arabia are filled with the tales of trading peoples like the Gerrhaeans, Minaeans and Nabataeans, whose star burned brightly for a time, then was eclipsed. 'They reigned, they prospered; yet their glory passed, now deep entombed they lie this many a year' (Tabari 1.854). Probably the most famous of the great Arabian merchant peoples were the Palmyrenes. Their city of Palmyra was a true caravan city, for it owed its prosperity entirely to its ability to channel the commerce passing

Plate 17 Limestone relief from a sarcophagus in the camp of Diocletian, Palmyra, showing two caravan leaders with camel (Palmyra Museum).

between the two empires either side of it (Pl. 17). 'Being traders they buy Indian and Arabian goods from the territory of the Persians and dispose of it in that of the Romans' (Appian 5.9). Whereas other peoples of Arabia almost never commented upon their mercantile activities, the Palmyrenes celebrated theirs with gusto, honouring their caravan chiefs and financiers with statues and inscriptions:

> This statue is that of Taymarsu, son of Tayme, son of Moqimu, son of Gabba, chief of the caravan (*synodiarch/rb shyrt'*), which has been made for him by the members of the caravan who came up with him from Charax, because he paid their expenses, three hundred gold coins, ancient currency, and was well-pleasing to them. To his honour and to the honour of Yaddai and 'Abdibol, his sons, in the month of May, the year 504.
>
> (PAT 0294, AD 193)

In the case of the Palmyrenes it was a change in the political situation which ruined their fortunes. The Sasanians, who replaced the Parthians in 224, were much more expansionist than their predecessors, and the tense relations that existed between them and the Romans made it impossible for an entity like Palmyra, which had truck with both, to survive for very long.

Local trade

The majority of the inhabitants of Arabia would not have been involved in the incense or international transit trade, but all would have participated to some degree in the local trade, that is, in the exchange of commodities of Arabian origin and destined for consumption in Arabia itself or on its fringes. Pastoralists bartered their surplus of animals and animal products (milk, clarified butter, wool, hides, skins, etc.) for the goods of agricultural communities (grain, oil, clothing, wine, arms, etc.). This could go on informally at any time; otherwise one could attend one or more of the grand markets staged at fixed times of the year in different parts of Arabia:

> The markets of the Arabs were ten, at which they would gather for their trading activities, and other people would attend them and would be safe in respect of their lives and their possessions. Among them was Dumat al-Jandal, taking place in the month of Rabi' I; its conveners were Ghassan and Kalb: whichever of the two tribes had the upper hand would run it. Then there was Mushaqqar in [the region of] Hajar [in east Arabia], the market of which took place in Jumada I and which was run by Tamim, the clan of Mundhir ibn Sawa. Then there was Sohar [in Oman], taking place in Rajab, on its first day, and not requiring any protection. Then the Arabs would travel from Sohar to Daba, at which Julanda and his tribe would collect the tithe. Then there was the market of Shihr in Mahra, and its market took place in the shade of the mountain on which was the tomb of the prophet Hud; there was no protection at it and Mahra would run it. Then there was the market of Aden, taking place on the first day of the month of Ramadan, at which the Persian nobles would collect the tithe and from which perfume would be conveyed to the rest of the provinces. Then there was the market of San'a, taking place halfway through the month of Ramadan, at which the Persian nobles would collect the tithe. Then there was the market of Rabiya in Hadramawt, to get to which protection was needed, for the land was not under anyone's authority, and whoever was strongest triumphed; once there Kinda provided protection at it. Then there was

109

the market of 'Ukaz in the highest part of Najd, taking place
in the month of Dhu l-Qa'da; Quraysh would go to it and
other Arabs, though most of them of [the tribal confederation
of] Mudar; and there would be boasting competitions of the
Arabs, [settlement of] blood-wits and truce negotiations.
Then there was the market of Dhu l-Majaz.
(Ya'qubi 1.313–14, cf. Ibn Habib, *Muh*. 263–68)

These markets were cooperative ventures. Safety of person and
goods at such events was guaranteed either by the holiness of the site
(e.g. Shihr under the wing of the prophet Hud), or by the prestige of
a strong tribe (e.g. Kinda at Rabiya), or else by its occurrence during
a holy month (e.g. 'Ukaz in Dhu l-Qa'da). Those in the last category
were particularly popular, for their timing in a holy month also
ensured ease of travel there and back and tended to promote a carnival-
like atmosphere. Many trekked considerable distances to reach them,
such as the envoys dispatched by king Nu'man of Hira every year to
purchase choice wares, such as Yemeni leather (Baladhuri 1.100–101).

Mining

Extraction and working of copper has been practised in the Oman
peninsula since the late third millennium BC. The textual witnesses
noted above are backed up by archaeological evidence in the form of
ancient slag heaps, fragments from the lining of smelting furnaces,
hammer stones for crushing ore, moulds for casting and a wide range
of copper objects intended for everyday use (pins, fish-hooks, needles,
chisels, awls, knives, etc.). This industry continued at different levels
of intensity throughout the pre-Islamic period (radiocarbon dating
shows copper mines around Sohar to have been worked in the fifth/
sixth centuries AD), and indeed is still carried on today.
    West Arabia was even more fortunate, for it possessed more valuable
ores:

Gold they discover in underground galleries, which have been
formed by nature, and gather in abundance. It is not that
which has been fused into artificial nuggets out of gold dust,
but the virgin gold which is called, from its condition when
found, 'unfired' gold ('for it is not smelted from ores, as is
done among other peoples, but is dug out directly from the
earth'). And as for size the smallest nugget found is about as
large as a fruit stone and the largest not much smaller than a

Persian walnut. This gold they wear about both their wrists and necks, perforating it and alternating it with transparent stones. And since this precious metal abounds in their land, whereas there is a scarcity of copper and iron, they exchange it with merchants for equal parts of the latter wares.

(Diodorus '2.50', 3.45)

And in south Arabia there was silver:

There is not in Khurasan or anywhere else a mine comparable to that of Radrad in Yemen, which is situated at the border between Nihm and the district of Yam in the land of Hamdan [northeast of San'a]. It has been abandoned since 270 [AD 883]. . . . The inhabitants of Radrad were all Persians, descendants of those who arrived there in the pre-Islamic period and in the days of the Umayyads and Abbasids, and they were called 'pit Persians'. . . . The village of the mine was large and there was flowing water and palm trees, and commodities would pass to and fro between it and Basra via Aqiq, Falaj, Yamama and Bahrain. . . . In one week a camel load of silver was extracted, 20,000 silver coins, making approximately a million per year. . . . There were 400 furnaces, and if a bird flew over the mining village it would fall down dead on account of the fire from the furnaces.

(Hamdani, *Jaw.* 145–57)

This mine has recently been located and studied. It covers some 10 hectares (25 acres) and comprises at least thirty tunnels longer than 10 metres. One tunnel is over 150 metres long, 30–40 metres wide and several metres high, and is linked to the surface (for purposes of ventilation and transporting the ore) by ten shafts of between 10 and 25 metres in height, each cut through solid rock. A charcoal sample from the bottom of an ore heap yielded a date, by radiocarbon techniques, of *c*.AD 600. All this makes more understandable the petulant reply of Sayf ibn Dhi Yazan to the Persian emperor (*c*.570), who had refused Sayf troops but offered him money instead: 'What do I want with money when the earth of my land is gold and silver?' (Nuwayri 15.310).

Modern scientific exploration has confirmed this mineral wealth and its past exploitation. About one thousand locations in west Arabia show signs of pre-modern mining activity, chiefly dating to early Islamic times. At one of the most famous sites, Mahd al-Dhahab ('cradle of gold') near Medina, radiocarbon dating of residual charcoal in slags suggests that gold and silver mining and smelting were carried out *c*.950 BC and again in the period AD 430–830. The earliest attempts were perhaps made in response to demand from east Mediterranean customers:

> King Solomon (*c*.970–931 BC) equipped a fleet at Ezion-Geber, which is near Aila on the shores of the Red Sea, in Edom. For this fleet Hiram [king of Tyre] sent men of his own, experienced sailors, to serve with those in Solomon's service. They went to Ophir and took on 420 talents of gold, which they brought back to Solomon.
>
> (1 Kings 9.26–28)

In the book of Genesis (10.29) Ophir is listed among the sons of Yoqtan, appearing between Sheba (southern Arabia) and Havilah (southern Palestine). If this genealogical idiom is a geographical mapping, then Ophir must be in west Arabia. And this is also where Agatharchides of Cnidus (*c*.200–131 BC) locates gold, his information going back to Ariston, who explored the west coast of Arabia for one of the early Ptolemies of Egypt:

> Down through the middle of their country there flows a river [meaning a dry river valley] which has three courses. It carries down gold dust in such great profusion that the mud which accumulates in the mouth shines in the distance. The inhabitants of the place are ignorant of how to work this metal. They are extremely hospitable, not to all men, but to those who cross over from the Peloponnese and Boeotia. This is because of some mythical story connected with Hercules.
>
> (in Photius 250)

Such reports make more believable statements by Muslim authors about the wealth accruing to the fledgling Islamic state from mining activities. For example it was said that 'much money came to [the caliph] Abu Bakr [632–34] from the mines of Qabaliyya and Juhayna [near Medina], and the mine of the Sulaym tribe was opened during the caliphate of Abu Bakr. He received alms money from it and deposited it in the treasury, thence distributing it to the people' (Ibn Sa'd 3.1.151).

5

SOCIETY

TRIBES[1]

Almost all the inhabitants of pre-Islamic Arabia were members of a tribe, that is, a mutual aid group bound together by a notion of kinship.[2] As one pre-Islamic poet astutely observed ('Amr ibn Qami'a 8), 'a man's tribe are his claws [with which he fends off enemies] and his props [which support him]'. Unlike a state, tribes have no specialised institutions of law and order, so a person's life, honour and goods were protected by his relatives, who were obliged to assist him in trouble and to avenge or seek compensation for him if he was wronged. 'When fighting comes, your kinsman alone is near; your true friend your kinsman is, who answers your call for aid with good will, when deeply drenched in bloodshed are sword and spear' (*Ham.* 225). And failure to fulfil these duties was lamented as the worst of crimes, for 'the cause of the destruction of tribes is the violation of the duties of blood' (Mubarrad 170):

> Had I belonged to [the tribe of] Mazin, there had not
> plundered my herds
> the sons of the foundling Dhuhl son of Shayban.
> Then there would have straightaway arisen to help me
> a firm-handed kin, quick to defend the weak and needy.
> Men who, when evil bares before them its hindmost teeth,
> fly out to meet it, in companies or alone.
> They ask not their brother, when he lays before them his
> troubles,
> to give them proof of the truth of what he says.
> But as for my people, though their number is not small,
> they are good for naught against evil, however light it be.
>
> (*Ham.* 1)

All adult men therefore had to be able to fight: 'Who holds not his foe away from his cistern with sword and spear, it is broken and spoiled; who uses not roughness, him men shall wrong' (*Mu.*: Zuhayr). This does not, however, mean that war and anarchy prevailed. The threat of retaliation would make any potential aggressor think twice, and there were numerous mechanisms – such as intermarriage, mediation, communal ceremonies and festivals, a strong code of hospitality, reciprocal gift-giving – that served to limit the use of force still further and to encourage peaceful coexistence.

The constituent units of tribal society make up a progressively inclusive series of groups, from the closely knit household to the whole tribe and even beyond to the confederation of tribes.[3] As an example let us take the family of Sa'd in the Jawf region of south Arabia. It was a well-known family and rich enough to equip caravans for participation in the incense trade. It belonged, together with others in the same region, to the lineage of Ab'amar. Ties of kinship linked this latter to the sub-clan of Aman. Going up a level, Aman belonged to the powerful clan of Gaba'an, which we know from inscriptions was responsible for the construction of towers and walls at Yathill. Twenty or so of these clans then formed the tribe of Ma'in, principally based at the city of Qarnaw. The tribe thus presents itself as a set of Chinese boxes or Russian dolls: the smallest units, such as households, are segments of more inclusive units, such as lineages, the lineages in turn segments of larger groups, and so on. Each level has its own set of responsibilities. The local community takes care of day-to-day labours: the production of subsistence goods, basic handicrafts, the rearing of the young and so on. More general issues are handled at higher levels, and in the case of events affecting all – drought, epidemic, crop failure, war and so on – the whole tribe may come together to combat the challenge to the common fate. Political behaviour is similarly qualified. Within the local community, not to mention the family, conflict must be speedily repressed for fear of breaking up the group. Among clans a prolonged feud may cause serious disruption in terms of access to resources and the like, and so should be resolved sooner rather than later. At the next level of segmentary integration groups usually occupy different ecological spaces, so there is no urgent necessity to make a settlement. And at the intertribal level enmity may be eternal, the original cause of the dispute lost to living memory.

The basic operating unit of a tribe is the independent local community, which is usually small, numbering no more than a few hundred people, and often many less. In form of settlement this community may be, as among the agropastoralist tribes of the Omani and Yemeni highlands, one or a few villages, clusters of households dwelling in houses of mud brick. Otherwise it may be, as among the camel-herding tribes of central and northern Arabia, one or a few encampments, clusters of households dwelling in tents of hair. The precise composition of the community varies too: a single lineage, an association of several lineages or a loose network of kith and kin. Whatever the case, it will be the same throughout all the communities of the tribe: all primary segments are structurally equivalent. Each local community engages in much the same economic activities, meaning that none is substantially dependent on another for specialised products (for which they turn to outsiders): all primary segments are functionally equivalent. At this local level the tie is of blood, all individual interests being subordinated to those of the kinship group. Indeed all relations of cooperation and moral obligations were regarded as properly deriving from unity of blood. So if a covenant were to be made between two parties involving them in duties of common blood feud, it would be accompanied by a sacramental ceremony at which their blood would be commingled:

> There are no men who respect pledges more than the Arabs. This is the manner of their giving them: a man stands between the two parties that would give security and cuts with a sharp stone the palms of the hands of the parties, by the thumb. Then he takes a piece of wool from the cloak of each and smears with the blood seven stones that lie between them, calling the while on Dionysus and the heavenly Aphrodite. When he has fully done this, he that gives the security commends to his friends the stranger (or his countryman if the party be such), and his friends hold themselves bound to honour the pledge.
> (Herodotus 3.8)[4]

Cohesion at higher levels of the tribal structure – that is, among persons who will only be distantly related, if at all, and will only rarely meet each other, if ever – might be promoted by one or more of a range of ties. In their early inscriptions each of the various south Arabian peoples appears bound by allegiance to the cult of their patron deity, of whom they are designated 'the children', and by loyalty to their king, who was the lord of his people. Likewise the Nabataeans came together in their worship of Dushara and their affection for their monarch, described in numerous inscriptions as 'king of the Nabataeans, lover of his people'. Otherwise attachment to a place might provide the basis for group cohesion. Hawshab son of Nafiy and

Wushuh daughter of Bagrat both made a point of recording on their tomb inscriptions that, though buried at Hegra, they were nevertheless Taymanites (H 1, 12). When Yedi'bel erected a statue in the city of Palmyra for his father 'Aziz son of Yedi'bel son of Barkai, he emphasised on the dedicatory inscription that his father was 'a Palmyrene' as well as 'of the tribe of Mattabol' (PAT 0271). In the highlands of south Arabia clans were normally qualified as 'the clan of such and such a place/town', and to specify an area one would habitually refer to the territory of a tribal group. One might, for example, say 'the land of [the tribe of] Ma'dhin' (CIS 4.323), 'to the east of [the tribe of] Yarsim' (Gl 1177), or 'on the frontiers of the tribe of Hashid' (Ir 12). For nomadic tribes, possessing no fixed abode nor supreme sovereign, it was common ancestry that afforded solidarity, one's identity and allegiance being determined by one's genealogy. Thus one Arab poet could state that 'our two tribes have always been enemies and always will be; to this day we have never started any relationship with you, nor do you find any with us when tracing back genealogies' (Tufayl 1).

The extent to which tribes might be integrated at higher levels varied greatly with time and place. Wealth was an important factor, for if there were sufficient means to maintain a political superstructure, a network of clan chiefs and even a paramount chief, then these could coordinate tribal members for collective action. Exposure to states also played a major part, for these were likely, often incidentally, to propel a tribe towards incipient statehood by demanding to deal with 'the leader', paying subsidies and encouraging trade relations. Poor remote communities, especially the camel-herding nomadic tribes of the inner deserts, were usually little more than a loose assemblage of small, local, autonomous groups. They hardly ever operated as wholes and made do with chiefs who had few functions and powers beyond being spokesmen of their own particular group and masters of its ceremonies. The rich agriculture-based kingdoms of south Arabia, on the other hand, possessed a hierarchy of chiefs who could levy goods and services from their people for building enterprises and for support of a retinue of ceremonial and executive personnel. This then made possible a considerable degree of integration of the whole tribe and a fairly high level of economic and cultural development. Tribes in the vicinity of states might be able to offer themselves as loyal military allies for a fee, especially in times of conflict. Thus, concerning the clash between Byzantium and Iran, it was observed that 'to the Arabs on both sides this war was a source of much profit' (Joshua the Stylite 79). The revenues would go to a dominant clan, such as the Jafnids of Ghassan and the Nasrids of Lakhm, who would establish a court for themselves, sponsor building and cultural projects, and organise their followers for large-scale military action. If contact were prolonged and earnings substantial, then centralised institutions might evolve that could command allegiance stronger than that to kin and the tribe might come to resemble a state. In late Roman Palmyra tribal affiliation featured less and less in inscriptions, probably because the bonds of citizenship and membership of the empire now carried increasing weight. And as Byzantium and Iran extended their influence further into west Arabia in the sixth century AD, they spawned ever more structured religio-political entities. Most famous of course was Muhammad's Islamic community, its members agreeing to accept God and Muhammad as their ultimate arbiters and to fight 'on God's behalf' against all unbelievers, even if they be kinsmen.

SOCIAL DIFFERENTIATION AND STRATIFICATION

It was frequently observed of Arab pastoralist tribes that they displayed a high level of social homogeneity. They disliked structures of authority: 'the distant Arabs dwelling in the desert . . . know neither overseers nor officials' (Sargon II, AR 2.17); 'they never at any time accept a man of another country as their overlord' (Diodorus 2.48); 'the Saracens . . . all alike are warriors of equal rank' (Ammianus 14.4). Their chiefs were expected to give support and to set an example, but not to compel, as is clear from the lament of the death of Kulayb, head of the powerful northeast Arabian tribe of Taghlib:

Who now will help the indigent when they cry out?
And who will stain the tips of supple spears with blood?
Who will cast lots for the slaughter camel
when the morning wind cuts through the knotted ropes?
Who will come forward with blood monies and gather them?
and who will succour us when calamities befall?

(Muhalhil 1.162)

Furthermore pastoralist tribes practised minimal division of labour: among them 'there is not a banker to be seen, nor modeller, nor painter, nor architect, nor geometer, nor singing-master, nor actor of dramatic poems' (Eusebius 6.10). Indeed craftsmen, such as metalworkers, weavers, tanners and the like, were held in contempt, and to be

117

designated such was a gross insult: 'Your father was a blacksmith' and, even worse, 'you are the slave of a blacksmith' (Hassan ibn Thabit 127, 48). These occupations were therefore usually the preserve of non-Arabs, especially slaves recruited from outside Arabia or Jews (who until recently provided most of the jewellers of Yemen). The principal social distinction was rather that between full members of a tribe and affiliated members/dependents. The latter could be: allies (*ḥulafā'*), individuals or groups who were to be spending a long time among foreigners and so had set up a protective relationship with a native host; protégés (*jîrân*), individuals or groups escaping vengeance, impoverishment or for some other reason in need of support; or else they could be slaves (*'abîd*), usually prisoners-of-war. If already members of other tribes, they could, if they wished (or, in the case of slaves, if manumitted and adopted), be incorporated fully into the host tribe, though most preferred to remain in the tribe of their birth. Those born outside the tribal commonwealth, however, found it hard to obtain tribal status, as the following text shows:

When [the Iranian commander] Basak son of Mahbudh began work on [the fortress of] Mushaqqar [in east Arabia], he was told: 'These workmen will not remain in this place unless they are provided with womenfolk.' . . . So he had whores brought for them from lower Iraq. . . . The workmen and the women married each other and begat children, and they soon constituted the majority of the population of the city of Hajar. They spoke Arabic and called themselves after [the tribe of] 'Abd al-Qays. When Islam came, they said to 'Abd al-Qays: 'You know well our numerical strength, our formidable equipment and weapons, and our great proficiency, so incorporate us among you and let us intermarry with you.' 'Abd al-Qays responded: 'No, remain as you are, as our dependent brethren.' But one 'Abdi said: 'People of 'Abd al-Qays, follow my advice and accept them, for the likes of these are highly desirable.' Another said: 'Have you no shame? Are you telling us to receive a people whose origins and ancestry are as you know?'

(Tabari 1.985–86)

This distinction also existed in the tribal kingdoms of Arabia; thus the Nabataean lady Wushuh and her daughters made a tomb for their protégés (*gryhm*) as well as for themselves (H 12). But these kingdoms exhibited far more degrees of differentiation: not a system of class, rather one of graded familial priorities in the control of wealth and force, in claims to others' services, in access to divine power and in material styles of life. Status positions were often very subtly demarcated, with the boundaries between nobility and commonality shifting according to the context of situation and speech. In south Arabia, for example, we very often encounter the antithesis *'bd* (pl. *'dm*) – *mr'* (pl. *'mr'*), which could designate any subordinate–dominant relationship: client–patron, tenant–landlord, subject–king, devotee–deity and so on. It did not therefore denote an absolute placing in the social hierarchy, but rather a relative one. Each tribe was dominated by a noble family, and these nobles (*qayls*) were simultaneously vassals (*'dm*) of the sovereign and seigneurs (*'mr'*) of the clans below them. The last were in no way slaves, but could erect their own monuments, plead in law, enter into contractual relationships with their overlords (e.g. lease lands off them, CIS 4.605bis), and even bring lawsuits against them (e.g. Hamilton 9). And a man who was a commoner in respect to some high chief was yet noble in relation to those kinsmen he outranked, even if it were merely the other members of his household (confirmed by CIAS 1.159, which thanks a deity for protecting all the family, 'the high and low members'/*'hrr w-'dm*). However, the same terms could refer to slaves and masters in the stricter sense, as is clear from an inscription that concerns 'mercantile transactions involving . . . a slave (*'bd*) or maidservant or head of cattle or other commodity' (RES 3910).

Kings emerged in various communities and at various times in pre-Islamic Arabia, but never were they absolute sovereigns; rather their function was to initiate and sponsor major public works, to see that the rulings of the legislative assembly were carried out and to serve as commander-in-chief in time of war. So though inferior to none, they were not considered far above all. Among the Nabataeans for example:

> The king is so democratic (*dēmotikos*) that, in addition to serving himself, he sometimes even serves the rest himself in his turn. He often renders an account of his kingship in the popular assembly; and sometimes his mode of life is examined. . . . The king has as chief administrator one of his companions, who is called 'brother'.
>
> (Strabo 16.4.26, 21)

A slightly bizarre account from Agarthicides of Cnidus (*c*.200–131 BC) suggests that the Sabaean monarch was also limited in his actions:

> The king of all the tribe holds his office from the people. Though it is prized, it is very hazardous. It is prized because the king is in command of many and he does whatever he wills in accordance with his judgements; it is hazardous because, although he has received the whole charge, he is not able thenceforth to leave the palace. Otherwise he is stoned by everyone in accordance with an ancient oracle, and thus his pre-eminence is deleterious.
>
> (in Photius 250)

This may refer to a period when the kingship was at a particularly low ebb, but it is true that at no point was it ever an absolutist office. Accession to the throne in Saba, during the early centuries AD at least, required the consent of 'the Sabaeans, the *qayls* and the army' (Ja 564). Ultimate authority rested in a legislative body of which the king was only one member, and edicts were regularly drafted in the name of the king plus a group of other functionaries. Moreover there was no state taxation system. The south Arabian monarchs received revenue from royal lands, war booty and rent from their clients, and they could compel military service and request aid for construction work, but tithes (paid as rent on temple lands or as tax on private lands) went to the temples.[5]

Arabian societies with good income from agriculture or trade were not only likely to be more hierarchical than pastoralist tribes, but also to have greater division of labour. In the inscriptions of Hatra, for example, we read about the professions of stonemasons, sculptors, metalworkers, carpenters, scribes, tutors, priests, physicians, accountants, doorkeepers, merchants and winesellers. In south Arabia a number of administrative offices are known, such as *kabîr*, *qayn* and *maqtawî*, though their exact nature and function is unclear. The first, literally 'elder', was a very senior figure. He might be the head of a tribe or professional group (e.g. 'chief of the cavalry'/*kabîr rkd̲*, Haram 2; 'chief of the stonemasons'/*kabîr nhmt*, Haram 16–17) or the agent of the king in an outlying city or region:

> Any *kabîr* holding office in Mayfa'a may appeal to [the deities] Sayin, Hawl and Halay'il and to the king of Hadramawt if the latter, through unawareness, does not keep the walls and tower of the folk of Mayfa'a in repair. In that

case let him [the *kabîr*] properly repair any damaged part which is collapsing, as well as what is not yet collapsing, and exercise royal authority as representative of the king of Hadramawt.

(RES 3869; cf. RES 3854, M 247)

Or else he might be the leader of a trading colony abroad, as is the case with the numerous Minaean *kabîr*s mentioned at Dedan and Timna (e.g. VL 9: 'elder of the Minaeans at Timna'). Before the first century AD the title of *qayn* occurs very frequently, relating the holder to a deity (e.g. Ja 554, 556), ruler (Gl 1717–19), city (Ja 555.3) or clan (Ja 550), and usually concerning the supervision of construction projects. After this time the term only appears as the name of a clan (perhaps because such administrators were originally drawn exclusively from this clan), and we hear much more of *maqtawî*s, personal assistants. They are most often encountered on military campaigns (e.g. Ja 632, 708, 713, 2113), but also performed secretarial duties, supervised building works (CIS 4.287) and the like. Though they are most commonly found in the service of kings and nobles, this is not always the case, which may mean that the system of administration in south Arabia was relatively informal (in the first few centuries AD at least).

LAW AND LEGISLATION

The renowned pre-Islamic Arab poet Labid once spoke of a leader from his own kin group as 'one of a tribe whose forefathers laid down for them a *sunna*, and every folk has a *sunna* and its *imâm*'. *Sunna* here refers to the established customary practice of the tribe, validated by tradition and by the deeds of the ancestors. The *imâm* is the tribal hero whose actions enshrine and articulate the law, that is, a precedent and an example. Thus when God said of Adam: 'We have made you an *imâm* for the people' (Quran 2.124), He meant: 'I shall make you such that you guide those who come after you. . . . You will go before them and they will follow your guidance and they will find their *sunna* in your *sunna*' (Tabari, *Tafsîr*). So tribal law was customary law, determined by ancient practice. It is therefore inherently conservative; 'We found our fathers on a path and we follow in their footsteps' was the reply of most Meccans to the Prophet Muhammad's new message (Quran 43.22, 24). And it is echoed by pre-Islamic Arab poets: 'We follow the ways of our forefathers, those who kindled wars and were

121

faithful to the ties of kinship' ('Abid 20). It could only be updated either by such aforementioned paragons of tribal virtue, who won the approval of all, or by the consensus of all full members of the community meeting together. Such gatherings were the means of most tribal decision-making and if efficacious they were a source of pride for a tribe:

> Among them are assemblies of fine men, councils from which
> follow decisive words and deeds . . .
> when you come to them, you will find them round their tents
> in session, at which impetuous action is often obviated by
> their prudent members.
>
> (Zuhayr 62)

Not only were rulings passed and policies determined in tribal councils, but also misdemeanours might be heard and their perpetrators examined: 'Excellent is the man upon whom you can call for defence when the plaintiff in the council brings his charge' ('Amr ibn Qami'a 1).

Innocence or guilt was proven either by 'oath or contest or evidence' (Zuhayr 12). However, in the absence of police, prison or the like, a man and his kinship group had to seek their own retribution. The motto was 'a slain for our slain, a prisoner for each one of us captured, and goods for our goods' (*Hudhaliyyun* 89). And we often observe this being put into practice:

> We obtained in requital for our slain an equal number
> of them, and for every one of our people fettered and
> shackled there was one shackled of theirs
> And for our robbed cattle the same number; for captive
> women, captive women and for every warrior, a warrior.
>
> (Tufayl 3)

Yet there were alternatives to retaliation. One was to pay compensation, though in the case of murder it might be felt that only the blood of the offender would suffice:

> If you will not seek vengeance for your brother,
> take off your weapons and fling them on the flinty ground.
> Take up the eye pencil, don the camisole, dress yourselves
> in women's bodices! What wretched kin you are
> to a kinsman oppressed!

122

You have been diverted from avenging your brother
by a bite of minced meat and a lick of meagre milk.
(*Ḥam.* 684)[6]

Another method was to seek the services of arbiters, ones respected
for their 'nobility, integrity, trustworthiness, leadership, seniority,
glory and experience' (Ya'qubi 1.299). Though they had no means to
enforce their judgements, their virtue added weight to their decision.
We find them acting in very different situations, sometimes helping
to resolve feuds:

> The conciliators from Ghayz ibn Murra laboured for peace
> after the tribe's concord had been shattered by bloodshed.
> So I swear, by the holy house about which circumambulate
> men of Quraysh and Jurhum, whose hands constructed it,
> A solemn oath I swear – you have proved yourselves fine
>   masters in all matters,
> be the thread single or twisted double.
> You alone mended the rift between 'Abs and Dhubyan
> after long slaughter, and much grinding of the perfume of
>   Manshim.
> And you declared: 'If we achieve peace broad and sure
> by ample giving and fair speaking, we shall live secure.'
> (*Mu.*: Zuhayr)

And at other times they gave their verdict on awkward points of law:

> The Arabs used to refer every serious and difficult case to
> 'Amir ibn Zarib for decision. Once it happened that a dispute
> in reference to a hermaphrodite was brought to him. They
> said: 'Are we to treat it as a man or a woman?' They had never
> brought him such a difficult matter before, so he said: 'Wait
> a while until I have reflected on it.' They agreed to wait, and
> he passed a sleepless night turning the matter over and
> looking at it from all sides without any result. Now he had a
> slave-girl, Sukhayla, who used to pasture his flock. . . . When
> this girl saw that he could not sleep and tossed about on his
> bed, she asked what his trouble was. 'Get out and leave me
> alone, for it is none of your business,' he retorted. However
> she was so persistent that he . . . told her: 'Well, I was asked
> to adjudicate on the inheritance of a hermaphrodite. Am I to
> make it a man or a woman? By God I do not know what to

do and I can see no way out.' She said: 'Good God, merely
follow the course of the urinary process.' . . . 'You have solved
my problem,' said he, and in the morning he went out to the
people and gave his decision in the way she had indicated.

(Ibn Hisham 78–79)

If a person had committed a crime within his own kinship group or
threatened their peace and stability, then that group might decide to
banish him from their presence and their protection. This meant that
a person's blood was licit and he was forced to live as an outlaw:

And somewhere the noble find a refuge afar from scathe,
the outlaw a lonely spot where no kin with hatred burn.
I, never a prudent man, night-faring in hope or fear,
hard-pressed on the face of the earth, but still have room to
turn.
To me now, in default of you [my kin], are comrades a wolf
untired,
a sleek leopard, and a fell hyena with shaggy mane.
True comrades, they never let out the secret in trust with
them, nor
forsake their friend just because he brought them bane.

(Shanfara, *lâmiyya*)

Among the wealthier sedentary polities of Arabia there existed a
more elaborate legal system with more of an institutional framework.
A number of the cities of south Arabia had a council (*mswd*), and at
each of the capital cities there was a supreme council where the king
sat along with delegates from a certain number of tribal groups,
representing the whole nation and issuing edicts on its behalf. Such
an edict might begin as follows: 'Thus have ordered and directed
and decreed Shahr Yagill Yuhargib, the son of Hawfa'amm, the king
of the Qatabanians, and the Qatabanians, the council, having its full
complement. . . . ' (RES 3566). In this particular text it would appear
that Shahr Yagill had to fight to maintain his position, for he goes on
to complain that 'some people from the council and community of
landowners determined and enforced their decisions by swearing oaths
between themselves in that temple in their very self-willed and loutish
manner without the sanction of [me] their lord'. Turning to Nabataea
we hear of their 'popular assembly' (*dêmos*), at which the king 'often
renders an account of his rule' (Strabo 16.4.26). In the earliest texts
from Palmyra decisions issue from 'the community (*polis/gbl*) of all the

Palmyrenes', PAT 0269). However, after AD 75 it is the city council (*boulê*) that deals with the promulgation of laws and decrees, though at least theoretically in conjunction with 'the people'. Here, for example, is the preamble to the issue of a new tax-law:

> A decree of the council, in the month of April, the eighteenth day, the year 448 [AD 137], during the presidency of Bonne son of Bonne son of Hairan, and the secretaryship of Alexander son of Alexander son of Philopator, secretary on behalf of the council and the people, and the magistracy of Maliku son of 'Ulayy son of Muqimu and Zebida son of Nesa. When the council was by law assembled, it established what is written below. . . .
>
> (PAT 0259)

In these three polities there was a system of fine-payment for infractions, usually to deities via their priests (see H 34 below and the list in CIS 4.548), and there also existed the possibility to sue those who had caused one harm, trauma or loss. Thus a Sabaean couple who 'made a journey to the land of Hadramawt' and nearly died of thirst on the way thanked the god Almaqah for 'having given them a favourable outcome in a lawsuit which was originated by them against the guide who had treacherously endangered their lives' (Ja 750). And it was said of Nabataea that:

> It is exceedingly well governed. At any rate Athenodorus, a philosopher and companion of mine, who had been to the city of the Petraeans, used to describe their government with admiration. For he said that he found both many Romans and many other foreigners sojourning there, and that he saw that the foreigners often engaged in lawsuits, both with one another and with the natives, but that none of the natives prosecuted one another, and that they in every way kept peace with one another.
>
> (Strabo 16.4.21)

In south Arabia there also existed the threat of being placed under a ban. For more minor offences one might 'rejoin the tribe' after making an expiatory offering (RES 4782), but in the case of major crimes one might be deprived of one's civil liberties, that is, one would no longer be able to regard one's life as protected by the king:

If anyone kills his fellow from Qataban and the said tribes, let him be banned [if guilty] . . . or subjected to an examination [if he claims innocence], as the king has directed and decreed and caused to be examined. . . . Whoever contravenes a proclamation of ban or an examination . . . let that man, who has [thereby] shown himself a transgressor, die, as is commanded, and his life is permissible. Whoever kills him need not fear death or examination in respect of the life of that man who has shown himself a transgressor.

(RES 3878)

Finally one might note that certain types of inscriptions in Arabia are often of a legal nature. For example tomb inscriptions often lay claim to ownership, transfer burial rights and spaces, stipulate what can or cannot be done with the tomb, and detail the penalties incurred by misuse of it:

No one shall ask of Bakr or his brothers or their sons of the clan of Maqar – no high or low person, no male or female dependent of Maqar – that they be buried in their tomb Ahram [near Marib] or in the tomb of its anteroom, whether with document or without.

(CIS 4.619)

This is the tomb belonging to Hinat, daughter of 'Abd Obodat, for herself and her children and her descendants and for whoever produces in their hand from the hand of this Hinat a document or deed of entitlement to the effect that they may be buried in this tomb. . . . And no one has the right to sell this tomb or to lease it or to draw up for themselves any document. And whoever does other than what is above will be liable for a fine to [the gods] Dushara and Manat in the sum of one thousand silver coins and to our lord Rabbel, king of the Nabataeans, for the same amount.

(H 34)

In one text from Hegra there is a reference to 'the copy of this deposited in the temple of Qaysha' (H 36) and in another from Palmyra an allusion to some sort of public registry office (*byt 'rk'*, PAT 2759). This suggests that it was standard practice to lodge a papyrus version in an official archive. Probably the latter would be the original deed, from which only the key elements (name, date, description of property, cession formula, penalty clause, etc.) were copied onto the walls of tombs where they have survived, long outlasting the perishable original. Then there are house deeds and land assignments:

> Ri'ab Alhan . . . built his house . . . with its guest hall and its lower storey and its two upper parts and its two walls and its two porticoes from foundation to top, with full legal title, by the law of Anbay. So let there be no infringement thereof. And he has committed it to the protection of [the gods] 'Amm and Anbay and of the kings of Qataban for himself and his children and his successors against anyone who may damage it.
>
> (Doe 7)

> This [inscribed stela] marks land which has been granted, leased, transferred and allotted by Hawfa'amm Yuhan'im son of Sumhuwatar and Yada''ab Yagill son of Dhamar'ali, joint kings of Qataban, to the tribe Adim in the valleys Akhirr and Baram. Payment for the land has been received and the documentary record has been engraved. The dimension of the whole territory as a unit, in value and extent, is . . . It is forbidden for Akhirr and Baram to be enlarged over and above these dimensions by any ploughing or planting. This document is based on ordinances and decrees which have been issued by 'Amm and Anbay, and on a code which has been applicable to Baram for many years, to all of which Yada''ab and Qataban have consented by grace. . . . As for the stock of any king or tribe that increases or fragments the extent of this territory, and anyone who presumes . . . to add to or diminish the details of the text of this announcement, let him and his children be consigned to oblivion.
>
> (VL 7)

And finally there are official edicts. A number of different authorities had the right to issue such texts, but most prominent were the gods, via an oracle transcribed by their temple servants, and kings, in consultation with tribal councils:

> Thus decreed Almaqah in His oracle that any man who stands under a ban must first offer a sacrifice before the priest shall cause his ban to be lifted, so the man who is under a ban should sacrifice and perform what is proper.
>
> (CIAS 1.15)

Thus has commanded, decreed, established and ordained King Shammar Yuhar'ish . . . for his subjects the tribe Saba, owners of the town Marib and its agricultural lands, with reference to all sales and transactions which they effect . . . that if anyone purchases a male or female slave, or head of cattle, or other commodity, then the cooling off period [before conclusion of the sale] shall be one month. If anyone, after ten days or twenty, returns a camel or ox or head of cattle, he shall pay its hire for the time that he shall have made use of it. And when a head of cattle dies in the possession of the purchaser when a seventh day has passed, then no responsibility rests on the vendor for its death and uselessness, and the purchaser must pay the vendor his legal claim. . . .

(RES 3910)

MARRIAGE AND THE ROLE OF WOMEN

Considerable variety of marital custom is attested in pre-Islamic Arabia, though we do not know the extent to which any one prevailed. Strict endogamy (people marry only their own stock) or exogamy (people marry only outside their own stock) does not seem to have existed (though at the town of Matira northeast of San'a permission was required to marry one's daughter to an outsider, Qutra 1). And it would in any case have been limited by the practice of marriage by capture:

They did not give us Tayyites their daughters in marriage,
but we wooed them against their will with our swords.
And with us captivity brought no abasement to them,
and they neither toiled in making bread nor boiled the pot.
But we commingled them with our noblest women,
and they bore us fine sons, of pure descent.
How often will you see among us the son of a captive bride,
who staunchly thrusts through heroes in the fray.

(Hatim al-Ta'i 66)

Most tribes would, however, at least have marked preferences. Some might favour cross-cousin marriages, others felt that marriage with outsiders produced hardier children and reduced the likelihood of

128

family quarrels. Most disliked unions with people of very different manners. Thus a poet of Hudhayl is indignant at a proposal that he should seek a bride among Himyarites, 'who do not circumcise their women and who do not think it disgusting to eat locusts', and Ta'abbata Sharra's kin are mocked for allowing their sister to wed into a tribe accused of cannibalism (*Hudhaliyyun* 57, 147, 164).

Newlyweds might join either the husband's or the wife's natal house. In the former case marriage challenges a woman's connection to her natural kin and in some sense captures her for her husband's (for which he pays a price, the dowry). He claims not merely wifely services but the woman as child-bearer and her progeny (whoever in fact may sire them). The children belong to him and his people, primarily to him but residually to his lineage, who may in the event of his demise perpetuate the group's interest by supplying another husband:

> In pre-Islamic times, when a man died and left a widow, his heir, if he came at once and threw his garment over her, had the right to marry her under the dowry of her deceased master or to give her in marriage and take her dowry. But if she anticipated him and went off to her own people, then they took charge of her.
>
> (Tabari, *Tafsîr ad* 4.23)

The second option imposes exactly opposite demands. A man's heirs are to be found only among his sister's children, not his own; and lineage continuity rests with his control of his sister and her offspring, not his wife and hers. Men therefore retain strong interests in their sisters even as against their wives, while women are bound to their brothers as against their husbands.

While descent through the male line would seem to have been the norm in pre-Islamic Arabia, we are occasionally given hints of matrilineal arrangements. In two south Arabian texts we find a king assigning a number of individuals to the overlordship of two noble families, one in Sirwah and one in Marib (Fa 3, 76). The lists of names are in each case preceded by the words 'the following men and women' and followed by 'and their children and descendants' with the pronoun 'their' being feminine plural. This suggests that the children were reckoned as belonging to the mother and not to a male progenitor, but this was evidently not a universal system in south Arabia, since similar expressions in other texts have a masculine pronoun. Another text describes a brawl between a woman's husband and an overlord of her clan, in which the former was killed and the latter wounded (Ja 700). The fight was occasioned by the woman's appeal to her kin's overlord for help in recovering from her husband custody of the child she had had by him, perhaps an indication of tension between two systems. In a Hasaean funerary inscription from east Arabia a woman recounts her ancestry through the female line for three generations: mother, grandmother, great-grandmother (HIT 16; cf. Ja 1048). And in Hegra in northwest Arabia a number of women erected tombs, cite only their female relatives and insist that the structure was intended for their daughters and their dependents:

> This is the tomb which Wushuh, daughter of Bagrat, and Qaynu and Nashkuyah, her daughters, Taymanites, made for themselves, each one, and for 'Amirat and 'Usra'nat and Al'alat, their sisters, daughters of this Wushuh, and for those under their protection, every one. . . .
>
> (H 12)

Finally we sometimes hear of a form of divorce that could only have occurred where the woman remained with her tribe:

> The women in pre-Islamic Arabia, or some of them, had the right to dismiss their husbands, and the form of dismissal was this. If they lived in a tent they turned it round, so that if the door faced east it now faced west, or if the entrance faced south they would turn it towards the north. And when the man saw this he knew that he was dismissed and did not enter.
>
> (Isfahani 17.387)

Diversity in marriage customs is also evident in the degree to which monogamy, polygyny (one man many wives) and polyandry (one woman many husbands) all crop up in our sources. The last seems hinted at by Strabo in his account of south Arabian mores:

> One woman is also wife for all [the sons of a family], and he who first enters the house before any other has intercourse with her, having first placed his staff before the door, for by custom each man must carry a staff; but she spends the night with the eldest. And therefore all children are brothers.
>
> (16.4.25)

And it receives probable confirmation from a south Arabian inscription that commemorates the building of a house by a woman with the aid of her two husbands (YMN 19). Furthermore, in a list of the different types of marriage found in Arabia before Islam, there is given the example of a group of men caring for and living with a single woman (Bukhari 3.427, *nikâḥ* 36).

In some places there also existed the phenomenon of temporary marriage, where women advertised for mercenary husbands when they wanted children:

> They [Saracens] have mercenary wives [since they give the men a dowry, the husbands must be mercenary, but this does not occur to Ammianus], hired under a temporary contract. But in order that there may be some semblance of matrimony, the future wife, by way of dowry, offers her husband a spear and a tent, with the right to leave him after a stipulated time, if she so elects. And it is unbelievable with what ardour both sexes give themselves up to passion.
>
> (Ammianus 14.4)

This practice may have chiefly taken place in the event of an existing husband's infertility. In the south Arabian sphere we find two childless women appealing to a deity for help. One of them subsequently conceived 'by means of a man who came and sheltered with their family on the sixth night'. And 'they then made it their duty to accept the bride-gift from this man and to dedicate the son born of him and this statuette as a thank-offering on their behalf' (CIS 4.581). Since he is not named, he was probably a passing stranger, which was an advantage in that he would not be in a position to claim the rights of a father over any child born, who would remain a member of the mother's family. And Muslim lexicographers describe the phenomenon of 'a woman's desiring sexual intercourse with a man only to obtain offspring by him' (*istibḍâ*):

> A man of them would say to his wife, when she had just finished menstruating [so there would be no doubt over parentage]: 'Send to such a one and demand of him sexual intercourse to obtain offspring', and her husband would separate himself from her and not touch her until her pregnancy by that man became apparent. As soon as it was apparent, her husband would resume sexual relations with her if he wished.
>
> (Bukhari 3.427, *nikâḥ* 36)

The aim was, it was said, to acquire a child sired by a man distinguished for bravery and generosity.

From all that has been said it is clear that we encounter women first and foremost as wives and mothers. This is not to say there was no differentiation among women. There was, for example, the distinction between freeborn and slave, the latter usually charged with the more menial tasks of cooking ('the maidservants set to roasting the little foal', *Mu.*: Tarafa), bearing messages ('I sent my slave girl to her', *Mu.*: 'Antara), and the like. Nor should it be thought that pre-Islamic Arabian women did not play a role outside the home. They might need, indeed demand, the protection of their menfolk, but could rally alongside them in times of trouble:

> Upon our tracks follow fair noble ladies,
> that we take care shall not leave us, nor be insulted;
> Howdah-borne ladies of Banu Jusham ibn Bakr
> who mingle, with good looks, high birth and obedience.
> They have taken a covenant with their husbands
> that, when they should meet with signal horsemen,
> They will plunder mail-coats and shining sabres
> and captives fettered together in irons.
> When they fare forth, they walk sedately
> swinging their gait like swaying tipplers.
> They provender our horses saying,
> 'you're not our husbands if you do not protect us'.
> If we do not defend them, may we not survive
> nor live on for any time after them.
>
> (*Mu.*: 'Amr)

Moreover in the settled communities of the south Arabians, Nabataeans and Palmyrenes we find women active in a number of different spheres. They commission inscriptions, make offerings to the gods in their own right,[7] act as administrative officers (Nami 14, Ja 487), take on a husband's overlordship upon his decease (CIS 4.95) and construct public buildings and tombs. The last activity points to the enjoyment of a considerable degree of financial independence, and it is also one which gave women a very visible presence in their community, for their faces stare out from many a statue and funerary relief (Pl. 18).

There are two particularly prominent roles that we find occupied by women pretty much throughout Arabia. The first is that of religious functionary, her authority then deriving from her ability to

Bust of Tamma, daughter of Shamshigeram, holding distaff and spindle.
Limestone.   Palmyra.   Early 2nd century A.D.

Plate 18 Funerary bust of the wealthy Palmyrene woman Tamna daughter of Shamsigeram, *c.*AD 150 (British Museum 125204).

commune with the other world (see chapter 6 below), which in turn empowered her to transcend petty rivalries and focus the energies of a large social grouping. The confederation of Qedar, for example, was at a loss without its divine images and their female guardian:

> Concerning Duma (*Adummatu*), the stronghold of Arabia which Sennacherib, king of Assyria, my own father, had conquered and whose goods, possessions and idols, together with the priestess (*apkallatu*),[8] the queen of Arabia, he had

carried off to Assyria. Haza'el, the king of Arabia, came with costly gifts to Nineveh, my lordly city, kissed my feet and implored me [Esarhaddon] to restore to him his idols. I had mercy upon him, repaired the damages [suffered by] these idols: Atarsamain, Daa, Nuha, Ruda, Abirillu and Atarquruma. I had written upon them [an inscription praising] the might of Assur, my lord, and my own name, and returned them to him. I made the woman Tabua, who was reared in my palace [taken there by Sennacherib], their queen and sent her back to her country together with her gods.

(IA 53)

The second role is that of entertainer (Pls. 19, 30). As noted above, she was a familiar feature at male wine feasts: 'the drinking of luxurious wine and the voice of a sweet singer' ('Abid, fr. 8), 'a charming girl plucking with nimble fingers the strings of her melodious lute' (*Mu.*: Labid). It is her skill at singing and playing the lute that is mostly spoken of, but there are also hints of more sensual attractions:

A singing-wench comes to us in her striped gown and
  saffron robe,
Wide the opening of her collar, delicate her skin
to my companions' fingers, tender her nakedness.
When we say 'let's hear from you', she advances to us
chanting fluently, her glance languid, in effortless song.

(*Mu.*: Tarafa)

FEASTING AND REVELLING

From all regions of Arabia we have evidence, sometimes archaeological and sometimes literary, for communal meals (Pl. 36). These might be joyous affairs, such as circumcision and marriage feasts, when whole communities came together to witness the rites and share in the repast. Others were more sombre, such as funerary banquets (*al-ṭaʿām ʿalā l-mayyit*, 'Abd al-Razzaq 3.550). But all such occasions of communal consumption served many functions beyond the immediate one of satiation. They often had social aims, for eating and drinking together promotes companionship, so confirming and reinforcing group identity and solidarity. If that group was a cultic entity, then commu- nal meals took on the significance of a declaration of confessional allegiance, and to eat the consecrated food of non-believers might be

Plate 19 Clay model from Petra of group of musicians, one man playing a double flute flanked by two women playing string instruments, *c*.1st century AD, 8.7 × 9.2 cm (Archaeological Museum of Petra 15768).

regarded as an abomination. As at the eucharistic meal of Christians, the divinities themselves might be present, and by admitting man to their table they bound him to them in a special relationship. There could also be a political dimension, for it was by sponsoring public feasts that an aspiring leader became a man of influence and renown, his cavalier generosity to others creating obligations of reciprocity as well as earning him repute.

A particularly long-lived form of feasting is the ritual banquet (*mrzḥ'*), a celebration attended by a select group of colleagues in honour of a particular deity or deities. It is attested as early as the thirteenth century BC in a text from Ugarit, which describes the preparations taken by the chief of the gods for his guests, the slaughtering of animals and the provision of wine. It frequently incurred the condemnation of Israelite prophets on account of its tendency towards excess and association with foreign gods:

> Lying on ivory beds and sprawling on their divans, they dine on lambs from the flock and stall-fattened veal. They bawl to the sound of the lyre. . . . They drink wine by the bowlful and lard themselves with the finest oils. . . . But the sprawlers' revelry (*mrzḥ'*) is over.
>
> (Amos 6.4–7)

It was a common event at Petra and Palmyra, its participants called 'children of the banquet' or, at Petra, 'companions of the banquet'. The event was dedicated to a deity (e.g. RES 1423: 'banquet of Obodat the god') and involved much eating and drinking:

> They prepare meals together in groups of thirteen persons; and they have two girl-singers for each banquet. The king holds many drinking-bouts in magnificent style, but no one drinks more than eleven cupfuls, each time using a different golden cup. The king is so democratic that, in addition to serving himself, he sometimes even serves the rest himself in his turn.
>
> (Strabo 16.4.26, on the authority of his friend Athenodorus 'who had been in the city of the Petraeans')

The convener bore the title 'chief of the banquet', rendered as 'symposiarch' in Greek. One such master of ceremonies, a certain Yarhai Agrippa, is honoured in a Palmyrene inscription together with those who helped him in his duties: his secretary, the head chef, the wine steward and all his aides (PAT 2743). It would seem to have been a rotating post, for Yarhai was congratulated at the end of 'a full year'. It was a great responsibility, since one 'served the gods', meaning that one oversaw all the preparations and supplied the wine 'from one's own house'. The banquets were generally held in a designated room within or near the temple precincts, which would be equipped with long benches for the guests to recline. Numerous such rooms have been found, though there is a marked difference between the Petran and the Palmyrene types (in particular those at Petra are smaller), which probably reflects a difference in their rituals and significance.

In the inscriptions of some of the ancient rulers of Saba there occurs a number of times the expression 'when he offered a banquet (*'lm*) to 'Athtar'. The most prestigious version of this event took place at the temple of Jabal al-Lawdh in the Jawf region, which comprises large courts with numerous rows of benches. The banquet there was convened by the Sabaean ruler and was linked to the 'pact of union' (*gw*), a ceremony that served to bind together the diverse tribes of the Sabaean federation and to guarantee the security of the sanctuaries under their common guardianship. It was under the aegis of 'Athtar that this pact was concluded, for he was above all local and tribal gods, and it was in his honour that the banquet was staged, and very likely at his expense in that it was probably paid for out of his dues.

Pliny (12.63) tells us that at the Hadramawt capital 'the tithe is drawn on to defray what is a public expenditure, for actually on a fixed number of days the god graciously entertains guests at a banquet'. This seems similar to an edict issued via an inscription to the tribe of Sam'ay by their patron god Ta'lab, who decrees that, among other things, 'he will provide banquets from [the proceeds of] the tithes' (RES 4176). It is not clear for what reason these gods offered this largesse, but possibly it is connected with the accomplishment of a pilgrimage to their holy places. In any case there certainly were ritual meals on such occasions. It happened, for example, at Marib, as attested by a number of sacrificial altars engraved with the name of the Sabaean pilgrimage month of Abhay.

Feasts might also be profane affairs, just plain revelry and cama-raderie. Allusions to gatherings for the purpose of enjoying wine, women and song are common in the poems of the pastoralists of north Arabia. Purveyors of wine apparently travelled great distances to sell their product:

> A captive, it dwelt in the jar for twenty revolving years,
> above it a seal of clay, exposed to the wind and sun
> Imprisoned by Jews who brought it from Golan in
>   lands afar and offered
> for sale by a vintner who knew well to follow gain.
>
> (*Muf.* 55)

They would then hoist a special flag to advertise to customers that they were open for business (*Mu.*: Labid, 'Antara). The expenses of transportation meant that the cost was high, and it therefore became a conventional item of boasting that one frequently hosted carousing sessions. The other ingredient of such occasions, the singing-girl, features in the inscriptions (*qnt, ghlmt*) and drawings of the tribes of the Harra, and was a permanent fixture in the taverns of the settled areas of Arabia:

> Many a time I hastened early to the tavern, while there ran
> at my heels a ready cook, a nimble active serving-man
> 'Midst a gallant troop, like Indian scimitars, of mettle
>   high;
> well they know that every mortal, shod and bare alike, must
>   die.
> Propped at ease I greet them gaily, them with myrtle boughs
>   I greet,

pass among them wine that gushes from the jar's mouth
  bitter-sweet.
Emptying goblet after goblet, but the source may no man
  drain;
never cease they from carousing save to cry, 'fill up again!'
Briskly runs the page to serve them: on his ears hang
  pearls, below
tight the girdle draws his doublet as he bustles to and fro.
'Twas as though the harp waked the lute's responsive note,
when the loose-robed chantress touched it, singing shrill
  with quavering throat.
Here and there, among the party, damsels fair superbly
glide: each her long white skirt lets trail and swings a
  wineskin at her side.

(A'sha)

Also in the category of profane feasts are the meals provided for the
poor and needy, for the stranger and wayfarer. Generosity and hospitality were considered the cardinal Arabian virtues, and to be thought
niggardly would be the ruin of a man:

When you have prepared the meal, entreat to partake
thereof a guest – I am not one to eat, like a churl, alone –
some traveller through the night, or protégé, for in truth
I fear the reproachful talk of men after I am gone.
                                        (Hatim al-Ta'i 62)

Munificence, on the other hand, would earn him and his tribe great
renown and allow him to hold his head high:

Many's the good companion, noble of ancestry, liberal,
  have I given
to drink before dawn a morning draught in a cup of wine
  bought dear . . .
And I tarried not, but sent my servant at once to seek
the best of my fat young she-camels with a large hump.
And she strove to rise, though resisted to be led along, and I
hamstrung her with my sharp-cutting Mashrafite sword.
And my fellow dallied long in luxury, waited upon, and
  later enjoyed a noble feast, to which all neighbours came.
                                        ('Amr ibn Qami'a 13)

6

RELIGION

POLYTHEISM

In monotheism the sacred is concentrated in one omnipotent and omniscient entity, whereas in polytheism it is diffused over a wide range of beings, places, objects, practices and human personnel. In reality there is both some seepage in most monotheisms, with saints and shrines and the like tending to proliferate, and some telescoping on the part of many polytheisms, with one god often being preferred above others. But the difference between the two is real and substantial. Firstly, in pre-modern societies that had not secularised public life and relegated religion to the private domain, monotheism is by nature intolerant and intransigent. For there to be only one true God all the rest must be impotent frauds, and those who worship them are not just in error, but damned, and should be fought or at the very least shunned. If you believe in many gods, however, there is no reason to be hostile to gods not your own, nor any bar to paying them and their faithful your respects. 'When you enter a village, swear by its god', as the old Arabian proverb goes. Secondly, the words of a unique omnipotent God must needs be the absolute Truth, in the light of which its recipients should therefore regulate their lives and interpret their world. Polytheism, on the other hand, is neither so unitary nor so coherent. It is rather a variegated worldview, one capable of eliciting a rich and subtle range of meanings from a multi-faceted reality, one desirous of understanding and influencing the many and varied ways the natural world impinges upon us.

Up until about the fourth century AD almost all the inhabitants of Arabia were polytheists. We know many of the names of their deities, since the most common aim of Arabian inscriptions was to invoke the gods in some way, usually petitioning them or thanking them. But names alone do not tell us much, and the brevity of most of these texts makes it difficult for us to understand the nature and function of the gods or to comprehend what they meant to their worshippers. They are also frequently assigned epithets (compare Christian designation of Mary as 'mother of God', 'the virgin', etc.), but without the myths and narratives to decode them these are not usually very informative. Loosely, of course, the gods represented those forces that were important to the lives of their devotees but beyond their control: rain, fertility, health, love, death and so on. By seeking the favour of the gods, typically making some votive gift, one might thereby influence these forces. Thus one member of the northwest Yemeni tribe of Amir 'dedicated to his lord Dhu Samawi in his temple . . . a bronze statuette of a she-camel that Dhu Samawi may grant him the wellbeing of himself and his children as well as the wellbeing and safety of his camel' (Ja 2956). But how exactly this tribesman conceived of his divine patron and to what degree the latter affected his life we do not know.

It was the view of the sociologist Emile Durkheim that spiritual beliefs mirror the structure of human societies. This might explain why the sophisticated civilisation of south Arabia had the most developed pantheon in Arabia with the names of over one hundred deities featuring in the surviving inscriptions, though many of these probably represent different aspects or manifestations of the same god. 'Athtar almost always occupies first place in lists and his cult was spread throughout the region. Moreover in one text we find a worshipper thanking another god for 'interceding on his behalf with 'Athtar' (CIAS 2.189), confirming that he enjoyed a certain primacy. Though he always bore the same name, he had a variety of manifestations, each distinguished by an added epithet, in many cases probably referring to one of his shrines (compare Christian use of 'our lady of Lourdes', 'our lady of Guadeloupe', etc.). The difference between the numerous deities of south Arabia seems not to lie in their function, but in their sphere of operation. Thus there was not one dedicated rain-god, but rather there were tutelary deities responsible for the irrigation of the village, patron deities for that of the tribal lands, and 'Athtar for the whole world.

The patron deity (*shym*) of a people was of more immediate significance in south Arabia than the remoter figure of 'Athtar. The four principal peoples had as their patrons Almaqah (Sabaeans), Wadd (Minaeans), 'Amm (Qatabanians) and Sayin (Hadramites), and each people was collectively termed the 'children' of their respective patron deity. The last would be characterised as the 'lord' of the shrine that served as the cultic centre for his people (e.g. 'Almaqah lord of

Awwam', the principal temple in Marib). These patron deities played a vital socio-political role in that their cults served as the focus of a people's cohesion and loyalty and functioned as an expression of communal will and activity. For example the tithes owing on land and its produce were paid to the gods (via their human servants), who also saw to its redistribution:

> Frankincense after being collected is conveyed to Shabwa on camels, one of the gates of the city being opened for its admission. The kings have made it a capital offence for camels so laden to turn aside from the high road. At Shabwa a tithe estimated by measure and not by weight is taken by the priests for the god they call Sayin, and the incense is not allowed to be put on the market until this has been done. This tithe is drawn on to defray what is a public expenditure, for actually on a fixed number of days the god graciously entertains guests at a banquet.
>
> (Pliny 12.63)

Tithes exacted on the same traffic by the Minaean deities could be discharged by public works, such as construction of town walls, undertaken by the tithe-payers (e.g. M 29). In Qataban, when the king 'requested' a regulation dealing with water supplies, the promulgation of it was made in the name of the god Anbay (Ry 478). The shared cult of 'Amm of Labakh enabled cooperation between a group of Qatabanian landlords and their tenants in far-off Dathinah (RES 3688–89, 3691–93). In Saba military campaigns were carried out 'for Almaqah and the Sabaeans' (e.g. RES 3945), and fines for all manner of offences were paid 'to Almaqah and the kings of Saba' (e.g. Ja 576). In other words it was the cult of the patron deity that allowed the community to function as a coherent entity (as opposed to a mass of discrete localised kinship groups), acting as a sort of social glue.

In less complex societies than south Arabia the pantheon might be much smaller and the patron deity might assume a particularly prominent place. Thus the inhabitants of the fertile oasis of Dedan turned to Dhu Ghaba, 'the master of the grove', for their needs and rarely to any other. The Minaean god Wadd appears in a few inscriptions, but these are presumably attributable to the Minaean colony that ran trade operations in the oasis. Then there is Kutba (or Aktab), god of writing, who is probably related to a Babylonian scribal deity, perhaps brought to northwest Arabia by the Babylonian monarch Nabonidus. But other gods are mentioned no more than once or twice, probably invoked by travellers passing through rather than native worshippers. The Nabataeans were similarly loyal to Dushara, 'the master of the Shara', the mountain range encompassing their capital Petra, and 'the god of our lord . . . the king of the Nabataeans' (H 11, 28, 36). At Petra itself the only other very popular deity was al-'Uzza, 'the mighty goddess', who is celebrated both in texts and in artistic representations (RES 1088, RB 42.413, 43.588).[1] However, the Nabataeans were rulers of a kingdom, and in the territories they controlled many other deities were worshipped, such as Hubal and Manat in the Hijaz, and Allat in the Hawran and the Syrian desert. Moreover, as international merchants, they were exposed to many foreign influences, and it is not therefore surprising to find that the cult of the Egyptian goddess Isis was widespread in Nabataea (Fig. 3). And there were also specialised deities, such as Shay' al-Qawm, 'the protector of the people', who looked after those away from home. In this capacity he was called upon in AD 132 by a certain 'Ubayd son of Ghanim son of Sa'dallat the Nabataean of the tribe of Rawah', who was a cavalryman doing service at Anat on the Euphrates (CIS 2.3973).

Palmyra was a special case, for it possessed a very cosmopolitan population, many members of which had brought their gods with them, and by virtue of its location had long been exposed to a number of different cultures, which had left their mark on its religious life. Hence a great diversity of deities jostle for position in the city's epigraphic record. The best documented cult, since AD 32 at least, was that of the divine triad Bel, Yarhibol and Aglibol (Pl. 20). Bel emerged as a supreme god, while Yarhibol, an ancestral deity of the oasis, and Aglibol, a deity of a north Syrian immigrant community, became his acolytes. However, Bel continued to associate with other divinities, such as the sun god Shamash and in particular his female partner Herta. We also hear of the ancient Canaanite/Phoenician deity Ba'alshamin, the Arab goddess Allat, the Mesopotamian deity Nergal and so on. And finally, as in most of the lands influenced by Greco-Aramaean culture, there were a number of fortune deities (*gad*), patrons of particular places (e.g. '*gad* of Dura', '*gad* of Palmyra', PAT 1094, 1097) and peoples (e.g. '*gad* of the oil merchants', PAT 2137–38).

Moving to east Arabia, the myth of Enki and Ninhursag tells us that 'Ninsikila shall become lord of Magan and Inzak shall become lord of Dilmun' (Enki 1.1.1.272–80). The latter, together with his consort Meskilak, feature in the greeting formulae of Kassite-period letters as 'the gods of Dilmun' (Ni. 615, 641), but we do not know if

Fig. 3 Clay figurine of the goddess Isis from Petra recognisable by her traditional double-feathered crown with sun disk (reconstruction by David Hopkins; the original is in the Archaeological Museum of Petra J.P.177).

Plate 20 Limestone relief representing another Palmyrene divine triad: Baʻalshamin (centre), Aglibol (right) and Malakbel (left), 1st century AD (P. & M. Chuzeville, Louvre AO19801).

they were the sole patrons of the polity or whether they had many companions. For the Greco-Roman period we have more evidence and it would seem that, as at Palmyra, foreign traders and visitors added their own gods to the local inventory. For example Bel, the Mesopotamian god Nabu, and the Greek deities Poseidon and Artemis are invoked by dedicants on the island of Ikaros (modern Failaka), and the west Arabian divinities Kahl and Manat appear on a funerary text from Mleiha in the modern Arab Emirates. There was also worship of the sun god Shamash in northeast Arabia, as is implied by the presence of the deity's name in south Arabian letters on Hellenistic-style coins issued in this region.

At another structural level there were the numerous tutelary deities who afforded protection to villages, encampments, families and individuals. In southern Arabia we hear of the anonymous guardian spirits (*mnḏḥ't*) of the local community and the ancestor spirits of the family, 'the sun (*shms*) of their ancestors'. In north Arabia there were the beings referred to as 'ginnaye', who are spoken of in an inscription from the environs of Palmyra: 'the ginnaye of the village of Beth Fasi'el, the good and rewarding gods' (PAT 1704). Probably related to these are the jinn, who feature in accounts of west and central Arabia. In the Quran they are frequently mentioned alongside mankind (*al-jinn wa-l-ins*), for they too were created beings, and so, though considered divine by mortals, were comparatively lowly: 'It is God who splits the seed and the fruit-stone. He brings forth the living from the dead and the dead from the living. . . . He kindles the light of dawn. . . . Yet they regard the jinn as God's partners, though He Himself created them' (6.95–100). Similarly 'they assert kinship between Him and the jinn, but the jinn well know that they will all be brought [to account] before Him' (37.158). People 'worshipped the jinn and it was in the jinn that most of them believed' (34.41), and what they most hoped to obtain thereby was security: 'individuals of humankind used to invoke the protection of individuals of the jinn' (72.6). A specific type of jinn was the companion jinn (called a *qarîn*), who is born when its human partners are born, dies when they die, remains with them at all times and exerts great influence, for better or for worse, on their behaviour, condition and accomplishments. In particular those who displayed an ability to manipulate the physical world or perform acts deemed beyond ordinary human capacity were thought to have been inspired or otherwise assisted by their *qarîn*.

Finally alongside benign spirits and benevolent gods there existed a suborder of malevolent beings ranging from the mischievous to the downright evil. They are, however, absent from the epigraphic record and alluded to only briefly, if frequently, in pre-Islamic Arabic poetry, but Muslim authors collected a mass of legends and tales about this shadowy world. Most commonly mentioned are ghouls which 'manifest themselves in different states to people in desolate places', particularly at night, and try to lead them off their course (Mas'udi 3.314). Their natural appearance is very ugly: 'two eyes in a hideous head like that of a tom-cat, with a cleft tongue; two legs with cloven hooves and the scalp of a dog' (Isfahani 21.129). Because its feet are like those of an ass, 'when one presents itself to the Arabs in the wastelands they utter the following couplet: "Oh ass-footed one, just bray away, we won't leave the desert plain nor ever go astray." . . . and it will then flee from them into valley bottoms and mountaintops' (Mas'udi 3.315–16).

145

MONOTHEISM

In the northwest of the Arabian peninsula there was a very ancient Jewish community. A certain Shubayt, who installed a family tomb in Hegra in AD 42, expressly designates himself as 'a Jew' (H 4). The name of Menasse son of Nathan appears inscribed on a sundial in the same town, and at nearby Dedan one Yahya bar Shim'un erected a tombstone for his father in AD 307 (JS Nab386). A few Jewish graffiti of this region comprise typically Jewish names such as Isaac and Samuel (JS Heb1–8),[2] and this epigraphic evidence can be supplemented with references from the Talmud. In south Arabia Judaism was to enjoy much greater prominence. When the missionary Theophilus the Indian accompanied the ambassadors of the Byzantine emperor Constantius (337–61) to the ruler of the Himyarites, he encountered 'no small number of Jews' (Philostorgius 3.4), who may have already been there for some time. Slightly later we hear of the conversion of the Himyarite king Abikarib As'ad (c.383–433) by two learned Jews from Yathrib, whom he brought with him to his country 'to summon its people to enter into the same religion as he had done':

> When he invited them to accept his religion on the ground that it was better than theirs, they proposed that the matter should be subject to the ordeal by fire. The Yemenis say that a fire used to settle matters in dispute among them by consuming the guilty and letting the innocent go unscathed. So his people went forth with their idols and sacred objects, and the two rabbis went forth with their sacred books hanging like necklaces from their necks until they halted at the place whence the fire used to blaze out. On this occasion when it erupted the Yemenis withdrew in terror, but their followers encouraged them and urged them to stand fast, so they held their ground until the fire covered them and consumed their idols and sacred objects and the men who bore them. But the two rabbis came out with their sacred books, sweating profusely but otherwise unharmed. Thereupon the Himyarites accepted the king's religion. Such was the origin of Judaism in the Yemen.
>
> (Ibn Hisham 17)

Though events may not have happened quite as described here, the speed and finality of the change in the religious phraseology in south Arabian inscriptions in the fourth century AD certainly suggests a revolution in the religious outlook of the ruling elite. References to the pagan deities of the ancient tradition disappeared almost completely in favour of mention of the one unique God, referred to as 'the Merciful' or simply as 'God' and usually qualified as 'Lord of heaven', 'Lord of heaven and earth'. And it is from this same period that we begin to find inscriptions containing Jewish expressions such as the concluding 'peace' (*slwm*).

In the Byzantine tradition, however, it was the missionary sent by Constantius who converted the Himyarite sovereign:

> Theophilus endeavoured to persuade the ruler of the tribe to become a Christian and to give up the deceits of heathenism. Hereupon the customary fraud and malice of the Jews was compelled to shrink into deep silence as soon as Theophilus had once or twice proved by his wonderful miracles the truth of the Christian faith. The embassy turned out successfully, for the prince of the nation, by sincere conviction, came over to the true religion, and built three churches in the district [one at Zafar, 'the metropolis of the nation', one at Aden, 'the Roman mart', and one 'where the Persian mart stands, hard by the mouth of the Persian sea'].
>
> (Philostorgius 3.4)

Whether this account be true or not,[3] it is certainly the case that in the fourth to sixth centuries Christianity made major inroads into Arabia. The church in the Sasanian realm was very dynamic and established offshoots in all the islands and coastlands of east Arabia in this period (see chapter 1 above). From the mid-fifth century Byzantium energetically promoted Christianity in south Arabia, chiefly via its ally Ethiopia, which sparked off violent clashes with the advocates of Judaism (see chapter 2 above). But it was particularly the inhabitants of north Arabia who were won over to Christianity in large numbers in this period. Most often they are portrayed as accepting the new faith as a result of the power of the Christian God, as demonstrated by the thaumaturgic deeds of various holy men:

> Some of the Saracens were converted to Christianity not long before the reign of Valens (364–78). Their conversion appears to have been the result of their intercourse with the priests and monks who dwelt among them and practised asceticism in the neighbouring deserts, and who were distinguished by the excellence of their life and by their miraculous works. It

147

is said that a whole tribe, and Zocomus their chief, were converted to Christianity and baptised about this period under the following circumstances. Zocomus was childless and went to a monk of great celebrity to complain to him of this calamity; for among Saracens, and I believe other barbarian nations, it was accounted of great importance to have children. The monk desired Zocomus to be of good cheer, engaged in prayer on his behalf, and sent him away with the promise that if he would believe in Christ he would have a son. When this promise was confirmed by God and when a son was born to him, Zocomus was initiated and all his subjects with him. From that period this tribe was peculiarly fortunate and became strong in point of number, and formidable to the Persians as well as to the other Saracens.

(Sozomen 6.38)

By their transition from paganism to 'true belief' the Saracens were considered to have entered the civilised fold: 'Those who were formerly called the wolves of Arabia became members of the spiritual flock of Christ' (Cyril of Scythopolis 24):

How many Arabs who have never known what bread is, but feed on the flesh of animals, came and saw the blessed Simeon and became disciples and Christians, abandoned the images of their fathers and served God. . . . It was impossible to count the Arabs, their kings and nobles, who came and received baptism, accepted the belief in God and acknowledged Jesus, and at the word of Simeon erected shrines in their tents.

(Simeon Stylites 108)

There were many peoples between the Tigris and Euphrates in the land of Mesopotamia who lived in tents and were barbarous and warlike. Numerous were their superstitions and they were the most ignorant of all the peoples of the earth until the moment when the light of Christ came to them. . . . The holy Ahudemmeh set himself with great patience to visit all the camps (*mashrîtê*) of the Arabs, instructing and teaching them in many sermons. . . . He had priests come from many regions . . . in order to establish in every tribe a priest and a deacon. He founded churches and named them after tribal chiefs so that they would support them. . . . Thus he inclined the hearts of the Arabs to the love of God and particularly to giving to the needy. . . . Their alms extended to all men and all places, but especially to the holy monasteries. . . . Nor do they confine their piety to making gifts to churches, monks, poor, and strangers, but they love fasting and ascetic life more than any other Christians, to such an extent that they begin the forty-days fast a week earlier than others. Many of them eat no bread during the whole time of the fast, not only the men but also many women.

(Ahudemmeh 21, 26–28)

This enthusiasm is forcefully illustrated by the deeds of a certain Mawia:

About this period [c.AD 370] the king of the Saracens died, and the peace which had previously existed between that nation and the Romans was dissolved. Mawia, the widow of the late monarch, after attaining to the government of her race, led her troops into Phoenicia and Palestine as far as the regions of Egypt lying to the left of those sailing up the Nile and which are generally denominated Arabia. This war was by no means a contemptible one, although conducted by a woman. The Romans, it is said, considered it so arduous and so perilous that the general of the Phoenician troops applied for assistance to the general of the entire cavalry and infantry of the east. This latter ridiculed the summons and undertook to give battle alone. He accordingly attacked Mawia, who commanded her own troops in person, and he was rescued with difficulty by the general of the troops of Palestine and Phoenicia. . . . As the war was still pursued with vigour, the Romans found it necessary to send an embassy to Mawia to solicit peace. It is said that she refused to comply with the request of the embassy unless consent were given for the ordination of a certain man named Moses, who practised asceticism in a neighbouring desert, as bishop over her subjects. This Moses was a man of virtuous life and noted for performing divine and miraculous signs. . . . He reconciled them to the Romans and converted many to Christianity, and passed his life among them as a priest.

(Sozomen 6.38)

This Moses adhered to a provincial (Monophysite) form of Christianity that differed subtly from the imperial (Chalcedonian) version and provided the medium for a degree of regional opposition to central authority, and so the issue here was not just about the appointment of a clergyman. The Christian Arab chiefs within the Byzantine empire mostly threw their weight behind the provincial creed, often becoming involved in church politics, and they are even portrayed as engaging in theological discussions:

> Harith ibn Jabala, king of the Christian Arabs, and his company were much offended by the synod and would not even break bread with the Chalcedonians. Ephraim, patriarch of Antioch [d. 545], was sent to them before his death by the emperor. He said to Harith: 'Why are you offended concerning us and the church?' Harith replied: 'We are not offended by the church of God, but by the evil which you have done to the faith. We distance ourselves from you because you introduce a quartet [saying Christ is both God and man] in place of the Trinity and oblige men to deny the true faith.' Ephraim added: 'Does it seem just to you then ... to scorn all those [six hundred and thirty bishops who accepted the creed of Chalcedon] and to embrace the small number who are heretics?' Harith responded: 'I am a barbarian and a soldier. I cannot read the scriptures, but let me give you an example. When I command my servants to prepare a feast for my troops, to fill the pots with fine lamb and beef and to cook it, and if there is then found in the pots a stunted rat, well patriarch, is not all the good meat tainted by this rat?' 'Yes,' was the reply. 'Then,' continued Harith, 'if a great mass of flesh is ruined by a little infected fat, how are all the assembly of those who adhered to that impure heresy [of Chalcedon] not soiled?'
>
> (Michael the Syrian 310–11)

MAGIC AND MEDICINE

Religious practices and beliefs, in this context referred to as magic, may often have as their goal the manipulation of natural or supernatural forces for practical ends. This will happen when the technical issue is beyond ordinary human competence and control, when the uncertain productive procedure involves serious risks to life and livelihood. One consults diviners and oracles, employs spells and potions and so on, when the usual man-made procedures and arrangements fail or are inadequate. Such recourse is not therefore instead of some natural process or in place of some matter-of-fact explanation, but rather is made in response to questions for which no people, we moderns included, have any good answer. We might not ourselves choose to employ sorceresses (*rqt*) to curtail a severe drought, but it is not because we could propose to the citizens of Marib who did so (Ja 735) any alternative method. And relieving the grief felt at the death of loved ones by drinking dust from their grave dissolved in water (Isfahani 1.332) might seem an unlikely cure to us, but again it is not that we have any better remedy to hand. Of course in different lands and different societies magic assumes different roles. It may rather, for example, be directed towards the regulation of human relationships and reduction of social tensions (thus Evans-Pritchard's Azande) or towards assigning value to communal activities and rituals (Radcliffe-Browne's Andamans). But in perilous or fragile environments, such as that of Arabia, propitiating and co-opting the powers of heaven and earth is likely to be a prime concern.

References to magic in inscriptions are rare, brief and uninformative about its nature and methods. For example one Safaitic text (WH 752) tells us that a certain Sharab ibn Ahbab had a period of derangement due to a magic spell (*'wdht rqwt*), but of its form, effects and manner of application we learn nothing. All that we do have is what we can glean from isolated incidents in later Muslim narratives, such as that recounted on the authority of the Prophet Muhammad's wife Aisha:

A man called Labid ibn al-A'sam from the tribe of Zurayq worked magic on (*sahara*) the Prophet Muhammad so that he began imagining that he had done things that he hadn't really done. Then one day or night, when he had been praying to God repeatedly, he said to me: 'Aisha, do you know that God has now given me a reply to what I was asking him about? Two men came to me and one of them sat near my head and the other near my feet. The one said to his companion: "What's wrong with this man?" The other answered: "He has been bewitched." "Who bewitched (*tabba*) him?" "Labid ibn al-A'sam." "With what?" "With a comb and the [Prophet's] hairs stuck to it placed in a skin of pollen of a male date palm." "Where is that?" "In the well of Dharwan."' So Muhammad and some of his friends went there and came back saying:

'Aisha, the colour of its water is like an infusion of henna leaves and the tops of the date-palm trees near it are like the heads of devils.'

(Bukhari 4.67, *ṭibb* 47)

Here we have an illustration of the so-called 'law of sympathy' identified by James Frazer (of *Golden Bough* fame): items that have been in contact with the victim, such as hair or nail clippings, may be magically manipulated to produce harm in the victim. The same principle also turns up in a positive context. It was, for instance, common to include some cuttings of one's hair in an offering to a god, the intention being to produce a magical identification between the offerer and the offering. Thus the faithful of Uqaysir in the Syrian steppe would shave their heads at his shrine, presenting to him their locks blended with fistfuls of flour (Ibn al-Kalbi 42d).

In the above account about the Prophet the word for bewitching also has the sense of 'to treat medically', and indeed magic and medicine are intimately connected in Muslim sources on pre-Islamic Arabia. Physical maladies are routinely ascribed to the workings of the jinn and other spirits, and the job of medicine/white magic was therefore to counter and neutralise these malevolent forces. Ubiquitous was the use of amulets, often inscribed with the names of deities, and spells, both intended to ward off misfortune, in particular the gaze of the evil eye, that invidious power that could blight the life of the person that it alighted upon. Thus a warrior might make sure that his steed was 'shielded by spells (*ruqâ*) so that she takes no hurt and amulets (*tamâ'im*) are tied on to her neck-gear' (*Muf.* 6). Both methods passed into Islam, though the pagan formulae were replaced with Muslim ones:

Aisha reported that when any person fell sick or had any sore or wound, the Prophet Muhammad would place his forefinger on the ground, then raise it saying: 'In the name of God, may the dust of our land (*turbatu arḍinâ*) with the saliva of one of our band (*bi-rîqati ba'ḍinâ*) render this patient sound (*la-yushfâ bihi saqîmunâ*), by our Lord's command (*bi-idhni rabbinâ*)', and rubbed this on the place of the ailment.

(Muslim 2.182, *salâm* 21)

Saliva was evidently deemed to have supernatural properties, as is indicated by the common use of the word 'to blow spittle' (*nafatha*) in magical contexts. For example it is connected with healing of the sick ('I did not blow spittle on him to revive him', *Muf.* 13) and averting evil ('the blowing of spittle by a sorcerer for fear of the evil eye', *Ikh.* 2; when the devil awakes you by a nightmare, 'blow spittle three times on the left side and seek refuge with God from its evil', Bukhari 4.63). And there is also the mysterious allusion in the Quran (113.4) to women who blow spittle on knots (*al-naffâthât fî l-'uqad*). Other medical treatments might seem more straightforward: cupping, cauterising, eating therapeutic substances (honey, camel's milk and urine, black cumin, costus, barley broth) and so on. Usually, however, magic would still be required to induce and ensure the efficacy of the desired natural process. For cupping to work properly it should be done on the nineteenth or twenty-first of the month (Ibn Maja 2.183, *tibb* 21). Shaving the head would dispel lice, but to keep it free of them one should fast for three days or give alms or slaughter a sheep (Bukhari 4.54). Acupressure might relieve pain, but only if coupled with an incantation (Muslim 2.183).

DIVINATION

This art aims to provide insight into the unknown, whether past, present or future. It is geared not so much towards the question of 'what will happen?' as towards that of 'what should be done?' It therefore assists in political and personal decision making, and it does this by removing the decision from contesting parties and giving it an objective legitimacy, both through its spiritual source and its convincing ritual drama. The underlying assumption is that the deities have developed forms of communication by which they instruct and advise mankind on how to act in the nether world, and it is up to us to unravel these signs and signals. The simplest way may be to consult deities directly, at their oracle, though the response – imparted by secret voices (*hawâtif*), by visions and dreams, or by a human medium – may still need interpretation. Otherwise one may resort to observation of the behaviour of birds, animals and heavenly bodies in the belief that their movements are governed by higher forces and so convey a message (omen). Or else one may turn to stratagems of chance, casting lots and the like, in the hope of receiving inspiration in one's choice. Finally one may rely upon the services of a spiritual diviner, who is able to see the unknown and know the unseen.

In southern Arabia an oracle was, logically enough, a 'place/ instrument of asking' (*ms'l*). The deity would often reply directly to interrogators by 'making them see' (*hr'yhw*) a vision (CIS 4.357, RES

4052) or a dream (RES 3929, Ja 567), even speaking personally to them (ZI 22). Otherwise deities might convey their message indirectly via a medium. At the sanctuary of Jar al-Labba, west of Bayda, two stones were found bearing inscriptions (CIS 4.460–66), unfortunately fragmentary, that detail the procedure for soliciting 'a divine response'. The method seems to have been to bring, and perhaps immediately sacrifice, an oblation, then to 'ask at the oracle over the sacrificial altar'. Next one must wait until the attendant 'delivered the oracular reply by the inspiration of 'Athtar', and finally offer a thanksgiving sacrifice upon receipt of 'a favourable response'. The ritual for this included such acts as a proclamation of 'a blood-offering poured out', 'turning towards the boundary marked by this pillar once and towards its corresponding one three times' and 'bowing down while turning about thrice'. The oracle was apparently not to be consulted at random: certain days of certain months are carefully specified on which the ceremonies took place. The mention in two places of a repetition of the sacrifices and of 'unpropitious omens or the evil eye' suggests that in some cases no pronouncement was forthcoming. The only recourse was then to repeat the sacrifices until an answer was given. A similar description is recorded in a Minaean inscription where sacrifices are offered in order to elicit from 'Athtar a decision regarding the day on which a feast is to be celebrated. Were no result to be achieved by this means, it was ordained that the sacrifices should be 'increased and made richer' until the god made his view known (M 293).

More familiar to us than oracles are omens, of which we have inherited a large stock (black cats, red skies, magpies, broken mirrors, etc.), even if we do not pay that much attention to them any more. They are natural phenomena or occurrences that are taken to be indicative of the likely future course of events, 'signs for the discerning' (Quran, *passim*). In his great work *On divination* Cicero opines that 'the Arabs, the Phrygians and the Cilicians are chiefly given over to the keeping of flocks; winter and summer they wander across plains and mountains, and so have ample opportunity to observe the voice and flight of birds' (1.42). Indeed 'the Arab people heed above all the signs of birds' (1.41). This is borne out by the first-century AD Jewish historian Josephus, who relates that the Nabataean king Haritat IV (8 BC–AD 40), on learning that the emperor Tiberius had dispatched an army to punish him for a raid against the Jewish king Herod, 'consulted the flight of birds' (*oiōnoskopia*). From this he learnt that 'his [Tiberius'] army could by no means enter Petra; one of the leaders would die, either the one who had given orders to make war or the one who had set forth to carry out his decision' (18.125). Sure enough Tiberius died shortly thereafter and the general whom he had empowered to march on Haritat was obliged to withdraw. Another example of this practice is given in the Quran, which describes the reaction of the tribe of Thamud to the prophet Salih sent to warn them against their corrupt ways. They informed him that 'from consultation of the flight of birds we augur evil from you (*iṭṭayyarnâ bika*)', and they plotted against him (27.47; cf. 36.18). Though in both cases the terms can refer to augury in general, the etymology of the words makes clear that the original meaning applied to birds in particular. Moreover the Quranic expression is always given the same general explanation by Muslim commentators and lexicographers: 'The Arabs, when they desired to set about an affair, passed by the places where birds lay upon the ground, and roused them in order to learn thence whether they should proceed or refrain'. The chief criterion was direction: whether they flew to the right (good omen) or to the left (bad omen), though there were further refinements. Not only the flight of birds was auspicious, but also the nature of their cries and the place of their alighting. And not only birds were portentous, but also animals and their behaviour, stars and planets and their movements.

Another widespread divinatory practice was that of deciding upon a course of action by resorting to techniques based on chance or lot. Again this has largely been relegated to the margins of our culture, though lingers on in such expressions as 'drawing the short straw'. There were three particularly popular methods in pre-Islamic Arabia. Of two of them, making marks in the sand and on rocks or throwing pebbles, we know very little,[4] but can surmise that the decision would be based on whether an odd (bad) or even (good) number emerged or on what patterns were formed. We have much more information about the third technique, namely randomly selecting from a group of arrows marked with instructions. The simplest form is illustrated by an anecdote about the famous poet Imru' al-Qays (d. *c*.AD 550), who sought advice on what to do about the murder of his father by the tribe of Asad:

> When Imru' al-Qays ibn Hujr was on his way to raid the tribe of Asad, he passed by Dhu l-Khalasa. This was an idol at Tabala [in west Arabia], which all the Arabs venerated. Before it were three arrows: one indicating 'do it', one indicating 'don't do it', and one indicating 'wait'. In its presence Imru' al-Qays three times made a random choice (*istaqsama*), and each time the 'don't do it' arrow came out. Thereupon he broke the arrows and threw them at the face of the idol,

saying: 'Confound you! If it had been your father who was killed, you wouldn't have been so obstructive.' Then he went off and successfully raided the tribe of Asad.

(Ibn al-Kalbi 41d; cf. Isfahani 9.92–93)

A more elaborate form is attested at the sanctuary at Mecca, presided over by the idol Hubal:

In front of Hubal there were seven arrows, each of them bearing some words. One was marked 'blood-price'. When they disputed about who should pay the blood-price they cast lots with the seven arrows and he on whom the lot fell had to pay the money. Another was marked 'yes' and another 'no' and they acted accordingly on the matter on which the oracle had been invoked. One was marked 'water'. If they wanted to dig for water, they cast lots containing this arrow and wherever it came forth they set to work. Another was marked 'of you', another 'affiliated', another 'not of you'. If they wanted to circumcise a boy, or make a marriage, or bury a body, or doubted someone's genealogy, they took him to Hubal with a hundred silver coins and a slaughter camel and gave them to the person who cast the lots. Then they brought forward the one with whom they were concerned, saying: 'O our god, this is A the son of B with whom we intend to do so and so; show the right course concerning him.' Then they would say to the man who cast the arrows, 'cast!' If there came out 'of you' then he was a true member of their tribe; if there came out 'affiliated' he was an ally; and if there came out 'not of you' he had no blood relation to them and was not an ally. Thus they used to conduct their affairs according to the decision of the arrows.

(Ibn Hisham 97–98)

The practice, though probably varying much in form and significance in different regions, seems to have existed throughout Arabia. We find it performed in Palmyra in the north, where we have mention of 'a basin of silver for [casting] lots (*lḥlq*)' on an honorific inscription from the temple of Allat. And it is also attested in Yemen in the south, where the expression 'to draw arrows by lot' (*tqrʿ slṭm*) crops up (NAG 12), as does the term 'a place of casting lots' (CIS 4.548: *mqsm*).

The ability to divine was not granted to all. It required 'a fine spiritual aptitude born of purity of natural constitution, strength of soul and sensitivity of feeling' and receptivity to the spirits 'who would inform them of what was hidden' (Mas'udi 3.349). There arose therefore specialists in divination, who were likely to be self-made, that is, their authority derived not from a hereditary office, but from their success in giving accurate information. This meant that they were as often women as men. Many of them were itinerant, offering their services at pilgrim fairs, perennial markets and tribal gatherings; a few were attached to such courts as existed; others had fixed abodes to which their customers would come, often from far away. They could tell when was the best time to marry, travel or engage in military action, where animals had strayed or who had killed them, who had stolen one's property, what the descent of an unknown person might be, what sort of future one's children might have, what would be the outcome of a military encounter, how one was going to die and so on. In times of great disaster or upheaval these diviners might serve as leaders, for their intercourse with the divine gave them the authority to transcend the petty rivalries between chiefs that could block collective action. In this case such persons would very often be women, since they were removed from the usual run of tribal politics not only by their supernatural sanction but also by virtue of their sex. Thus a certain Tarifa predicted the collapse of the Marib dam and led her people north, dispensing advice along the way (Nuwayri 15.334–37). Another visionary known as Zarqa' bint Zuhayr united sundry dispersed clans of Quda'a under the name of Tanukh and recommended them to depart from Bahrain and establish themselves in lower Iraq (Isfahani 13.82). And the seeress Sajah brought diverse groups of Tamim together in an attempt to counter the growing strength of Muhammad's Medinan polity in the 620s (Tabari 1.1908–21).

SACRED PLACES, SACRED OFFICES, SACRED TIMES

The idea that certain spaces – whether because of their great height, outstanding beauty, lush vegetation or the like – are occupied by divinities is very ancient, and such spaces were legion in Arabia. The terms for them had usually to do with protection and prohibition (*hima, haram, mahram*), for within them all living things were considered inviolable and all use of violence was forbidden. In much of Arabia sanctuaries would be open-air, the natural features of the spot being sufficient to distinguish it. This might be a spring with its margin of rich vegetation, a patch of forest haunted by lions, a shady cleft in the mountainside or a solitary eminence rising from the desert. The borders of the holy ground would usually be drawn somewhat widely, skirting the sacred centre on all sides, the whole roughly marked off by pillars or cairns. In cities and where money was available, the sacred place might be bounded by walls and filled with ornate structures, then constituting what we would call a temple. The suspension within them of the usual state of human competition served two major functions. In the first place it was a way of eliminating potential conflict over scarce resources, and so places of dense vegetation and abundant water might well be made into sanctuaries:

> Directly after the innermost recess [of northwest Arabia] is a region along the sea which is especially honoured by the natives because of the advantage which accrues from it to them. It is called the Palm Grove and contains a magnitude of trees of this kind which are exceedingly fruitful and contribute in an unusual degree to enjoyment and luxury. But all the country round about is lacking in springs of water and is fiery hot because it slopes to the south. Accordingly it was a natural thing that the barbarians made sacred the place, which was full of trees and, lying as it did in the midst of a region utterly desolate, supplied their food. And indeed not a few springs and streams gush forth there, which do not yield to snow in coldness; and these make the land on both sides of them green and altogether pleasing. Moreover an altar is built there of hard stone and very old in years, bearing an inscription in ancient letters of unknown tongue.
>
> (Diodorus 3.42)

In the second place it provided a venue for the accomplishment of activities by individuals and groups free from any interference:

> Thus has ordered and ordained [the god] Nakrah in an oracle . . . that the borders of the sanctuary ('wthn mhrm) be established. . . . As also he has ordered in an oracle . . . that if anyone molests the one who is having a miscarriage or the one who is giving birth or the one who is fatally ill, let that person be barred from this place of refuge.
>
> (Darb al-Sabi 1)

The sick and needy could petition the resident deity for relief and succour, the guilty make confessions and expiation, the perplexed

158

request advice and a resolution of their problem, the harassed seek refuge and asylum. Pacts and agreements were concluded, with the deity called upon to act as witness and guarantor; sundry rituals were practised and numerous ceremonies were staged.

Sacred areas need not be staffed, but at many there would at least be a guardian or some performer of cultic functions (Pl. 21), as was the case in the aforementioned Palm Grove:

> The oversight of the sacred precinct is in the care of a man and a woman who hold the sacred office for life. The inhabitants of the place are long-lived and have their beds in the trees because of their fear of the wild beasts.
>
> (Diodorus 3.42)

And it was also the case at a mountain in the desert of Sinai:

> On this mountain there is a place where the Saracens have set up an idol for themselves, which is of snow-white marble. Their priest (sacerdos) also lives there, and he wears a dalmatic and linen cloak.
>
> (Antoninus Placentinus 148)

And the same situation obtained at numerous other sites, though inscriptions only ever record the existence of such functionaries, not their job description. The word for the office varies, probably reflecting the cultural–linguistic preference rather than the duties involved. In the Hijaz *afkal* was the usual term (e.g. *afkal* of Allah at Rawwafa, BIA 10.58; *afkal* of Wadd, of Kutba, and of Allat at Dedan, JS Lih49, 55, 277; *afkal* linked with Dushara, Hubal and Manat at Hegra, H 16).[5] In the Sinai–Negev–Hisma region it was *kâhin* (e.g. *kâhin* of Allat at Ramm, RB 41.591; *kâhin* of al'Uzza in Sinai, CIS 2.611, 1236). And in areas of Aramaic influence it was *kumrâ* (e.g. *kumrâ* of Allat at Hebran in the Hawran, CIS 2.170; *passim* at Palmyra and Hatra). The principal task of such officials was presumably to maintain the sacred area and attend to visitors, receiving their offerings, aiding them in their rituals, collecting their fines and dues (from which they would themselves be paid) and providing divinatory services. At major sanctuaries, and especially in city temples, there might be more specialised religious staff. The Sabaean goddess Dhat Ba'dan forbade invocation of her 'when there was not present in the sanctuary any priestess or seeress', the term for the latter, literally 'dreamer' (*ḥlmt*),

Plate 21 Limestone stele from Tayma bearing a 23-line Aramaic inscription on its front and the scene illustrated here on one side. The upper register shows a person in profile with long robe, conical hat and staff standing beneath a winged solar disc, probably representing the god Salm. The lower register portrays an altar with bull's head and before it, according to the inscription, the priest Salm-shezib who is performing the installation of a manifestation of Salm (Salm of Hagam) in Tayma (P. & M. Chuzeville, Louvre AO1505).

suggesting some type of medium (Nami 74). And a similar office is attested at Hatra by an inscription which regulates against theft from a temple and concludes that 'the dreamer (*ḥlm'*) has shown that [the offender] should be stoned' (IIH 281). At Raybun in Hadramawt priestesses apparently also undertook social work, such as adjudicating in cases of marital disputes (SOYCE 706). Nowhere do we discern a priestly caste, but offices might be hereditary and were sometimes the preserve of a particular tribal group. For example the lineage of Qasiy seem particularly connected with the cult of the goddess Allat at Salhad in the Hawran. In AD 56 Rawah son of Malik son of Aklab son of Rawah son of Qasiy rebuilt her temple which, he says, had been founded by his ancestor Rawah son of Qasiy. And in AD 95 it underwent further restoration at the hands of another family member (CIS 2.182, NIN 1).

To a number of these holy places pilgrimages would be made at certain fixed times of the year. The Sabaeans were, for example, cemented by an annual procession to the temple of Almaqah in Marib at the time of the summer rains. Not only did the people of Saba attend, but also all their allies were at least expected to send delegations, as the tribe of Sam'ay were reminded in an edict of their patron god Ta'lab (RES 4176). The Tal'ab was also an object of pilgrimage at his mountain abode in the land of Hamdan (Gl 1361; Hamdani 8.82–83). And people went in honour of Dhu Samawi at Yathill (CIS 4.547) and of Sayin at Shabwa (Ir app. B3). For as long as these ceremonies lasted pilgrims were obliged to set aside their weapons (CIS 4.548) and to abstain from sexual relations (CIS 4.533), and they would don special garments or adornments to advertise that they were temporarily exempt from the usual rules of tribal behaviour. In central and northern Arabia such events might form part of a much larger phenomenon, pilgrim fairs, which took place in months specially designated as holy and violence-free:

> Most of the Saracens, both those in the Palm Grove and those beyond it and the so-called Taurenian mountains, consider as sacred a spot dedicated to one of the gods, gathering there twice each year. The first of these assemblies extends over a whole month and takes place about the middle of the spring, when the sun passes through the sign of Aries, while the other assembly lasts two months; this they celebrate after the summer solstice. In these assemblies they observe a complete peace, not only towards each other, but also towards all men living in their country. They claim that wild animals are at

peace with man, and not only this, but that they are at peace with each other.

(Nonnosus cited in Photius 3)[6]

This suspension of hostilities allowed a whole range of activities to flourish and a carnival-like atmosphere prevailed:

Then they [the Arabs] would journey to ʻUkaz and Dhu l-Majaz in the holy months and would hold their markets in them. They would stage poetry competitions and debating contests and settle their differences. Whoever had a prisoner would work to ransom him, and whoever had a lawsuit would submit it to the member of Tamim who was in charge of legal affairs. Then they would stop at ʻArafa and perform the required rites, and after that they would head for their home-lands.

(Tawhidi 1.85)

In some places only exchange was permitted, not trade:

We went on foot through the desert for five or six days. Camels carried our water of which each of us received a pint in the morning and a pint at night. When the water in the skins turned bitter, we put sand in to sweeten it. Moreover families of Saracens, or rather their women, came from the desert and sat by the wayside, half-clothed, crying and begging for food from travellers. Their husbands appeared and brought skins of cold water from the inner desert and offered some to us and received bread in return. They also brought bunches of roots, the sweet smell of which was beyond all perfumes. Nothing was sold, for they considered that anathema while they were celebrating their holy days.
. . . And because the Saracen holidays were now drawing to a close, the announcement was made [since the moratorium on violence was now also at an end] not to remain in or to return through the desert.

(Antoninus Placentinus 147, 149).

OFFERINGS TO THE GODS

The most prevalent means of establishing a link with, and thereby influencing, the divine was by setting apart something from one's own disposal and dedicating it to a deity (Pl. 22). Practically anything could be presented to a deity, but the greater the effect desired the more precious it should be. The most common offerings were animals, crops, food, liquids (milk and wine as libations), inscribed metal plaques or stone tablets, aromatics (usually burned to produce fragrant odours), edifices (walls, roofs, temples, wells, pillars, etc.) and manufactured objects (altars, incense burners, libation tables, metal tablets, statues, figurines, etc.). Camel-herding Arabs would devote certain of their beasts to deities, excluding them from being worked by man and allowing them to die a natural death. The Quran (5.103) gives a number of examples, such as the female camel that is the last in a series of females borne by one mother (*baḥîra*) and a she-camel that has lived to see her offspring bear offspring (*sâ'iba*). Their ears would be slit to indicate that they were in a state of taboo and they would be left to pasture without a herdsman. In ancient times south Arabians would make over themselves and their immediate family to deities; since many such dedicants were of high status, this probably did not mean any sort of sacred slavery, but rather full allegiance to the cult community. A subject of the king of Hadramawt, for example, offered to Sayin and the gods of Shabwa 'his soul, his faculties, his children, his goods, the light of his eyes and the thoughts of his heart, trusting in divine protection' (RES 2693). At a later date worshippers would dedicate statuettes of themselves rather than themselves directly, though the aim probably remained much the same, to receive the protection of a divinity. Human sacrifice was occasionally practised in Arabia, the victims generally being prisoners-of-war, who represented the victory-giving deity's share in the booty (Mi'sal 7, 9; Jidhma 2–3),[7] though other forms may have existed.[8]

At temples and holy places offerings would be made on a regular basis, especially in more developed cultures where service was organised more along the lines of that at a royal court. It was noted of the Nabataeans, for example, that 'they worship the sun, building an altar on the top of the house, and pouring libations on it daily and burning frankincense' (Strabo 16.4.26). And in south Arabia it is common to read on an altar the like of the following: 'On this the king will slaughter a bull on the ninth day of the month of Dhu Thawr' (RES 3104). The agricultural/pastoral calendar would also provide its own set of dates for offerings; in particular there was the very widespread

Plate 22 Alabaster stele made by 'Lahay'athat the Sabaean' on behalf of 'Abibahath wife of Tubba' son of Subh' for the goddess Shams. The standing male figure, presumably Tubba', is equipped with bow, spear and dagger, and is presenting together with his wife, the seated woman, the 'spoils' (the oryx and vase) that they had promised to the goddess. There is an incense-altar between the two and a crescent moon and disc above them; *c.*1st century AD, 20.6 × 10.5 cm (National Museum of San'a).

practice of making first-fruit/first-born offerings (*fr'*), presenting to the relevant deity a proportion of the crops harvested/young animals born in gratitude for that deity's bounty. And there were various occasions in the life of the individual that usually entailed offerings, such as birth, puberty, marriage and death, for these were times of transition, and transition was always regarded as a phenomenon rife with potential danger that was best minimised by involving the gods on one's side. The commemoration of some great event, historical or otherwise, might also become a set part of the calendar and inevitably require its own offerings:

> In the above-mentioned Palm Grove a festival was celebrated every four years, to which the neighbouring peoples thronged from all sides, both to sacrifice to the gods of the sacred precinct large numbers of well-fed camels and also to carry back to their native lands some of the water of the place, since the tradition prevailed that this drink gave health to such as partook of it.
>
> (Diodorus 3.43)

> [There should be dedicated] a burnt offering every year on the good day for ever, the year 474 [AD 163], on the sixth day of April [namely the founding day of the temple of Bel in Palmyra, inaugurated 6 April AD 32].
>
> (RES 2157)

There would also be extraordinary occasions for offerings, which were provided by special or exceptional occurrences in the life of the community and the individual and have no fixed times. These might be joyous occasions, in which the workings of divine providence could be detected, though all too often it was crises that demanded such action, in the hope that the gods may be propitiated and the disasters with which mankind is periodically visited be kept away. Given the importance of rain everywhere in Arabia, droughts would necessitate sacrifices, and in south Arabia there was a special ceremony involving sacrifice carried out by certain specialised religious personnel (*rshw*; e.g. CIS 4.967, Gl 1766). If benefits were forthcoming or misfortunes were averted, then this would be a natural occasion for a thanksgiving offering. And after committing some offence or violating some taboo an expiatory offering would help to restore the normal good relationship between man and deity. This practice is attested in south Arabia, where the exact nature of the infraction, often to do with breaching purity laws, was described on the accompanying inscription.[9]

Among the peoples of Arabia, and particularly among the pastoral tribes, animal sacrifice was a very commonly practised form of offering. It was principally domestic beasts that were selected, especially camel, sheep and oxen; game is rarely mentioned, and poultry never. The rite of sacrifice was not tied to a particular location, though we mostly hear of it being performed in some sort of sacred place. Nor was the execution of the rite restricted to a priestly group, but could be carried out by the dedicants themselves (though probably not women) or, in the case of a communal sacrifice, by the head of the relevant social grouping (household, lineage, clan etc.). Of the actual mechanics of the rite we know very little. There must have been special words pronounced and actions performed to convey the drama of the event, as is indicated by the following account:

> They make a white unblemished camel kneel on the ground and all together walk around it three times in a broad circle. One of their leaders or holy priests of suitable age and rank leads both the procession and a hymn composed to honour the morning star. After the third revolution, while the people have not yet ceased to sing, but are still carrying the last words of the hymn on their lips, the leader draws his sword and vigorously strikes it on the camel's neck, and he is the first to take eagerly a taste of the blood. Then in the same manner all the others run up with their knives, some cutting off some small piece of the skin together with the hair, others grasping whichever part they come to and chopping off pieces of the flesh. They continue right to the entrails and innards, leaving behind nothing of the sacrifice unprocessed to be seen by the rising sun.[10] They do not even abstain from the bones and marrow, conquering with perseverance their toughness and gradually overcoming their obduracy.
>
> (Nilus 613)

The blood of the victim, according to pre-Islamic Arabic poetry and certain south Arabian inscriptions (e.g. CIS 4.464), is also 'poured out' on to the altar-stones, thus forming a bond between the human participants (who have 'tasted' it) and the deity. And Muslim sources confirm that most sacrifices did, as here, conclude with a communal meal. When, for example, two disputants went before a diviner or arbiter to resolve their quarrel, the winner would always have to slaughter a camel, whereupon he would share out its meat (*aṭʿamahu*) to anyone present and to the poor and needy (e.g. Ibn Habib, *Mun.* 108, 114).

7

ART, ARCHITECTURE AND ARTEFACTS

ARABIAN MATERIAL CULTURE?

One might expect that just as monographs on Islamic history open with an excursus on the pre-Islamic Arabian background, so studies on Islamic material culture would follow suit. This is not, however, the case, for such works tend to assume that pre-Islamic Arabia was an aesthetic *tabula rasa*, that it did not possess 'anything worthy of the name of architecture', but was 'an architectural vacuum'. It is emphasised that 'the Arabs of Arabia had very few indigenous traditions of any significance' and that 'any modification of this impression of poverty in the artistic development of pre-Islamic Arabia is hardly likely to be significant'. Indeed it is pointed out that Islamic art was held back while the Muslims ruled from Arabia, for it was 'an environment in which the visual arts . . . had no very significant role'.[1] It is certainly true that much of the country does not possess sufficient resources to permit sponsorship of monumental buildings or lavish artwork, but there is more than the traditional view allows for and this chapter will attempt to give at least some impression of this.

It is first necessary to stress once more that pre-Islamic Arabia, though remote, did interact with the rest of the Middle East, and indeed came to do so more and more as time progressed. Economic and political links inevitably brought in their wake new artistic products and styles. Since the different regions of Arabia had different trading partners and political allies, and were at varying distances from centres of state power, they were exposed to different foreign influences. They also had different local traditions and different raw materials available to them. Hence the art and architecture of Arabia exhibits much regional diversity. East Arabia was greatly affected by Mesopotamian and later by Iranian ideas, and Hellenism had an impact in the northeast. South Arabia initially cultivated its own local forms, but became progressively more influenced by Hellenistic and Roman art, and north Arabia was of course bound to feel the pull of the great empires of the Middle East that often sought to bring it into their orbit. Yet there was no aping of imperial art, but rather a blending of foreign styles with local tastes.

A major reason for Islamic art experts' indifference to pre-Islamic Arabia is that they feel it has no bearing on the development of their subject. This may well turn out to be true, but it is perhaps rash to be so categorical when Arabian art has, to date, received so little detailed examination. One recent characterisation of south Arabian aesthetics has underlined its tendency 'towards abstraction and geometrisation' (Fig. 4), a feature also of Islamic art. And it has been argued that 'the non-figurative representation of the gods among the Nabataeans and other pre-Islamic pagan Arabs of north and central Arabia determined a non-figurative course for the art of Islamic monotheism'.[2] All this would require further demonstration, but there is at least room for discussion. For the moment we must content ourselves with the general observation that 'the pre-Islamic Arab tribes' acquaintance with Sasanian and Roman–Byzantine traditions at an early stage made possible the relatively short process of emergence of Umayyad art that was nourished by these sources'.[3]

Fig. 4 Relief on the lintel of the portal of a temple at Haram with stylised representation of female figures, palm trees with bird, and rows of ibex, *c.*mid-1st millennium BC (David Hopkins).

SETTLEMENTS

In his *Geography*, completed *c*.AD 150, Ptolemy 'recorded noteworthy information concerning the peoples and their relations to one another, and we have noted the chief cities, rivers, gulfs and mountains' (1.19). His register of people and place-names is more extensive than Strabo and Pliny combined, and he supplies maps, so we get a very useful presentation of Arabia and its relation to the Roman empire. However, it is not a prose descriptive geography, but, as one might expect of a mathematician, a guide to creating an accurate set of maps. In all Ptolemy lists 218 settlements in Arabia (Petraea, Deserta and Felix), many of which were presumably quite small. As regards the peninsula, for which he gives by far the most information (6.7), most of the 151 settlements named are described as villages (*kômai*), some as towns (*poleis*), even fewer as market-centres (*emporia*) and only six as cities (*mêtropoleis*). These last are Marib (*Mara*), Najran (*Nagara*), Shabwa (*Sabbatha*), Mayfa'a (*Maepha*), Zafar (*Sapphar*) and possibly modern Qaryat al-Faw (*Maocosmos*).[4] All these cities are in south Arabia, which was probably the only region of Arabia that could be characterised as to some degree urbanised. South Arabians did not themselves have a specialised word for city, but applied the term *hagar*, the fortified assembly-place of a tribe, to all sizes of settlement. The places named by Ptolemy, and possibly a few others, merit the term city, however, in that they all possessed monumental architecture, a high level of literacy (evidenced by inscriptions) and political institutions (especially councils).

There is considerable variation in the makeup and layout of Arabian settlements, depending upon the form and extent of outside cultural influences, the type of materials and skills available, local traditions and history, the nature of the terrain and so on. Petra and Palmyra, for example, were for a long time under the cultural thrall of Rome, and came to acquire many of the trappings of a Roman city (e.g. colonnaded street, theatre, nymphaeum, baths), which were absent from settlements elsewhere in Arabia. Since the earliest cities of south Arabia were adjacent to the open desert and were often at odds with one another, fortifications were regarded as essential. And what began as a necessity soon became a source of pride and a sign of wealth and status, with cities competing with one another in the might and scope of their surrounding walls and bastions. But though they might attain great heights (14 metres in the case of Yathill), they were not very extensive, for the average south Arabian city was a compact affair. Of the four capitals the walls of Qarnaw were 1150 m in length, at Timna

169

1850 m, at Shabwa 1500 m (though with a further defensive line beyond this) and at Marib, by far the largest town in south Arabia, 4500 m. The settlements of west Arabia, by contrast, were of an expansive nature. Only a few were enclosed, like Tayma, where massive walls encompassed an area of eight square kilometres. Most were unbounded, like Medina, which covered an area of about fifty square kilometres, divided into small discrete clan districts consisting of both individual houses and residential compounds. In between were 'open spaces' (*fuṣaḥ al-Madina*) dotted with farming plots, palm groves, gardens, pastures, springs and wells, and comprising a great deal of wasteland (Ibn Hisham 733; Ibn Saʿd 1.2.182; cf. Hassan ibn Thabit 9.7).

The settled inhabitants of Arabia favoured stone or mud-brick dwellings. The type most frequently mentioned by pre-Islamic poets and Muslim writers is the residential compound (*qaṣr*). This was probably little different from the type still in use in the nineteenth century:

> The high-walled *qaṣr* of this ground was a four-square building in clay, sixty paces upon a side, with low corner towers. In the midst is the well of seven fathoms to the rock, steyned with dry masonry, a double camel-yard, and stalling for kine and asses; chambers of a slave-woman caretaker and her son, rude store-houses in the towers, and the well-driver's abode. . . . An only gateway into this close was barred at nightfall. Such redoubts, impregnable in the weak Arabian warfare, are made in all outlying properties. The farm beasts were driven in at the going down of the sun.[5]

Each compound might shelter a number of people: 'a desert *qaṣr* forms a square courtyard enclosed with a high wall, against which abut the dwellings of several families; thus the whole kin lives together'.[6] In the event of any hostilities they would quickly withdraw into their compounds, though they might be brought to surrender with the threat of destruction of their crops or date palms (Ibn Hisham 653, 673–74). The structure and layout of these compounds would vary from region to region. Often, as was the case until recently in certain parts of Arabia, a tower-house (*uṭum*)[7] would be incorporated in the perimeter wall, partly for defensive purposes, and partly for prestige. Mud brick was the basic building material, combined with stone if it were easily available, for else it would fall victim to the harsh elements.

Thus at Tayma the poet Imru' al-Qays (d. *c*.550) once watched a violent storm that 'left not one trunk of a date-palm standing, not a single tower-house, save those fortified with stone' (*Mu.*: Imru' al-Qays).

When the Nabataeans first arrived at Petra in the fourth century BC, 'it was their custom . . . not to construct any house' (Diodorus 19.94), but having shed their nomadic ways 'their homes, through the use of stone, are costly' (Strabo 16.4.26). Excavations lend credence to these reports, for the earliest dwellings do not antedate the third century BC and are built on virgin soil. They are simple affairs, with clay floors and walls of rough stone and clay, but later, as Strabo intimates, they are of carefully worked and evenly coursed masonry, covered with plaster that has evidently been painted or decorated with classical mouldings. Often too they would be hewn into the rock faces of the city in the same manner as tombs. The best evidence for domestic architecture in east Arabia comes from Saar in Bahrain. Here we get whole rows of stone houses, many built to the same basic plan, namely a rectangular building with a small covered room in one corner and an L-shaped outer area and often an open yard at the rear. The L-shaped area contained water basins, ovens and pits, the last used for storing household equipment (especially large jars) and liquid substances (then carefully plastered). The most dramatic residential buildings of Arabia are to be found in the south. Here a tradition of high-rise housing was initiated (Pl. 23). On top of a base of cut stones 2–4 metres in height were raised up multi-storey dwellings constructed from a framework of wooden beams filled in with mud brick. Thus Muhabiyyih Atkan 'built, founded, prepared and completed the stonework of their house from the bottom to the top, six ceilings with six floors' (IMT 1). Entry was by means of an outside staircase, which took one up to the ground floor elevated a couple of metres above the street. This gives these abodes the aspect, and presumably also the function, of refuges and fortresses; the Yemeni's home really was his castle.

Arabia's cities were few, but its encampments were innumerable. And so to many outsiders Arabia's inhabitants were by definition 'tent-dwellers', a people 'who have no gates, no bars, who live in a remote place' (Jeremiah 49.31). Yet though their residences were minimal and mobile, they still left marks of their occupation, as was recorded by many a melancholy minstrel:

Still to see are the traces at Dafin . . .
every valley and pasture once full of people.

The abode of a tribe whom past time has smitten,
their dwellings show now like patterns on sword sheaths,
Desolate all, save for ashes extinguished,
and leavings of rubbish and ridges of shelters,
Shreds of tethering ropes, and a trench round the camp,
and lines plotted out, changed by long years' lapse.

('Abid 11)

And from such verses we are able to obtain much information about
the material life of pre-Islamic Arab pastoralists and the structure of

Plate 23 Mud-brick house in old Marib (author).

their camps. We hear of 'the blackened stones laid in order where the pot was set' (*Mu.*: Zuhayr), 'the places where the huts built of boughs were set up' (*Muf.* 49), 'the pegs to which were tied the troop of horses' ('Amr ibn Qami'a 7), and so on. About the tents themselves we are very ill informed (but see Pl. 24). They are often mentioned in poetry, but never really described except to say that they are supported by poles (*mu'ammad*), stretched out by ropes (*mumaddad*), anchored by pegs (*muwattad*) and made either of leather or animal hair (cf. Pliny 6.144: 'tents made of goat-hair cloth'). However, we do have accounts of temporary shelters raised for men on expedition:

> Many a tent[8] in whose sides the fresh wind blows,
> in a spacious country, the door of which is never closed,
> Its awning made of worn-out embroidered garments
> while the inner covering is of striped Athami cloth,
> Having for ropes the halters of short-haired horses,
> straight like lance-shafts, returning from a first or second
> raid
> Such tents have I raised over men both young and hoary,
> whose lances cause blood to flow from the enemies' veins.
>
> (Tufayl 1)

Plate 24 Assyrian relief, *c*.650 BC, showing Assyrians burning round tents of an Arab camp (British Museum 124927).

FUNERARY BUILDINGS AND OBJECTS

The most ubiquitous architectural item in Arabia is the tomb. For most Arabians burial was a simple affair: 'In a grave, dug where the valley is bent, swathed in white I shall lie, white like an antelope's back' ('Abid 28). If persons were of some importance or belonged to a social group possessing means, then some sort of funerary monument might be created for them, whether an edifice built up or a space carved out. Of the former type the most common example was a heap of stones (cairn), often arranged in circular fashion, over the grave. Such structures have been the Arabian nomad's preferred memorial for thousands of years, its form therefore associated with death: 'My camel started when she spied the cairn on the stony waste, built over one who was open of hand, most quick to give' (*Ham.* 308).[9] More elaborate are tombs built from unworked or occasionally worked stones put together in such a way as to form funerary chambers of various shapes (circular, beehive, rectangular, thimble), sometimes for individual (especially Bahrain) and sometimes for collective burial (especially Oman/Emirates). These are particularly numerous along the eastern littoral (Pl. 25a), most famously on the island of Bahrain, where large burial complexes are known, ranging in date from the late third millennium BC to at least the Parthian period. More ostentatious are the tower-tombs of Palmyra. The earliest examples resemble simple lookout towers with an internal staircase and the graves located at the base or around the outside. Gradually they acquired many storeys, each stacked high with compartments for corpses, and became beautified with ornamental niches outside and rows of fluted columns inside. Then there are the imposing and opulent funerary constructions of south Arabian cities, what we might call mausoleums, which would house the deceased of the noblest lineages. Variety is also evident in the second genre of funerary structure (space carved out), ranging from cist graves cut into rock floors and wadis in a narrow rectangular shape just big enough for a body and sealed with stone slabs, to spacious subterranean chambers, and on to the magnificent rock-cut tombs of the elite of Petra and northwest Arabia (Pl. 25b). The last have grand facades with elegant entrances, often crenellations and columns, all adeptly fashioned out of the bare rock faces.

Traditionally certain belongings of the deceased would be interred alongside them. This could include anything intimately associated with them: their clothes, personal adornments (jewellery, amulets etc.), tools, weapons (swords, blades, arrowheads etc.) and household implements (especially glass, ceramic and bronze vessels). Sometimes their riding animal, most often a camel (though horses have been found), would be buried either together with them or in an adjacent tomb. The camel would usually be interred in a seated position with its head pulled back; this is the modern slaughtering position, which suggests that the animal was killed upon the death of its owner. Pre-Islamic Arab poets refer to a similar practice, namely tethering a camel or confining it in a pit by its master's grave until it died of hunger or thirst (*Mu.*: Labid, *baliyya*; Tirimmah 49, *ḥufar al-muballâ*). In addition some monument evoking the spirit of the deceased (*nfs*) might be placed by the grave. This would commonly be a stone slab bearing their name and/or an outline of their face or figure (Pl. 25c), but for the rich and powerful it could mean finely carved busts and statuettes (Pls. 6, 18, 25d), or, as in south Arabia, reliefs showing scenes pertinent to the life of the deceased (Pls. 13, 16b, 36). The corpse would undergo some preparations before being interred. One poet, imagining himself dead, describes how his kin 'combed my hair . . . and clad me in clothes that bore no signs of wear. They sprayed me with sweet odours . . . and wrapped my form in a white sheet closely folded around' (*Muf.* 80; cf. Waqidi 527, who says lote-tree leaves and camphor were used). Otherwise, as in south Arabia and Palmyra, embalming might be practised.

PALACES AND TEMPLES

Eratosthenes of Cyrene (*c*.284–202 BC) informs us that 'all these cities [the four capitals of south Arabia] are ruled by monarchs and are prosperous, being beautifully adorned with both temples and royal palaces' (in Strabo 16.4.3). And, given the myths current among Greeks and Romans about the fabulous wealth of Arabia, it was assumed that their monumental buildings must have been spectacularly decked out:

> Since they [the south Arabians] have never for ages suffered the ravages of war because of their secluded position, and since there is an abundance of both gold and silver in their country, especially in Saba, where the royal palace is situated, they have embossed goblets of every description, made of silver and gold, couches and tripods with silver feet, and every other furnishing of incredible costliness, and halls encircled by large columns, some of them gilded, and others having

(a)

(b)

(c)

(d)

Plate 25 (a) The great Hili tomb (reconstructed) now in a park in al-'Ain oasis, *c.*2500–2000 BC, diameter 12 m (author); (b) tomb facade from Hegra bearing inscription (H 38), AD 63–64 (A. al-Ansary); (c) stone grave marker from region of Tayma with outline of human form wearing belt and dagger (A. al-Ansary); (d) limestone funerary statuette of woman from al-Maqsha cemetery, *c.*2nd–3rd century AD, 37 × 17 cm (Bahrain National Museum).

silver figures on the capitals. Their ceilings and doors they have decorated with sunken recesses set with close-packed gems. Thus they have made the structure of their houses in every part marvellous for its opulence, for some parts they have constructed of silver and gold, others of ivory and the most showy precious stones or of whatever else men esteem most highly.

(Diodorus 3.47)

177

The only palace to have been excavated is that at Shabwa, the Hadramite seat, from which we have some beautiful stonework (Pl. 26). It is an imposing building and, with its high foundations, windowless base, many storeys and impenetrable inner courtyard, was clearly constructed with defensive purposes in mind. And in such a capacity it served during a campaign c.AD 220 when the king of Saba sent troops against Hadramawt to rescue his sister, which necessitated infiltrating the 'palace of Shaqir' as it was called where many of the leading citizens of Shabwa had sought refuge (Ir 13). Otherwise we have only literary remains. For example vestiges of the palaces of Salhin at Marib and of Ghumdan at San'a, which are mentioned together in a number of inscriptions of the third century AD (Ja 577, NAG 12,

Plate 26 Capital from the palace of Shabwa, possibly carved at the time of the palace's reconstruction in the 230s AD (National Museum of Aden).

178

Ir 18), were still to be seen in Islamic times, the latter in particular provoking much wonder:

> Foremost among the palaces of Yemen and having the most remarkable history and the most widespread reputation is Ghumdan . . . [the ruin of] which still stands in San'a. . . . Ghumdan was twenty storeys high, one on top of the other. . . . At each of the palace's four corners stood a copper statue of a lion. These were hollow so that whenever the wind blew through them a voice similar to the actual roaring of lions would be heard. . . . The palace was a four-sided edifice, one of which was made of white stones, the second of black, the third of green and the fourth of red. On the top of the palace was a room that had several windows, each made with a marble frame and ebony woodwork, with silk curtains. The roof of the room was made of one single slab of marble.
>
> (Hamdani 8.5, 15, 22–25)

The Nasrid kings of Lakhm followed their Persian masters and constructed a number of palaces, but by the early seventh century they too were already deserted:

> What can I hope for after Muharriq's folk [i.e. Lakhm] have abandoned their residences? What after Iyad?
> And what after those who dwelt in [the palaces of] Khawarnaq, Bariq and Sadir, and the high-pinnacled palace that stood beside Sindad . . .
> Now sweep the winds over their desolate homes,
> as though their lords had been set a time
>   and no more to be.
> Once indeed they lived there a life most ample in wealth
> and delight beneath the shade of a kingdom firm and stable.
>
> (*Muf.* 44: Aswad ibn Ya'fur)

A related type of building that is commonly mentioned in south Arabian inscriptions is the 'fortress' (*mṣn't*), the fortified residence of a tribal overlord, which would be equipped with 'apartments, bastions, encircling wall and cisterns' (Ir 40). The solidity of these structures means that the remains of many have survived until today, perched atop the heights of Yemen's mountains. For the same reason they are frequently alluded to in pre-Islamic Arabic poetry, a metaphor for durability: 'We mortals perish, but the stars on high will never fade and the mountains and fortresses (*maṣâni‘*) will long endure' (Labid 24). And this same quality even earned them a place in the Quran: 'You raise strong fortresses hoping that you may last for ever' (26.129).

Pliny alleges that Timna posessed sixty-five temples and Shabwa sixty (6.153, 155). Though these figures may be somewhat exaggerated, the considerable number of deities that feature in inscriptions suggests that major settlements would certainly have harboured a good many temples. In ancient Arabia these were not so much congregational buildings where devotees gathered to celebrate their faith as houses of the gods where they would watch over their faithful; 'Make me a sanctuary so that I can reside among my people' (Exodus 25.8), as Yahweh told Moses. They might be located within or just outside a settlement, or else far from any habitation. Local diversity is most to the fore, dictated by available materials and resources, local architectural traditions, exposure to foreign influence and intended function, but there are a number of recurrent features. Besides the temple itself, where the cultic objects could be stored (including the representation of the deity) and the required rituals performed by the servants of the deity in seclusion from the eyes of the multitude, there would usually be a courtyard. This served as the venue for the sacrifice of animals, the presentation of offerings and the consumption of sacred meals. And the whole sanctuary would commonly be marked off either by boundary stones or a perimeter wall.

The temple could be a very simple affair; that at Mecca seems initially to have been no more than a walled open-air chamber:

> The temple (*ka‘ba*) was built in pre-Islamic times with loose stones, without clay. Its height was such that young goats could leap into it. It had no roof and its drapes were merely laid upon it, hanging down.
>
> ('Abd al-Razzaq 5.102)

But it could also be an ornate and monumental edifice. The temple of Bel at Palmyra was raised up on a podium, encompassed by enormous columns bearing carved crossbeams and approached via a grand staircase (Pl. 27a). The temple of Dushara (Qasr el-Bint) at Petra was subdivided into an initial portico, which marked the transition from the realm of mankind to the realm of the gods, a central chamber and at the back two private rooms, one housing the deity and one for initiation ceremonies. The temple of the winged lions at Petra was elaborately decorated with lavish use of colour and a proliferation of mouldings, frescoed niches, drum-built columns and marble

(a)

(b)

Plate 27 (a) Temple of Bel at Palmyra (David Hopkins); (b) Pillars remaining from the monumental entrance to the Awwam temple in Marib (Merilyn Hodgson).

finishings, all intended to induce a feeling of awe in those privileged enough to be admitted into the holy of holies. And in the Sabaean realm the entrance to the sanctuary was frequently embellished with an imposing facade consisting of a squared limestone roof atop monolithic pillars (Pl. 27b), which led, via a courtyard surrounded by a colonnaded portico on three sides, to a tripartite sacred chamber at the rear.

In addition there are temples of substantially different design, the nature and function of which we do not fully understand. The temples of the Minaean Jawf usually avoid the directional tendency of the aforementioned type (oriented along a central axis from entrance to holy of holies) and emphasise a contrapuntal balance in the arrangement of the interior. A surrounding wall would be breached on one side by a monumental portal opening onto a hall filled with an array of pillars distributed regularly across the whole ground area or partially filled by pillars on either side allowing space in the centre for a courtyard (Fig. 5). The so-called Barbar temple (c.2200–1500 BC) on Bahrain consists of four principal elements. There is an oval

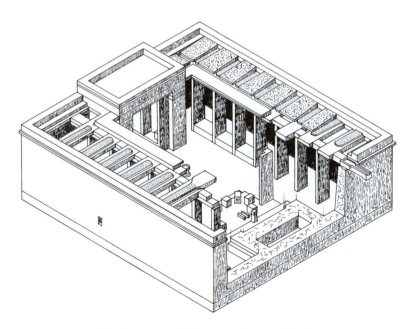

Fig. 5 Temple of 'Athtar at Nashshan, *c.* mid-1st millennium BC, 15.5 × 14.1 m (reconstruction by David Hopkins on the basis of Breton, 'Le Sanctuaire de 'Athtar dhu-Risaf', 437).

platform supporting a four-sided upper terrace (thought to contain the sanctuary proper), which led via a ramp on the east side to a small oval enclosure and via steps on the west side to a stone-lined well incorporating a natural spring (Fig. 6). The temple at Saar, also on Bahrain, is different again: a simple trapezoidal building with a roof supported by three stone pillars placed on the long axis of the temple and comprising a storage area and two built-in altars.

CULT OBJECTS

Within the temple or sacred area were stored a number of objects that related to the resident deity's cult. Most important was some sort of representation of the deity. This might take the form, especially in periods when and places where Greco-Roman influence was strong, of an anthropomorphic statue (Pls. 20, 28a), but in general an unworked stone block was favoured:[10]

> The god Dushara is worshipped by them [the Nabataeans], for him they honour above all others. The image is a black stone, square and unshapen, four feet high by two feet broad. It is set on a base of wrought gold. To this they offer sacrifice and for it they pour forth the victim's blood, that being their form of libation.
>
> (Suidas, 'Theus Ares')[11]

> There was no actual man-made statue of the god [of the Emesenes], the sort Greeks and Romans put up. But there was an enormous stone, rounded at the base and coming to a point on the top, conical in shape and black. This stone is worshipped as though it were sent from heaven.
>
> (Herodian 5.3)

> On this mountain [in Sinai] there is a place where the Saracens have set up an idol for themselves which is of snow-white marble. . . . When the new moon comes and it is time for their festival, this stone begins to change colour, before the moon rises on the feast day. As soon as the moon appears and their worship begins, the stone turns black as pitch. And when the time of the festival is over, it changes back to its original colour. This seemed very marvellous to us.
>
> (Antoninus Placentinus 148–49)

183

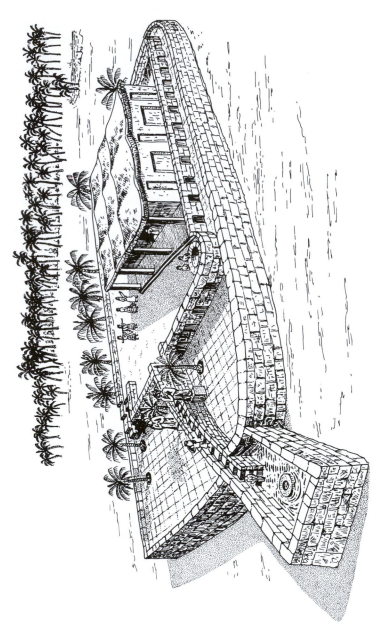

Fig. 6 The Barbar temple of Dilmun, upper platform *c.*23–25 × 15–17 m (reconstruction by David Hopkins).

The clans of Quraysh gathered stones for the rebuilding [of the *ka'ba*], each clan collecting and placing them by itself until the building was finished up to the black stone, when controversy arose, each clan wanting to lift it to its place. . . . Muhammad came to them and they informed him of the matter, and he said: 'Give me a cloak.' When it was brought to him, he took the black stone, put it inside it, and said that each clan should take hold of an end of the cloak and lift it together.

(Ibn Hisham 125)

The most common name for such god-stones comes from the Semitic root *nṣb*, meaning to be stood upright. Other terms reflect different aspects of their use; thus in Nabataean they could be called *masgida*, meaning place of prostration, and in pre-Islamic Arabic poetry *dûwâr*, object of circumambulation, commonly occurs. As in the texts cited above, the god-stone is usually a free-standing slab, or it may be, as sometimes in the Nabataean realm, carved into a rock-face. It may be positioned on the ground or on the floor of a specially fashioned niche, or else, as in the first text quoted above, on some sort of base, either just a rock or a more elaborate structure such as a throne or a raised platform. There was a clear preference for crude stones, shaped only by nature/god (cf. Exodus 20.25: 'If you make me a stone altar, do not build it of dressed stone; for if you use a chisel on it, you will profane it'). But we also encounter many incised with the rudiments of a face (especially in Nabataea; e.g. Pl. 28b) or with astral symbols (especially in south Arabia). The external form of the god-stone seems to have been important: 'Whenever a traveller halted at a place, he would pick out four stones, then would select the finest among them and adopt it as his god, and the remaining three he would use as supports for his cooking pot' (Ibn al-Kalbi 29c). Different deities seem to have been represented by different sizes and shapes: 'Allat . . . was a cubic stone', 'Sa'd . . . was a long stone' (Ibn al-Kalbi 12d, 32c). And it is noticeable that where god-stones of al-'Uzza and Dushara ('Lord of the House') appear together the former is always bigger (e.g. RES 1088, RB 42.413, 43.588).

Given the importance to Arabian religions of presenting gifts and sacrifices to the gods, some sort of altar was obviously essential. The god-stone could serve this purpose. The third-century AD philosopher Porphyry in his account of human sacrifice notes that 'the inhabitants of Duma in Arabia used each year to sacrifice a boy whom they buried beneath an altar that they treat as a cult-statue' (2.56). A south

Arabian worshipper receives an oracular message from his god to erect a standing stone (*qyf*) on his property and to sacrifice on it once every year (CIS 4.392). Moreover pre-Islamic poetry frequently mentions sacrifice and blood libation over the god-stone (e.g. 'the sacrificial stone with its top reddened by the outpoured blood of victims', Zuhayr 50; 'the stones about which blood is poured', Tarafa 10).[12] And the Quran expressly forbids the Muslims to eat animals 'that have been slaughtered over the god-stone' (5.3). Among the well-to-do, however, the two were usually distinguished. Indeed altars became very ornate (Pl. 28c), and many different types evolved in order to suit better the different types of dedication. Thus there were incense altars for aromatic offerings libation tables for liquid offerings, sacrificial altars for animal offerings and so on. The most sophisticated bore not only a dedicatory inscription, but were also adorned with geometric designs, animal-heads, star and crescent moon and so on.

Just as crucial for execution of dedications to the gods were the votive gifts themselves. Very often these were perishable items (aromatics, foodstuffs, animals etc.), but there are two types that have survived in considerable numbers. One is the stone tablet or bronze plaque, on which is inscribed a person's dedication and usually some expression of entreaty or thanksgiving. The other is the figurine or statuette (south Arabian/Aramaic *ṣlm*, Arabic *ṣanam*), usually human or animal in form (Pl. 28d). They are fashioned out of a variety of different substances, most frequently stone (e.g. steatite, talc, limestone), metal (bronze, silver or gold), alabaster, wood or clay. Numerous Arabian inscriptions contain the statement that so-and-so dedicates to such-and-such a deity a statuette in the hope of obtaining/in gratitude for receiving such-and-such a blessing. In this case the figurine may take the place or represent the nature of the sacrifice (e.g. CIS 2.157: dedication of two camel figurines to Dushara). Otherwise it may be an image of the petitioner or related to the subject of the petition; for instance a likeness of a sick child for whom a cure is sought, or the following:

> Ilighazz Ayawkan and his son 'Ali, cavalrymen of the king, have dedicated to their lord Almaqah . . . this horse and its rider of bronze . . . in gratitude because He protected the horse of the king . . . and in gratitude because He saved their two horses . . . while they were riding them from the Bariyan valley to take up their positions in Khabtan.
>
> (Ja 745)

(a)

(b)

(c)

(d)

Plate 28 (a) Basalt stele portraying the goddess Allat in the form of Athena with coat of mail, shield and spear, from Kharaba in the Hawran, 2nd century AD, 52 × 25.5 cm (P. & M. Chuzeville, Louvre AO11215); (b) god-stone with anthropomorphic features representing, according to the inscription on the base, 'the goddess of Hayyan son of Nibat', *c*.1st century AD, height 32 cm (Temple of the Winged Lions, Petra); (c) south Arabian altar from Bar'an temple in Marib inscribed with name of dedicants, *c*.5th–4th century BC, 72 × 35 cm (Museum of Marib); (d) bronze votive statuette of warrior (note helmet, lion skin and attachment for shield on left hand), named Ma'dikarib in the accompanying inscription, *c*.6th century BC, height 93 cm (National Museum of San'a).

WEAPONRY AND WARFARE

Excavations in east Arabia have uncovered substantial numbers of weapons, especially in tombs, where they were buried with their owner. And inscriptions, drawings and poetry in west Arabia often convey images of hunting, fighting and raiding. Together these two sources can teach us much about pre-Islamic Arabian weaponry and its usage. Most commonly encountered are the bow, spear and sword. Bronze arrowheads are attested abundantly in second- and first-millennium BC east Arabia, and at Rumeilah (in modern al-'Ain oasis) the base of a quiver was found with holes into which the arrows would have slotted. From the Hellenistic period onwards iron arrowheads begin to turn up in large quantities, many of which are likely to have been manufactured locally (621 discovered at Mleiha and ed-Dur in the Emirates, both of which have deposits of iron ore nearby). The bow and arrow was obviously most useful at a distance, whether in battle ('now my horse darts forth for the lance-thrusting, now retreats to the great host of archers', *Mu.*: 'Antara) or in hunting (Pl. 29a).

How many a marksman of Thu'al sliding out his hands
　　from his sleeves, lifting his strong-made bow with a
　　twang in its idle string,
Has drawn and taken aim as the quarry came to drink,
　　shot it straight in the chest as it stood at the water's brink
With a shaft from the quiver drawn, flashing like sparks
　　from the blaze, feathered with eagle plumes, sharp from
　　the whetting stone.

(Imru' al-Qays 29)

Most frequently mentioned in pre-Islamic Arabic poetry is the spear, which appears for the first time in the late third millennium BC in east Arabian archaeological sites. Depending on the length to weight ratio it could serve either as a projectile, like a javelin, or as a thrusting implement. The latter function became more popular once the horse had been introduced into Arabia, during the fourth–second centuries BC, for the spear could be wielded more easily on horseback than the sword. Rock drawings and poetry illustrate the use of the spear in this manner for hunting and fighting, and also for raiding, when it was used for claiming one's spoils (Pl. 36).[13] Poets very often refer to spears as the product of Khatt in east Arabia, where many were reportedly assembled from bamboo imported from India.

The most prized of all weapons was the sword: 'My friends there were twain: a camel light-hearted, nimble of pace, and a blade marked with grooves, a fellow whose company none dislikes' (*Muf.* 41). It is often mentioned in the same breath as the spear: 'This mare of mine shall carry me and a bright keen blade, and a sharp spear-head set on a pliant shaft five cubits long' ('Abid 12). And they would commonly be used together: 'I thrust him with my spear, then I came on top of him with a trenchant Indian blade' (*Mu.*: 'Antara). But whereas the spear was used at a slight distance from the enemy, the sword only came into play when right up close: 'When the ranks stand apart from us we thrust with spears, and we strike with swords when they are upon us' (*Mu.*: 'Amr). For this reason it was deemed the most noble of arms and its skilful manipulation earned one the highest praise. Furthermore it was employed for slaughtering animals to host a dinner and so stood for generosity and hospitality. The form of swords in use in Arabia changed much over time, from long two-piece bronze swords in the second millennium BC, to short single-piece bronze swords in the first millennium BC (Pl. 29b), to the long heavy iron swords of the Roman and Sasanian periods. Each development is likely to have entailed fundamental alterations in the region's modes of combat, though we have no evidence of this for the pre-Roman period.

As well as tools of aggression there were instruments of defence. Fragments of an iron coat of mail have been discovered in a first-second-century AD grave at Janussan on Bahrain and shields are illustrated on a bronze bowl of the third/second century BC from Mleiha in the Emirates. These meagre remains can be abundantly supplemented by the numerous references in pre-Islamic poetry. The full complement is given as follows: 'We wore helmets and Yemeni leather shields . . . and glittering coats of mail having visible folds above the belt' (*Mu.*: 'Amr). The first two items do not receive much attention from the poets, but coats of mail were frequently and variously described. They were 'of David's weave', a reference to a legend that is also alluded to in the Quran: 'We bestowed upon David Our favours . . . and made hard iron pliant for him, telling him to make coats of mail and measure their links with care' (34.10–11, 21.80). They are wide and loose-fitting (*sâbigha*), ample (*fadfâḍa*) and spreading (*nathra*). They are most often long and their skirts might need to be 'hoisted up on the sheath of a shining sword' (*Muf.* 75). The individual rings are set close together, bound firm by nails, so that it might prove impenetrable to any missile or assault. A coat of good metal, it is often said, will shimmer and ripple like a silvery pool blown by the wind and glitter like lightning.

(a)

(b)

Plate 29 (a) Rock drawing from Jabal Says showing men hunting with bow and arrow (David Hopkins); (b) lost Assyrian relief from Nineveh showing Arabs bearing bows and short swords (British Museum Or. Dr. 7.28); (c) rock drawing from Burqu', now in Amman Museum, showing men fighting with bow, spear and shield (M.C.A. Macdonald); (d) Assyrian relief, *c.*650 BC, showing Arabs retreating on camelback, one steering and one firing at pursuers (British Museum 124926).

(c)

(d)

The manner of deployment of this arsenal is elucidated by battle scenes in the rock art of pastoralist tribes (Pl. 29c) and by their poetry, which commonly narrates whole incidents. Both, incidentally, make clear that the camel was ridden to battle and in retreat (Pl. 29d), but the horse was used during the battle itself:

191

We led the horses alongside [while riding on our camels]
from the sand-hills of Ghamra and of Lubna . . .
Then when the hills of Qanan and Sara came into sight
and we were in the neighbourhood of the highland to the
 east of mount Salma,
We made the camels lie down and offered the horses the
 remains which were in the water-skins,
some drinking, others not at all.
They were compelled to have the bit of the bridle put into
 their mouth,
[their necks outstretched] like a palm-trunk having its top
 lopped off,
And the grooms made the saddles firm; then they were
handed to men armed for war, accustomed to making raids
 in the morning.
Those on the lookout do not see them till they are upon
them in a wadi bordered by acacia, into which streams drain
. . . Our infantry shot from masikhi-bows,
the best that can be bought in Yathrib . . .
When the supply of arrows in the quivers was exhausted,
 they took to sword-play on shields
made from the hides of well-bred camels.

(Tufayl 1)

ROCK ART

Almost everywhere in Arabia that stones are abundant (i.e. not dune deserts) drawings and doodlings will be found. These will be partic- ularly numerous where the rock surfaces are amenable to incising (fairly flat and smooth) and where human beings are apt to congre- gate (e.g. watering holes, sheltered spots, high places etc.). Recent excavations at Dhuweila in the basalt desert of east Jordan have revealed carvings of human and animal figures on stones incorporated into Neolithic structures of the late seventh millennium BC. Evidently, then, this art is very ancient, and continued for millennia, being attested also for the Islamic period. There are three principal methods of producing such images. The simplest is 'pecking', that is, the percussive use of a pointed stone held in the hand, directly striking the rock with repeated blows that penetrate the patina and affect the surface at the point of impact. Slightly more complex is 'chiselling', employing a stone as a hammer to drive a sharp implement, also usually a stone. The latter technique allows more precision and gives greater depth of relief. Finally there is scratching on the rock surface with a stone so that the patina of the rock is removed and figures appear prominently in contrast to the dark patina of the original rock surface. None of these drawings can be dated precisely, though some idea can be gained from the degree of weathering. Moreover some are accompanied by an inscription in which the author claims the credit for their artistic creation, and this can then give us a very approximate time of composition derived from what we know about the language used. It might also be possible to assign particular styles to particular peoples, but this would require much more study than has been carried out to date.

The interest to the historian of these pictures is that they have the potential to make a valuable contribution to our knowledge of everyday life in Arabia. Most depict persons (men and women, singly and in groups), animals (especially camels, horses, asses, ibexes, lions, gazelles and ostriches) and diverse symbols (e.g. stick figures, dots arranged in patterns, suns, stars and numerous unidentified marks). These may appear individually or form part of a composition portraying a number of figures engaged in a variety of activities. Hunting scenes are very common, either a chase (men pursuing an animal on horseback, often accompanied by dogs, shooting with bows and brandishing a spear) or trapping (driving game into an enclosure or the like). Representations of armed combat are also popular, usually involving a small number of participants armed with shield and a spear or sword. Raids are rarer, but do occur, the participants being shown on horseback and laying claim to an animal (usually a camel) by touching it with their spears. Of particular interest are scenes of dancing and playing instruments, either a group of men watching a female perform or else two or more persons acting together (Pl. 30).

COINS AND SEALS

It is not only as a means of economic exchange that coins are important. Their issuing also constitutes a declaration of political power, or at least of a pretension to political power. One of the first acts therefore of a would-be ruler or fledgling state will usually be to mint their own coins. Moreover the fact that they can bear images and writing and enjoy wide circulation means that they may serve as an effective instrument of propaganda. Thus the Palmyrene queen Zenobia made clear her ambitions by striking coinage in the name of her son

Plate 30 Rock drawing from northeast Jordan showing female musician and male dancer; text reads 'by Aqraban son of Kasit son of Sa'd; the beautiful woman played the reed pipes' (G. Lankester Harding; see *ADAJ* 2, 1953, no. 79).

'Emperor Caesar Wahballat Augustus' and of herself as 'Zenobia Augusta' (Pl. 12). Yet, occasional tumultuous periods notwithstanding, coins are a highly conservative medium. They must inspire confidence in their users that they really are worth what they say they are, and that they will still be accepted by others a few years down the line. If they do not inspire this confidence, people will shun them in favour of internationally recognised types (compare the use of the American dollar in some unstable regimes today). For this reason all Arabian coinage started off as an imitation of some more illustrious model. In south Arabia the earliest coins (fourth/third century BC) are imitations of Athenian tetradrachms, the dollar of their day: the obverse shows the head of Athena with helmet, the reverse has an owl, olive branch, crescent moon and the Greek letters AΘE. In east Arabia they turned to the coinage of Alexander the Great: on the obverse the head of Heracles wearing the pelt of the Nemean lion and on the reverse Zeus seated on his throne, in his left arm a sceptre and on his outstretched right arm an eagle. And about the beginning of the first century BC, when the Seleucid empire was sufficiently weakened, minor powers under their influence, including the Nabataeans, began to assert themselves and to strike their own coins, using issues of their former overlords as a model.

Gradually attempts were made to nativise the coinage, to introduce features more relevant to the issuing culture. On many east Arabian coins, for example, the name of Alexander is replaced by that of Abyatha' in south Arabian letters or Abi'el in Aramaic letters (Pl. 3), evidently the names of local monarchs. Moreover the imagery of the reverse is frequently reworked in accordance with local tastes (e.g. Zeus' beard removed, eagle replaced by horse or reed pipe, palm tree or south Arabian letters inserted). Otherwise symbols meaningful and particular to the local population might be employed. For example the extended palm of the raised hand had a distinctly religious and ceremonial significance in the life of the Nabataeans and its appearance on coins is exclusive to them. Finally there might also be technical innovations answering some local need and effected in local style. Thus in south Arabia four different denominations of the original Athenian coins were minted, their respective weights (and so values) indicated by a south Arabian letter placed on the cheek of Athena.

A seal is an object (often worn on a ring) made of hard material – generally stone, but sometimes bone, ivory or glass – on which a design is engraved so that when it is pressed on clay or wax it will leave an imprint. For thousands of years this act of sealing has guaranteed authenticity, marked ownership, indicated participation in a legal transaction or protected goods against theft. Not many seals have been found in Arabia except in the east where approximately one thousand have been recovered, over four hundred of which come from the island of Failaka in the bay of Kuwait. Most are fabricated from stone (chlorite or steatite), though some are made from seashells (which seem primarily, however, to have been used in burials). The designs presumably conveyed some special significance to their users, but this is mostly now lost to us. Astral and solar symbols are popular, as are humans, birds and animals, particularly the gazelle and those identified with constellations (bull, goat, scorpion, lion, snake). Either these are portrayed individually or in some sort of scene, whether of daily life or drawn from ritual and mythic contexts (Pl. 31).

ARTISANS AND CRAFTS

Like many pre-modern societies, pre-Islamic Arabians valued those who worked in the domains of agriculture/pastoralism, religion and war, but looked down upon craftspeople (see chapter 5 above). This is

Plate 31 Impression made by chlorite/steatite stamp seal of Dilmun, representing (mythological?) scene involving human figures (enthroned deity?) and bull, *c.*2000–1800 BC, diameter 2.54 cm (Bahrain National Museum).

evident from inscriptions, which treat the former three at length, but almost never mention crafts. As one might expect from the huge quantity of inscriptions and relief sculpture discovered in Arabia, the one type of artisan to feature with any frequency in Arabian texts are stonemasons. At Hegra they would even sometimes append their name to funerary inscriptions, thirteen of which would seem to have been executed by members of the same clan. Otherwise we are forced to rely upon pre-Islamic Arabic poetry, which never discusses crafts directly, but often uses elements from them to form a simile or metaphor. Thus it is asserted that 'the spears riddled his body as the comb passes through the weaver's web' (*Ham.* 272). And the markings on a smooth mountain slope are likened to the patterns on 'a Yemeni garment which [the inhabitants of the south Arabian towns of] Rayda

196

and Suhul have embroidered' (Tarafa 4). Particularly important was tanning and leather-working, for it could provide such diverse articles as tents, buckets, saddles, clothes, containers for water and oil, belts, cushions, writing material and even boats (the Sabaeans 'sail across the straits in leather boats', Strabo 16.4.19). So when Quraysh were preparing to send a deputation to the ruler of Ethiopia, it seemed obvious to them that the best present they could give him, 'the most excellent of what they produced', was leatherware (Ibn Hisham 218). But besides these and other scattered references we have only the products themselves, or rather only those which have survived, to tell us about Arabian crafts, such as the pottery of Nabataea, the seals of Dilmun, the textiles of Palmyra and the alabaster statuettes of south Arabia.

8

LANGUAGE AND
LITERATURE

SCRIPTS

There are two great alphabetic traditions from which all alphabets are derived: the northwest Semitic (normally called Phoenician, from which the Greek alphabet is descended) and the Arabian. Both are thought to have originated in the Levant and to have separated some time in the second millennium BC. The Arabian group is divided into two branches, the southern and the northern. The former consisted of twenty-nine letters, which were written as capitals in monumental inscriptions on stone and bronze and in minuscule in documents on wood and palm stalks. In its early stages it was written from left to right or from right to left, or a long inscription might even switch from one direction to the other from line to line; gradually, however, the preferred direction, right to left, became the only possibility. This south Arabian script continued in use until the early Islamic period, when it was occasionally used to write Arabic, but was abandoned soon thereafter in favour of the Arabic script. It was also used, with minor modifications, in the coastal region of northeast Arabia (the Hasa). The north Arabian group comprised twenty-eight letters and is found, with local variations in letterform and orthographic practice, throughout north and central Arabia and also among the Arabian diaspora communities settled in Babylonia and elsewhere (Fig. 7).

As well as these Arabian scripts a number of imported types are attested. The earliest was cuneiform, used in the second millennium BC on the islands of Failaka and Bahrain. The most important was Aramaic, used in northwest and east Arabia during the Persian period (539–334 BC) and later adopted by all the polities scattered around the edges of the Syrian desert. The success of the Nabataeans led to the spread of their version of the Aramaic script far and wide, and even after the Roman annexation of their realm in AD 106 it continued in

Phonetic value	South Arabian	Taymanitic	Dedanitic	Hismaic	Safaitic	Arabic
ʾ						
b						
t						
th						
ǧ						
ḥ						
kh						
d						
dh						
r						
z						
s						
sh						
ṣ						
ḍ						
ṭ						
ẓ						
ʿ						
gh						
f						
q						
k						
l						
m						
n						
h						
w						
y						
ś						

Fig. 7 Arabian scripts; note that letter forms can vary considerably, especially in the case of scripts known only from graffiti.

use for a couple of centuries. Subsequently the Arab tribes affiliated to Rome and Iran employed it to write their language, namely Arabic. The process of conveying a language with different sounds and extra consonants caused the Nabataean script (which had only twenty-two letters) gradually to evolve until by the sixth century AD it had become what we would recognise as the Arabic script (Pl. 32b).

LANGUAGES

Almost all the languages used in Arabia belong to the Semitic family, the members of which bear a close resemblance to one another, most obviously in the sphere of word structure. The vast majority of words in a Semitic language consist of three root letters. In each case these three root letters can be modified by the addition of vowels and a limited range of other consonants to give a variety of words of similar meaning. For example in a number of Semitic languages the letters *ktb*, in that order, evoke the concept of writing; thus in Arabic *kataba* means to write, *kâtaba* to correspond, *kitâb* a book, *kâtib* a scribe, *maktab* an office, *maktaba* a library, and so on. The modification of the root letters is not arbitrary, but highly schematic, and each schema makes clear the grammatical form of the word and its specific sense. Though the practice is a bit messier, this theoretical overview works well enough to allow us to distinguish non-Semitic languages very clearly from Semitic languages.

Like the Arabian scripts, the Arabian languages divide into a southern group and a northern group. The former, known from some ten thousand inscriptions, are distinguished by the existence of three non-emphatic sibilants (letters pronounced with a hissing sound) and a definite article attached to the end of the word. The principal members of the southern group of languages are: Sabaic, Minaic (or Madhabic), Qatabanic and Hadramitic, these being the languages used by the four principal peoples of the region. Various other languages were spoken in south Arabia, but they were never, or only very rarely, written down. The Himyarites, for example, used Sabaic in their inscriptions, yet frequently made mistakes and introduced alien words and foreign grammatical features which presumably derived from their own spoken language. The irregularities in the inscriptions of the Minaeans suggest that they, too, spoke one language and wrote another, the latter being the language employed in the area (the Wadi Madhab, modern Jawf) into which they moved around the sixth century BC. Finally there are the modern non-Arabic languages of south Arabia (Mehri, Harsusi, Socotri, Bathari, Jibbali, Hobyot), which presumably have ancient ancestors, but for which the extant inscriptions of south Arabia offer no parallels.

The northern group of Arabian languages can be recognised by the presence of only two non-emphatic sibilants and a definite article attached to the beginning of the word. They are represented by some forty thousand inscriptions mostly located in and around the oasis-towns of northwest Arabia, the sandy desert of the Hisma and the basalt desert of the Harra, and the highlands of central Arabia.[1] These north Arabian languages are all fairly close to one another and would have been to a considerable degree mutually comprehensible. Among them is to be found the ancestor of classical Arabic, which is usually referred to by scholars as Old Arabic and which is readily distinguishable by its use of the definite article *al* (other languages use *h/han*). From the observation of Herodotus (3.8) that the Arabs call Aphrodite *Al-ilat* ('the goddess') we can probably infer that Old Arabic existed as early as the fifth century BC, but it seems to have been seldom written down until a century or so before the advent of Islam. On the very few occasions that it was committed to writing, the script of prestige in the locality concerned was employed. Thus at Dedan from before the time of the Nabataeans (end of the first century BC) an inscription advertises 'the funerary monument of 'Abdsamin son of Zaydharim which (*allati banâhâ*) Salma daughter of Aws built' (JS Lih384). The language is Old Arabic, but the script is one that had long been in use in Dedan. At Qaryat al-Faw, the capital of Kinda and other Arab tribes, a certain 'Igl son of Haf'am wrote the dedicatory text for his brother's tomb in Old Arabic using the script of the nearby Sabaean kingdom (Pl. 3):

'Igl son of Haf'am constructed for his brother Rabibil son of Haf'am the tomb: both for him and for his child and his wife, and his children and their children's children and womenfolk, free members of the folk Ghalwan. And he has placed it under the protection of [the gods] Kahl and Lah and 'Athtar al-Shariq from anyone strong or weak, and anyone who would attempt to sell or pledge it, for all time without any derogation, so long as the sky produces rain or the earth herbage.

And in AD 328 at Nemara in the basalt desert southeast of Damascus a tomb was built for Imru' al-Qays and his deeds celebrated in a text composed in Old Arabic using the script of the Nabataeans (Pl. 32a),

(a)

(b)

Plate 32 (a) Lintel from the tomb of Imru' al-Qays in Nemara, Syria, bearing Arabic inscription in Nabataean script, dated AD 328 (P. & M. Chuzeville, Louvre AO4083); (b) Arabic graffito from Jabal Says, Syria, written by 'Ibrahim ibn al-Mughira al-Awsi' on the occasion of his dispatch by 'al-Harith the king', now in Arabic script, dated AD 528 (David Hopkins).

still the script of prestige in that region (see chapter 3 above). Features of Old Arabic often surface in texts written in other north Arabian dialects or in Nabataean from various parts of Arabia, making it clear that Old Arabic was widely spoken throughout the region. Nevertheless it remained primarily a vernacular, employed by non-literate peoples and by those who, for whatever reason, preferred to write in other languages. Texts written wholly in Old Arabic are so rare that the commissioning of them must have been a conscious and deliberate choice. Presumably the intention was to make a statement about their ethnic and/or cultural affiliation, about their Arab identity. It is also possible that there were political connotations to using the spoken tongue rather than a foreign language, for it is noticeable that Imru' al-Qays exerted influence over a sizeable region and 'Igl ibn Haf'am came from a city used as a capital by a number of Arab tribes.

Of the linguistic situation in east Arabia we are very ill informed, since only a paltry number of texts has come down to us. Fifty or so engraved tombstones have been found in the northeast coastal region known as the Hasa (hence modern scholars call the language of the epitaphs Hasaitic). However, these are all very brief and mostly consist of a stereotyped funerary formula plus a personal name ('monument and tomb of . . . '), so it is difficult to say anything meaningful about

Plate 33 Arabic inscription in Sabaean script from Qaryat al-Faw on limestone tombstone by 'Igl son of Haf'am, *c.*1st century BC (A. al-Ansary; see his *Qaryat al-Faw*, 146).

203

this language beyond the fact that it belongs to the north Arabian group. It may even be the case that it is not an indigenous language; rather these tombstones might be the monuments of an immigrant group of west Arabians operating the east–west trade route by way of the Wadi Sirhan.

As well as these Arabian languages a number of foreign tongues were in use in this land. There are a handful of Akkadian documents of the second millennium BC and a few Greek texts of the Hellenistic period from the islands of Failaka and Bahrain. A very few Greek and even Latin rock inscriptions have been found in northwest Arabia. But it is only the Aramaic language (together with its script) that is attested with any frequency. As is to be expected, it is most often encountered in areas under Nabataean and Palmyrene influence. It was also important in east Arabia, as is proven by a growing corpus of texts on a variety of materials such as coins, bronze plaques and potsherds, and by the surviving correspondence (in the Aramaic dialect known as Syriac) between church authorities in Babylonia and east Arabian clergy.

DOCUMENTS

Inscribing on stone or metal is an arduous task. Moreover the former is unwieldy and the latter expensive to prepare. Not surprisingly therefore neither was much used for recording everyday transactions. For these purposes there were available handier and cheaper materials on which one could write with ink or dye or incise with ease. Abundant references in pre-Islamic Arabic poetry give us some idea of the principal surfaces employed. Thus we read about animal skins, from which one can make parchment (untanned skin) and leather (tanned skin); plants, notably papyrus and the stalks of palm and ben trees; cloth, chiefly cotton and linen; bones, of which some fragments bearing the south Arabian script have been unearthed at Qaryat al-Faw; and pieces of pottery (ostraca), for which we have Aramaic examples from Nabataea and east Arabia. In addition clay tablets and seals were used in east Arabia for texts written in cuneiform script, particularly official stamps and receipts for goods. However, what these materials gain in user-friendliness they lose in durability. Whereas tens of thousands of texts on rock have weathered the centuries, only a few hundred on palm stalks have been found, and no more than a few dozen texts written on other media. The documents on palm stalks are all in south Arabian script and shed light on aspects of that society

2 cm

Plate 34 Palm stalk bearing Sabaic text by Yu'allil of the clan of Giraf instructing Wahar of the clan of Hubran to 'take charge of the client of the clan of Dawr who has been sent with Siba' and not to abuse him', 1st–3rd century AD (Jacques Ryckmans; see *id. et al.*, *Textes du Yémen antique*, no. 6).

for which inscriptions leave us totally in the dark (Pl. 34). They include, for example, writing exercises, private letters (usually to do with commercial matters) and acknowledgements of services rendered. Most likely these documents were once part of archives, probably kept in temples. Their discovery is recent, and it is to be hoped that many more will be located, offering further new perspectives on what is otherwise a mysterious world to us.

INSCRIPTIONS

The durability of inscriptions was observed by pre-Islamic Arab poets who compared them to the traces left by their desert encampments, which seemed in like manner able to defy the ravaging effects of time. And because of this same property inscriptions had long been used by Greco-Roman and Middle Eastern peoples to note down their deeds and resolutions, their hopes and aspirations, their prayers and supplications. Often a fine monumental script was developed in order to convey these messages, imparting dignity and authority both to the text and to the medium onto which it was carved. For certain civilisations little else remains of their literary heritage bar the epigraphic record. This is particularly true of pre-Islamic Arabia, the inhabitants of which scribbled on the rocks around them with gay abandon.[2] The visibility of inscriptions meant that they were all, to a greater or lesser degree, public texts. Many were officially so, a proclamation by a representative of the political or religious establishment on behalf of the whole community, expressing the principles by which it was governed and conducted itself. Others were deliberately so, a declaration by a wealthy patron vaunting his magnanimity and virtue. Others again (notably epitaphs and graffiti) were more subtly so, a personal statement by individuals seeking to demonstrate their credentials, affirming their membership of a community and their adherence to its moral precepts and guiding tenets. Given this intention and the need for ease of comprehension, inscriptions tend to draw upon a common repertoire of phrases, which, though each genre and each cultural group has expressions peculiar to it, remain fairly limited and exhibit a high degree of recurrence of set formulae. The number of genres is also relatively few, though each is fairly broad in scope and an inscription may combine elements from more than one genre.

Commemorative/declarative

This is a very extensive category. In the case of monumental texts it will most often mean the recording of a successful undertaking: victories won in war, profits gained in commerce, imposing edifices completed, binding treaties concluded. In the case of graffiti it entailed committing to words the actions, thoughts and feelings of everyday existence, and so the range of subjects is much wider. In Safaitic and Hismaic inscriptions, for example, we receive a general outline of the life of their nomadic authors. In the spring they left the by now hot inner desert with their herds in search of the new pastures spawned by the rains. There the animals gave birth: 'the goats have borne young amidst the new growth (*bql*)' (WH 1673), while their owners warded off predators, constructed folds into which the animals were gathered at nightfall, and sometimes erected rough shelters for themselves as a protection against the elements. As the heat intensified, they would seek somewhere to spend the summer (*qyẓ*), ideally a cool location with permanent water supplies. With the first rains of autumn they returned to the warmth of the inner desert (*shrq mdbr*), for the cold of the steppe in winter could kill their young animals. With the coming of spring the cycle began again: 'this is his camping place year after year' (WH 1193, SIJ 171). Life must have been hard, and occasionally we do hear of 'a year of misery' (WH 2110), yet some declared that they 'shepherded and lived in ease' (WH 597). The day-to-day activities most commonly mentioned are herding (*r'y*), keeping a lookout (*nẓr*), drawing (*khṭṭ*), building (*bny*, especially enclosures, shelters, cairns) and fighting (*ghzz*).

With regard to emotions it is of their sorrows and their loves that our authors most often write. The former prevail in the Safaitic texts, which exhibit a rich vocabulary for expressing sadness. Usually it is sorrow upon the decease of their nearest and dearest, which may haunt the living 'year after year' (SIJ 72, 119, 785) and be recalled by some chance reminder: 'He found the inscription of his grandfather and he grieved (*wjd sfr 'mh f-wjm*)' (WH 1273). Hismaic texts, on the other hand, more often inform us of amorous exploits and many a young tribesman proclaims that 'he loved (*wdd*) a beautiful young girl' (KJA 23) or that 'he was very love-sick (*sqm srr*) for a maiden and had joyous sex with her' (KJA 24). Those inscribing in the north Arabian dialect in use around Najd were wont to point out that emotions are a gift of the gods: 'by Nuha is the flying into a rage', 'by Nuha is the jealousy of a lover', 'o Allah, by you are love and tranquillity'. And indeed all things, good or bad, are recognised as being manifested through the agency of the gods: 'by Dathan are our bread and pasture', 'by Ruda are we', 'by Kahl is the love of animals', 'by Ruda is weeping', 'by Nuha is bowel-disease and measles'.[3]

Invocatory

It is a feature of a large proportion of Arabian inscriptions that they call upon a deity for some favour. Of the thousand or so inscriptions of Petra six hundred advance simple requests: 'may so-and-so be well' (*shlm* + name), 'may so-and-so be remembered' (*dkyr* + name), and 'may so-and-so be blessed' (*bryk* + name). And the same short pleas are found in thousands more graffiti in the rest of the Nabataean realm. Otherwise the petitioners may have something specific in mind that is of relevance to them/their community at that time, whether to be relieved of a particular affliction or to receive a particular boon. In Safaitic texts the deity most frequently invoked is the goddess Allat. She is asked to extend solicitude and to display mercy. Of her are expected wellbeing, ease and prosperity. Travellers pray that she might accompany them in their migrations and provide clement weather. She is entreated for protection against the enemy, vengeance on the aggressor, booty for her faithful in their raids and infliction of blindness and lameness upon whomsoever defaces their inscriptions.

Votive

A request for a favour or thanksgiving for its accomplishment will very often be supported by a gift or sacrifice presented to the pertinent deity (Pl. 35). And among sedentary people an accompanying inscription will often record this act.

Plate 35 Bronze votive plaque from Timna with oil lamp held by a hand, dedicated by Hamati'amm Dhirhan to 'his god and lord, the master of Yaghil', *c.*1st century BC, 20 × 11.6 cm (AFSM).

Mani' has dedicated to his lady, the mistress of Mafrash, this incense altar, so that she may grant him an oracular decision which is satisfactory, and that she may grant him the safety of his brothers and the safety of their children, and that she may grant them spring- and autumn-crops on their land, and that she may repel all their enemies.

(Ja 2897)

The inscription may also set out the reasons for making the dedication, usually an expression of the hope or gratitude of the dedicant for what the deity will do or has already done. These reasons might be detailed at length if the dedicant were a king or noble, able to afford the fees of a professional scribe and stonemason and wishing to parade their exploits and receipt of divine blessings to all passers-by. Otherwise the offering may be made without any strings attached, simply out of devotion and respect and 'for their life and the life of their children and brethren' (a common Palmyrene formula).

Funerary

Inscriptions on gravestones and tombs tend to be very simple affairs in Arabia. In the south it is common just to note the name of the deceased and their lineage. Among the tribes of the Harra the builders of a tomb might record their action and for whom it was intended, and simply say that they 'felt grief'. Only from the elite of the Nabataean realm (and then chiefly from Hegra) do we have substantial tomb texts, and these are rather in the nature of legal documents, specifying what may or may not be done with the tomb and what will happen to those who violate these specifications:

> This is the tomb which 'Aydu son of Kuhaylu son of Alkasi made for himself and his children and his descendants and for whoever produces in his hand a deed of entitlement from the hand of 'Aydu, valid for him, and for whoever 'Aydu during his lifetime grants permission to bury in it. In the month of April, the ninth year of Haritat, king of the Nabataeans, lover of his people. And may [the god] Dushara and [the goddesses] Manat and Qaysha curse anyone who sells this tomb or buys it or gives it in pledge or makes a gift of it or leases it or draws up for himself any document concerning it or buries in it anyone apart from those inscribed above. And the tomb and this its inscription are inviolable according to the nature of inviolability among the Nabataeans and Salamians for ever and ever.
>
> (H 8)

Honorific

These are very much a Palmyrene phenomenon, imitating the Greco-Roman custom of singling out and praising those who have exerted themselves in the service of society. The following is a particularly effusive example:

209

The council and people honour Soados son of Boliades son
of Soados son of Taymisamos for his piety and love of his city,
and for the nobility and munificence that he has on many
important occasions shown to the merchants and the caravans
and the citizens at Vologesias. For these services he received
testimonial letters from the divine Hadrian and from the most
divine emperor Antoninus his son, similarly in a proclamation
of Publicius Marcellus and letters from him and successive
consular governors. He has been honoured by decrees and
statues by the council and people, by the caravans on various
occasions, and by individual citizens. And now he alone of
all citizens of all time is on account of his continuous and
cumulative good services honoured by his city at public
expense by four statues mounted on pillars in the tetradeion
of the city, and by decision of the council and people another
three, at Spasinou Charax, Vologesias and the caravanserai of
Gennaes.

(Sy 12.106–107)

Juridical

It was quite common in the sedentary regions of Arabia to inscribe
texts of a legal nature on stone (see chapter 5 above for examples).
The advantage of this was that these texts were then easily available
for all to read (or have read for them) and would endure for many
lifetimes. The subjects are diverse: commercial ordinances (such as
the list of taxes owing on goods sold in Palmyra put up by the
city council, and the regulations concerning trade in the market of
Timna established by the king of Qataban), sanctions against
criminals, hydrological legislation, cultic prescriptions, boundary
settlements, property claims and so forth. The issuing authority was
most often a deity (whose edicts were effected by means of an oracle
and received and transcribed by a religious functionary), a king or
his representative, or a city or tribal council. And even individuals
might avail themselves of this practice, laying down conditions
for use of their tombs, asserting their ownership of houses and the like.
A special type of juridical inscription, so far known chiefly from
the Jawf region of south Arabia and Raybun in Hadramawt, is the
penitential text, in which persons confess their infraction of a law,
usually to do with purity, and make an offering in atonement. Here
is a typical example:

Hawliyyat, slave of [the clan of] Sulaym, has confessed and done penance to Dhu Samawi, lord of Bayan, for having worn an unclean cloak and a soiled woollen garment. And she hid from her masters what she had committed. As for Dhu Samawi may he reward her with favour. [For her part] she has submitted and humbled herself, and she has made an offering in expiation and paid a fine.

(Haram 35; cf. nos. 8, 10, 33–36, 40, 56)

LITERATURE: POETRY

Physical evidence of poetry in Arabia before Islam is limited to two examples. One was discovered recently in the Wadi Qaniya to the southeast of San'a. It is a poem addressed to the sun goddess, Shams 'Aliyyat, whose mountaintop shrine lies close by. Though written in the south Arabian script, probably of the late first/early second century AD, it is not in any of the known tongues of south Arabia, though it may be in the native language of the Himyarites, in whose territory it lies. The text has twenty-seven lines, each line containing three word-dividers, which suggests a verse-form with four beats to the line. Moreover it is rhymed, every line ending with the letters *hk*. It begins and concludes as follows:

> I seek your protection, for all events are by you accomplished.
> In the Khinwan hunt the blood of hundreds [of beasts] to flow
>   have you caused.
> The head of the tribe of Dhu Fasad aloft have you raised
> And the breast of 'Alhan of Yahir have you expanded . . .
> You have made fragrant the steady rain, for you have been
>   open-handed.
> You have aided us, oh Shams, for it is you who have the rain
>   provided.
> And we beseech you that with constant rain may your people
>   ever be anointed.[4]

From roughly the same period but the other end of Arabia, 'En 'Avdat in the Negev desert, we have a second text, much shorter and this time in Arabic. It forms part of a Nabataean inscription, in which a certain Garmallahi son of Taymallahi records his offering of a statue to the god Obodat. He then switches into the Arabic language, though still using the Nabataean script. At the festival of Venus in Petra the

211

citizens would apparently 'praise the virgin with hymns in the Arabic language' (Epiphanius 51.22), and it may be that what we have here is part of a hymn or well-known verse in praise of the deity:

> For He [Obodat] acts [expecting] no reward nor predilection.
> Though death has often sought us out, He afforded it no occasion;
> Though I have often encountered wounding, He has not let it be my destruction.

Except for these two pieces we are forced to rely for our knowledge of pre-Islamic Arabian poetry on compositions mostly of the sixth century, which began to be collected in the eighth century. For a long time it was fiercely debated whether these poems were genuine or not, but recent studies have demonstrated how pre-literate peoples can effectively preserve their traditions over the course of centuries, and this has constrained the discussion to the issue of minor contamination rather than that of major fabrication. Moreover the sceptical view ignored the high status accorded poetry in Arab society:

> When there appeared a poet in a family of the Arabs, the other tribes round about would gather together to that family and wish them joy of their good luck. Feasts would be got ready, the women of the tribe would join together in bands, playing upon lutes, as they were wont to do at bridals, and the men and boys would congratulate one another. For a poet was a defence to the honour of them all, a weapon to ward off insult from their good name, and a means of perpetuating their glorious deeds and of establishing their fame for ever.
>
> (Ibn Rashiq 1.65)

And in Islamic times there was an additional incentive to preserve this material, namely that it provided an indispensable resource for understanding the Quran and for codifying Arabic grammar ('if you read anything in the book of God and you do not understand it, then seek its meaning in pre-Islamic Arabic poetry, for this is the archive of the Arabs', Ibn Rashiq 1.30).

Pre-Islamic Arabic poetry is subject to an elaborate set of conventions with regard to both content and form. The basic building blocks are motifs (stock images, similes, metaphors) which the poet uses to compose larger thematic units. A short poem comprising only one such unit is called a *qiṭ'a* (literally 'a segment'), while a longer poem (25–120 lines) including many units is known as a *qaṣîda* (usually translated as 'ode'). At the beginning one must set the mood for the poem, 'enter through the door and place one's foot in the stirrup'. To a people so much on the move it was often deemed appropriate to open on a note of nostalgia, with mention of the deserted campsite, the scenery pertinent to it, the memories associated with it and the joys once experienced in it. Otherwise one might begin with love, whether painful recollections, eager anticipation or amorous allusions. More often than not the two would blend together, for reflections on a past abode inevitably evoked thoughts of the love that one had found there:

> Desolate are the encampments in Mina, places of but a
> week or month's stay; the wilderness has reclaimed Ghawl
>   and Rijam.
> Runnels of Rayyan, stripped of all trace, rubbed smooth
> like letterings long since scored on a stony slab.
> Sites whose tenant-time is long passed; years have gone by,
> each with its holy season and its months of freedom . . .
> I stopped to question them – yet how can we question
> dumb things and immovable? One cannot interpret their
>   speech.
> They are left bare, where once the whole clan was, but
>   departed one morning,
> abandoned now are their trenches and litter.
> Love-longing came over you for the women of that clan,
>   as they mounted their camels,
> sheltering under cotton awnings, on creaking howdahs,
> Each with its trappings, framework hidden by a folded rug
> overlaid with coverlet and tapestry,
> In a dense mass, like wild cows of Tudih riding there, or
>   the gazelles of Wajra as they bend graceful necks
> to their young.
>
>   (*Mu.*: Labid)

> How many singers before me! Are there yet songs unsung?
> do you, my sad soul, remember where was her dwelling
>   place?
> Tents in Jiwa, the fair wadi, will you speak to me of her?
> fair house of Abla, my true love, blessing and joy to thee!

Doubting I paused in the pastures, seeking her camel-
tracks, high on my swift-trotting she-camel, tall as a
citadel, weaving a dream of the past days, days when she
dwelt in them.

(Mu.: 'Antara)

Love might also constitute a major theme, then treating of courting,
flirtation and conquests, of unfulfilled passion and unrequited love, of
heart-enthralling beauty and soul-bewitching charms.

Many's the fair veiled lady, whose tent few would think of
   seeking, I've enjoyed sporting with at my leisure,
Slipping past packs of watchmen to reach her, with a whole
   tribe hankering after my blood,
   eager every jack-man to slay me.
At the time that the Pleiades showed themselves broadly
   in the heavens,
glittering like the folds of a woman's bejewelled scarf,
I came, and already she'd stripped off her garments for
   sleep
beside the tent-flap, all but a single flimsy slip.
She cried: 'God's oath, man, you won't get away with this!
I see that your errant ways have not yet left you.'
Out I brought her, and as she stepped she trailed behind us
to cover our footprints the skirt of an embroidered gown.
Then when we had crossed the camp-lines
and were hidden by a high-ridged undulating hollow,
I twisted her side-tresses to me, and she leaned over me;
slender-waisted she was, and tenderly plump her ankles,
Shapely and taut her belly, white-fleshed, slim; polished
the lie of her breast-bones, smooth as a burnished mirror.

(Mu.: Imru' al-Qays)

So gone is Umayma, gone, and leaves here a heart in pain:
my life was to yearn for her, and now its delight is fled.
She won me whenas, shamefaced – no maid to let fall her
   veil, no wanton to glance behind – she walked forth with
   steady tread.
Her eyes seek the ground, as though they looked for a
   thing lost there;
she turns not to left or right, her answer is brief and low.
She rises before day dawns to carry her supper forth

to wives who have need – dear alms when such gifts are few
  enough.
Afar from the voice of blame her tent stands for all to see,
when many a woman's tent is pitched in the place of
  scorn . . .
And slender is she where meet, and full where it so
  beseems, and tall,
straight, a fairy shape, if such upon earth there be.

(Muf. 20: Shanfara)

From a loved one or a campsite one inevitably one day will part, which
gives us a third topic, departure or travelling, which may serve simply
to lubricate the passage from one idea to another, or may, in the
account of the journey, constitute a major part of the poem.

Ah, but when grief assails me, straightaway I ride it off,
mounted on my swift lean-flanked camel, night and day
  racing.
Sure-footed, like the planks of a litter, I urge her on
down the bright highway, that back of a striped mantle.
She vies with the noble hot-paced she-camels, shank on
  shank, nimbly plying over a path many feet have beaten.

(Mu.: Tarafa)

The departure might then entail description, whether of the one left
behind or repaired to, of the riding animal, or of the scenery passed
on the way, or again this might form a topic in its own right.

She [my mare] is like an eagle, swift to seize her quarry,
in her nest are the hearts of her victims gathered.
Night long she stood on a way-mark, still, upright,
like an old woman whose children are all dead.
And at dawn she was there in the piercing cold,
the hoar-frost dropping from her feathers.
Then she spied on the moment a fox far off,
between him and her was a droughty desert.
Then she shook her feathers and stirred herself,
ready to rise and make her swoop.
He raised his tail and quailed as he saw her,
so behaves his kind when fright possesses them.
She rose, and swiftly towards him she sped,
gliding down, making for him her prey.

215

He creeps, as he spies her coming, on his belly;
his eyes show the whites as they turn towards her.
Then she swoops with him aloft, and casts him headlong,
and the prey beneath her is in pain and anguish.
She dashes him to earth with a violent shock,
and all his face is torn by the stones.
He shrieks, but her talons are in his side; no help!
with her beak she tears his breast.

('Abid 1)

She stood up displaying herself, between two curtains of a
    howdah of red wool, like the sun when it rises in Aries.
Or like a pearl in an oyster shell for which the diver,
overjoyed, praises god and prostrates himself
whenever he looks at it.
Or like a statue of marble raised [on a plinth]
built of baked brick, plastered, and of tile.
Her headscarf dropped unintentionally; she picked it up,
    shielding herself from us with her hand.

(Nabigha 107, depicting the king of Hira's wife)

The meatiest themes of a poem are eulogy (whether of oneself
or another) and satire (often abusive), and it is these which are most
revealing of the moral principles and cultural values of the pre-Islamic
Arabs. The former holds up as a model those who maintain and
defend the virtues most highly prized by society (collectively named
muruwwa) – generosity, courage, fidelity to covenant, loyalty to kin,
protection of the weak – while the latter exposes those who fail to live
up to them. In other words through these themes poetry contributed
to the enunciation and enforcement of social norms. Illustrative of
both genres is the very first poem of the famed Labid, who was charged
by his clan to avenge an insult proffered to them by the closest
confidant of Nu'man, king of Lakhm. He promised to compose a
satirical piece 'so biting that Nu'man would never again pay attention
to him' (Isfahani 15.364–65) and was brought before the monarch
just as he and his confidant were finishing dinner:

Must I shave my head every day for battle?
ah, but frequent warring is better than repose.
We, the four sons of Umm al-Banin,
are trenchant swords and bowls broad and full.

216

We are the best of the 'Amir ibn Sa'sa'a,
the strikers of skulls right through their helmets.
You provider of a filling meal, hold on –
may you be spared all evil – don't eat with him!
His anus is blotched with leprosy and he inserts his finger
up it all the way to the knuckle, as though trying to find
   something he lost.[5]

Two other popular themes, also very revealing of the ethical aspects
of Arabian society, are wisdom, whether admonition or observation,
and elegy. Poems of the latter type are particularly interesting in that
they were often composed by women, and indeed probably began as
rhymed chants intoned at funerals by 'female mourners carrying their
waving cloths' (Labid 11):

Who gathers not friends by giving aid in many a case of
need is torn by the blind beast's teeth, or trodden beneath
   its foot.
And he who his honour shields by the doing of kindly deed
grows richer; who shuts not the mouth of reviling, it lights
   on him.
And he who is lord of wealth and is niggardly with his
   hoard,
alone is he left by his kind; nought have they for him but
   blame.
Who keeps his word, no blame he earns; and that man
   whose heart is led to goodness unmixed with guile
   gains freedom and peace of soul . . .
Who will not yield to the spears when their feet turn to
him in peace, shall yield to the points thereof,
   and the long flashing blades of steel.
Who holds not his foe away from his cistern with sword
   and spear it is broken and spoiled;
   who uses not roughness, him men shall wrong.
Who seeks far away from kin for housing takes foe for
   friend;
who honours himself not well, no honour gains he from
   men . . .
If a man be old and a fool, his folly is past all cure; but a
   young man may yet grow wise and cast off his
   foolishness.

(*Mu.*: Zuhayr)

217

In the evening remembrance drives away sleep,
and I wake wearied by the weight of my woe,
My loss of Sakhr. And what young man could
match Sakhr in skilful warring and spear-sparring,
And in opposing the refractory transgressor,
championing the case of the oppressed.
His death, in my eyes, occasioned greater misfortune
than that of any man or jinn.
Truly strong was he against the vicissitudes of fate
and decisive in action, never afflicted by confusion;
Most generous in his labours, when hardship struck,
towards the needy, the neighbour and his wife.
Many was the night-guest and refuge-seeker,
their hearts afright at the least sound,
Whom he offered kindness and security,
freeing their mind of all care and distress.
No indeed, oh Sakhr, I shall never forget you until
my heart's blood dries up and my grave is cut.

(Khansa' 41, for her brother)

These thematic units could be of very different lengths and be combined in a variety of different ways. Though certain sequences are
more popular than others (most famously: nostalgic overture, journey,
eulogy), this did not become a defining feature of poems. And the
most important thing to note is that while the basic ingredients
were largely determined by convention, there was much latitude in
the manner of their blending. This amalgam of freedom and constraint
also characterises the formal aspects of pre-Islamic Arabic poetry, for
though there was a wide range of available metres and rhymes, once
chosen they could not be varied: a *qaṣīda* is a poem in monometre and
monorhyme.

A mood of heroic-cum-pessimistic resignation pervades this poetry.
Time/fate (*al-dahr*) worries and harries man throughout the all too
short passage to his death and the occasions of relief and repose are
but few and fleeting. This mood is well captured by one poet who,
developing the motif of the contemplation of the deserted campsite,
has the gravestones speak as follows:

He that sees us should tell himself
that he is about to be impaled on the horn of extinction.
Even hard mountains cannot outlast Time
nor withstand the depredations it inflicts.

Many riders have made their camels kneel around us,
drinking wine mixed with limpid water.
Their wine vessels had cloth strainers,
their thoroughbred horses were dressed in fine blankets.
They lived a good life for a time,
trusting restfully in their lot.
Then Fate turned against them in the same manner
that it destroys mountains.
Thus Fate fires at the man in quest of livelihood
circumstance after circumstance.

('Adi ibn Zayd 15)

The most obvious and most lamented sign of Time's ravaging effects on a person is the appearance of grey hairs, for they signal the end of adolescent pleasures: 'You think of youth and love, and yet how can you dally when grey hairs have already warned you' ('Abid 1). And they are 'a forerunner of One that comes later; when he knocks, no doorkeeper can bar his entrance' (*Muf.* 17). The only solution is stoic acceptance ('Indeed I know, and there is no averting it, that I am destined to be the sport of fate, and yet do you see me worry?', *Muf.* 9) and the adoption of a hedonistic attitude towards mortality:

If you cannot fend off my death,
then let me hasten towards it using up what money I've got.
But for three things that are the joy of a youth
I assure you I wouldn't care when my deathbed visitors arrive.
The first is to forestall my critics with a good swig
of crimson wine that foams when the water is mingled in.
Second, to dash to the call of one in trouble on a bow-legged
    steed,
streaking like the wolf disturbed at the waterhole.
And third, to while away the day of showers, an admirable
    season,
with a beautiful maid under the pole-propped tent . . .
So let me take my fill whilst I live, since I tremble
at the thought of the scant draught I'll get when I'm dead.
A noble man satiates himself in life, for you will know,
if we die tomorrow, which of us is thirsty.

(*Mu.*: Tarafa)

219

LITERATURE: PROSE

The tens of thousands of inscriptions bequeathed to us by the inhabitants of pre-Islamic Arabia divulge something of these peoples' private sentiments and public pronouncements, but they cannot really be called literature (with the exception of the two poems mentioned above). Of pre-Islamic Arabian creative expression in languages other than Arabic we are therefore totally ignorant. In the case of Arabic we do at least have the collections of both poetry and prose made by Muslim scholars. Prose was not, however, valued so highly as poetry and it was not subject to the preservative constraints of metre and rhyme, and so most of the material was recast as time went on into the idiom of later generations. Hence the most we can probably do is to identify the principal genres of pre-Islamic Arabic prose. In this we are to some degree aided by another resource, namely the Quran, which was revealed to the Prophet Muhammad in the course of his later life. It incorporates a number of different narrative styles which were presumably fairly recognisable to his audience (some portions they mistook for direct imitations of contemporary styles), and so can give us some clues as to the sort of Arabic prose material that was circulating before Islam.

Supernatural speech

When, after communion with the spirits, diviners gave their response to those who had sought them out, they did so in a highly stylised language, in rhymed prose of lofty style and cryptic diction. This distinctive style of divinatory speech was evidently employed to highlight the supernatural origin of the message, for the diviners were but the mouthpiece of a spirit. Often they would begin with a string of oaths, issued fast and hard like a drum roll, which formed the prelude to their verdict. It was a common practice to test prospective diviners by challenging them to identify a concealed object. Here is the reply of Salma al-'Udhri to such a challenge by two members of the tribe of Khuza'a, who are considering employing him to adjudicate in a contest of honour between them about who has the better horse (Ibn Habib, *Mun.* 110):

> I swear by the light and the moon (*aḥlifu bin-nûri wa-l-qamri*)
> by the lightning flash and by fate (*was-sana wad-dahri*)
> by the winds and the cleaving (*war-riyâḥi wa-l-faṭri*)
> You have hidden for me a vulture's corpse (*la-qad khaba'tum lî
> juththata nasri*)

in a bundle of hair (*fi 'ikmin min sha'ri*)
in the possession of the youth from the Banu Nasr
(*ma'a l-fatâ min banî Nasri*)

Having passed this test, the diviners would then proceed to give their answer to the question set before them. Here, for example, is the reply of a diviner of 'Usfan to two members of the tribe of Quraysh, who had asked which of them was the more noble (Ibn Habib, *Mun.* 108):

I swear by dust-coloured gazelles (*ḥalaftu bi-azbin 'ufri*)
in mirage-glinting deserts (*bi-lamma'ati qafri*)
roaming among thorn-trees and lote-trees (*yarudna bayna
silmin wa-sidri*)
The highest degree of glory and honour (*inna sana' al-majdi
thumma l-fakhri*)
is ever to be found in 'A'idh (*la-fî 'A'idh ilâ âkhiri d-dahri*)

Though the Quran vigorously asserts that it is 'not diviner's speech' (*lâ bi-qawli kâhin*), one can understand why Muhammad's contemporaries regarded it as such, since the same rhythmic drive is present, though the content has of course been adapted to the new message. Here is a particularly fine example (91.1–10):

By the sun and its midday brightness (*wash-shamsi wa-ḍuḥâ-hâ*)
By the moon which rises after it (*wa-l-qamari idhâ talâ-hâ*)
By the day which reveals its splendour (*wan-nahâri idhâ
jallâ-hâ*)
By the night which veils it (*wal-layli idhâ yaghshâ-hâ*)
By the heaven and Him that built it (*was-samâ'i wa-mâ banâ-hâ*)
By the earth and Him that spread it (*wa-l-arḍi wa-mâ ṭaḥâ-hâ*)
By a soul and Him that moulded it (*wa-nafsin wa-mâ sawwâ-hâ*)
And gave it knowledge of sin and piety (*fa-alhama-hâ fujûra-hâ
wa-taqwâ-hâ*)
Blessed shall be the man who has kept it pure (*qad aflaḥa man
zakkâ-hâ*)
And ruined he that has corrupted it (*wa-qad khâba man
dassâ-hâ*)

Like the characters of Greek and Latin histories, pre-Islamic heroes were made to utter speeches felt by the later Muslim historian to be appropriate to the event or subject being treated, deemed to be similar to what would have been uttered by such a figure on such an occasion.

These are usually long and fulsome, packed with rhetorical devices, whereas it may be that pre-Islamic Arabic oratory was, by contrast, not so different from the short staccato-like expression of the diviners. Here is one of God's first addresses to Muhammad (74.1–7):

> You, enveloped in your cloak (*yâ ayyuhâ l-muddaththir*)
> Arise and warn (*qum fa-andhir*)
> Magnify your Lord (*wa-rabbaka fa-kabbir*)
> Purify your attire (*wa-thiyâbaka fa-ṭahhir*)
> Shun pollution (*war-rujza fa-hjur*)
> Do not grant favours in expectation of gain
>   (*wa-lâ tamnun tastakthiru*)
> For your Lord's sake be patient (*wa-li-rabbika fa-ṣbir*)

This may be compared with the words of Hadrami ibn 'Amir, orator of the tribe of Asad, who represented them to the Prophet (Ibn al-Athir, *Usd* 2.29):

> We have come to you (*innâ ataynâka*) journeying through
> a black night (*nataḍarra' al-layla al-bahîma*)
> in a sterile white year (*fî sanatin shahbâ'*)
> of our own accord (*wa-lam tursil ilaynâ*)
> We are of your ilk (*wa-naḥnu minka*)
> united by [our common ancestor] Khuzayma (*tajma'unâ*
>   *Khuzayma*)
> Our sacred territories are well protected (*ḥimânâ manî'*)
> our women are virtuous (*wa-nisâ'unâ mawâjid*)
> our sons brave and noble (*wa-abnâ'unâ anjâd amjâd*)

Similar also are the sermons of the famed bishop of Najran, Quss ibn Sa'ida, of whom Muhammad is said to have memorised the following excerpt (Isfahani 14.40):

> Oh people, assemble (*ayyuhâ n-nâsu jtami'û*)
> listen and pay heed (*wa-sma'û wa-'û*)
> All who live die (*man 'âsha mât*)
> and all who die are lost (*wa-man mâta fât*)
> and everything that is coming will come
>   (*wa-kulla mâ huwa âtin ât*)

Legends

In the Quran it is mentioned a number of times how people came to listen to the preaching of Muhammad, but went away concluding that 'this is nothing but tales of the ancients' (*asâtîr al-awwalîn*). By this is meant the accounts of peoples of the past that are interspersed throughout the Holy Book. It would appear from the audience's reaction that these were well-known stories, and indeed all are either famous Biblical narratives (Noah and the Flood, Abraham the religious reformer, Moses and Pharaoh, Lot and licentiousness) or Arabian traditions that had already achieved, judging from the allusions to them in pre-Islamic Arabic poetry, legendary status. In the Quran all are constrained into one genre, the punishment story, and adduced as examples of how God vents his wrath upon those who fail to heed his warnings. The Arabian pieces are, however, relics of something very different, namely accounts of mythical origins. Genealogists divided Arab tribes into the extinct (*bâ'ida*) and the extant (*bâqiya*). The former, some seven or eight tribes, were the true Arabs, who spoke pure Arabic (*al-'arab al-'âriba*), but who had been wiped out or dispersed, whether by internecine strife (Tasm and Jasim), natural disasters ('Abil, Jurhum), oppressive foreign powers ('Amlak) or, as the Quran would have it, by divine intervention ('Ad and Thamud):

To the tribe of 'Ad we sent their compatriot Hud. He said: 'Serve Allah, my people, for you have no god but Him. Will you not be warned?' The unbelievers of the elders of his tribe said: 'We can see you are a foolish man, and what is more, we think that you are lying.' 'I am not foolish, my people,' he replied. 'I am sent forth by the Lord of Creation to make known to you His will and to give you honest counsel. . . .' They said: 'Would you have us serve Allah only and renounce the gods which our fathers worshipped? Bring down the scourge with which you threaten us if what you say be true.' . . . . We delivered Hud and all who were with him through Our mercy, and annihilated those that disbelieved Our revelations 'by a howling violent gale which We let loose on them for seven nights and eight long days. You might have seen them lying dead as though they had been hollow trunks of palm-trees.'

(7.65–72, '69.6')

And to Thamud We sent their compatriot Salih. He said: 'Serve Allah, my people, for you have no god but him. A veritable proof has come to you from your Lord. Here is Allah's she-camel, a sign for you. Leave her to graze at will in Allah's land and do not molest her lest you incur a woeful punishment. Remember that He has made you the heirs of 'Ad and provided you with dwellings in this land. You have built mansions on its plains and hewed out houses in its mountains. Remember Allah's favours and do not corrupt the earth with wickedness.' The haughty elders of his people said to the believers whom they oppressed: 'Do you really believe that Salih is sent forth from his Lord?' . . . They slaughtered the she-camel and defied the commandment of their Lord, saying to Salih: 'Bring down the scourge with which you threaten us if you truly are an apostle.' Thereupon an earthquake felled them, and when morning came they were prostrate in their dwellings, 'like the dry twigs of the sheep-fold builder'.

(7.73–78, '54.31')

Both tribes are familiar to pre-Islamic Arab poets, 'Ad a byword for antiquity ('ever since the time of 'Ad . . . ') and Thamud the supreme example of the transience of all things ('men that were of outstanding generosity and courage are now the company of the people of Thamud', *Ikh.* 87: Abu Zubayd al-Ta'i). But these early references to 'Ad, Thamud and the other extinct Arab tribes have been so cross-woven with and overlaid by later traditions that it is now difficult to say anything concrete about them beyond the fact that in the allusions to their wanderings and their confrontations we have echoes of a more mythic age.

Battle narratives

The Quran speaks of the 'days of God' (14.5), meaning the many confrontations between God and ungrateful peoples. And there is reference to the last of the 'days of God', namely the Day of Judgement, the final showdown between God and the unbelievers, which will be the 'day of victory' (32.29). The word could also be applied to conflict between believers in God and their enemies:

On the day of Hunayn you [the Muslims] set great store by your numbers, but they availed you nothing; the earth,

for all its vastness, seemed to close in on you and you turned
your backs and fled. Then God caused His tranquillity
to descend upon His apostle and the faithful. He sent to
your aid invisible warriors and sternly punished the unbelievers.

(9.25–26)

The sense of the term is patently 'battle-day' and it frequently crops
up in pre-Islamic poetry: 'We'll tell you of the days long and glorious
we rebelled against the king and would not serve him' (*Mu.*: 'Amr);
'Don't you know of those days when men were raided and plundered,
and every tribe was howling?' (*Mu.*: Harith); 'Our days are famous
amongst our foes, branded and blazed with glory like noble horses'
(*Ḥam.* 16: Samaw'al).

A considerable proportion of the vast Muslim literature on pre-
Islamic Arabian life is taken up with the wars that the Arab tribes
fought among themselves, known collectively as 'the days of the Arabs'
(*ayyām al-'arab*). Like all other forms of pre-Islamic Arabic prose we
know of these battle accounts only from later collections, in which
they have come to acquire a rather formulaic nature and sometimes to
have been multiplied and confounded with one another. But though
their worth for historical reconstruction may therefore be question-
able, they often have high literary value. The narrative style is usually
very accomplished, the language colourful and vivid, and above
all they are entertaining. Some recount raids, small-scale strikes
performed for the sake of seizing animals and winning prestige. Others
tell of wars waged for the sake of honour. The incidents that trigger
the latter type of conflict often appear trivial, as in the following
example:

The reason for this [particular battle-day] was that some
young men of [the tribes of] Quraysh and Banu Kinana were
feeling amatory when they espied a pretty graceful girl from
the [tribe of] Banu 'Amir. She was sitting at the market of
'Ukaz, wearing a single long gown, with nothing underneath,
and a veil. . . . The youths of Quraysh and Kinana came and
surrounded her, and they asked her to unveil. She refused,
then one of them took up position behind her. He worked
free one edge of her garment and fastened it above her waist
with a thorn without her knowing. So when she stood up her
bottom was exposed. The youths laughed and said: 'You
prevented us from seeing your front, but you granted us a

view of your rear.' She at once called out: 'oh people of 'Amir!', whereupon these stirred themselves and took up arms. Kinana did likewise and they fought a fierce battle and blood flowed between them. Then Harb ibn Umayya stepped in to mediate and he took upon himself the blood money of the people, and he gave Banu 'Amir satisfaction with respect to the insult of their kinswoman.

(Isfahani 22.55–56)

However, since honour was at stake, the matter was important, for the people are shamed that cannot defend their rights and safeguard their interests. In the above incident the question is protection of dependents, a fundamental duty of any tribesman and the root of many a feud. Thus the famous Basus vendetta, which set at odds the previously friendly northeast Arabian tribes of Taghlib and Bakr, was started when Kulayb ibn Rabi'a, chief of Taghlib, shot an arrow at the camel of a protégée of Bakr, thinking that its herder, his brother-in-law Jassas, had deliberately let it disturb his own camels. Jassas' aunt Basus, a companion of the protégée, 'tore the veil from her head, beating her face, and cried out, "oh shame, shame . . . this people for their guests have no care"'. Stung by this worst of imputations, Jassas slew Kulayb, sparking off forty years of strife and bloodshed between the two groups. Other provocations might be a dispute over access to grazing or water sources, burdensome taxation in a lean year or a sacred area violated. Or else it might be that a harmless raid led to a skirmish, blood flowed and a feud was unleashed. The renowned fighter Durayd ibn al-Simma, chief of Jusham, had led a successful foray against a clan of Ghatafan and carried off many camels, but their owners overtook them and in the ensuing skirmish Durayd's brother was killed. For this affront Durayd took stern vengeance, visiting each of the tribes of the Ghatafan confederation and slaying several of their men in requital.

It is also on the subject of warfare that south Arabian inscriptions, especially those from the second and third centuries AD, are most expansive and come close to being literary compositions. In the following text, for example, the narrative moves along chronologically and at a lively pace, allowing us to observe the evolution of the king of Saba's plan to effect a pincer movement. Furthermore the motivation of the two principal actors is explained and there is a subtle degree of characterisation: the wise king of Saba who outwits the aggressive king of Hadramawt who at the end is forced to 'retire in defeat, rout and disorder':

The king of Hadramawt and his forces campaigned in the Yathill district. . . . They marched against the Nashq–Nashshan district, but the militia of these two towns and the garrison posted by the king of Saba for their defence proved too much for them and fought them off. Thereupon the Sabaean king ordered his vassal Nasha'karib together with Sumyafaʿ of Bataʿ and an infantry column and cavalry from the Sabaean royal army to go to the relief of Nashq and Nashshan. When the king of Hadramawt got news of this relief force, he and all his troops retired from Nashq and Nashshan. Back at Yathill, a spy came to them with the information that the Sabaean king and the forces under his command were on the march against him from Marib, while Nasha'karib and Sumyafaʿ and the forces under their command were doing the same from Nashq and Nashshan. So the king of Hadramawt began to fear that he, in his position at Yathill, was being threatened by the combination of the two forces, and so he abandoned Yathill and retired to Hanan. There they were brought to a confrontation by the Sabaean king and the forces who had been summoned to join him at Marib. The king of Hadramawt and all his troops abandoned Hanan in defeat and rout, and withdrew to a strongpoint where they had established their supply depot.

(Ja 643, 643bis)

Wisdom narratives

In early Islamic times it became popular to put together collections of wise Arab sayings (*amthāl al-'arab*), in all of which a considerable number would be assigned a pre-Islamic Arabian origin. Many might seem to suit well such a context: 'fresh herbage and no camel', 'what could bring a mountain goat and an ostrich together' (said of two incompatible things), 'he is trickier than a hunted lizard', 'the one urinated on by foxes is indeed contemptible', 'he who is mightiest takes the spoil', 'like the ostrich who wanted horns and ended up with cut-off ears' (Abu 'Ubayd, nos. 581, 898, 1229, 319, 285, 796). But, as is inevitable with such a genre, fixing a time or place of emergence is impossible. The same is true for an equally popular genre, that of the last will and testament (*waṣiyya*), wry comments and advice about life uttered by famous figures at their deathbed to their progeny. All that one might note is that such material is already found in pre-Islamic Arabic poetry and that the concept of 'wisdom' (*ḥikma*) is

227

prominent in the Quran. In the latter, however, it is not astute observations on life that are offered, but ethical precepts: 'Do not behave as if your hand were tied to your throat [i.e. don't be miserly] nor stretch it out completely [i.e. don't be prodigal], for then you will either be reproached or be reduced to penury' (17.29); 'Do not pursue a matter of which you are ignorant' (17.36); 'Do not stride arrogantly over the earth, for you cannot cleave the earth nor can you rival the mountains in stature' (17.37). And it is as a dispenser of such wisdom that the ancient Arab hero Luqman, mentioned in pre-Islamic Arabic poems as a paragon of sagacity, is presented to us:

> We bestowed wisdom on Luqman saying: 'Give thanks to Allah'. . . . Luqman admonished his son. 'My son,' he said, 'serve no other god besides Allah, for idolatry is an abominable sin. . . . My son, Allah will bring all things to light, be they as small as a grain of mustard seed, be they hidden inside a rock or in heaven or earth. . . . My son, be steadfast in prayer, enjoin justice and forbid evil. Endure with fortitude whatever befalls you. That is a duty incumbent on all. Do not treat men with scorn, nor walk proudly on the earth; Allah does not love the arrogant or the vainglorious. Rather let your gait be modest and your voice low; the most disagreeable of voices is the braying of the ass.'
>
> (31.12–19)

9

ARABHOOD AND
ARABISATION

In his history of the pre-Islamic Arabs the Muslim scholar Asma'i (d. 213/828) transmits a speech by the Prophet Muhammad's grand-father 'Abd al-Muttalib delivered to the last Yemeni ruler Sayf ibn Dhi Yazan:

> 'Abd al-Muttalib entered into the presence of Sayf ibn Dhi Yazan, who was ringed by his princes and nobles and their offspring, had his drawn sword before him, and was perfumed with ambergris and musk from head to toe. 'Abd al-Muttalib then addressed him as follows: 'God has granted you a realm fine, firm and fair. . . . You are the head of the Arabs whom they will follow, their prop on whom they can rely, their stronghold in whom they can find refuge, and their spring who makes their land fertile. You have the most worthy ancestors and you are the best able to supply their place for us.'
>
> (52; cf. Wahb ibn Munabbih 306–308)

Though cast here as an Arab hero, Sayf in fact belonged to an ancient Hadramite family who would certainly not have considered themselves as Arabs (ancient south Arabian inscriptions draw a clear distinction between Arabs and native peoples of Yemen). But by Asma'i's day there existed a very clear conception of Arab identity and it was applied retrospectively to all the inhabitants of pre-Islamic Arabia. There is some awareness that they may not all have possessed the same racial origins, but none doubted that they had come to form a single ethnic (socio-cultural) community:

> Our reply [to the question of whether, 'in view of the difference in their ancestry', one can speak of a coherent grouping

229

called 'the Arabs'] is that the Arabs have come to constitute a unity assimilated to one norm in regard to their native soil, language, temperament, ambition, pride, zeal, manners and disposition, fused into a single body and all cast alike into a single mould. And the parts of that unity are so concordant and the constituent elements so harmonious that, whether one considers broad outline or detail, similarities or dissimilarities, the resultant entity is more integrated than are, in some cases, groups which have real genealogical affinity.

(Jahiz, *Atrâk* 11)

The author of this passage is writing in the early ninth century AD when the elaboration of Arab identity was well advanced and the Arabisation of Arabia was complete. In this chapter we will try to elucidate the earlier stages of these processes.

THE FIRST MILLENNIUM BC

Biblical and Assyrian texts of the ninth to fifth centuries BC are best acquainted with the Arab tribes in the Syrian desert between Palmyra and Duma, but they are aware that there were Arab tribes beyond these parts. The territory of Nabayoth, for example, is known to the Assyrians, but it is outside their sphere of influence (hence King Uaite of Qedar flees there to escape Assyrian retribution) and seemed to them particularly remote: 'a far-away desert where there are no wild animals and where not even the birds build their nests' (AR 2.823). Since Arabs also feature in one very early inscription of south Arabia, most probably of the seventh/sixth century BC (RES 3945), we can assume that they ranged as far as the borders of that country. The Arab homeland was therefore north and central Arabia (the area treated in chapter 3 above). It extended from the edges of the Fertile Crescent southwards to the borders of Yemen, from the west Arabian mountains eastwards to the Dahna and Rub' al-Khali deserts (east of which lay the coastlands of the Gulf, a separate cultural region).

What linked the Arabs together and distinguished them from other peoples was their language.[1] Most spoke one of a number of north Arabian dialects, as is attested by the approximately forty thousand graffiti found all over their homeland (see chapter 8 above). These are very closely related, to the point that they would have been to a considerable degree mutually intelligible, so facilitating interaction between the various tribes. There were also many social and religious practices and institutions shared by various Arab tribes (see chapters 4 to 7 above), but none were so pervasive nor so unifying as the language. Many tribes, for example, were animal herders, yet a good number practised agriculture, especially in the oasis towns of northwest Arabia and the highlands of Najd. The god Ruda was very popular in the north but ignored in the south, whereas Yaghuth was worshipped in the south but little appreciated in the north. And while the Arabs in the north felt the pull of the empires of the Mediterranean and Mesopotamian worlds, those in the south were influenced by the polities of Yemen (Pl. 36).[2]

THE FIRST AND SECOND CENTURIES AD

In this period a number of Arab groups in the south of Arabia (roughly the area between modern Riyad and Najran) began to migrate from their homeland. Literary and epigraphic evidence indicates that they went to the north (Syrian desert), to the east (Bahrain/Oman) and to the south (Yemen). Why they went is unclear, but it is probably connected with upheavals in the kingdoms of Yemen. By the end of the first century BC the Minaeans had ceased to exist as a political power and the Sabaeans had been weakened so severely that they were forced to form a coalition with the Himyarites (see chapter 2 above). Muslim histories of pre-Islamic Arabia begin with this dispersal of tribes from the south of Arabia to its far corners and offer various reasons for its occurrence. Sometimes they propose a Malthusian explanation, namely population growth placing a strain on limited resources and so necessitating the departure of a part of the population to seek out new pastures:

> When the progeny of Ma'add and the Arab tribes multiplied and filled their land in the Tihama and adjoining areas, they were dispersed by wars that occurred among them and evils that befell them. They therefore moved out in quest of space and fertile land into the neighbouring regions of Yemen and the Syrian marches.
>
> (Tabari 1.745)

More commonly a specific event is adduced as cause, namely a breaching of the dam of Marib, which ushered in a period of instability and want. 'The water overwhelmed the lands, gardens, edifices and

Plate 36 Alabaster funerary stele showing the deceased engaged in a feast
(top) and camel raiding (bottom) with Sabaic inscription: 'image and
monument (ṣwr w-nfs) of 'Igl ibn Sa'dallat of Qaryat; may 'Athtar Shariqan
strike down whoever destroys it'. Note that though the name is Arab
(most probably from Qaryat al-Faw), the deity invoked is south Arabian;
c.1st–3rd century AD, 55 × 29 cm (P. & M. Chuzeville, Louvre AO1029).

homes until the inhabitants of the country had perished and its
citizens been wiped out' (Mas'udi 3.371).

Besides the explicit reports of the Muslim sources, the principal
evidence for the migrations of some southern Arab groups is the
occurrence of Arab tribal names in places where they had not
previously been attested. For example Muslim historians relate that

'a number of Arab tribes [who had left Yemen] gathered in Bahrain; they became allies known as Tanukh . . . and pledged themselves to assist and support one another under the joint name of Tanukh' (Tabari 1.746). This receives confirmation from the *Geography* of Ptolemy, written *c*.AD 150, which places Tanukh in the region of Bahrain, whereas Pliny's *Natural history*, completed in AD 77, does not know of them there (see chapter 1 above). And in the Yemeni inscriptions of about the second century AD a host of new tribal names appears, such as Murad, Madhhij, Kinda and Sufl (see chapter 2 above). That these are Arab tribes (and not Sabaean, Himyarite etc.) is clear from a number of terms applied to them which are previously unattested and are evidently taken from Arabic, such as tribe/'*ashîra*, clan or lineage/*âl*, nomads/*a'râb*. Moreover the Arabic definite article *al* is used in certain personal and tribal names; thus we read of a king named *al*-Harith ibn Ka'b (CIAS 2.33) and of 'the land of *al*-Azd' (Ja 635). Evidently a number of these southern Arab tribes spoke Arabic, as indeed is asserted by all Muslim historians, who call them 'the Arabic-speaking Arabs' (*al-'arab al-'âriba*). It is also suggested by the existence in this region of Sabaic graffiti with Arabic features and by the Arabic funerary inscription of 'Igl ibn Haf'am discovered at Qaryat al-Faw (see chapter 8 above).

It seems likely that what we have in the Muslim accounts of the dispersal of the Arab tribes is the remains of a *Volksepos*, the collective memory of an epic journey undertaken by groups which began their trek as motley bands and finished it as united peoples. The surviving accounts certainly display many of the hallmarks of such literature, such as the focus on specific persons and events rather than on environment and processes and the predilection for supernatural signs. Thus the whole venture begins when 'Amr ibn 'Amir, chief of the Azd, or his wife, foresees in a dream that Marib will be engulfed by a flood, which prompts them to sell up and move out with as many of their tribe as will join them. Then there are the hardships of the journey, for they are such a multitude that 'his clan and those with him did not come to a water source without draining it nor enter a land without making it barren' (Asma'i 82). They settled first on the coastal plain of Tihama, but it did not suit them, so they headed northwards to the Hijaz. Once there 'every clan went its own way, some occupying the mountains of northwest Arabia, some staying behind in the environs of Mecca, some leaving for Iraq and some proceeding to Oman' (Asma'i 85). And in each case there would be confrontation with local tribes, battles that each group could remember and embellish with pride.

THE THIRD CENTURY AD

In order to pursue his war against the Parthians, the emperor Marcus Aurelius (AD 161–80) moved troops from the Rhone and Danube eastward. He did not take many – probably only three legions and those from widely separated regions – but it was enough. During the Parthian war various Germanic tribes, notably the Marcomanni, crossed the Danube and began to devastate the rich agricultural lands beyond it. In 166 they were repelled, but in 170 they reached Italy itself before being defeated. Rome's drive to the east in the first two centuries AD meant that its military resources were now barely sufficient to meet the needs of east and west, and this situation was worsened by the accession to power in AD 224 of the Sasanians, an Iranian dynasty with expansionist designs. Its second ruler, Shapur (242–73), led a series of devastating campaigns into Roman territory, culminating in the capture of the emperor Valerian in 259. To deal with these new challenges the provincial armies were expanded and their pay raised, leading to increasing militarisation of the empire and particularly of the provinces. The demand for troops was met chiefly by filling the ranks with peoples from outside the empire, leading to increasing barbarisation of the empire and again particularly of the provinces.[3]

In the east the Romans and Iranians had relied on client states (Nabataeans, Palmyrenes, Hatrans, Characenes etc.) to look after the frontier regions for them. By the second half of the third century, however, both powers had incorporated these clients within their respective domains and now had to deal directly with the nomads on their borders. It is at this point that the various tribes who had migrated from southern Arabia began to enter into relations with the two great empires:

> The southern tribes were compelled to leave their homes and dispersed in the land. Quda'a . . . were the first to settle in Syria. They allied themselves with the emperors of the Romans, who made them kings, after they had become Christians, over the Arabs who had gathered in Syria.
>
> (Mas'udi 3.214–15)

> These Arabs of Bahrain looked towards the land of Iraq; they were desirous of overpowering the non-Arabs in order to seize the area adjoining Arabia or to share it with them. Taking advantage of the discord among the [Parthian] princes, the

Arab chiefs resolved to march to Iraq. . . . Many of Tanukh settled at Anbar and Hira. . . . The first ruler from among them was Malik ibn Fahm . . . then his brother 'Amr ibn Fahm . . . then Jadhima al-Abrash.

(Tabari 1.747–49)

Jadhima himself features as 'king of Tanukh' in the epitaph of his tutor, recorded on a bilingual Greek–Nabataean inscription from Umm al-Jimal (PAES 4A.41). His nephew, 'Amr ibn 'Adi of the tribe of Lakhm, appears in a bilingual Persian–Parthian inscription (Paikuli 92) listing the vassals of the Sasanian emperor Narseh (293–302) as "Amru king of the Lakhmids (*'Amrw lhm'dyn mlk'*)'. This sits nicely in time with the fact that 'Amr's son Imru' al-Qays, 'governor . . . over the frontier region of the land of the Arabs' (Tabari 1.833–34), is stated in his epitaph to have died in AD 328. Finally a south Arabian inscription of the late third century mentions the dispatch by the Himyarite ruler Shammar Yuhar'ish of delegations to the Sasanian capitals in Iraq to 'the land of Tanukh' and to the 'king' of the tribe of al-Azd (Sharaf 31).[4]

The arrival of these new peoples is also reflected in the change in the way imperial citizens referred to the inhabitants of Arabia. Classical authors had employed the generic terms 'Arabs' and 'tent-dwellers', but now that the old client states had gone, subjects of Rome and Iran who lived on the borders of the Syrian desert came to have direct knowledge of tribes and began to use instead the names of those closest to them. In the former Nabataean lands the most conspicuous were the Saracens,[5] who are registered in the *Geography* of the second-century writer Ptolemy (6.7) as a tribe of the northern Hijaz–Sinai area. The inhabitants of upper Mesopotamia had dealings first with Tayyi' (rendered Tayyaye in the local Aramaic dialect of Syriac), an Arab tribe that had joined the migrations from south Arabia and settled in central and northeast Arabia. Both terms begin to feature in the writings of sedentary peoples in the third century when, for example, we find one author using the expression 'the region of the Tayyaye and Saracens' (Bardaisan 50). By the fourth century their names have become generic terms for Arabs (Saracens used by the Romans,[6] Tayyaye by Syriac-speaking Christians), even though they were subsequently eclipsed by other tribes (the Saracens so completely that they were no longer remembered by Muslim genealogists).

By their own account the tribes who participated in the exodus from south Arabia displaced a number of native groups:

They did not enter a land without robbing its people of it. Khuza'a wrested Mecca from Jurhum; Aws and Khazraj wrested Medina from the Jews; the clan of Mundhir seized Iraq from its people; the clan of Jafna seized Syria from its people and ruled it; and the progeny of 'Imran ibn 'Amr ibn 'Amir [of al-Azd] seized Oman from its people. Up till then all of these [southern tribes] had been in obedience to the kings of Himyar.

(Asma'i 88)

Though there is probably much self-glorification in this claim, it is plausible that large-scale migrations would have entailed many disputes, relocations and assimilations. This may in part explain the cessation of ancient north Arabian inscriptions at about this time, as older tribal groups were subsumed within new ones or were ousted from their traditional haunts, and new dialects emerged. Since, as noted above, many of the southern Arab tribes spoke Arabic, this language grew in popularity. As Muslim scholars would later put it, the original northern Arabs became 'Arabicised Arabs' (*'arab muta'arriba*). In the area of the Saracens, for example, texts often contain Arabisms (e.g. use of the Arabic passive participle *madhkûr* rather than the Aramaic *dkîr*; CIS 2.1331, 2662, 2768).[7] And from Hegra we have an epitaph of AD 267 that has been described as 'the earliest dated Arabic document', though it still has Aramaic features. Then in the fourth century we encounter our first purely Arabic inscription in north Arabia, an epitaph for the aforementioned Imru' al-Qays, who considered himself to be 'king of all the Arabs' (see chapter 3 above).

THE FOURTH TO SIXTH
CENTURIES AD

There had always been two aspects to the term Arab. From Assyrian times onwards we hear not just of nomad Arabs, but also of settled Arabs, those who had chosen to make a life for themselves within the borders of civilisation rather than outside them. Probably most became fully assimilated to the prevailing culture, but there are occasional hints that some still thought of themselves as Arabs. There is, for example, the diviner (*oiônoskopos*) Rufinus, a native of Canatha in the Hawran, but subsequently resident on the Greek island of Thasos, who wrote an epitaph in Greek for his son in the third century AD and

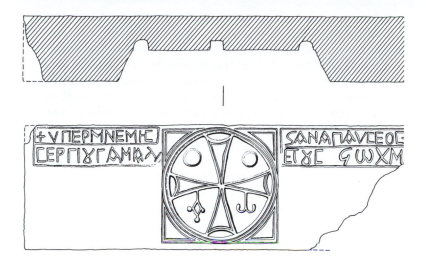

Fig. 8 Inscription from the tomb of 'Sergius Jammal' found by the author at Hamdaniyya, near Andarin, Syria, 'of the year 890', AD 572/3 (David Hopkins).

who specifies that he is an Arab (*araps*). What exactly he meant by this is not clear, but he may have been thinking of enhancing his professional reputation, since the Arabs had long been renowned for their skill in the science of augury.[8] And in the inscriptions of the fourth–sixth centuries AD from the outlying provinces of the Roman empire (the Negev, Transjordan, the Hawran and Syria) there is a very high proportion of distinctively Arab names (e.g. Fig. 8). Increased spending in these areas on soldiers' pay and military installations meant that there was a greater demand there for goods and services and this gave rise to an economic boom in the fourth to sixth centuries. Places like Umm al-Jimal (southwest of Bosra) and Andarin (northeast of Emesa), which had begun their life as quiet fortified outposts protecting trade routes, became thriving towns, boasting fine houses, baths, taverns, churches and a galaxy of satellite villages. Arabs, whether from near or afar, were attracted by this rise in prosperity and the strong demand for labour. It is also possible that they were settled, or encouraged to do so, by the government in areas depopulated by war or plague, a very common practice of the Roman and Iranian empires. Once settled, these Arabs adopted in some measure the imperial culture, and this is most obvious in their conversion to Christianity, which facilitated their integration with the urban population:

Aspebetos, though a pagan and a Persian subject, became an ally of the Romans [by converting after having had his son healed by the monk Euthymius]. . . . On hearing that the great Euthymius [d. 473] had eventually returned, he came to him with a great number of Saracens, men, women and children, and begged him to preach to them the word of salvation. The holy elder catechised them all and received them into the lower monastery where he baptised them. After remaining with them for the whole week, he then ascended with them to his own cave. Aspebetos brought along skilled workmen and constructed a great cistern . . . and nearby he built a bakehouse. . . . Moreover these people who had previously been wolves of Arabia but had then joined the spiritual flock of Christ begged to remain near him. . . . Taking them to an appropriate spot he said to them: 'If you want to be very near me, settle here'. . . . Marking out [the site of] a church for them and tents round it, he told them to build the church and settle there. He frequently made visits to them and assigned them a priest and deacons. Those who had already been baptised came and settled there, and others too who arrived gradually were baptised by him. Since in consequence they became extremely numerous and spread out to form various encampments, our great father Euthymius wrote to Juvenal, patriarch of Jerusalem, requesting the ordination of a bishop and, when he consented, sent him Aspebetos as most capable of drawing souls to salvation. So it was that Aspebetos [now named Peter] was the first to be ordained in Palestine bishop of the encampments.

(Cyril of Scythopolis 18.24–25)

The literary sources for this period, however, are much more interested in the nomadic Arabs, for at this time these were serving in the armies of Rome and Iran in ever greater numbers. Imperial foreign policy had constantly sought to bring the leadership of tribes along the frontiers under imperial influence by bribing them with citizenship, gifts and military and economic support in order to use them to keep their own members pacific and as buffers against other tribes. Treaties were established with these groups, providing their chiefs with gold and titles and the masses with grain. In the fourth century this practice grew enormously, as can be seen very clearly in the Roman sphere where army units recruited from throughout the empire carried the names of barbarian peoples. A document of c.AD 400, for example, lists Saracen cavalry units at locations in Egypt, Phoenicia and Palestine (*Notitia dignitatum* Or. 28.17, 32.27–28, 34.22). And we often read accounts of the likes of 'Atfar the Saracen king', who 'was a warlike and able man, and who had had much experience in the use of Roman arms, and who in various places had won distinction and renown in battle' (Zacharias 9.2). The Iranians employed principally the Nasrid clan of the Lakhm tribe and delegated them to make arrangements with other tribes themselves. The Romans, however, who had a much greater share of Arabia, made use of a number of different clans, which they assigned to specific provinces. Thus, when an Arab vassal of Iran killed one of the Arab leaders loyal to the Romans, the emperor Justinian (527–65) 'wrote to the commanders of Phoenicia, Arabia and Mesopotamia and to the tribal chiefs of the provinces [named as Arethas, Gnouphas and Naaman] to go after him and pursue him and his army' (Malalas 18.16). And when Abikarib, chief of an Arab tribe in the Hijaz, made Justinian a present of some palm groves, 'he was appointed by the emperor chief over the Saracens in Palestine' (Procopius 1.19.7–11).

The continual hostilities between Rome and Iran meant that both needed manpower and also wished to rally effective tribes to their side rather than let them join the enemy. This can be observed in the following account of how Ghassan, another tribe that originally hailed from southern Arabia, entered Syria in the reign of Anastasius (491–518):

> [The tribe of] Salih would tax those of Mudar and other Arab tribes who settled in their territory on behalf of the Byzantines. Ghassan approached in a great multitude heading for Syria and then settled in it. Salih said to them: 'If you agree to pay the tax you can stay, if not we will fight you.' Ghassan refused and so Salih fought and defeated them. . . . The chief of Ghassan at that time was Tha'laba ibn 'Amr. . . . Then Ghassan accepted to pay the tax to them. They would tax them one, one and a half or two dinars per head annually according to their rank. They continued to tax them until Jidh' ibn 'Amr of Ghassan killed the tax-collector of Salih. . . . Then Salih called one another to arms, as did Ghassan, and they engaged at a place called Muhaffaf, and Ghassan destroyed them. The king of the Byzantines feared that they would side with Iran against him, so he sent to Tha'laba saying: 'You are a very courageous and numerous people and you have destroyed this tribe who were the most

vigorous and numerous of the Arabs. I now appoint you in
their place and shall write an agreement between us and you:
if a raiding party of Arabs raid you I will support you with
40,000 armed Roman soldiers, and if a raiding party of Arabs
raid us then you must provide 20,000 soldiers, and you must
not interfere between us and the Iranians.'

(Ibn Habib, *Muḥ* 370–71; cf. Ya'qubi 233, 235)

Like their fellow Arabs who were settled in the countryside, these
tribes who served in the military were affected by their contact with
the imperial powers. Again most converted to Christianity and some
took an active interest in its promotion. Moreover the desire for the
material culture of Rome and Iran, which could be acquired only
by trade or by warfare, transformed the range of activity and extent
of interaction among Arab peoples. As tribes were drawn into the
imperial commercial network, their leaders were necessarily drawn
into political relationships with the empires, a result specifically
sought by imperial officials. From their perspective it was highly
desirable to have Arab tribes led by chiefs who could negotiate on
behalf of their tribes binding treaties with the empire and whose
personal loyalty could be maintained by gifts, as also it was desirable
to have these tribes dependent on imperial merchandise. Thus imperial
policy aimed at the stabilisation, in their terms, of barbarian political
structures and the development of barbarian economies in order to
secure markets for their goods. However, the net result of this imperial
policy was to destabilise Arab society, to accentuate social and
economic differentiation within Arab tribes, and to form within these
peoples pro- and anti-imperial factions that often led to the splintering
of old tribal units and the formation of new groupings. Since Rome
and Iran were in competition with each other, they encouraged their
Arab allies to win over to their side as many tribes as they could. For
example 'the emperor Justinian put Harith ibn Jabala in command of
as many clans as possible' (Procopius 1.17), and the emperor Khosro
appointed Mundhir ibn Nu'man 'over the lands extending from
Oman, Bahrain and Yamama to Ta'if and the rest of the Hijaz and all
the Arabs of the intervening lands' (Tabari 1.958). And this led to the
emergence of ever larger confederations (Mudar, Rabi'a etc.). Imru'
al-Qays was perhaps rather precipitate in styling himself 'king of all
the Arabs' already in the fourth century, but his boast was a harbinger
of things to come.

The emergence of these Arab dynasties had its roots in military
leadership. Clans such as the Nasrids and Jafnids, who were vassals of

Iran and Rome respectively, possessed no inherent authority to impose their will on other tribal groups. But success in war gave them prestige and the means to find resources beyond those of pastoralism, in particular the exaction of tribute and protection money. And if, as in the above quotation, they could by their prowess attract the attention of states, they might also win substantial subsidies. With this revenue these dynasties would try to do two things. The first was to transform their military force from one based on kinsmen and allied tribes, who were, however, autonomous and might or might not remain loyal to them, to a professional paid army of townspeople, slaves, and others over whom they could exercise effective control. Thus it was known that 'Ghassan is a tribe whose strength lies in other folk [i.e. not their own tribesmen]; both lightly armed men and squadrons of cavalry fight on their behalf' (*Muf.* 41). And indeed Mundhir ibn Harith (a Jafnid chief) wrote to the emperor Justin (565–78) requesting 'that he send him gold so that he might hire troops' (John of Ephesus 6.3).

The second objective of these dynasties when spending their income was to imitate their imperial masters in patronising culture. To this end they would erect buildings and import all manner of artists to their luxurious courts:

> I [an observer at the Jafnid court] have seen ten singing-girls, five of them Byzantines, singing Greek songs to the music of lutes, and five from Hira who had been presented to [the Jafnid] king Jabala by [the chief of Tayyi'] Iyas ibn Qabisa [602–11], chanting Babylonian melodies. Arab singers used to come from Mecca and elsewhere for his delight. And when he would drink wine he sat on a couch of myrtle and jasmine and all sorts of sweet-smelling flowers, surrounded by gold and silver vessels full of ambergris and musk. During winter aloes-wood was burned in his apartments while in summer he cooled himself with snow. Both he and his courtiers wore only light, single garments in the hot weather and fenek fur or the like in the cold season. And by God I was never in his company but he gave me the robe which he was wearing on that day, and many of his friends were thus honoured. He treated the rude with forbearance; he laughed without reserve and lavished his gifts before they were sought.
>
> (Isfahani 17.166–67)

In particular these Arab chiefdoms promoted Arabic language and poetry. They chose to pen their correspondence in Arabic, making use of the Nabataean alphabet, which over time became transformed into what would subsequently be called the Arabic script (see chapter 8 above). The documents of these Arab polities have all perished except for a handful of inscriptions and so we cannot now trace this development, but we can witness its final stages in three texts from the sixth century engraved on stone in pretty much standard Arabic letters. The customary practice for newcomers in this part of the world was to write at least their official texts in the local language of prestige, whether Greek or Aramaic. The decision of these Arab principalities to write in their own native tongue was therefore new and must have been a deliberate choice. It suggests that they had a sense of the worth of their own language and a strong attachment to it and that it was intimately bound up with their identity and self-perception.

Pre-Islamic Arabic documents might be rare, but pre-Islamic Arabic poetry is abundant, for these Arab dynasties sponsored poetry with gusto and each had its own panegyricist. According to one Muslim literary critic 'the early Arabs had no poetry other than a few lines which someone composed on certain occasions; lengthy epic poems were first recited in the time of 'Abd al-Muttalib and Hashim ibn 'Abd Manaf', that is, in the early sixth century (Ibn Sallam 1.26). Simple poetry had long existed (perhaps the light short style of verse known as *rajaz*), and indeed a victory of the Saracen queen Mawia in the 370s was 'celebrated in songs (ôdai) by the Saracens' (Sozomen 6.38). But all Muslim scholars agreed that complex poems (*qaṣīdas*) were 'newly born and of a tender age' (Jahiz, Ḥay. 1.74) and that this new form had been born around AD 500. This nicely coincides with the rise of more powerful client kingdoms such as the Jafnids and Nasrids, and it seems reasonable to conclude that it was their patronage that had helped to bring about this development.

This new poetry was extremely important in promoting a sense of Arab identity. Firstly it gave life and currency to an ideal of Arabian virtue (*muruwwa*), for generosity to the needy, courage in battle, fidelity to covenant and loyalty to kin are championed and advocated in almost every poem. Though based on tribal groups and insisting that only ties of blood were sacred, this ideal nevertheless became an invisible bond between diverse clans and laid the foundations, whether consciously or not, for a wider moral community. Secondly the distinctive Arabic diction in which this poetry was drafted transcended dialects and united those who understood it in a broad linguistic community. Lastly it served as a tool of collective memory, for 'every nation relies on one means or another to preserve and protect its glorious deeds, and the Arabs strove to immortalise theirs by means of poetry, which constituted their public archive' (Jahiz, Ḥay. 1.72). And indeed innumerable mighty battles and great events of Arab tribal history are recorded in the surviving corpus of pre-Islamic Arabic poetry. But though appreciable to a sedentary Arab audience, it was to nomadic Arabs that it was principally addressed, as is clear from the air of nostalgia for the abodes now deserted and the theme of constant travelling that so thoroughly pervade it.

THE SEVENTH AND EIGHTH CENTURIES AD

Islam was born among town-dwellers and started out with a town-dweller's stereotyped image of nomads as unreliable and deceitful. 'The nomads (al-a'râb) who stayed behind [and did not participate in the holy war] will say to you: "We were occupied with our goods and families, so ask pardon for us." They will say with their tongues what they do not mean in their hearts' (Quran 48.11). In early Islamic literature nomadic Arabs are often represented as uncouth, given over to hypocrisy and covert sensuality, and addicted to pagan practices. For this reason they should not act as prayer leaders, marry settled Muslim women or give testimony against a sedentary. All this was soon to change, however, and they would become characterised as 'the root of the Arabs and a reinforcement for Islam' (aṣl al-'arab wa-mâddat al-islâm).[9]

One reason for this rehabilitation of the nomad is that the Muslim town-dwellers, who were the mainstay of Islam, were strong on religion but short on identity. Muhammad evidently thought of his faith as being open to all: 'We have sent you as a messenger to mankind' (Quran 4.79); 'Say [o Muhammad], I am the messenger of God to you all' (7.158), 'We have only sent you as a herald and warner to all mankind' (34.28). Consequently the Quran makes no attempt to identify the early Muslim community along national lines. Yet the Muslims were entering a land of very ancient peoples with venerable traditions, and they needed to make some reply when questioned about their own particular history and their defining characteristics. As regards history they took up an idea that had circulated at least since the time of the Jewish historian Josephus (d. c.AD 110), that the Arabs were descendants of Ishmael (Ant. 1.214, 221). With it they fashioned a religious pedigree for themselves, narrating how Ishmael and his father Abraham had gone to Mecca together and founded the original Muslim sanctuary. As regards characteristics they turned to the nomadic Arabs, who were short on religion but strong on identity, and so it was nomadic culture that came to form the core of Arab identity in Islamic times. This can be seen in the vast number of anecdotes that aim to set out the nature and customs of the Arabs:

> An Arab skilled in oratory was sent to [the Persian emperor] Khosro who asked him about the Arabs, why they lived in the desert and chose the nomadic life. The Arab replied: 'O king, they are masters of their land rather than mastered by it, and they have no need for fortification walls, since they can rely on trenchant blades and pointed lances for their protection and defence.' . . . 'And what is the Arabs' main sustenance?' 'Meat, milk, date-wine and dates.' 'And what are their qualities?' 'Might, honour, magnanimity, extending hospitality to the guest, providing security to the client, granting refuge to the weak, repaying favours and dispensing generosity. They are travellers of the night, masters of the stealth attack, denizens of the desert, the good hosts of the wilderness. They are accustomed to temperance and averse to subservience; they practise vengeance, disdain ignominy, and preserve their honour.'
>
> (Mas'udi 3.248–49)

Though this left them open to such taunts as that 'the Arabs never had a king who could unite them . . . they achieved nothing at all in art and technology and made no mark in philosophy' (Ibn 'Abd Rabbihi 3.353), these could easily be silenced by reference to their military achievements:

> [Asma'i at the court of the caliph Harun al-Rashid]: al-Rashid asked me if I knew the poem of 'Adi ibn Riqa' with the line 'he knew the dwellings instinctively and visited them repeatedly'. I replied 'yes' and he said 'go ahead then.' So I started reciting it until I got to where he describes his camel, when Fadl ibn Yahya al-Barmaki [an Iranian courtier] exclaimed: 'I beseech you by God not to interrupt our enjoyment of this nightly gathering of ours by describing a scabby camel!' 'Shut up!' said al-Rashid. 'It is the camels who have driven you from your home and power, taking away the crown of your kingship.'
>
> (Marzubani 130)

A second reason for the rehabilitation of the nomadic Arabs is that they came to be regarded by scholars as a crucial source for the Islamic sciences. The wealth accumulated by the early Muslims in taxes and plunder meant that their new cities attracted peoples of diverse origin, creed and status, who hoped to win a share in these riches by offering their services to the new rulers. Moreover the latter's 'robber bands went annually to distant parts and to the islands, bringing back captives from all the peoples under the heavens' to the new cities (John bar Penkaye 147). And these melting pots were stirred by the wide-spread phenomena of conversion and apostasy, of inter-confessional marriage and festival attendance, of commercial contacts and public debate. Inevitably all this upheaval led to rapid and substantial transformation of the early Islamic world within two or three generations after the death of the Prophet Muhammad. This posed a problem for scholars of later times who sought to understand the Quran and its language, to compose laws in conformity with the precepts of Muhammad's community, and to write the history of the birth of their religion. However, there were nomadic Arabs who had chosen not to participate in the conquests or else had subsequently returned to their camps rather than settle in the new garrison cities. They had therefore lived outside the maelstrom and were well known to preserve the traditions of their tribes, and it was not long before the idea suggested itself of consulting them on these matters.

The first to have practised this systematically was probably Abu 'Amr ibn al-'Ala' (d. 154/770), who promoted Quranic and gram-matical studies at Basra. Allegedly he would dispatch his students to nomad informants to resolve a point of grammar, to ask about 'the speech of the nomadic Arabs' (*kalâm al-'arab*), and would himself take notes when in conversation with nomads, especially elderly sheikhs who had been alive before Islam (Suyuti 278, 304, 321).[10] Many of his disciples adopted this method. Thus 'Abd al-Malik al-Asma'i (d. 213/828), one of his last protégés, begins the preface to his history of the Arabs before Islam, commissioned by the celebrated caliph Harun al-Rashid, as follows:

> You commanded . . . that I collect what has reached me of the reports of ancient Arab kings. . . . I perceived that the full accomplishment of this would be arduous owing to the paucity of what had come to me and that its adequate execution would be difficult because of the discontinuity of their reports and the effacement of many of their traditions. I therefore travelled widely among the tribes, seeking out

transmitters of reports and keepers of the histories of bygone ages, interrogating all the genealogists whom I befriended and learning the traditions conveyed to me by old men about their forefathers. In the end I had collected therefrom this meagre measure in compliance with your august command.

Another student of Abu 'Amr (and more particularly of Khalil ibn Ahmad and Yunus ibn Habib, themselves also students of Abu 'Amr) was Sibawayh (d. 180/796), author of the first Arabic grammar, who can be clearly seen to adhere to his master's tradition. His grammar contains a description and analysis of the Arabic language, as well as some linguistic theorising. It is based on three main sources: the Quran, ancient Arabic poetry and the ordinary speech of the nomadic Arabs (al-'arab). In Sibawayah's view many of the last, in contrast to the urban population of Iraq, still spoke dialects close to how Arabic was before Islam and, unlike the Quran or ancient poetry, they were to hand and could be interrogated. His work is therefore littered with observations about what the nomads do and do not say, and his general principle is that one should 'use those expressions which the nomads use and endorse what they endorse' (Sibawayh 1.174–75).

The origins of Arab identity are still unclear to us, but we can see how it became reinforced through migrations and interaction with states, then taken in a new direction by the rise of Islam. The link between Islamic religion and Arab identity took time to forge, but it was already strong by the end of the first century after Muhammad's death. Thus the caliph Walid (86–96/705–15) emphasised to Sham'allah, a chief of the Christian Arab tribe of Taghlib, that 'while you are a chief of the Arabs, you shame them all by worshipping the cross' (Michael the Syrian 11.17). He was allowed to live, but by the time of the caliph Mahdi (159–69/775–85) the question was no longer up for debate. The Christian Arab tribe of Tanukh was given the stark choice of conversion or death, as is recorded in a local inscription: 'In the year 1091 [780] the commander of the faithful came . . . and ordered that the churches be torn down and that the Tanukh become Muslims (nhaggrûn)'.[11] And indeed it was at this time, in the first century of the Abbasid dynasty (133–236/750–850), that the issue of Arab identity was to receive greatest attention. The Muslim Arabs now had their capital at Baghdad, which exposed them to the challenge of the strong and well-articulated identity of Iran, whereas before, at Damascus, they had only to contend with the numerous parochial and etiolated identities of the Levant. Moreover Iraq was a very cosmopolitan land with a large cultural elite, whose members now set about debating the cultural orientation of the Muslim empire (Arab or multi-ethnic?), the foundations of Islamic sciences (traditional Arabian lore or more rationality-based?), and the respective merits of the world's great peoples and religions (what had Arabs achieved, was Muhammad a true prophet, etc.).

Inevitably the fact that the Holy Book was in Arabic and that the Prophet was an Arab born in Arabia meant that many a good Muslim, even if not of Arab ancestry, would acknowledge the link between matters Arab and Islam and even seek to strengthen that link. Thus the first comprehensive work on Arabian history and the life of Muhammad was by Ibn Ishaq (d. 150/767), whose grandfather was a prisoner-of-war from 'Ayn al-Tamr in Iraq. The earliest surviving Quranic commentary was by Muqatil ibn Sulayman (d. 150/767), who was born of Persian parents. And the first Arabic grammar was by Sibawayhi (d. 180/796), a native of Balkh in modern Afghanistan. The forging of this link meant that the pre-Islamic Arabs, who had initially been reviled as pagans, became an acceptable topic of scholarship. It was not therefore considered amiss when the caliph Mansur (136–58/754–75), proud of his son's achievements in learning pre-Islamic Arabic poetry, instructed the tutor to 'select for your young charge the best of what each Arab poet has expressed' (Qali 132). Numerous histories of the pre-Islamic Arabs, like that of Asma'i, soon followed, seeking to give a proper account of this people for the first time and to fit them into a general picture of human cultures. Now that more archaeological work is being undertaken in Arabia and more inscriptions being uncovered it is to be hoped that this task will be continued and that the inhabitants of pre-Islamic Arabia will be accorded their proper place in world history.

NOTES

INTRODUCTION

1 There has also been a number of short essays, most famously I. Guidi, *L'Arabia antéislamique*, Paris, Geuthner, 1921; C.A. Nallino, 'L'Arabie preislamica' in his *Raccolta di scritti 3*, Rome, Istituto per l'Oriente, 1941, 1–47; G. Levi della Vida, 'Pre-Islamic Arabia' in N.A. Faris ed., *The Arab heritage*, Princeton, PUP, 1944, 25–47; H. St J. Philby, *The background of Islam*, Alexandria, Whitehead Morris, 1947.

2 Arabia seldom, and south Arabia almost never, appear in histories of the Near East. To take a very recent example, Sicker's *The pre-Islamic Middle East* has no chapter or even section on Arabia, and its inhabitants only feature as 'treacherous', 'marauding Arab tribes' and 'tribes harassing the Byzantine provinces' (pages 159, 183, 202).

3 For a recent discussion see Retso, 'The earliest Arabs'.

4 Robin (*AAKM*, 72) argues that Shaqab 3 mentions Arabs, but it should be read rather as the verb to offer (thus Walter Müller in *Bibliotheca Orientalis* 51, 1994, 472).

5 An ethnic group is defined by its social structures, history and culture. So ethnicity, unlike race (which is biologically determined), is a human construct, but that does not mean that it is any the less real in the eyes of its members or less able to bind and motivate them.

6 See further I. Goldziher, 'What is meant by al-Jahiliyya' in *id.*, *Muslim studies 1*, Chicago, Aldine, 1967, 201–208 (original German: Halle 1889).

1 EAST ARABIA

1 These identifications of the location of Dilmun and Magan are now generally accepted, but there had been a long debate about their whereabouts; for references see Potts, *Arabian Gulf*, 85–92, 133–50.

2 I use such terms as Bronze Age and Iron Age for chronological purposes, not to say anything about material culture. In fact there was

248

very little iron used in east Arabia in this period; the abundance of copper delayed its introduction until Seleucid times.

3 This people of the Syria/Middle Euphrates region will feature often in this book, for, though never a unified political power like the Assyrians and Babylonians, they came to have a major cultural influence on the Middle East, particularly via their language, which gradually became a lingua franca in the second half of the first millennium BC. For further information see the works by Dion and Hoerth listed in the background reading section of the bibliography.

4 The texts cited in this paragraph are conveniently assembled and references given in Potts, *Arabian Gulf*, 1.333–49.

5 The ruler whom we encounter most often is Abi'el. Sometimes the full name is given; it is difficult to read, but always begins with *brt*/'daughter of', so Abi'el was a queen (this will be demonstrated in a forthcoming study by Michael Macdonald).

6 Its exact location has been much debated; all we can say for sure is that it is in east Saudi Arabia, slightly inland and not far from Bahrain.

7 The text has Carrae; since talk is of Arabia, aromatics and Characene, it would seem that Gerrha is meant; see Potts, *Arabian Gulf*, 2.90–97, for discussion and further references.

8 For the loss of the final 'kh' compare the bilingual Greek/Nabataean inscription of Umm al-Jimal: *Thanouênoi/Tnwḥ* (PAES 4A.41).

9 Cf. *Epistulae* 261: 'You took the statement of your rebellion to the court of the secular rulers' (to the bishops of Qatar). Given that Isho'yahb was patriarch in the 640s and 650s, the references must be to the Muslims.

10 Thus George of Resh'aina 313. From this base 'Ali launched his bid for the rulership of the whole Middle East; to subsequent followers, the Shi'ites, he had been the sole legitimate ruler.

2 SOUTH ARABIA

1 Or it is argued that a north Arabian queen is meant (see chapter 5 below), but the only ones known, those of Qedar, were priestesses, and south Arabia had priestesses. Moreover the author, at whatever time he or she were writing, evidently had in mind an equal to the kingdom of Israel, and this could only be a major sedentary power, not some pastoralist tribe.

2 Cf. Theophanes 144: 'In this year [502–503] Anastasius made a treaty with Harith [known as the son of a woman of Tha'lab], the father of Ma'dikarib and Hujr, after which all Palestine, Arabia and Phoenicia enjoyed much peace and calm'. Robin (*CRAIBL* 1996, 696–97) and Shahid (*BASIC*, 5–6) reject this account, saying that tribesmen might bear their mother's personal name, but not her tribal name; this is, however, untrue (e.g. Tabari 1.755: "Amr ibn 'Adi, son of a woman of

Tanukh, of Lakhm'). Malalas 18.434–35 has Mundhir, the Persians' Arab ally, kill Harith in AD 528.

3 The date of AD 523 is given by the Greek martyrdom account. This event allows us to fix the Himyarite era, for this and the following inscription, both dated year 633, clearly describe the same events as the Greek martyrdom account.

4 This Esimiphaeus is presumably the Sumyafa' Ashwa' of south Arabian inscriptions and possibly the Aryat of Muslim sources (Tabari 1.927–33). That the Ethiopian king launched a second expedition against Himyar is indicated in Greek and Syriac sources (Huxley, 'On the Greek *Martyrium*', 46–48).

5 In late Roman and Byzantine sources Saracen, originally the name of an Arab tribe, came to be the general term for Arabs (see chapter 9 below).

6 Mundhir and Harith were the most powerful Arab vassals of Iran and Byzantium respectively; see chapter 3 for discussion.

3 NORTH AND CENTRAL ARABIA

1 For the references in this paragraph and further discussion see Eph'al, *Ancient Arabs*, 93–100.

2 The Geshem of this text is usually identified with the Biblical 'Geshem the Arab' who opposed Nehemiah's rebuilding of the walls of Jerusalem in 444 BC (Neh. 2.19, 6.1), and with the Geshem son of Shahr who appears on an inscription from the north Arabian oasis town of Dedan as a political figure of some importance (JS Lih349), but this remains speculative.

3 For the changing meanings of Arabia Felix see Retso, 'Where and what was *Arabia Felix?*'.

4 Shahid, following Rosenthal, reads *sharbat*/'tribe' (*EI*, *s.v.* 'Saracen'); Milik reads *shirkat*, meaning a squadron drawn from the tribe of Thamud, which makes good sense (see Macdonald, 'Saracènes').

5 Modern scholars usually identify ßZenobia with the Arab queen Zabba' of Muslim tradition. This may be so, but the many legends that have gathered around Zabba' have made her biography very different from that of Zenobia.

6 This is the translation of Beeston, but there have been other renderings (see bibliography), for the text is in many places difficult to read.

7 Possibly this is the Abikarib ibn Jabala of Ghassan who sends an embassy to Abraha in Yemen (CIS 4.541; see chapter 2 above).

4 ECONOMY

1 For modification of this statement see the section on weapons and warfare in chapter 7 below.

2 Though A. Jamme, *A propos des rois Hadramoutiques de al-'Uqlah*,

Wahington, 1965, 16–17, sees them, against Müller and Beeston, as members of the south Arabian clans *Tdhmr*, *Kshd* and *Hnd*.

3 Though they suffered severe punishment if caught by the authorities. E.g. 'the Persian Arabs . . . crossed over into Byzantine territory without the Persian army and captured two villages. When the Persian governor at Nisibis learned this, he took their chiefs and executed them. The Byzantine Arabs too crossed over without orders into the Persian territory and captured a hamlet. When the general heard this . . . he sent to Timostratus, governor of Callinicum, and he seized five of their chiefs, slaying two with the sword and impaling the other three' (Joshua the Stylite 88).

4 Cf. Zacharias 7.2–3 (Arabs flock to Amida as a result of locusts and famine); Marcellinus 943 (pastures of Persia ruined by drought in 536 and 'about 15,000 Arabs' cross into Byzantine lands).

5 Cf. p. 68 above (Sargon settles Arabs in Samaria) and Plutarch, *Lives*, Cambridge (Ma.), Leob, 1959, 2. 536 (Tigranes settles 'the tent-dwelling Arabs . . . to employ them in trade and commerce').

6 Strabo has it the other way round, but this must be a scribal error, for Hadramawt is the source of frankincense while myrrh came from areas further west such as Qataban.

7 The figure varies in the different manuscripts and this is just the variant closest to the actual distance, *c.*2220 km (a Roman mile is just under 1.5 km).

5 SOCIETY

1 Our most vivid source for this form of social organisation in Arabia comes from pre-Islamic Arabic poetry (see chapter 8 below), but it must be borne in mind that this derives chiefly from the sixth century AD and we cannot be sure how representative it is of earlier times.

2 The kinship might be very real (Safaitic texts often record a person's genealogy going back as many as fifteen generations, and in a genetic study of two tribes of Sinai sixty-five out sixty-seven males tested had the same haplotype) or it might be fictional (the four civic tribes of Palmyra were formed for administrative and cultic ends), but in all cases kinship provided the idiom for group cooperation.

3 This is evident from poetry, which has a rich vocabulary for distinguishing tribal subdivisions (e.g. *ahl*, *raht*, *batn*, *fakhdh*, *'imâra*, *hayy*, *qawm*, *'ashîra*, *qabîla*, *ma'shar*, *âl*), whereas inscriptions are much less forthcoming (south Arabian texts mostly just use the term *sha'b* and Safaitic texts *âl* whatever size of tribal fraction is intended).

4 The same sort of practice is described in pre-Islamic Arabian poetry from 1000 years later, which argues for a certain continuity of social structures over this period.

5 That it was not a covert state tax is clear from the fact that one could make a votive gift instead. It should be noted here that we do also have

references to east Arabian kings in Mesopotamian documents (Potts, *Arabian Gulf*, 135–41, 229) and on Hellenistic coins, but we know nothing of the nature and extent of their rule.

6 Meaning livestock taken as bloodmoney. This poem is by a woman of the murdered man's clan.

7 The degree to which this occurs varies greatly: at the temple of Hadran in Raybun 44% of inscribed offerings are from women whereas at the Awwam temple in Marib it is only 5.3%.

8 This is Te'elhunu, here referred to by her title (Borger, 'Miszellen', *Orientalia* 26, 1957, 9–10); elsewhere she is also described as 'priestess'/*kumirtu* (AR 2.943). For the meaning and further instances of the title see chapter 6 below and note 5 thereto.

6 RELIGION

1 Their prime position is clear from bilingual inscriptions, which equate them with Zeus and Aphrodite (see Roche, 'Les Nabatéens en Méditerranée'). Assumed to be about al-'Uzza is the notice of Epiphanius (d. 403) that 'in the idolatrous temple at Petra . . . they praise the virgin with hymns in the Arabic language and call her khaabu (*ka'ba?*) . . . in Arabic; and the child who is born of her they call Dusares. And this is also done that night in the city of Elusa' (51.22). As also is the remark of Jerome that Saint Hilarion (d. 371) 'arrived at Elusa on the very day that a solemn festival had brought all the people of the town to the temple of Venus; for the Saracens worship this goddess as the Morning Star and their race is dedicated to her cult' ('Vita Hilarionis' 42–43).

2 Though their language is not Hebrew as Jaussen and Savignac thought, but Nabataean and Arabic; e.g. no. 3 reads 'this is what he wrote'/*hâdha mâ kataba* (pointed out to me by Simon Hopkins).

3 The earliest monotheist inscriptions are not explicit (which has led some to posit an indigenous brand of monotheism), but there are overtly Jewish texts before there are overtly Christian texts.

4 References in pre-Islamic poetry are always too brief; e.g. Labid 24: 'neither the women who cast pebbles nor those who scare away birds know what Allah is going to do'.

5 The term also occurs once in east Arabia (Ja 1052) and in south Arabia (RES 3945). It is ultimately of Sumerian origin and is attested in Akkadian mythology, meaning 'a sage', whence it entered Arabian languages. It can also be used of women (e.g. J.S. Lih64, *afklt*).

6 Cf. Procopius 2.16: 'It was the season of the vernal equinox and at this season the Saracens always dedicated about two months to their god, and during this time never undertook any inroad into the land of others.'

7 It is thus that one should understand King Mundhir's sacrifice of 400 virgins to the goddess al-'Uzza in 527 (Zacharias 8.5). Cf. Procopius

2.28.13 (Mundhir sacrifices a son of Harith to Aphrodite/al-'Uzza); Nilus 612: 'they prostrate themselves to the morning star and sacrifice the best of their spoils to it'.

8 Nilus 611–13 (Sinai, boys sacrificed); Eusebius 4.16 (Arabia, boy sacrificed and buried under altar); Porphyry 2.56 (Duma, annual victim buried at foot of idol-altar).

9 More will said about such texts in the section on inscriptions in chapter 8 below.

10 That is, the ceremony had to be performed while the morning star was visible. This text was disdained by most early scholars, but now see Christides, 'Once again the "Narrations" of Nilus', and Mayerson, 'Observations on the Nilus *Narrationes*'.

7 ART, ARCHITECTURE AND ARTEFACTS

1 Creswell, *Muslim architecture*, 1; repeated by Allan's revision of Creswell, 3; Ettinghausen and Grabar, *Art and architecture of Islam*, 17–18; Hillenbrand, *Islamic art and architecture*, 11 (he does note that it was 'by no means absent', but offers no survey of its contents).

2 Schmidt in *Yemen 3000*, 88; Patrich, *Nabataean art*, 191.

3 Talgam, *Origins*, 'conclusion'. Umayyad is the name of the first dynasty of Islam (656–750).

4 Ptolemy places it north of Najran and southwest of mountains, probably the Tuwayq range. However, it must be noted that Ptolemy's calculations are not exact and that he uses an eclectic mix of sources.

5 Doughty, C.M., *Travels in Arabia deserta*, Cambridge, CUP, 1888, 2.417. The long gap between Doughty and pre-Islamic times is bridged by Muslim travellers such as Ibn al-Jubayr who also speak of 'the kind of stronghold known in these parts [Arabia] as a *qaṣr*', 'a large enclosure containing small buildings' (*Riḥla* 206).

6 Musil, A., *The manners and customs of the Rwala Bedouins*, New York, American Geographical Society, 1928, 160.

7 The height is suggested by its comparison to a corpulent she-camel (e.g. 'Abid 12: *jalâla wajnâ' ka-uṭum maṭîn*), usually described as tall (e.g. Tufayl 9: *ka-rukn al-bâb*/'like the pillar of a gate').

8 Here *bayt* ('house'); many other words are used, especially *qubba*, which Muslim commentators explain as a round leather tent, and *khibâ'*, said to be of hair or skin.

9 Though not every cairn is a tomb; e.g. 'cairns appeared, and it seemed as though their heads were the heads of mountains plunging down into a water-course; when I left behind one cairn by which one finds the way another one appeared, dim in the heat-haze' (*Muf.* 47).

10 Both types are also encountered in a private context; pocket-size god-stones are known from excavations and full-size ones still stand at ancient campsites (Avner, 'Nabataean standing stones'). Statuettes

of deities, what we might call idols, were kept about the home, presumably to ward off malign spirits and for private devotions (Waqidi 870–71; Kalbi 28c; Ibn Hisham 54).

11 This is a tenth-century Byzantine lexicon, but it draws on earlier writers, to whom it was well known that the Nabataeans worshipped their god in the guise of a stone; e.g. Maximus of Tyre (d. c.AD 185) 19 ('their image I have seen; it was a rectangular stone/*lithos tetragônos*').

12 The pouring out of the blood of sacrifices was evidently very important, as is clear from the fact that the word for it (*nusuk*) came to mean religious ceremonies in general.

13 Cf. Musil, *Rwala*, 524: 'Everyone tries to reach an animal with his spear, calling at the same time on his comrades to witness that it was he who captured it; he then drives it before him to a second and third, which he also makes his own. A long spear is very useful for this kind of work.'

8 LANGUAGE AND LITERATURE

1 The languages identified so far are labelled by modern scholars as Taymanitic, Dedanitic, Dumaitic (spoken in or around Tayma, Dedan and Duma respectively), Hismaic (from the Hisma) and Safaitic (from the Harra). All the rest (represented by some 15,000 graffiti from all over Arabia) are for the moment called Thamudic (after the name of the famous Hijazi tribe, though few would be by them) pending further research.

2 Except in the east where, except for some short informal texts (as yet undeciphered) painted on the roofs and walls of caves in Dhofar, very few inscriptions have been found.

3 These examples are all to be found in Winnett, 'Thamudic religious texts' in illustration of the construction *b* + name of god + noun(s).

4 This is based on Abdallah, 'Naqsh al-qaṣîda al-ḥimyariyya', and Beeston, 'Antecedents', but it is intended only as a hint of the nature of the poem, not a certain reading, for the language is not yet much understood. Another inscription preserves what might be part of a hymn (Z I 11; see M.A. Bafaqih and C. Robin, 'Min nuqûsh maḥram Bilqîs', *Raydan* 1, 1978, 16–22).

5 Labid's tribe and the king, providers of food, are contrasted with the confidant who searches for it.

9 ARABHOOD AND ARABISATION

1 This was the most important condition, but not a necessary and sufficient one; other attributes (e.g. residence in Arabia, allegiance to deities perceived as Arab, practice of Arab-style divination etc.) might suffice for a person to claim Arab identity. On the ways of

defining on ethnic group see S.L. Armstrong and C.K. Mahmood, 'Do ethnic groups exist?', *Ethnology* 31, 1992, 1–14.

2   These and other differences may justify the Muslim genealogists' division of the Arabs into northerners (descended from 'Adnan) and southerners (descended from Qahtan), but in our period the latter group must be distinguished from the Yemeni peoples (to the Muslims they were all one).

3   Greco-Romans used the term 'barbarian' to designate peoples outside their borders, so by 'barbarisation of the empire' I mean that the distinction between the Roman provinces and the lands beyond them became less and less as the former became more barbarised and the latter more Romanised.

4   The latter had become allied with a section of Tanukh by virtue of the marriage of Jadhima, originally of al-Azd, into the Tanukh clan of Fahm ibn Taymallah (Tabari 1.746–47).

5   There have been various explanations of the name Saracen, such as easterners (*sharqiyyîn*), plunderers (*sâriqîn*), inhabitants of barren lands (from the Aramaic root *srq*), federates (from *shirka*). But it seems simpler to assume it is the name of a tribe, as with Tayyaye.

6   Note Ammianus 22.15.2: 'the Scenite [tent-dwelling] Arabs whom we now call the Saracens' (cf. 23.6.13).

7   A few Arabisms are also attested in Syriac (Segal, 'Arabs in Syriac literature', 104) and some snippets of Arabic expressions are noted in Jewish sources (A. Brüll, *Fremdsprachliche Redensarten in den Talmud und Midraschim*, Leipzig, Fritsch, 1869, 40–59).

8   For this inscription and further references to Arabs as diviners see L. Robert, 'L'Epitaphe d'un Arabe à Thasos', *Hellenica* 2, 1946, 43–50. Another self-designated Arab is Parates, a barber from Ptolomaic Egypt (J. Lesquier, *Papyrus grecs de Lille 2: Papyrus de Magdola*, Paris, Leroux, 116, 15, 220 BC).

9   References for this paragraph are to be found in Bashear, *Arabs and others*, 10–13, 32.

10 *A'râb qad adrakû l-jâhiliyya*. Since Abu 'Amr was born sixty years after the death of Muhammad, there would have been few such sheikhs around. But one can imagine the young scholar being ushered into the tent of some wizened old bedouin, who would claim to be a hundred years old or more and regale him with tales of the good old days of paganism.

11 Edited in H. Pognon, *Inscriptions sémitiques*, Paris, Imprimerie Nationale, 1907, 84. Another reason for this action was that being Christian could, in times of Muslim–Byzantine conflict, be perceived as tantamount to being pro-Byzantine.

BIBLIOGRAPHY

Since the source material for pre-Islamic Arabia is so little known and because almost every hypothesis I have advanced is contested or contestable, it is necessary for me to give in full the primary and secondary literature upon which I have directly relied. To keep it manageable, however, I will exclude works from before 1970 unless they are still fundamental. Those interested in earlier studies can consult the *Corpus des inscriptions et antiquités sud-Arabes: bibliographie générale systématique*, Louvain, Peeters, 1977, and Stephen D. Ricks, *Western language literature on pre-Islamic central Arabia*, Denver, American Institute of Islamic Studies, 1991. Those wishing to do more advanced research can consult the very full bibliography of D.T. Potts, 'The Gulf and Arabia, 3000 BC–600 AD', *Handbuch der Orientalistik*, forthcoming, and the annual update on south Arabian studies by Walter Müller in *Archiv für Orientforschung*. For the general reader I include a background reading list and at the beginning of the bibliography for the first three chapters I have listed survey works that provide an introduction and orientation to the main issues.

SELECTED BACKGROUND READING AND REFERENCE WORKS

Ali, Jawad, *Al-mufaṣṣal fī ta'rīkh al-'arab qabl al-Islām*, 10 vols, Baghdad, Maktabat al-Nahda, 1968 (the most famous and comprehensive modern Muslim history of pre-Islamic Arabia).

Ball, Warwick, *Rome in the east: the transformation of an empire*, London, Routledge, 2000.

Briant, Pierre, *Histoire de l'empire Perse de Cyrus à Alexandre*, Paris, Fayard, 1996.

Bulliet, R., *The camel and the wheel*, Cambridge (Ma.), Harvard UP, 1975.

Calvet, Yves, and Robin, Christian, *Arabie heureuse, Arabie déserte*, Paris, Musée du Louvre, 1997 (catalogue of the Louvre's Arabian items with a helpful introduction).

Cameron, Averil, *The Mediterranean world in Late Antiquity AD 395–600*, London, Routledge, 1993.

Chelhod, Joseph, *Le Sacrifice chez les Arabes*, Paris, Presses Universitaires, 1955.

—— *Les Structures du sacré chez les Arabes*, Paris, Maisonneuve et Larose, 1964 (an anthropologist's view).

Civilizations of the Ancient Near East (CANE), 5 vols, ed. J.M. Sasson, New York, Charles Scribner, 1995.

Daum, Werner, *Ursemitische Religion*, Stuttgart, Kohlhammer, 1985 (examines south Arabian religion in light of modern Yemeni myths and folktales).

Dion, P.E., *Les Araméens à l'âge du fer: histoire politique et structures sociales*, Paris, Librairie Lecoffre, 1997.

Dostal, Walter, 'Die Araber in vorislamischer Zeit', *Der Islam* 74, 1997, 1–63 (examines degree to which Arabs integrated into the high cultures of the Near East).

Encyclopaedia Islamica (EI), new edition, ed. H.A.R. Gibb *et al.*, Leiden, Brill, 1960–2001 (has numerous entries on aspects of pre-Islamic Arabia).

Groom, Nigel, *Frankincense and myrrh: a study of the Arabian incense trade*, London, Longman, 1981 (the classic study).

Hamdani, Hasan ibn Ahmad al-, *Ṣifat jazîrat al-'arab*, 2 vols, ed. D.H. Müller, Leiden, Brill, 1884–91 (famous description of Arabia by a tenth-century AD visitor).

Harding, G. Lankester, *An index and concordance of pre-Islamic Arabian names and inscriptions*, Toronto, University of Toronto, 1971.

Hawting, Gerald, *The idea of idolatry and the emergence of Islam*, Cambridge, CUP, 1999 (argues that the environment in which Islam arose was monotheist not polytheist).

Hetzron, Robert, ed., *The Semitic languages*, London, Routledge, 1997.

Hoerth, Alfred, *et al.*, eds, *Peoples of the Old Testament world*, Grand Rapids (Mi.), Baker Books, 1994.

Höfner, Maria, Gese, H., and Rudolph, K., *Die Religionen Altsyriens, Altarabiens und der Mandäer*, Stuttgart, Kohlhammer, 1970.

Isaac, Benjamin, *The limits of empire: the Roman army in the east*, Oxford, Clarendon, 1990.

Jabbur, Jibrail S., *The bedouins and the desert* (tr. L.I. Conrad), Albany, SUNY, 1995 (blends modern observation and ancient references).

Kaiser, O., ed., *Texte aus der Umwelt des Alten Testaments*, Gütersloh, Mohn,

1982– (contains translations by Walter Müller of a number of Arabian inscriptions).

Khazanov, Anatoly, *Nomads and the outside world*, Cambridge, CUP, 1984 (a classic study of the subject).

Kitchen, K.A., *Documentation for ancient Arabia (DAA)*, 4 vols, Liverpool, LUP, 1994– (chronology, concordance of south Arabian inscriptions, gazetteer, anthology of texts).

Kuhrt, Amelie, *The ancient Near East c. 3000–330 BC*, London, Routledge, 1995.

Masry, A.H., *Prehistory in northeastern Arabia*, London, KPI, 1997.

Millar, Fergus, *The Roman Near East 31 BC–AD 337*, Cambridge (Ma.), Harvard UP, 1993.

Nayeem, M.A., *Prehistory and protohistory of the Arabian peninsula*, 5 vols, Hyderabad, 1990–98.

Nicholson, Reynold, *A literary history of the Arabs*, Cambridge, CUP, 1930.

Noja, Sergio, *I primi arabi*, Milan, Jaca, 1994; *L'Arabie avant l'Islam*, Aix-en-Provence, Edisud, 1994.

Obrycht, Marek J., *Parthia et ulteriores gentes: die politischen Beziehungen zwischen dem arsakidischen Iran und den Nomaden der eurasischen Steppen*, Munich, Tuduv, 1998.

Peters, F.E., *Muhammad and the origins of Islam*, New York, SUNY, 1994.

Pritchard, James, ed., *Ancient Near Eastern texts relating to the Old Testament*, Princeton, PUP, 1969.

Robertson Smith, W., *Lectures on the religion of the Semites*, London, Adam and Charles Black, 1894 (now dated, but still influential).

Sartre, M., *L'Orient romain: provinces et sociétés provinciales en Méditerranée orientale d'Auguste aux Sévères*, Paris, Seuil, 1991.

Sass, Benjamin, *Studia alphabetica: on the origin and early history of the northwest Semitic, south Semitic and Greek alphabets*, Göttingen, Vandenhoeck and Ruprecht, 1991.

Sherwin-White, Susan, and Kuhrt, Amelie, *From Samarkhand to Sardis: a new approach to the Seleucid empire*, London, Duckworth, 1993.

Sicker, Martin, *The pre-Islamic Middle East*, Westport (Ct), Praeger, 2000.

Soden, Wolfram von, *The ancient Orient: an introduction to the study of the Ancient Near East* (tr. D.G. Schley), Grand Rapids (Mi.), Eerdmans, 1994.

Stetkevych, Suzanne, *The mute immortals speak: pre-Islamic poetry and the poetics of ritual*, Ithaca (NY), Cornell, 1993 (rich commentary on the most famous poems and their milieu).

Teixidor, J., *The pagan god: popular religion in the Greco-Roman Near East*, Princeton, PUP, 1977 (has chapters on north Arabia and Palmyra).

Thompson, Andrew, *Origins of Arabia*, London, Stacey International, 2000 (geological formation).

Versteegh, Kees, *The Arabic language*, Edinburgh, Edinburgh University, 1997 (discusses origins and development).

Yarshater, Ehsan, ed., *The Cambridge history of Iran, 3.1: the Seleucid, Parthian and Sasanian periods*, Cambridge, CUP, 1983.

Zwettler, Michael, *The oral tradition of classical Arabic poetry*, Columbus, Ohio State University, 1978 (on the language and transmission of these poems).

USEFUL JOURNALS AND COLLECTIONS OF ARTICLES

(These items are abbreviated as follows in the bibliography below.)

AA = Robin, Christian, and Gajda, Iwona, eds, *Arabia antiqua: early origins of south Arabian states*, Rome, IsMEO, 1996.

AAE = *Arabian Archaeology and Epigraphy*.

AAEI = Peters, F.E., ed., *The Arabs and Arabia on the eve of Islam*, Aldershot and Brookfield, Variorum, 1999.

AAKM = Robin, Christian, *L'Arabie antique de Karib'il à Mahomet*, Aix-en-Provence, Edisud, 1991.

AAW = Altheim, Franz, and Stiehl, Ruth, *Die Araber in der alten Welt*, Berlin, Walter de Gruyter, 1964–69.

ABADY = *Archäologische Berichte aus dem Yemen* (Deutsche Archaeologische Institut San'a).

ADAJ = *Annual of the Department of Antiquities of Jordan*.

AF = Nebes, Norbert, ed., *Arabia Felix: Festschrift Walter Müller*, Wiesbaden, Harrassowitz, 1994.

AMB = Salles, J.F., *L'Arabie et ses mers bordières 1: itinéraires et voisinages*, Paris, Maison de l'Orient, 1988.

ANBC = Phillips, C.S., *et al.*, eds, *Arabia and its neighbours: essays in honour of Beatrice de Cardi*, Brepols, Abiel II, 1998.

AOMIM = Boucharlat, R., and Salles, J.F., eds, *Arabie orientale, Mésopotamie et Iran méridional de l'âge du fer au début de la période islamique*, Paris, Recherche sur les Civilisations, 1984.

AP = Fahd, T. ed., *L'Arabie préislamique et son environnment historique et culturel: colloque de Strasbourg 1987*, Leiden, Brill, 1989.

ASB = Gabrieli, Francesco, ed., *L'antica società beduina*, Rome, Centro di Studi Semitici, 1959.

ASMG = Ibrahim, Moawiyah, *Arabian Studies in honour of Mahmoud Ghul*, Wiesbaden, Harrassowitz, 1989.

ATB = Potts, D.T., ed., *Araby the blest: studies in Arabian archaeology*, Copenhagen, Carston Niebuhr Institute, 1988.

BAA = Khalifa, H.A. al-, and Rice, Michael, eds, *Bahrain through the ages: the archaeology*, London, Kegan Paul, 1986.

BASOR = *Bulletin of the American School of Oriental Research.*

BSOAS = *Bulletin of the School of Oriental and African Studies.*

CRAIBL = *Comptes Rendus de l'Académie des Inscriptions et Belles-Lettres.*

ESA = *Etudes Sud-Arabes: recueil offert à Jacques Ryckmans*, Louvain, Institut Orientaliste, 1991.

Hudhud = Stiegner, Roswitha, ed., *Al-Hudhud: Festschrift Maria Hofner*, Graz, Karl-Franzens-Universität, 1981.

JSS = *Journal of Semitic Studies.*

NESE = Degen, Rainer, *et al.*, eds, *Neue Ephemeris für Semitische Epigraphik*, 3 vols., Wiesbaden, Harrassowitz, 1972–78.

PA = Lozachmeur, Hélène, ed., *Présence arabe dans le Croissant fertile avant l'Hégire: table ronde international 1993*, Paris, Editions recherche sur les Civilisations, 1995.

PSAS = *Proceedings of the Seminar for Arabian Studies* (London, Institute of Archaeology).

Sayhadica = Robin, Christian, and Bafaqih, Muhammad, eds, *Sayhadica: recherches sur les inscriptions de l'Arabie pré-Islamique offertes au Professeur A.F.L. Beeston*, Paris, Geuthner, 1987.

SHA = Ansary, A.T., ed., *Studies in the history of Arabia*, 2 vols, Riyad, University of Riyad, 1979–84.

Südarabien = Stiegner, R.G., ed., *Südarabien: in memoriam Maria Hofner*, Graz, Leykam, 1997.

ZDMG = *Zeitschrift der Deutschen Morgenländischen Gesellschaft.*

PRIMARY SOURCES: TEXTS FROM OUTSIDE ARABIA

Ancient texts (3000–330 BC)

ABC = Grayson, A.K., *Assyrian and Babylonian chronicles*, Locust Valley (NY), J.J. Augustin, 1975.

Ahiqar, *The Aramaic proverbs of*, ed./tr. James M. Lindenberger, Baltimore, Johns Hopkins, 1983.

AR = Luckenbill, D.D., *Ancient records of Assyria and Babylonia*, 2 vols, Chicago, University of Chicago, 1927.

Bible: cited according to *The New Jerusalem Bible*, London, Darton, Longman and Todd, 1985.

CHLI = Hawkins, J.D., *Corpus of hieroglyphic Luwian inscriptions*, 3 parts, Berlin, de Gruyter, 2000.

CSL = Black, J.A., *et al.*, *The electronic text corpus of Sumerian literature*, *http://www.etcsl.orient.ox.ac.uk*, Oxford, 1998–

Harran Inscription = Gadd, C.J., 'The Harran inscriptions of Nabonidus', *Anatolian Studies* 8, 1958, 35–92.

Herodotus, *History*, 4 vols, ed./tr. A.D. Godley, Cambridge (Ma.), Loeb, 1926.

IA = Borger, Riekele, *Die Inschriften Asarhaddons Königs von Assyrien*, Graz, Archiv für Orientforschung, 1956.

ITP = Tadmor, H., *The inscriptions of Tiglath-Pileser III king of Assyria*, Jerusalem, Israel Academy of Sciences and Humanities, 1994.

La = Cooper, J.S., *Sumerian and Akkadian royal inscriptions, I: pre-Sargonic inscriptions*, New Haven, AOS, 1986, 22–30 (Lagash texts).

Ni = Goetze, A., 'The texts Ni. 615 and Ni. 641 of the Istanbul Museum', *Journal of Cuneiform Studies* 6, 1952, 142–45 (Nippur texts).

RIM = Frayne, Douglas, *The royal inscriptions of Mesopotamia, 2: Sargonic and Gutian periods*, Toronto, University of Toronto, 1993.

Sappho = Page, Denys, ed./tr., *Sappho and Alcaeus*, Oxford, Clarendon, 1955.

Suhu = Cavigneaux, A., and Ismail, B.K., 'Die Statthalter von Suhu und Mari im 8. Jh. v. Chr.', *Baghdader Mitteilungen* 21, 1990, 321–456.

UET = Ur Excavation Texts; the letter of Ea-Nasir cited in ch. 1 is translated in W.F. Leemans, *Foreign trade in the Old Babylonian period*, Leiden, Studia et Documenta, 1960, 39.

VAT 5600 = Weippert, Manfred, 'Die Kämpfe des assyrischen Königs Assurbanipal gegen die Araber', *Die Welt des Orients* 7, 1973–74, 74–85.

Xenophon, *Anabasis/Cyropaedia*, ed./tr. C.L. Brownson/W. Miller, Cambridge (Ma.), Loeb, 1922/1914.

Classical texts (330 BC–AD 400)

Aelian, *On the characteristics of animals*, 3 vols, ed./tr. A.F. Scholfield, Cambridge (Ma.), Loeb, 1958–59.

Ammianus Marcellinus, *History*, 3 vols, ed./tr. J.C. Rolfe, Cambridge (Ma.), Loeb, 1950.

Appian, *Roman history*, 4 vols, ed./tr. Horace White, Cambridge (Ma.), Loeb, 1912.

Arrian, *Anabasis Alexandri* and *Indica*, 2 vols, ed./tr. P.A. Brunt, Cambridge (Ma.), Loeb, 1976.

Athenaeus, *The deipnosophists*, 7 vols, ed./tr. C.B. Gulick, Cambridge (Ma.), Loeb, 1928.

Cassius Dio, *Roman history*, 9 vols, ed./tr. E. Cary, Cambridge (Ma.), Loeb, 1914.

Cicero, *De divinatione*, 2 vols, ed. A.S. Pease, Urbana, University of Illinois, 1920–23.
—— *Epistulae ad familiares*, 4 vols, ed./tr. V. Glynn Williams, Cambridge (Ma.), Loeb, 1926.
Delos = Durrbach, F., *et al.*, *Inscriptions de Délos*, Paris, Académie des Inscriptions et Belles-Lettres, 1926–.
Diodorus Siculus, *History*, 12 vols, ed./tr. C.H. Oldfather *et al.*, Cambridge (Ma.), Loeb, 1933.
Festus, *Breviarum*, ed. J.W. Eadie, London, Athlone, 1967.
Herodian, *History*, 2 vols, ed./tr. C.R. Whittaker, Cambridge (Ma.), Loeb, 1969.
Josephus, *Antiquities*, 6 vols, ed./tr. H. St J. Thackeray *et al.*, Cambridge (Ma.), Loeb, 1930.
Maximus of Tyre, *Dissertationes*, ed. M.B. Trapp, Stuttgart and Leipzig, Teubner, 1994.
Nicander of Colophon, *Poems and political fragments*, ed. A.S.F. Gow and A.F. Scholfield, Cambridge, CUP, 1953.
Notitia dignitatum, ed. Otto Seeck, Berlin, Weidemann, 1876.
Periplus maris Erythraei, ed./tr. Lionel Casson, Princeton, New Jersey, PUP, 1989.
Pliny, *Natural history*, 10 vols, ed./tr. H. Rackham *et al.*, Cambridge (Ma.), Loeb, 1942.
Polybius, *The histories*, 6 vols, ed./tr. W.R. Paton, Cambridge (Ma.), Loeb, 1954.
Porphyry, *De abstinentia*, 3 vols, ed./tr. J. Bouffartigue and M. Patillon, Paris, Belles Lettres, 1977–95.
Ptolemy, *The geography*, ed. K.F.A. Nobbe, Leipzig, Otto Holtze, 1888–1913; tr. E.L. Stevenson, New York, NY Public Library, 1932.
Scriptores historiae Augustae, 2 vols, ed. E. Hohl, Leipzig, Teubner, 1927.
Strabo, *The geography*, 8 vols, ed./tr. H.L. Jones, Cambridge (Ma.), Loeb, 1917.
Theophrastus, *Enquiry into plants*, 2 vols, ed./tr. A. Hort, Cambridge (Ma.), Loeb, 1916.
Zenon papyri, 4 vols, ed. C.C. Edgar, Cairo, Musée du Caire, 1925–31.

Christian and Zoroastrian texts (200–AD 700)

Ahudemmeh, 'Histoire', ed./tr. F. Nau, *Patrologia Orientalis* 3, 1909, 52–96.
Anastasius of Sinai = Nau, F., ed., 'Le Texte grec des récits du moine Anastase sur les saints pères du Sinaï', *Oriens Christianus* 2, 1902, 58–89.
Antoninus Placentinus, *Itinerarium*, ed. P. Geyer, Turnhout, Brepols, 1965,

127–53; tr. J. Wilkinson in his *Jerusalem pilgrims before the crusades*, Warminster, Aris and Phillips, 1977, 79–89.

Bardaisan, *The book of the laws of countries*, ed./tr. H.J.W. Drijvers, Assen, Van Gorcum, 1964.

Chron. Khuzistan = Guidi, I., ed., *Chronicon anonymum*, Paris, CSCO, 1903.

Chronicle of Siirt (10th century, but citing earlier writers), ed./tr. A. Scher, *Patrologia Orientalis* 4–5, 7, 11, 1908–19.

Cosmas Indicopleustes, *Topographie chrétienne*, 3 vols, ed./tr. W. Wolska-Conus, Paris, Cerf, 1968–73.

Cyril of Scythopolis, *Lives of the monks of Palestine*, ed. E. Schwartz, Leipzig, Texte und Untersuchungen 49, 1939; tr. R.M. Price, Kalamazoo (Mi.), Cistercian Publications, 1991.

Epiphanius of Salamis, *Panarion*, 3 vols, ed. K. Holl, Leipzig, Hinrichs, 1915–33; tr. F. Williams, Leiden, Brill, 1987–94.

Eusebius of Caesarea, *Praeparatio evangelica*, 5 vols, ed./tr. E.H. Gifford, Oxford, Clarendon, 1903.

George of Resh'aina, 'An early Syriac life of Maximus the Confessor', ed./tr. Sebastian Brock, *Analecta Bollandiana* 91, 1973, 299–346.

Isho'yahb III, *Epistulae*, ed. R. Duval, Paris, CSCO, 1904–1905.

Jerome, 'Vita Hilarionis', *Bibliotheca patrum latina* (ed. J.P. Migne) 23, 1845, 29–53.

—— 'Vita Malchi', *Bibliotheca patrum latina* (ed. J.P. Migne) 23, 1845, 53–60.

John bar Penkaye, *Ktâbâ d-rîsh mellê*, partial ed./tr. A. Mingana (*Sources syriaques*), Leipzig, 1907.

John of Ephesus, *Ecclesiastical history III*, ed./tr. E.W. Brooks, Louvain, CSCO, 1952.

Joshua the Stylite, *Chronicle*, ed./tr. W. Wright, Cambridge, CUP, 1882.

Malalas, *Chronicle*, ed. L. Dindorf, Bonn, Weber, 1831; tr. E. Jeffreys *et al.*, Melbourne, Australian Association for Byzantine Studies, 1986.

Malchus, *Byzantine history*, ed./tr. R.C. Blockley in *The fragmentary classicising historians of the later Roman empire II*, Liverpool, Francis Cairns, 1983, 402–55.

Marcellinus Comes, 'Chronicle', *Bibliotheca patrum latina* (ed. J.P. Migne) 51, 1846, 913–48.

Menander the Guardsman, *History*, ed./tr. R.C. Blockley, Liverpool, Francis Cairns, 1985.

Michael the Syrian (12th century, but citing earlier writers), *Chronique*, ed./tr. J.B. Chabot, 4 vols, Paris, Ernest Laroux, 1899–1910.

Nilus Monachus, 'Narrations', *Bibliotheca patrum graeca* (ed. J.P. Migne) 79, 1865, 583–694.

Paikuli = Humbach, H., and Skjaervo, P.O., *The Sassanian inscription of Paikuli 3.1*, Wiesbaden, Reichert, 1983.

Philostorgius, *Historia ecclesiastica*, ed. J. Bidez, rev. F. Winkelmann, Berlin, Akademie-Verlag, 1972; tr. E. Walford, London, Bohn's Ecclesiastical Library, 1855.

Photius (9th century, but citing earlier writers), *Bibliotheca*, 8 vols, ed./tr. R. Henry, Paris, Belles Lettres, 1959–77; partial tr. N.G. Wilson, London, Duckworth, 1994.

Procopius, *History of the wars* and *Buildings*, 7 vols, ed./tr. H.B. Dewing, Cambridge (Ma.), Loeb, 1914 (references are to *Wars* unless B is prefixed).

Pseudo-Dionysius of Tel-Mahre, *Chronicle II*, ed. J.B. Chabot, Paris, CSCO, 1933; tr. Witold Witakowski (part III), Liverpool, LUP, 1996.

Simeon Stylites, *Das Leben*, ed. (of Greek texts) H. Lietzmann/tr. (of Syriac texts) H. Hilgenfeld, Leipzig, Texte und Untersuchungen, 1908.

Sozomen, *Ecclesiastical history*, ed. R. Hussey, Oxford, Clarendon, 1860; tr. C.D. Hartranft in *Nicene and Post-Nicene fathers of the Christian church*, 2, Oxford, Parker and co., 1891, 239–427.

Stephen of Byzantium, *Ethnikôn*, ed. A. Westermann, Leipzig, Teubner, 1839.

Suidas (10th century, but citing earlier writers), *Lexicon*, 5 vols, ed. A. Adler, Leipzig, Lexicographi graeci, 1928–38.

Synodicon orientale, ed./tr. J.B. Chabot, Paris, Bibliothèque Nationale, 1902.

Theophanes Confessor, *Chronicle*, ed. C. de Boor, Leipzig, Weber, 1883–85; tr. C. Mango and R. Scott, Oxford, Clarendon, 1997.

Theophylact Simocatta, *History*, ed. C. de Boor, rev. P. Wirth, Stuttgart, Teubner, 1972; tr. M. and M. Whitby, Oxford, Clarendon, 1986.

Zacharias Rhetor, *Historia ecclesiastica*, 2 vols, ed./tr. E.W. Brooks, Paris, CSCO, 1919–24.

Muslim texts (written after AD 700, but containing material on pre-Islamic Arabia)

'Abd al-Razzaq al-San'ani, *Muṣannaf*, 11 vols, ed. H. al-A'zami, Beirut, al-Majlis al-'Ilmi, 1970–72.

Abu 'Ubayd, Qasim ibn Sallam, *Amthâl*, ed. A. al-Qatamish, Damascus, Markaz al-Bahth al-'Ilmi, 1980.

Asma'i, 'Abd al-Malik al-, *Ta'rîkh al-'arab qabl al-islâm*, ed. M.H. Al Yasin, Baghdad, al-Maktaba al-'Ilmiyya, 1959.

Awtabi, Salma ibn Musallim al-, *Kitâb ansâb al-'arab*, Bibliothèque Nationale, Ms. arabe 5019.

Bukhari, Muhammad ibn Isma'il al-, *Al-ṣaḥîḥ*, 4 vols, ed. L. Krehl, Leiden, Brill, 1862–1908.

Dinawari, Ahmad ibn Da'ud al-, *Al-akhbâr al-ṭiwâl*, ed. M.S. al-Rafi', Cairo, Matba'at al-Sa'ada, 1910.

Hamdani, Hasan ibn Ahmad al-, *Kitâb al-iklîl*, vol. 8, ed. A.M. al-Karmali, Baghdad, Dar al-Salam, 1931; tr. N.A. Faris, Princeton, PUP, 1938 (as *The antiquities of south Arabia*).

—— *Kitâb al-jawharatayn*, ed./tr. C. Toll, Uppsala, Acta Universitatis Uppsaliensis, 1968.

Ibn 'Abd Rabbihi, Ahmad ibn Muhammad, *Al-'iqd al-farîd*, 9 vols, ed. M.M. Qumayha and A.M. Tarhini, Beirut, Dar al-Kutub al-'Ilmiyya, 1983.

Ibn al-Athir, 'Ali ibn Muhammad, *Usd al-ghâba*, 5 vols, Cairo, Jam'iyyat al-Ma'arif, 1869–71.

Ibn Habib, Muhammad, *Kitâb al-muhabbar*, ed. I. Lichtenstadter, Hyderabad, Da'irat al-Ma'arif al-'Uthmaniyya, 1942.

—— *Kitâb al-munammaq*, ed. K.A. Fariq, Hyderabad, Da'irat al-Ma'arif al-'Uthmaniyya, 1964.

Ibn Hisham, 'Abd al-Malik, *Sîrat rasûl Allâh*, ed. F. Wüstenfeld, Göttingen, Dieterichsche Universitäts-Buchhandlung, 1858–60; tr. A. Guillaume (as *The life of Muhammad*), Karachi, OUP, 1955.

Ibn Jubayr, *Rihla*, ed. W. Wright, rev. M.J. de Goeje, Leiden, E.J.W. Gibb Memorial, 1907.

Ibn al-Kalbi, Hisham, *Kitâb al-asnâm/Les Idoles*, ed./tr. W. Atallah, Paris, Klincksieck, 1969.

Ibn Maja, Muhammad ibn Yazid, *Sunan*, 2 parts in 1, Cairo, al-Matba'a al-'Ilmiyya, 1895.

Ibn Qutayba, 'Abdallah ibn Muslim, *'Uyûn al-akhbâr*, 4 vols, Cairo, Dar al-Kutub, 1925–30.

Ibn Rashiq, Hasan, *Al-'umda*, 2 vols, Cairo, Matba'at al-Sa'ada, 1963.

Ibn Sa'd, Muhammad, *Kitâb al-tabaqât al-kabîr*, 8 vols, ed. E. Sachau *et al.*, Leiden, Brill, 1905–40.

Ibn Sallam al-Jumahi, *Tabaqât fuhûl al-shu'arâ'*, 2 vols, ed. M.M. Shakir, Cairo, Madani, 1974.

Isfahani, 'Ali ibn Husayn al-, *Kitâb al-aghânî*, 24 vols, Cairo, Dar al-Kutub, 1927–74.

Jahiz, *Hayawân*, 7 vols, ed. A.M. Harun, Cairo, Mustafa Albabi al-Halabi, 1940–45.

—— '*Amr ibn Bahr al-, 'Manâqib al-Atrâk', ed. A.M. Harun in *Rasâ'il al-Jâhiz*, Cairo, Khanji, 1964, 1.5–86.

Kalbi, Hisham ibn Muhammad al-, *Ǧamharat al-nasab*, 2 vols, ed. W. Caskel, Leiden, Brill, 1966.

Marzubani, Muhammad ibn 'Imran, *Kitâb nûr al-qabas/Die Gelehrtenbiographien*, ed. R. Sellheim, Wiesbaden, Bibliotheca Islamica, 1964.

Mas'udi, 'Ali ibn Husayn al-, *Murûj al-dhahab/Les Prairies d'or*, 9 vols, ed./tr.

C. Barbier de Meynard and J.B. Pavet de Courteille, Paris, Société Asiatique, 1861–77.

Mubarrad, Muhammad ibn Yazid al-, *Al-kitâb al-kâmil*, 3 vols, ed. W. Wright, Leipzig, Brockhaus, 1874–92.

Muslim ibn al-Hajjaj, *Al-ṣaḥîḥ*, 2 parts in 1, Bulaq, 1873.

Nuwayri, Ahmad ibn 'Abd al-Wahhab, *Nihâyat al-arab*, 31 vols, Cairo, Dar al-Kutub, 1924–92.

Qali, Isma'il ibn al-Qasim al-, *Dhayl al-amâlî wa-l-nawâdir*, Cairo, Dar al-Kutub, 1926.

Quran: I use the text of M.M. Pickthall, London, George Allen and Unwin, 1976, and the translation of N.J. Dawood, Harmondsworth, Penguin, 1956.

Sibawayh, *Al-kitâb/Le Livre*, 2 vols, ed. Hartwig Derenbourg, Paris, Imprimerie Nationale, 1881–89.

Suyuti, 'Abd al-Rahman al-, *Al-muzhir fî 'ulûm al-lugha*, 2 parts in 1, Cairo, 1907.

Tabari = Tabari, Muhammad ibn Jarir al-, *Ta'rîkh al-rusul wa-l-mulûk*, 3 series, ed. M.J. de Goeje *et al.*, Leiden, Brill, 1879–1901; tr. *The history of al-Tabari*, 39 vols, Albany, SUNY, 1985–99.

―――― *Tafsîr al-qurân*, 30 vols, Bulaq, 1905–12.

Tawhidi, Abu Hayyan al-, *Kitâb al-imtâ' wa-l-mu'ânasa*, ed. A. Amin and A. al-Zayn, Cairo, 1953.

Wahb ibn Munabbih, *Kitâb al-tîjân*, Hyderabad, Da'irat al-Ma'arif al-'Uthmaniyya, 1929.

Waqidi, Muhammad ibn 'Umar al-, *Kitâb al-maghâzî*, 3 vols, ed. Marsden Jones, London, OUP, 1966.

Ya'qubi, Ahmad ibn Abi Ya'qub al-, *Ta'rîkh*, 2 vols, ed. M.T. Houtsma, Leiden, Brill, 1883.

PRIMARY SOURCES: TEXTS FROM WITHIN ARABIA

Inscriptions and papyri

'Abadan = Robin, Christian, and Gajda, Iwona, 'L'Inscription du Wadi 'Abadan', *Raydan* 6, 1994, 113–37.

AH = Abu l-Hasan, Husayn b. Ali, *Qirâ'a li-kitâbât Lihyâniyya min Jabal 'Akma bi-manṭiqat al-'Ulâ*, Riyad, King Fahd National Library, 1997.

Askoubi, Khalid M., *Dirâsa taḥlîliyya muqârina li-nuqûsh min manṭiqat Rum junûb gharb Taymâ'*, Riyad, Wakalat al-Athar wa-l-Matahif, 1999.

BIA = *Bulletin de l'Institut de l'Archéologie* (re: vol. 10, 1972, containing the 'Preliminary survey in N.W. Arabia, 1968' of P.J. Parr *et al.*).

CIAS = *Corpus des inscriptions et antiquités sud-arabes*, Louvain, Peeters, 1977–.

CIS = *Corpus inscriptionum semiticarum*, Paris, e Reipublicae Typographeo, 1881–.

Darb al-Sabi = Robin, Christian, *et al.*, 'Le Sanctuaire Minéen de *Nkrh* à Darb as-Sabi', *Raydan* 5, 1988, 91–159.

Doe 1–7 = Beeston, A.F.L., 'Miscellaneous epigraphic notes', *Raydan* 4, 1981, 9–14; 5, 1988, 5–10.

Fa = Fakhry, A., *An archaeological journey to Yemen, part II: epigraphical texts* (by G. Ryckmans), Cairo, Government Press, 1952.

Gl = 'Sammlung Eduard Glaser', *Osterreichische Akademie der Wissenschaften*, philosophisch-historische Klasse, 1913–81.

H = Healey, John, *The Nabataean tomb inscriptions of Mada'in Salih*, Oxford, JSS, 1993.

Hamilton = Brown, W.L., and Beeston, A.F.L., 'Sculptures and inscriptions from Shabwa', *Journal of the Royal Asiatic Society* 1954, 43–62 (deposited by Major Hamilton in the Ashmolean, Oxford).

Haram = Robin, Christian, *Inventaires des inscriptions sud-arabiques*, Paris/Rome, Boccard/Herder, 1992, 1.9–126.

HIT = Livingstone, A., 'A linguistic, tribal and onomastical study of the Hasaean inscriptions', *Atlal* 8, 1984, 86–108 (pp. 87–90 = Hasaean inscriptions from Thaj).

IGLS = Jalabert, L., *et al.*, *Inscriptions grecques et latines de la Syrie*, Paris, Geuthner, 1929–.

IIH = Aggoula, B., *Inventaire des inscriptions Hatréennes*, Paris, Geuthner, 1991.

IMT = Müller, Walter, 'Sabäische Inschriften aus dem Museum in Ta'izz', *NESE* 1.87–102.

Ingrams 1–3 = Philby, H. St J., 'Three new inscriptions from Hadramaut', *Journal of the Royal Asiatic Society* 1945, 124–32.

Ir. = Iryani, M.A., *Fî ta'rîkh al-Yaman. Sharḥ wa-ta'lîq 'alâ nuqûsh lam tunshar*, Cairo, Dar el-Hana, 1973.

ISB = Oxtoby, W.G., *Some inscriptions of the Safaitic bedouin*, New Haven, American Oriental Society, 1968.

Ja 550–850 = Jamme, A., *Sabaean inscriptions from Mahram Bilqis*, Baltimore, Johns Hopkins, 1962.

Ja 910–1006 = Jamme, A., *The al-'Uqlah texts*, Washington, Catholic University of America, 1963.

Ja 1008–62 = Jamme, A., *Sabaean and Hasaean inscriptions from Saudi Arabia*, Rome, Istituto di Studi del Vicino Oriente, 1966.

Ja 2106–20 = Jamme, A., and Doe, D.B., 'New Sabaean inscriptions from South Arabia', *Journal of the Royal Asiatic Society* 1968, 2–25.

Ja 2830–69 = Jamme, A., *1974–75 Yemen expedition*, Pittsburgh, Carnegie Museum, 1976.

Ja 2892–900 = Jamme, A., 'Pre-Islamic Arabian miscellanea', *Hudhud* 95–112.

Jidhma = Robin, Christian, "Amdan Bayyin Yuhaqbid, roi de Saba et de Dhu Raydan', *ESA* 187–88.

JS = Jaussen, P., and Savignac, P., *Mission archéologique en Arabie*, Paris, Geuthner, 1909–22.

KJA = King, Geraldine, *Early north Arabian Thamudic E: a preliminary description based on a new corpus of inscriptions from the Hisma desert*, 2 vols, London, SOAS, 1990, 1.176–252.

M = *Iscrizioni sudarabiche, vol. 1: iscrizioni minee*, Napoli, Istituto Orientale, 1974.

Mi'sal 7–9 = Robin, Christian, "Amdan Bayyin Yuhaqbid, roi de Saba et de Dhu Raydan', *ESA* 176–77.

MNA = Macdonald, M.C.A., *North Arabian inscriptions and drawings*, forthcoming.

NAG 1–20 = Nami, K.Y., 'Nuqûsh 'arabiyya ǧanûbiyya', *Kulliyyat al-âdâb* (Cairo) 9, 16, 20, 22–24, 1947–66.

Nami = Nami, K.Y., *Nashr nuqûsh sâmiyya qadîma*, Cairo, al-Ma'had al-'Ilmi al-Faransi, 1943.

Nessana Papyri = Kraemer, C.J., ed./tr., *Excavations at Nessana*, vol. 3, Princeton, PUP, 1958.

NIA = Negev, A., 'Nabatean inscriptions from 'Avdat (Oboda)', *Israel Exploration Journal* 11, 1961, 127–38; 13, 1963, 113–24.

NIN = Milik, J.T., 'Nouvelles inscriptions Nabatéennes', *Syria* 35, 1958, 227–51.

PAES = Littmann, Enno, *Semitic inscriptions*, Leiden (Publications of the Princeton University Archaeological Expeditions to Syria 1904–5 and 1909, division 4), 1914–49 (parts A–D).

PAT = Hillers, Delbert R., and Cussini, Eleonora, *Palmyrene Aramaic texts*, Baltimore, Johns Hopkins, 1996.

Qutra 1 = Robin, Christian, *AAKM*, 141–43.

RB = *Revue Biblique* (re: R. Savignac, 'Le Sanctuaire d'Allat à Iram', 41–43, 1932–34).

RES = *Répertoire d'épigraphie sémitique*, 8 vols, Paris, Académie des Inscriptions et Belles-Lettres, 1900–68.

Ry = Ryckmans, G., 'Inscriptions sud-arabes', in numerous articles in *Le Muséon* between 40, 1927, and 78, 1965.

Sharaf = Sharafaddin, A.H., *Ta'rîkh al-Yaman al-thaqâfî 3*, Cairo, 1967.

SIJ = Winnett, F.V., *Safaitic inscriptions from Jordan*, Toronto, University of Toronto, 1957.

SOYCE = Soviet Yemenite Complex Expedition; see S.A. Frantsouzoff, 'The inscriptions of the temples of Dhat Himyam at Raybun', *PSAS* 25, 1995, 15–27.

Sy = *Syria* (re: R. Mouterde and A. Poidebard, 'Palmyre et Hit au II siècle ap. J.C.', and J. Cantineau, 'Textes palmyréniens du temple de Bêl', 12, 1931, 101–15, 116–41).

VL = Van Lessen collection. For VL 7 see Beeston, A.F.L., 'Notes on old south Arabian lexicography X', *Le Muséon* 89, 1976, 420–23; for VL 9 see M. Ghul, 'New Qatabani inscriptions', *BSOAS* 22, 1959, 419–23.

WH = Winnett, F.V., and Harding, G. Lankester, *Inscriptions from fifty Safaitic cairns*, Toronto, University of Toronto, 1978.

WR = Winnett, F.V., and Reed, W.L., *Ancient records from north Arabia*, Toronto, University of Toronto, 1970.

YMN = Abdallah, Y.M., 'Mudawwanat al-nuqûsh al-yamaniyya al-qadîma', *Dirâsât yamaniyya* (San'a) 3, 1979, 45–50 (no. 13); *al-Iklil* (San'a) 8, 1990, 76–78 (no. 19).

ZI = 'Inan, Zayd, *Ta'rîkh hadârat al-Yaman al-qadîm*, Cairo, Salfiyya, 1976.

Pre-Islamic Arabic poetry (*c*.500–630 AD)

'Abid ibn al-Abras, *Dîwân*, ed./tr. Charles Lyall, Leiden and London, E.J.W. Gibb Memorial, 1913.

'Adi ibn Zayd, *Dîwân*, ed. M.H. al-Mu'aybid, Baghdad, Wizarat al-Thaqafa wa-l-Irshad, 1965.

'Amr ibn Qami'a, *Dîwân/The poems of*, ed./tr. C.J. Lyall, Cambridge, CUP, 1919.

A'sha: the piece I quote is edited in C.J. Lyall, *A commentary on ten ancient Arabic poems*, Calcutta, 1894, 146–47, and translated in Nicholson, *Literary history of the Arabs*, 125.

Ham. = Salih, A.A., ed., *Dîwân al-Hamâsa ta'lîf Abî Tammâm*, Baghdad, Dar al-Shu'un al-Thaqafiyya al-'Amma, 1987.

Hassan ibn Thabit, *Dîwân*, ed. H. Hirschfeld, Leiden and London, E.J.W. Gibb Memorial, 1910.

Hatim al-Ta'i, *Dîwân*, ed./tr. Friedrich Schulthess, Leipzig, Hinrichs, 1897.

Hudhaliyyun, *Dîwân*, ed. J.G.L. Kosegarten, London, Oriental Translation Fund, 1854 (nos. 1–138); ed./tr. J. Wellhausen in his *Skizzen und Vorarbeiten I*, Berlin, Georg Reimer, 1884 (nos. 139–).

Ikh. = Akhfash al-Asghar, *Kitâb al-ikhtiyârayn*, ed. F. Qabawa, Damascus, Majma' al-Lugha al-'Arabiyya, 1974.

Imru' al-Qays, *Dîwân*, ed. W. Ahlwardt in his *The diwans of the six ancient poets*, London, Trubner, 1870, 115–62.

Khansa', *Dîwân*, ed. A. Abu Suwaylim, Amman, Dar 'Ammar, 1988.

Labid, *Dîwân*, ed. I. Abbas, Kuwait, Wizarat al-Irshad wa-l-Anba', 1962.
Mu. = *Mu'allaqât*, the seven most famous pre-Islamic Arabic poems. I use the edition of C.J. Lyall, *A commentary on ten ancient Arabic poems*, Calcutta, 1894, and the translations of A.J. Arberry, *The seven odes*, London, George Allen and Unwin, 1957 (Imru' al-Qays, Tarafa, 'Antara, 'Amr, Haritha); C.J. Lyall, *Translations of ancient Arabian poetry*, London, Williams and Norgate, 1930, 111–15 (Zuhayr); A.F.L. Beeston, 'An experiment with Labid', *Journal of Arabic Literature* 7, 1976, 1–6 (Labid).
Muf. = Lyall, C.J., ed./tr., *The mufaḍḍaliyât*, Oxford, Clarendon, 1918.
Muhalhil = Cheikho, L., ed., *Shu'arâ' naṣrâniyya*, 2 vols, Beirut, Jesuit Fathers, 1890, 1.160–81; see Stetkevych, *Mute immortals,* 206–38.
Nabigha al-Dhubyani, *Dîwân*, ed. A. 'Abd al-Satir, Beirut, Dar al-Kutub al-'Ilmiyya, 1984.
Shanfara, *Dîwân*, ed. I.B. Ya'qub, Beirut, Dar al-Kitab al-'Arabiyy, 1991 (the passage of his *Lâmiyya* translated in chapter 5 is from Nicholson, *Literary history of the Arabs*, 80).
Tarafa ibn al-'Abd, *Dîwân*, ed. D. al-Khatib and L. al-Saqqal, Damascus, Majma' al-Lugha al-'Arabiyya, 1975.
Tufayl ibn 'Auf, *Dîwân/The poems of*, ed./tr. F. Krenkow, London, E.J.W. Gibb Memorial, 1927.
Zuhayr ibn Abi Sulma, *Dîwân*, ed. K. al-Bustani, Beirut, Dar al-Sader, 1964 (references are to page numbers).

SECONDARY SOURCES

1 East Arabia

Survey works

Hellyer, Peter, *Hidden riches: an archaeological introduction to the United Arab Emirates*, Abu Dhabi, Union National Bank, 1998.
Potts, D.T., *The Arabian Gulf in antiquity*, 2 vols, Oxford, Clarendon, 1990.
Rice, Michael, *The archaeology of the Arabian Gulf*, London, Routledge, 1994.
Traces of paradise: the archaeology of Bahrain 2500 BC–300 AD: an exhibition at the Brunei Gallery, London, July–September 2000, London, Bahrain National Museum, 2000.

Bronze Age

BAA (all articles relevant; see also review and update by H.I. Macadam, 'Dilmun revisited', *AAE* 1, 1990, 49–87). J. Reade's article, pp. 332–3, discusses cylinder seal of Ubalisu-Marduk.

Calvet, Yves, 'Le Pays de Dilmoun au II millénaire: découvertes récentes', *AP* 15–24.

Chakrabarti, D.K., 'The Indus civilisation and the Arabian Gulf: an Indian point of view', *ANBC* 303–14.

Cleuziou, Serge, 'Dilmoun–Arabie', *AMB* 27–58 (urges caution on identification and chronology).

Crawford, Harriet, 'Dilmun, victim of world recession', *PSAS* 26, 1996, 13–22.

—— *Dilmun and its Gulf neighbours*, Cambridge, CUP, 1998.

Durand, Capt., 'Extracts from report on the islands and antiquities of Bahrein', *Journal of the Royal Asiatic Society* 12, 1880, 6–7 (stone mentioning 'palace of Rimum. . . . ').

Hojlund, F., 'The ethnic composition of the population of Dilmun', *PSAS* 23, 1993, 1–7.

Hruška, B., 'Dilmun in den vorsargonischen Wirtschafttexten aus Šuruppak und Lagaš' in Potts, ed., *Dilmun*, 83–85.

Millard, A.R., 'Cypriot copper in Babylonia c. 1745 BC', *Journal of Cuneiform Studies* 25, 1973, 211–13.

Oljidam, Eric, 'Nippur and Dilmun in the second half of the 14th c. BC: a re-evaluation of the Ili-ippasra letters', *PSAS* 27, 1997, 199–204.

Potts, D.T., ed., *Dilmun: new studies in the archaeology and early history of Bahrain*, Berlin, Dietrich Reimer, 1983.

—— 'The booty of Magan', *Oriens Antiquus* 25, 1986, 271–85.

—— 'The late prehistoric, protohistoric and early historic periods in eastern Arabia (c.5000–1200 BC)', *Journal of World Prehistory* 7, 1993, 163–212.

—— 'Rewriting the late prehistory of southeastern Arabia: a reply to J. Orchard', *Iraq* 59, 1997, 63–71.

Iron Age

Bienkowski, Piotr, *Early Edom and Moab*, Sheffield, J.R. Collis, 1992 (re: Iron Age tribal kingdoms).

Boucharlat, R., 'Les Périodes pré-Islamiques récentes aux Emirats Arabes Unis', *AOMIM* 189–97.

Ferrara, A.J., 'An inscribed stone slab of Nebuchadnezzar II', *Journal of Cuneiform Studies* 27, 1975, 231–32.

Finkelstein, I., and Na'aman, Nadav, eds, *From nomadism to monarchy: archaeological and historical aspects of early Israel*, Jerusalem, Yad Izhak Ben-Zvi, 1994 (re: Iron Age tribal kingdoms).

Graf, David, 'Arabia during Achaemenid times', *Achaemenid History* 4 (Leiden, Nederlands Institut voor het Nabije Oosten), 1990, 131–48 (re: Hagar).

Liverani, M., 'The collapse of the Near Eastern regional system at the end of the Bronze Age' in M. Rowlands *et al.*, eds, *Centre and periphery in the ancient world*, Cambridge, CUP, 1987, 66–73.

Lombard, Pierre, 'Ages du fer sans fer: le cas de la péninsule d'Oman au 1 millénaire avant J.C.', *AP* 25–37.

MacDonald, Burton, and Younker, Randall W., eds, *Ancient Ammon*, Leiden, Brill, 1999 (re: Iron Age tribal kingdoms).

Magee, Peter, and Carter, Rob, 'Agglomeration and regionalism: southeastern Arabia between 1400 and 1100 BC', *AAE* 10, 1999, 161–79.

Müller, Walter, 'Zur Inschrift auf einem Krugfragment aus Muweilah', *AAE* 10, 1999, 51–53.

Potts, D.T., 'From Qadê to Mazûn: four notes on Oman 700BC–700AD', *Journal of Oman Studies* 1, 1975, 81–94.

Roaf, M., 'The subject peoples on the base of the statue of Darius', *Cahiers de la Délégation Archéologique Française en Iran* 4, 1974, 73–160.

Salles, J.F., 'Les Echanges commerciaux et culturels dans le Golfe arabo-persique au 1 millénnaire avant J.C.', *AP* 67–96.

—— 'Les Achéménides dans le Golfe arabo-persique', *Achaemenid History* 4 (Leiden, Nederlands Institut voor het Nabije Oosten), 1990, 111–30.

Sass, Benjamin, *The genesis of the alphabet and its development in the second millennium BC*, Wiesbaden, Harrassowitz, 1988.

Schmidt, E.F., *Persepolis*, 3 vols, Chicago, University of Chicago, 1953–70 (3.108: province lists; 3.111: status of Arabians; 3 figs. 47, 50: portrayal of Macians, Arabians).

Sherratt, Susan, 'Commerce, iron and ideology: metallurgical innovation in 12–11th century Cyprus' in *Proceedings of the international symposium 'Cyprus in the 11th century BC'*, Nicosia, Leventis Foundation, 1994, 59–106.

Sherratt, Susan and Andrew, 'From luxuries to commodities: the nature of Mediterranean Bronze Age trading systems' in N.H. Gale, ed., *Bronze Age trade in the Mediterranean*, Jonsered, Paul Astroms, 1991, 351–86.

—— 'The growth of the Mediterranean economy in the early first millennium BC', *World Archaeology* 24, 1993, 361–78.

Ungnad, A., *Neubabylonische Rechts- und Verwaltungskunden I*, Leipzig, Hinrichs, 1935 (pp. 550–51 translate and discuss the text relating to 'administrator of Dilmun').

Zarins, J., 'Persia and Dhofar: aspects of Iron Age international politics and trade' in G.D. Young *et al.*, eds, *Crossing boundaries and linking horizons*, Bethesda, CDL, 1997, 615–89.

Greco–Roman/Parthian period

AAW, 'Omana und Gerrha', 1.107–13; 'Bahrain und der Untergang Gerrha's', 5.1.163–69; 'On the location of Gerra', 5.2.36–57 (by W.E. James).

Blau, O., 'Die Wanderung der sabäischen Völkerstämme im 2. Jahrhundert n. Chr.', *ZDMG* 22, 1868, 654–73.

Boucharlat, R., 'Les Périodes pré-Islamiques récentes aux Emirats Arabes Unis', *AOMIM* 189–97.

—— and Mouton, M., 'Cultural change in the Oman peninsula during the late 1st millennium BC as seen from Mleiha, Sharjah Emirate', *PSAS* 21, 1991, 23–33.

—— and Salles, J.F., 'The history and archaeology of the Gulf from the fifth century BC to the seventh century AD', *PSAS* 11, 1981, 65–84.

Fahd, T., 'Gerrhéens et Ğurhumites', in Hans Roemer and Albrecht Noth, eds, *Studien zur Geschichte und Kultur des Vorderen Orients: Festschrift für B. Spuler*, Leiden, Brill, 1981, 67–78.

Groom, N. St J., 'Gerrha – a "lost" Arabian city', *Atlal* 6, 1982, 97–108.

Haerinck, E., 'Abi'el, the ruler of southeastern Arabia', *AAE* 10, 1999, 124–28.

Högemann, Peter, *Alexander der Grosse und Arabien*, Munich, C.H. Beck, 1985.

Jeppesen, Kristian, 'The Ikaros inscription', in *Ikaros: the Hellenistic settlements, 3*, Moesgaard, Jutland Archaeological Society, 1989, 82–103.

Lombard, Pierre, 'The salt mine site and the "Hasaean period" of north-eastern Arabia', *ATB* 117–35.

Mouton, Michel, 'Les Echanges entre l'Arabie du Sud et la péninsule d'Oman du 3 s. av. J.C. au 4 s. ap. J.C.' in A. Avanzini, ed., *Profumi d'Arabia*, Rome, 'L'Erma' di Bretschneider, 1997, 297–311.

Potts, D.T., 'Thaj in the light of recent research', *Atlal* 7, 1983, 86–101.

—— 'Northeastern Arabia in the later pre-Islamic era', *AOMIM* 85–123.

—— 'Thaj and the location of Gerrha', *PSAS* 14, 1984, 87–91.

—— 'Arabia and the kingdom of Characene', *ATB* 137–67.

—— 'The Roman relationship with the *Persicus sinus* from the rise of Spasinou Charax (127 BC) to the reign of Shapur II (AD 309–79)' in Susan Alcock, ed., *The early Roman empire in the east*, Oxford, Oxbow, 1997, 89–107.

Salles, J.F., 'Bahrain "hellénistique": données et problèmes', *AOMIM* 151–62.

Seray, Hamad bin, 'Spasinou Charax and its commercial relations with the East through the Arabian Gulf', *Aram* 8, 1996, 15–23.

Byzantine/Sasanian period

AAW, 'Die Araber an der oströmisch–persischen Grenze im 4. Jahrhundert', 2.312–32; 'Šapur II. und die Araber', 2.344–56.

Abu Ezzah, A., 'The political situation in eastern Arabia at the advent of Islam', *PSAS* 9, 1979, 53–64.

Beaucamp, J., and Robin, Christian, 'L'Evêche nestorien de Mâšmâhîg dans l'archipel d'al-Bahrayn' in D.T. Potts, ed., *Dilmun*, Berlin, 1983, 171–95.

Bernard, V., and Salles, J.F., 'Discovery of a Christian church at al-Qusur, Failaka', *PSAS* 21, 1991, 7–21.

Boucharlat, R., and Salles, J.F., 'The history and archaeology of the Gulf from the fifth century BC to the seventh century AD', *PSAS* 11, 1981, 65–84.

Calvet, M.A., 'Les Ecrivains chrétiens de l'antiquité et le Golfe', *AOMIM* 347–50.

Cardi, Beatrice de, 'A Sasanian outpost in northern Oman', *Antiquity* 46, 1972, 305–10.

Donner, Fred, 'The Bakr b. Wa'il tribes and politics in northeastern Arabia on the eve of Islam', *Studia Islamica* 51, 1980, 5–37.

Frye, Richard N., 'Bahrain under the Sasanians' in D.T. Potts, ed., *Dilmun*, Berlin, 1983, 167–70.

Healey, John F., 'The Christians of Qatar in the 7th century AD', in I.R. Netton, ed., *Studies in honour of C.E. Bosworth*, Leiden, Brill, 2000, 1.222–37.

Kennet, Derek, 'Evidence for 4th/5th century Sasanian occupation at Khatt, Ras al-Khaimah', ANBC 105–16.

Kervran, Monik, 'A la recherche de Suhar: état de la question', *AOMIM* 285–97.

Langfeldt, J.A., 'Recently discovered early Christian monuments in northeastern Arabia', *AAE* 5, 1994, 32–60.

Lecker, M., 'The levying of taxes for the Sasanians in pre-Islamic Medina', *Jerusalem Studies in Arabic and Islam* forthcoming (Persians govern Hijaz via governor in Bahrain, then via a local Arab vassal).

Maricq, A., 'Res gestae divi Saporis', *Syria* 35, 1958, 295–360 (re: Naqsh-i Rustam inscription).

Piacentini, V.F., 'Ardashir I Papakan and the wars against the Arabs', *PSAS* 15, 1985, 57–77.

Potts, D.T., 'Nestorian crosses from Jabal Berri', *AAE* 5, 1994, 61–65.

Rothstein, G., *Die Dynastie der Lahmiden in al-Hira*, Berlin, Reuter und Reichard, 1899.

Seray, Hamad bin, 'Christianity in east Arabia', *Aram* 8, 1996, 315–32.

—— 'The Arabian Gulf in Syriac sources', *New Arabian Studies* 4, 1997, 205–42.

Tardieu, M., 'L'Arabie du Nord-Est d'après les documents manichéens', *Studia Iranica* 23, 1994, 59–75 (discusses a reference to Manichaeans in Khatt).

Wilkinson, J.C., 'Arab–Persian land relationships in late Sasanid Oman', *PSAS* 3, 1973, 40–51.

—— 'The Julanda of Oman', *Journal of Oman Studies* 1, 1975, 97–107.

Archaeology

(See also relevant references in the sections above and in chapter 7.)

Cleuziou, Serge, 'Hili and the beginning of oasis life in eastern Arabia', *PSAS* 12, 1982, 15–22.

Hassell, Jonathan, 'Alabaster beehive-shaped vessels from the Arabian peninsula', *AAE* 8, 1997, 245–81.

Orchard, J., 'Third millennium oasis towns and environmental constraints on settlement in the al-Hajar region', *Iraq* 56, 1994, 63–88.

Potts, D.T., 'Nabataean finds from Thaj and Qatif', *AAE* 2, 1991, 138–44.

—— 'A new Bactrian find from southeastern Arabia', *Antiquity* 67, 1993, 591–96 (re: bone comb).

Whitehouse, D., *Excavations at ed-Dur (Umm al-Qaiwain, U.A.E.) I: the glass vessels*, Louvain, Peeters, 2000.

2 South Arabia

Survey works

Breton, J.F., *L'Arabie heureuse au temps de la reine de Saba*, Paris, Hachette, 1998.

Doe, Brian, *Southern Arabia*, London, Thames and Hudson, 1971.

Jemen, 3000 Jahre Kunst und Kultur des glücklichen Arabien, München 1987, Innsbruck, Pinguin, 1987.

Robin, Christian, 'Sheba dans les inscriptions d'Arabie du sud', *Dictionnaire de la Bible, supplément* 1996, 1047–1254.

Schippmann, Klaus, *Geschichte der altsüdarabischen Reiche*, Darmstadt, Wissenschaftliche Buchgesellschaft, 1998.

Yémen au pays de la reine de Saba: exposition présentée à l'Institut du monde arabe 1997–98, Paris, Flammarion, 1997 (an exhibition that has since gone to Vienna, Munich and Rome, spawning more catalogues).

Iron Age

Avanzini, A., 'Saba' and the beginning of epigraphic documentation of the Jawf', *AAE* 7, 1996, 63–68.

—— 'La Chronologie "courte": un réexamen', *AA* 7–14.

Beek, Gus van, *Hajar bin Humeid: investigations at a pre-Islamic site in south Arabia*, Baltimore, Johns Hopkins, 1969.

Beeston, A.F.L., 'Problems of Sabaean chronology', *BSOAS* 16, 1954, 37–56.

Dion, Paul, and Daviau, P.M., 'An inscribed incense altar of Iron Age II at *Khirbet el-Mudeyine* (Jordan)', *Zeitschrift des Deustchen Palästina-Vereins* 116, 2000, 1–13.

Edens, Christopher, and Wilkinson, T.J., 'Southwest Arabia during the Holocene: recent archaeological developments', *Journal of World Prehistory* 12, 1998, 55–119.

Garbini, Giovanni, 'La successione dei "Mukarrib" di Saba', *ESA* 93–99.

—— 'La Chronologie "longue": une mise au point', *AA* 15–22.

Korotayev, Andrey, 'The earliest Sabaeans in the Jawf: a reconsideration', *AAE* 9, 1998, 118–24.

Lemaire, A., 'Histoire du proche-orient et chronologie sudarabique avant Alexandre', *AA* 35–48.

—— 'Les Minéens et la Transeuphratène à l'époque perse', *Transeuphratène* 13, 1997, 123–39.

Magee, Peter, 'Writing in the Iron Age: the earliest south Arabian inscription from southeastern Arabia', *AAE* 10, 1999, 43–50.

Maigret, Alessandro de, *The Sabaean archaeological complex in the Wadi Yala*, Rome, IsMEO, 1988.

—— and Robin, Christian, 'Les Fouilles Italiennes de Yalâ: nouvelles données sur la chronologie de l'Arabie du Sud préislamique', *CRAIBL* 1989, 255–91.

Pirenne, Jacqueline, 'Des Grecs à l'aurore de la culture monumentale sabéenne', *AP* 257–69.

Robin, Christian, 'Les Premiers Etats du Jawf et la civilisation sudarabique', *AA* 49–66.

—— 'Sumhuriyam, fils de Karib'il le grand, et le mukarribat', *Südarabien* 155–69.

Ryckmans, Jacques, *L'Institution monarchique en Arabie méridionale avant l'Islam (Ma'in et Saba)*, Louvain, Publications universitaires, 1951.

—— 'Biblical and old south Arabian institutions: some parallels', in R. Bidwell and G.R. Smith, eds, *Arabian and Islamic studies: articles presented to R.B. Serjeant*, London, Longman, 1983, 14–25.

Saqqaf, H.M. al-, 'Awwal naqsh yadhkuru mkrb Awsân', *Raydan* 6, 1994, 111–20.

Sayed, Abdel Monem, 'Were there direct relationships between Pharaonic Egypt and Arabia?', *PSAS* 19, 1989, 155–64 (no!).

Singer-Avitz, Lily, 'Beersheba: a gateway community in southern Arabian long-distance trade in the eighth century BC', *Tel Aviv* 26, 1999, 3–75 (see also references in pastoralism section of ch. 4).

Wissmann, Hermann von, *Das Grossreich der Sabäer bis zu seinem Ende im frühen 4. Jht. v. Chr.*, Vienna, Osterreichischen Akademie der Wissenschaften, 1982 (ed. Walter Müller).

Greco–Roman/Parthian period

Bafaqih, M.A., *L'Unification du Yémen antique: la lutte entre Saba', Himyar et le Hadramawt du 1 au III s. de l'ère chrétienne*, Paris, Geuthner, 1990.

—— and Arbach, M., 'Nouvelles Données sur la chronologie des rois du Hadramawt', *Semitica* 48, 1998, 109–26.

Beeston, A.F.L., 'Notes on old south Arabian lexicography VIII', *Le Muséon* 86, 1973, 443–53 (tr. of Ja 576).

—— 'The Himyarite problem', *PSAS* 5, 1975, 1–7.

—— 'The settlement at Khor Rori', *Journal of Oman Studies* 2, 1976, 39–42.

—— 'Some observations on Greek and Latin data relating to south Arabia', *BSOAS* 42, 1979, 7–12.

—— 'Old South Arabian era datings', *PSAS* 11, 1981, 1–5.

—— 'Further remarks on the Zayd-'il sarcophagus text', *PSAS* 14, 1984, 100–102.

—— 'Chronological problems of the Ancient South Arabian culture', *SHA* 2.3–6.

—— 'Sabaeans in Tihama', *AAE* 6, 1995, 236–45.

Bron, F., 'A propos de l'éponymie Qatabanite', *Sayhadica* 21–27.

Casson, Lionel, 'South Arabia's maritime trade in the first century AD', *AP* 187–94.

—— 'The Greek and Latin sources for the southwestern coast of Arabia', *AAE* 6, 1995, 214–21.

Gnoli, Gherardo, 'Il sincronismo Mineo–Persiano', *AA* 23–34 (re: RES 3022/M247).

Groom, Nigel, 'The *Periplus*, Pliny and Arabia', *AAE* 6, 1995, 180–95.

Müller, Walter, 'Arabian frankincense in antiquity according to classical sources', *SHA* 1.79–92.

—— 'Das Ende des antiken Königreichs Hadramaut: die sabäische Inschrift Schreyer-Geukens = Iryani 32', *Hudhud* 225–56.

Potts, D.T., 'Augustus, Aelius Gallus and the Periplus: a reinterpretation of the coinage of San'a class B', *AF* 212–22.

Robin, Christian, 'Le Calendrier himyarite: nouvelles suggestions', *PSAS* 11, 1981, 43–53.

—— 'Les Inscriptions d'al-Mi'sal et la chronologie de l'Arabie méridionale au III siècle de l'ère chrétienne', *CRAIBL* 1981, 315–39.

—— *Les Hautes-terres du nord-Yémen avant l'Islam*, 2 vols, Leiden, Nederlands Instituut voor het Nabije Oosten, 1982.

—— 'Aux origines de l'état Himjarite: Himyar et Dhu-Raydan', *ASMG* 104–12.

—— 'Première Mention de Tyr chez les Minéens d'Arabie du Sud', *Semitica* 39, 1990, 135–47.

—— 'La Pénétration des Arabes nomades au Yémen', *AAKM* 71–88.

—— 'A propos d'une nouvelle inscription du règne de Sha'r Awtar: un réexamen de l'éponymat sabéen à l'époque des rois de Saba et de dhu-Raydan', *AF* 230–49.

—— 'La Fin du royaume de Ma'in', *Res Orientales* 11, 1998, 177–88.

Rodinson, Maxime, 'L'Arabie du sud chez les auteurs classiques', in Chelhod, J., ed., *L'Arabie du sud I*, Paris, Maisonneuve et Larose, 1984, 55–89.

Rougé, Jean, 'La Navigation en mer Erythrée dans l'antiquité', *AMB* 59–74.

Ryckmans, Jacques, 'Les "Hierodulenlisten" de Ma'in et la colonisation Minéene', *Scrinium Lovaniense: mélanges historiques E. van Cauwenbergh*, Louvain, Université de Louvain, 1961, 51–61.

Salles, J.F., 'La Circumnavigation de l'Arabie dans l'antiquité classique', *AMB* 75–102.

Sayed, Abdel Monem, 'Reconsideration of the Minaean inscription of Zayd'il', *PSAS* 14, 1984, 93–99.

Sedov, Alexander, 'Sea-trade of the Hadramawt kingdom from the 1st to the 6th centuries AD', in A. Avanzini, ed., *Profumi d'Arabia*, Rome, 'L'Erma' di Bretschneider, 1997, 365–79.

Wissmann, Hermann von, 'Himyar, ancient history', *Le Muséon* 77, 1964, 429–97.

Zwettler, Michael, 'The "era of NBT" and "YMNT": two proposals', *AAE* 7, 1996, 95–107.

Byzantine/Sasanian period

AAW, 'Dhu Nuwas', 5.1.305–91 (and related topics).

Ansary, A.T., 'Aḍwâ' jadîda 'alâ dawlat Kinda min khilâl âthâr Qaryat al-Faw wa-nuqûshihâ', *SHA* 3–15 (includes epitaph of Mu'awiya ibn Rabi'a).

Bafaqih, M.A., 'New light on the Yazanite dynasty', *PSAS* 9, 1979, 5–9.

—— 'Abraha . . . tubba'an! Ta'ammulât fî 'ahdih fî daw' naqshihi l-kabîr', *ASMG* 91–105 (re: CIS 4.541).

Beeston, A.F.L., 'Notes on the Mureighan inscription', *BSOAS* 16, 1954, 389–92 (tr. of Ry 506).

—— 'A note on Ma'dikarib's Wadil Masil text', *Annali dell'Istituto Orientale di Napoli* 42, 1982, 307–11 (re: Ry 510).

—— 'Two Bi'r Hima inscriptions re-examined', *BSOAS* 48, 1985, 42–52 (tr. of Ja 1028, Ry 507).

—— 'The martyrdom of Azqir', *PSAS* 15, 1985, 5–10.

—— 'The chain of al-Mandab', in *On both sides of al-Mandab, studies presented to Oscar Löfgren*, Stockholm, Swedish Research Institute in Istanbul, 1989, 1–6.

Blois, F. de, 'The date of the martyrs of Nagran', *AAE* 1, 1990, 110–28.

Frézouls, Edmond, 'Cosmas Indicopleustes et l'Arabie', *AP* 441–60.

Gajda, Iwona, 'Huǧr b. 'Amr roi de Kinda et l'établissement de la domination himyarite en Arabie centrale', *PSAS* 26, 1996, 65–73.

Huxley, G.L., 'On the Greek *Martyrium* of the Negranites', *Proceedings of the Royal Irish Academy* 80, 1980, 41–55.

Kister, M.J., 'The campaign of Huluban: a new light on the expedition of Abraha', *Le Muséon* 78, 1965, 425–36.

Müller, Walter, 'Eine sabaeische Gesandtschaft in Ktesiphon und Seleukeia', *NESE* 2, 155–65.

—— 'Survey of the history of the Arabian peninsula from the 1st c. AD to the rise of Islam', *SHA* 2.125–31 (chiefly south Arabia).

—— 'CIH 325: die jüngste datierte sabäische Inschrift', ESA 117–31.

Olinder, Gunnar, *The kings of Kinda*, Lund, Gleerup, 1927.

Robin, Christian, 'Du nouveau sur les Yaz'anides', *PSAS* 16, 1986, 181–97.

—— 'La Tihama yéménite avant l'Islam: notes d'histoire et de géographie historique', *AAE* 6, 1995, 222–35.

—— 'Le royaume hujride, dit "royaume de Kinda", entre Himyar et Byzance', *CRAIBL* 1996, 665–714.

Rubin, Z., 'Byzantium and southern Arabia: the policy of Anastasius', in D.H. French and C.S. Lightfoot, eds, *The eastern frontier of the Roman empire II*, Oxford, BAR, 1989, 383–420.

Ryckmans, Jacques, *La Persécution des chrétiens Himyarites au sixième siècle*, Istanbul, Nederlands Historisch–Archaeologisch Instituut, 1956.

—— 'Some remarks on the late Sabaean inscriptions', *SHA* 1.57–68.

—— 'A confrontation of the main hagiographic accounts of the Najran persecution', *ASMG* 113–33.

Sayed, Abdel Monem, 'Emendations to the Bir Murayghan inscription Ry 506', *PSAS* 18, 1988, 131–43.

Shahid, Irfan, *The martyrs of Najran: new documents*, Brussels, Société des Bollandistes, 1971.

—— 'Further reflections on the sources for the martyrs of Najran', *ASMG* 161–72.

Shitomi, Y., 'Réexamen de deux lettres attribuées à Siméon de Beth-Aršam relatives à la persécution de Naǧran', *ESA* 207–24.

3 North and central Arabia

Survey works

(There are no survey works for all the peoples of this region during the pre-Islamic period, but only for specific peoples, especially Nabataeans, and specific places, especially Palmyra.)

Dussaud, René, *La Pénétration des Arabes en Syrie avant l'Islam*, Paris, Geuthner, 1955 (covers Nabataeans, Palmyrenes, Lihyan, Thamud, Safaites, without considering whether all are Arabs).

Eph'al, Israel, *The ancient Arabs: nomads on the borders of the Fertile Crescent 9th–5th centuries BC*, Jerusalem, Magnes, 1982.

Glueck, Nelson, *Deities and dolphins: the story of the Nabataeans*, London, Cassell, 1966.

Hammond, Philip, *The Nabataeans: their history, culture and archaeology*, Gothenburg, Paul Aströms, 1973.

Knauf, E.A., *Ismael: Untersuchungen zur Geschichte Palästinas und Nordarabiens im 1. Jahrtausend v. Chr.*, Wiesbaden, Harrassowitz, 1985.

Levy, Udi, *Die Nabatäer: versunkene Kultur am Rande des heiligen Landes*, Stuttgart, Urachhaus, 1996.

Macdonald, M.C.A., 'North Arabia in the first millennium BCE', *CANE* 2.1355–69.

Starcky, J., and Gawlikowski, M., *Palmyre*, Paris, Librairie d'Amérique et d'Orient, 1985.

Stoneman, Richard, *Palmyra and its empire: Zenobia's revolt against Rome*, Ann Arbor, University of Michigan, 1992.

Will, Ernest, *Les Palmyréniens: la Venise des sables*, Paris, Armand Colin, 1992.

Iron Age

Bawden, G., 'Continuity and disruption in the ancient Hejaz', *AAE* 3, 1992, 1–23 (argues against Parr's view that there was a break in settlement 11–6th centuries BC).

Dalley, S., and Goguel, A., 'The Sela' sculpture: a neo-Babylonian rock relief in southern Jordan', *ADAJ* 41, 1997, 169–76 (a relief on a cliff near Petra effected by Nabonidus on his way to Tayma).

Deller, K., and Parpola, S., 'Ein Vertrag Assurbanipals mit dem arabischen Stamm Qedar', *Orientalia* 37, 1968, 464–66.

Dumbrell, William J., 'The Tell el-Maskhuta bowls and the kingdom of "Qedar" in the Persian period', *BASOR* 203, 1971, 33–44.

Gerardi, Pamela, 'The Arab campaigns of Assurbanipal: scribal reconstruction of the past', *State Archives of Assyria Bulletin* 6, 1992, 67–103.

Graf, David, 'Arabia during Achaemenid times', *Achaemenid History* 4 (Leiden, Nederlands Institut voor het Nabije Oosten), 1990, 131–48.

Knauf, E.A., 'The Persian administration in Arabia', *Transeuphratène* 2, 1990, 201–17.

—— 'Südarabien, Nordarabien und die hebräische Bibel', *AF* 115–22.

Livingstone, A., 'Arabians in Babylonia/Babylonians in Arabia', *AP* 97–105.

Parr, P.J., 'Pottery of the late second millennium BC from northwest Arabia', *ATB* 73–89.

—— 'Aspects of the archaeology of northwest Arabia in the first millennium BC', *AP* 39–66.

—— 'The early history of the Hejaz: a response to Garth Bawden', *AAE* 4, 1993, 48–58.

Rabinowitz, Isaac, 'Aramaic inscriptions of the fifth century BCE from a north-Arab shrine in Egypt', *Journal of Near Eastern Studies* 15, 1956, 1–9 (re: Tell el-Maskhuta bowl).

Reade, Julian, 'Assyrian illustrations of Arabs', *ANBC* 221–32.

Retso, Jan, 'The earliest Arabs', *Orientalia Suecana* 38–39, 1989–90, 131–39.

—— 'Xenophon in Arabia', *Studia graeca et latina gothoburgensia* 54, 1990, 122–33 (against F.M. Donner, 'Xenophon's Arabia', *Iraq* 48, 1986, 1–14).

Rouillard-Bonraisin, H., 'Présence et représentations des Arabes dans les écrits bibliques', *PA* 23–35.

Sack, Ronald, 'Nabonidus of Babylon', and Weisberg, D.B., 'Polytheism and politics: some comments on Nabonidus' foreign policy', in G.D. Young *et al.*, eds, *Crossing boundaries and linking horizons*, Bethesda, CDL, 1997, 455–74, 547–56 (put the religious and political cases respectively for Nabonidus' move to Tayma and list the voluminous earlier literature on this topic).

Zadok, Ran, 'Arabians in Mesopotamia during the late Assyrian, Chaldean, Achaemenian and Hellenistic periods', *ZDMG* 131, 1981, 42–84.

BIBLIOGRAPHY

Greco-Roman/Parthian period: writers of north Arabian texts

AAW, 'Die Lihyan', 1.93–106.

Abu Duruk, Hamid, and Murad, Abd al-Jawad, 'Preliminary report on Qasr al-Hamra excavations, Tayma', *Atlal* 9, 1985, 55–64; 10, 1986, 29–35; 11, 1988, 29–36.

Caskel, Werner, *Lihyan und Lihyanisch*, Cologne and Opladen, Westdeutscher Verlag, 1954.

Dalley, S., 'Stelae from Teima and the god Slm (Salmu)', *PSAS* 15, 1985, 27–33.

Edens, C., and Bawden, G., 'History of Tayma and Hejazi trade during the first millennium BC', *Journal of the Social and Economic History of the Orient* 32, 1989, 48–103.

EI, *s.v.* 'Thamud'.

Fares-Drappeau, Saba, *Dedan et ses inscriptions*, 3 vols, Aix–Marseilles, Université d'Aix, 1999.

Graf, David, 'The Saracens and the defense of the Arabian frontier', *BASOR* 229, 1978, 1–26.

Gysens, J. Calzini, 'Safaitic graffiti from Pompeii', *PSAS* 20, 1990, 1–7.

Höfner, Maria, 'Die Beduinen in den vorislamischen arabischen Inschriften', *ASB* 53–68.

Khraysheh, Fawwaz al-, 'Safaïtische Inschriften mit Jahresangaben', *Südarabien* 69–80.

Lemaire, A., 'Les Inscriptions araméennes anciennes de Teima', *PA* 59–72.

Macdonald, M.C.A., 'The distribution of Safaitic inscriptions in northern Jordan', *Studies in the History and Archaeology of Jordan* 4, 1992, 303–307.

—— 'Nomads and the Hawran in the late Hellenistic and Roman periods: a reassessment of the epigraphic evidence', *Syria* 70, 1993, 303–403.

—— 'Quelques réflexions sur les Saracènes, l'inscription de Rawwafa et l'armée romaine', *PA* 93–101.

—— 'Herodian echoes in the Syrian desert', in S. Bourke and J.P. Descoeudres, eds, *Studies in honour of J. Basil Hennessy*, Sydney, *Mediterranean Archaeology Supplement*, 1995 (Safaitic texts mentioning Herodian rulers of the Hawran).

Maraqten, Mohammed, 'The Aramaic pantheon of Tayma', *AAE* 7, 1996, 17–31.

Potts, D.T., 'Tayma and the Assyrian empire', *AAE* 2, 1991, 10–23.

Retso, Jan, 'Where and what was *Arabia Felix?*', *PSAS* 30, 2000, forthcoming.

Salles, J.F., 'Al-'Ula-Dédan: recherches récentes', *Topoi* 6, 1996, 565–607.

Scagliarini, Fiorella, 'La Chronologie dédanite et lihyanite: mise au point', *PA* 119–32.

282

Sima, Alexander, 'Aramaica aus Dedan und Tayma', *AAE* 10, 1999, 54–57.

Theeb, S.A. al-, *Dirâsa taḥlîliyya li-l-nuqûsh al-ârâmiyya al-qadîma*, Riyad, King Fahd National Library, 1994.

Winnett, F.V., 'The revolt of Damasi: Safaitic and Nabataean evidence', *BASOR* 211, 1973, 54–57 (an example of some precisely datable Safaitic texts).

—— 'A reconsideration of some inscriptions from the Tayma area', *SHA* 1.69–77 and *PSAS* 10, 1980, 133–40.

Greco–Roman/Parthian period: writers of Aramaic/Greek texts

AAW, 'Berichte über die Anfänge der Nabatäer', 1.31–39; 'Ptolemäer und Nabatäer', 1.65–79; 'Odainat und Palmyra', 2.251–73.

Aggoula, Basile, 'Arabie et Arabes en Mésopotamie (du III siècle av. JC. au III siècle apr. JC.)', *PA* 73–79 (re: Hatra and its hinterland).

Aram 2, 1990: *The Nabataeans* (proceedings of a conference held in Oxford 1989).

Aram 7, 1995: *Palmyra and the Aramaeans* (proceedings of a conference held in Oxford 1994).

Bowersock, G.W., *Roman Arabia*, Cambridge (Ma.), Harvard UP, 1983.

Briquel-Chatonnet, F., 'La Pénétration de la culture du Croissant fertile en Arabie: à propos des inscriptions nabatéennes', *PA* 133–41.

Dijkstra, K., 'State and steppe: the socio-political implications of Hatra inscription 79', *JSS* 35, 1990, 81–98.

Dodgeon, Michael, and Lieu, Samuel, *The Roman eastern frontier and the Persian wars AD 226–363*, London, Routledge, 1991 (ch. 4: 'The rise and fall of Palmyra').

Drijvers, H.J.W., 'Hatra, Palmyra und Edessa', *Aufstieg und Niedergang der römischen Welt* 2.8, 1977, 799–906.

Freeman, Philip, 'The annexation of Arabia and imperial grand strategy', *Journal of Roman Archaeology* suppl. 18, 1996, 91–118.

Gatier, P.L., and Salles, J.F., 'Aux frontières méridionales du domaine Nabatéen', *AMB* 174–90.

Gawlikowski, M., 'Les Arabes en Palmyrène', *PA* 103–108.

—— 'The Syrian desert under the Romans', in Susan Alcock, ed., *The early Roman empire in the East*, Oxford, Oxbow, 1997, 37–54.

Hamarneh, Salih, 'The Nabataeans after the decline of their political power', *Aram* 2, 1990, 425–36.

Hauser, Stefan R., 'Hatra und das Königreich der Araber', in J. Wiesehöfer, ed., *Das Partherreich und seine Zeugnisse*, Stuttgart, Franz Steiner, 1998, 493–528.

Healey, John F., 'The Nabataeans and Mada'in Salih', *Atlal* 10, 1986, 108–16 (ancient Hegra).
—— 'Were the Nabataeans Arabs?', *Aram* 1, 1989, 38–44.
Isaac, Benjamin, 'Trade-routes to Arabia and the Roman presence in the desert', *AP* 241–56.
Kammerer, A., *Pétra et la Nabatène: l'Arabie Pétrée et les Arabes du nord dans leurs rapports avec la Syrie et la Palestine jusqu'à l'Islam*, Paris, Geuthner, 1929.
Kasher, Aryeh, *Jews, Idumaeans and ancient Arabs 332 BCE–70 CE*, Tübingen, J.C.B. Mohr, 1988.
Knauf, E.A., 'Nabataean origins', *ASMG* 56–61 (from ancient Edom).
MacAdam, Henry I., 'Strabo, Pliny the Elder and Ptolemy of Alexandria: three views of ancient Arabia and its peoples', *AP* 289–320.
Macdonald, M.C.A, 'Personal names in the Nabataean realm: a review article', *JSS* 44, 1999, 251–89 (on the value of names to Nabataean cultural history).
Nasiriyy, S.A. al-, 'Al-ṣirâ' 'alâ l-bahr al-ahmar fî 'asr al-Baṭâlima', *SHA* 2.401–28.
Retso, Jan, 'Nabataean origins once again', *PSAS* 29, 1999, 115–18 (a social rather than ethnic term).
Roche, M.J., 'Les Débuts de l'implantation nabatéenne à Pétra', *Trans-euphratène* 8, 1994, 35–46.
Segal, J.B., 'Arabs at Hatra and the vicinity', *JSS* 30, 1986, 57–80.
Sidebotham, S.E., *Roman economic policy in the Erythra Thalassa 30 BC–AD 217*, Leiden, Brill, 1986.
Starcky, J., 'Pétra et la Nabatène', *Dictionnaire de la Bible*, supplément 1966, 886–1017.
Wenning, Robert, 'The Nabataeans in the Decapolis/Coele Syria', *Aram* 4, 1992, 79–99.
Zakeri, M., 'Arabic reports on the fall of Hatra to the Sasanids', in S. Leder, ed., *Story-telling in the framework of non-fictional Arabic literature*, Wiesbaden, Harrassowitz, 1998, 158–67.

Byzantine/Sasanian period

Beeston, A.F.L., 'Nemara and Faw', *BSOAS* 42, 1979, 1–6 (re: translation of Nemara text).
—— 'A further note on the Nemara inscription', *al-Abhath* 29, 1981, 3–5.
Bosworth, C.E., 'Iran and the Arabs before Islam', in E. Yarshater, ed., *The Cambridge history of Iran, 3.1: the Seleucid, Parthian and Sasanian periods*, Cambridge, CUP, 1983, 593–612.
Gaube, Heinz, 'Arabs in sixth-century Syria: some archaeological

observations', *Proceedings of the First International Conference on Bilad al-Sham*, Amman, 1984, 61–66.

Greatrex, G., and Lieu, S., eds, *The Roman eastern frontier and the Persian wars AD 363–630* (forthcoming).

Kropp, Manfred, 'Vassal – neither of Rome nor of Persia: Mar' al-Qays the great king of the Arabs', *PSAS* 23, 1993, 63–93.

Letsios, D.G., 'The case of Amorkesos and the question of the Roman foederati in Arabia in the Vth century', *AP* 525–38.

Peters, F.E., 'The Arabs on the frontier of Syria before Islam', *Proceedings of the First International Conference on Bilad al-Sham*, Amman, 1984, 141–75.

Pohl, Walter, ed., *Kingdoms of the empire: the integration of barbarians in late antiquity*, Leiden, Brill, 1997.

Qathami, H.D. al-, *Shimâl al-Ḥijâz*, Beirut, Al-'Asr al-Hadith, 1991 (vol. 1: *al-âthâr*; vol. 2: *mu'jam al-mawâḍi' wa-l-qabâ'il*).

Sartre, M., 'Le Trophéus de Gadhimat, roi de Tanukh: une survivance en Arabie d'une institution hellénistique', *Liber Annuus* 29, 1979, 253–58.

—— *Trois études sur l'Arabie romaine et byzantine*, Brussels, Revue d'études latines, 1982.

—— 'Deux phylarches arabes dans l'Arabie byzantine', *Le Muséon* 106, 1993, 145–53.

Shahid, Irfan, 'Ḥamlat Imru' al-Qays 'alâ Najrân: al-maṣâdir ghayr al-'arabiyya', *SHA* 1.73–79.

—— *Byzantium and the Arabs in the fourth century*, Washington DC, Dumbarton Oaks, 1984.

—— *Byzantium and the Arabs in the fifth century*, Washington DC, Dumbarton Oaks, 1989.

—— *Byzantium and the Arabs in the sixth century*, Washington DC, Dumbarton Oaks, 1995.

—— 'The Syriac sources for the history of the Arabs before the rise of Islam', *Orientalia Christiana Analecta* 256, 1998, 323–31 (Symposium Syriacum VII).

Smith, Sydney, 'Events in Arabia in the 6th century AD', *BSOAS* 16, 1954, 425–68.

Whittow, Mark, 'Rome and the Jafnids: writing the history of a 6th-c. tribal dynasty', *Journal of Roman Archaeology* suppl. 31, 1999, 207–24.

Zwettler, Michael, 'Imra'alqays, son of 'Amr: king of . . . ?', in M. Mir, ed., *Literary heritage of classical Islam*, Princeton, Darwin, 1993, 3–37 (argues for 'of Arabia' rather than 'of the Arabs').

4 Economy

Agriculture and water management

ABADY 5–7, 1991–95: 'Die sabäische Wasserwirtschaft von Marib'.

Bowen, R. LeBaron, 'Irrigation in ancient Qataban', in *id.* and F.P. Albright, *Archaeological discoveries in south Arabia*, Baltimore, Johns Hopkins, 1958, 43–131.

Brunner, Ueli, 'The history of irrigation in the Wadi Marhah', *PSAS* 27, 1997, 75–85.

Costa, Paolo M., 'Notes on traditional hydraulics and agriculture in Oman', *World Archaeology* 14, 1983, 273–95.

Hehmeyer, Ingrid, 'Irrigation farming in the ancient oasis of Marib', *PSAS* 19, 1989, 33–44.

Irvine, A.K., *A survey of old Arabian lexical materials connected with irrigation techniques*, Oxford, University of Oxford, 1962 (tr. of CIS 4.540).

Muheisen, Zeidoun al-, 'Maîtrise de l'eau et agriculture en Nabatène: l'exemple de Pétra', *Aram* 2, 1990, 205–20.

Nasif, Abdallah A., 'An ancient water system in Sakaka, al-Jawf, Saudi Arabia', *PSAS* 17, 1987, 127–35.

—— *Al-'Ula: an historical and archaeological survey with special reference to its irrigation system*, Riyad, King Saud University Press, 1988.

Pirenne, Jacqueline, *La Maîtrise de l'eau en Arabie du sud antique*, Paris, Imprimerie nationale, 1977.

—— 'La Juridiction de l'eau en Arabie du sud antique', in F. and J. Metral, eds, *L'Homme et l'eau en Méditerranée et au Proche Orient II*, Lyon, Maison de l'Orient, 1982, 81–102.

Potts, D.T., 'Contributions to the agrarian history of eastern Arabia I: implements and cultivation techniques', *AAE* 5, 1994, 158–68.

—— 'Contributions to the agrarian history of eastern Arabia II: the cultivars', *AAE* 5, 1994, 236–75.

Roberts, N., 'Water conservation in ancient Arabia', *PSAS* 7, 1977, 134–46; 8, 1978, 29–32.

Robin, Christian, 'Quelques observations sur la date de construction et la chronologie de la première digue de Ma'rib d'après les inscriptions', *PSAS* 18, 1988, 95–105.

Sedov, A.V., 'On the origin of the agricultural settlements in Hadramawt', *AA* 67–86.

Serjeant, R.B., 'Observations on irrigation in southwest Arabia', *PSAS* 18, 1988, 145–53.

Wilkinson, J.C., 'The origins of the *aflâj* of Oman', *Journal of Oman Studies* 6, 1983, 177–94.

Pastoralism

Artzy, Michal, 'Incense, camels and collared rim jars: desert trade routes and maritime outlets in the second millennium', *Oxford Journal of Archaeology* 13, 1994, 121–47.

Bar-Yosef, Ofer, and Khazanov, Anatoly, eds, *Pastoralism in the Levant*, Madison (Wi.), Prehistory Press, 1992.

Betts, A.V.G., 'The Solubba: nonpastoral nomads in Arabia', *BASOR* 274, 1989, 61–69 ('a useful example of the potential diversity of lifestyles' even in Arabia deserta).

—— 'The Neolithic sequence in the east Jordan *Badia*: a preliminary overview', *Paléorient* 19, 1993, 43–53.

Dayton, J.E., 'Midianite and Edomite pottery', *PSAS* 2, 1972, 25–37.

Finkelstein, I., 'Arabian trade and socio-political conditions in the Negev in the 12–11th centuries BC', *Journal of Near Eastern Studies* 47, 1988, 241–52.

Gauthier-Pilters, H., and Dagg, A.I., *The camel: its evolution, ecology, behaviour and relationship to man*, Chicago, University of Chicago, 1981.

Köhler-Rollefson, I., 'Camels and camel pastoralism in Arabia', *Biblical Archaeologist* 56, 1993, 180–88.

—— and Rollefson, G.O., 'The impact of Neolithic subsistence strategies on the environment: the case of 'Ain Ghazal, Jordan', in S. Bottema *et al.*, eds, *Man's role in the shaping of the eastern Mediterranean landscape*, Rotterdam, Balkema, 1990, 3–14.

—— and —— 'PPNC adaptations in the first half of the 6th millennium B.C.', *Paléorient* 19, 1993, 33–41.

Liverani, M., 'Early caravan trade between south Arabia and Mesopotamia', *Yemen* (IsMEO, Rome) 1, 1992, 111–15.

Maigret, Alessandro de, 'The Arab nomadic people and the cultural interface between the Fertile Crescent and Arabia Felix', *AAE* 10, 1998, 220–24.

Parr, P.J., 'The early history of the Hejaz: a response to Garth Bawden', *AAE* 4, 1993, 48–58.

Retso, Jan, 'The domestication of the camel and the establishment of the frankincense road from south Arabia', *Orientalia Suecana* 40, 1991, 187–219.

Schwartz, Glenn, 'Pastoral nomadism in ancient western Asia', *CANE* 1.249–58.

Sherratt, Andrew, 'The secondary exploitation of animals in the old world', *World Archaeology* 15, 1983, 90–104.

Wapnish, Paula, 'The dromedary and bactrian camel in Levantine historical settings: the evidence from Tell Jemmeh', in J. Clutton-Brock and C. Grigson, eds, *Animals and archaeology 3*, Oxford, BAR, 1984, 171–200.

Wengrow, David, 'Egyptian taskmasters and heavy burdens: highland exploitation and the collared rim pithos of the Bronze/Iron Age Levant', *Oxford Journal of Archaeology* 15, 1996, 307–26.

Hunting

Beeston, A.F.L., 'The ritual hunt: a study in old south Arabian religious practice', *Le Muséon* 61, 1948, 183–96 (tr. of CIS 4.571 and Ingrams 1).
—— 'Observations on the texts from al-'Uqlah', *PSAS* 12, 1982, 7–13.
—— 'The Sayhadic hunt at Ši'b al-'Aql', *ESA* 49–57.
Doe, Brian, 'Anwad, Jabal al-'Uqla', *PSAS* 12, 1982, 23–25.
Fowden, Garth, '"Desert kites": ethnography, archaeology and art', *Journal of Roman Archaeology* suppl. 31, 1999, 107–36.
Höfner, Maria, 'Ta'lab und der "Herr der Tiere" im antiken Südarabien', in *Al-Bahit: Festschrift Joseph Henninger*, Bonn, Anthropos-Institut, 1976, 145–53.
Müller, Walter, 'The meaning of Sabaic KRWM', *ASMG* 89–96.
Ryckmans, Jacques, 'An ancient stone structure for the capture of ibex in western Saudi Arabia', *PSAS* 6, 1976, 161–66.
—— 'La Chasse rituelle dans l'Arabie du sud ancienne', in *Al-Bahit: Festschrift Joseph Henninger*, Bonn, Anthropos-Institut, 1976, 259–307.
Serjeant, R.B., *South Arabian hunt*, London, Luzac, 1976 (p. 36: 'if we did not hunt . . . ').
Stetkevych, Jaroslav, 'The hunt in the Arabic *Qaṣîdah*', in J.R. Smart, ed., *Tradition and modernity in Arabic language and literature*, Richmond (Surrey), Curzon, 1996, 102–19.

Nomad–settled relations

Athamina, K., '*A'râb* and *muhâjirûn* in the environment of *amṣâr*', *Studia Islamica* 66, 1987, 5–25.
Bosworth, C.E., 'A note on *ta'arrub* in early Islam', *JSS* 34, 1989, 355–62.
Briant, Pierre, *Etat et pasteurs au moyen orient ancien*, Cambridge, CUP, and Paris, Maison des sciences de l'homme, 1982.
Bronson, B., 'The role of barbarians in the fall of states', in N. Yoffee and G. Cowgill, eds, *The collapse of ancient states and civilizations*, Tucson, University of Arizona, 1988, 196–218.
Caskel, W., 'Zur Beduinisierung Arabiens', *ZDMG* 103, 1953, 36–58; English tr. ('The Bedouinization of Arabia') in AAEI 34–44.
Christides, V., 'Saracens' *Prodosia* in Byzantine sources', *Byzantion* 40, 1970, 5–13.

Crone, Patricia, 'The first century concept of *hiǧra*', *Arabica* 41, 1994, 352–87.

Donner, Fred, 'The role of nomads in the Near East in late antiquity', in F.M. Clover and R.S. Humphreys, eds, *Tradition and innovation in late antiquity*, Madison, University of Wisconsin, 1989, 73–88 (repr. in AAEI 21–33).

Dostal, Walter, 'The evolution of bedouin life', *ASB* 11–34 (new saddle developed in 2nd–3rd c. AD allowed Arabian camel-herders to develop their military powers and become 'full bedouin').

—— 'The development of bedouin life in Arabia seen from archaeological material', *SHA* 1.125–44.

Finkelstein, I., *Living on the fringe: the archaeology and history of the Negev, Sinai and neighbouring regions in the Bronze and Iron Ages*, Sheffield, Sheffield Academic Press, 1995.

—— and Perevolotsky, Avi, 'Processes of sedentarization and nomadization in the history of Sinai and the Negev', *BASOR* 279, 1990, 67–88 (see reply thereto in Rosen below).

Geyer, Bernard, 'Des fermes byzantins aux palais omayyades', in L. Nordigiwan and J.F. Salles, eds, *Aux origines de l'archéologie aérienne: A. Poidebard (1878–1955)*, Beirut, Saint Joseph, 2000, 109–22.

Graf, David, 'Rome and the Saracens: reassessing the nomadic menace', *AP* 341–400.

Haiman, Mordechai, 'Agriculture and nomad–state relations in the Negev desert in the Byzantine and early Islamic periods', *BASOR* 297, 1995, 29–53.

Isaac, Benjamin, 'The meaning of "limes" and "limitanei" in ancient sources', *Journal of Roman Studies* 78, 1988, 125–47.

Labianca, O.S., *Sedentarization and nomadization: food system cycles at Hesban and vicinity in Transjordan*, Berrien Springs (Mi.), Andrews University, 1990.

Lancaster, William and Fidelity, 'Thoughts on the bedouinisation of Arabia', *PSAS* 18, 1988, 51–62 (argues against Caskel and Dostal's concept of predatory bedouin).

Macdonald, M.C.A., 'Was the Nabataean kingdom a "bedouin state"?', *Zeitschrift der deutschen Palästina-Vereins* 107, 1991, 102–19.

Mayerson, Philip, 'The Saracens and the Limes', *BASOR* 262, 1986, 35–47.

—— 'Saracens and Romans: micro–macro relationships', *BASOR* 274, 1989, 71–79.

Nelson, Cynthia, *The desert and the sown*, Berkeley, University of California, 1973.

Parker, S. Thomas, *Romans and Saracens: a history of the Arabian frontier*, Winona Lake (In.), ASOR, 1986.

Rosen, Steven, 'Nomads in archaeology: a response to Finkelstein and Perevolotsky', *BASOR* 287, 1992, 75–85 (but see comments of Finkelstein on pp. 87–88).

Rowton, M., 'Enclosed nomadism', *Journal of the Economic and Social History of the Orient* 17, 1974, 1–30.

—— 'Dimorphic structure and the tribal elite', in *Al-Bahit: Festschrift Joseph Henninger*, Bonn, Anthropos-Institut, 1976, 219–57.

Segal, J.B., 'Arabs in Syriac literature before the rise of Islam', *Jerusalem Studies in Arabic and Islam* 4, 1984, 89–123 (tr. of 'Vita Malchi' and Bar Sauma passages).

Webster, Roger, 'The bedouin in southern and southeastern Arabia: the evolution of bedouin life reconsidered', *PSAS* 22, 1992, 124 (based on modern data).

Whittaker, C.R., 'Where are the frontiers now?', *Journal of Roman Archaeology* suppl. 18, 1996, 25–40.

Zarins, J., 'Mar-tu and the land of Dilmun', *BAA* 233–50 (pastoral nomads around northeast Arabia).

Trade

Avanzini, A., ed., *Profumi d'Arabia*, Rome, 'L'Erma' di Bretschneider, 1997 (a very useful collection of articles on all aspects of Arabian aromatics).

Beeston, A.F.L., 'Pliny's Gebbanitae', *PSAS* 2, 1972, 4–8 (and see his 'Greek and Latin data').

Crone, Patricia, *Meccan trade and the rise of Islam*, Oxford, Blackwell, 1987.

Dirven, Lucinda, 'The nature of the trade between Palmyra and Dura-Europos', *Aram* 8, 1996, 39–54.

During Caspers, E., 'Harappan trade in the Arabian Gulf in the third millennium BC', *PSAS* 3, 1973, 3–20.

Eidem, Jesper, and Hojlund, Flemming, 'Trade or diplomacy? Assyria and Dilmun in the eighteenth century BC', *World Archaeology* 24, 1993, 441–48.

Gawlikowski, M., 'Le Commerce de Palmyre sur terre et sur eau', *AMB* 163–72.

—— 'Palmyra as a trading centre', *Iraq* 56, 1994, 27–33.

Gogte, V.D., 'Petra, the Periplus and ancient Indo-Arabian maritime trade', *ADAJ* 43, 1999, 299–304 (pottery evidence for interaction between Nabataea and India).

Healey, John F., 'Palmyra and the Arabian Gulf trade', *Aram* 8, 1996, 33–37.

Lecker, M., 'On the markets of Medina in pre-Islamic and early Islamic times', *Jerusalem Studies in Arabic and Islam* 19, 1995, 133–47.

Macdonald, M.C.A., 'A dated Nabataean inscription from southern Arabia', *AF* 132–41 (a Nabataean in south Arabia in AD 87/88 , possibly trading).

Mango, M.M., 'Byzantine maritime trade with the east (4–7th centuries)', *Aram* 8, 1996, 139–63.

Maraqten, Mohammed, 'Dangerous trade routes: on the plundering of caravans in the pre-Islamic Near East', *Aram* 8, 1996, 213–36.

Mattingly, Gerald, 'The Palmyrene luxury trade and Revelation 18:12–13', *Aram* 7, 1995, 217–31.

Mildenberg, Leo, 'Petra on the frankincense road?: again', *Aram* 8, 1996, 55–65.

Müller, Walter, 'Notes on the use of frankincense in south Arabia', *PSAS* 6, 1976, 124–36.

—— 'Weihrauch: ein arabisches Produkt und seine Bedeutung in der Antike', 'Pauly–Wissowa', *Realencyclopädie der classischen Altertumswissenschaft*, C.H. Beck, Munich 1978, suppl. XV, 700–77.

O'Dwyer Shea, M., 'The small cuboid incense-burner of the ancient Near East', *Levant* 15, 1983, 76–109.

Palmyra and the Silk Road, special issue of *Annales Archéologiques Arabes Syriennes* 42, 1996.

Potts, D.T., 'Trans-Arabian routes of the pre-Islamic period', *AMB* 127–62 (repr. in AAEI 45–80).

—— 'Rethinking some aspects of trade in the Arabian Gulf', *World Archaeology* 24, 1993, 423–40.

—— 'Distant shores: ancient Near Eastern trade with south Asia and northeast Africa', *CANE* 3.1451–63.

Rashid, N.S., 'Ta'āmul al-'arab al-tijāriyy wa-kayfiyyatuhu fī l-'aṣr al-jāhiliyy', *SHA* 2.210–49.

Rey-Coquais, J.P., 'L'Arabie dans les routes de commerce entre le monde Méditerranéen et les côtes Indiennes', *AP* 225–39.

Sahhab, Victor, *Ilāf Quraysh riḥlat al-shitā' wa-l-ṣayf*, Beirut, Kumbyu nashr, 1992.

Salles, J.F., ed., *L'Arabie et ses mers bordières*, Lyon, Maison de l'Orient, 1988.

Saud, Abdullah al-, 'The domestication of camels and inland trading routes in Arabia', *Atlal* 14, 1996, 129–36.

Sidebotham, Steven E., 'Ports of the Red Sea and the Arabia–India trade', *AP* 195–223.

Speece, Mark, 'The role of eastern Arabia in the Arabian Gulf trade of the third and second millennia', *SHA* 2.167–76.

Teixidor, J., *Un port romain du désert: Palmyre et son commerce*, Paris, Semitica 34, 1984.

Will, Ernest, 'Marchands et chefs de caravane à Palmyre', *Syria* 34, 1957, 262–77.

Yon, J.B., 'Remarques sur une famille caravanière à Palmyre', *Syria* 75, 1998, 153–60.

Mining

Heck, Gene W., 'Gold mining in Arabia and the rise of the Islamic state', *Journal for the Social and Economic History of the Orient* 42, 1999, 364–92.
Prentiss, S., Zarins, J., Hester, J., *et al.*, 'Preliminary report on the ancient mining survey', *Atlal* 6, 1982, 63–79; 7, 1983, 76–84; 8, 1984, 115–42.

5 Society

Tribes and social differentiation/stratification

For understanding tribal structure in general, it can be helpful to read modern anthropological studies (e.g. Sahlins, Marshall D., *Tribesmen*, Englewood Cliffs, NJ, Prentice-Hall, 1968; Khoury, Philip S., and Kostiner, Joseph, eds, *Tribes and state formation in the Middle East*, Berkeley, University of California, 1990; Lancaster, William and Fidelity, 'Tribal formations in the Arabian peninsula', *AAE* 3, 1992, 145–72) and ethnographic studies (e.g. C.M. Doughty, *Travels in Arabia deserta*, 2 vols, Cambridge, CUP, 1888; Musil, A., *The manners and customs of the Rwala Bedouins*, New York, American Geographical Society, 1928).

Beeston, A.F.L., 'Kingship in ancient south Arabia', *Journal for the Social and Economic History of the Orient* 15, 1972, 256–68.
—— 'Epigraphic South Arabian nomenclature', *Raydan* 1, 1978, 13–21.
—— 'Notes on Old South Arabian lexicography XI', *Le Muséon* 91, 1978, 195–209 (tr. of RES 3869).
—— 'Some features of social structure in Saba', *SHA* 1.115–23.
—— 'Free and unfree: the Sayhadic case', *PSAS* 16, 1986, 1–6.
Caskel, Werner, 'Der arabische Stamm vor dem Islam und seine gesellschaftliche und juristische Organisation', *Convegno internazionale sul tema 'Dalla tribu allo stato'*, Accademia dei Lincei 359, 1962, 139–51.
Crone, Patricia, *Roman, provincial and Islamic law,* Cambridge, CUP, 1987 (ch. 4 looks at clientage in pre-Islamic Arabia).
Dostal, Walter, 'Mecca before the time of the prophet', *Der Islam* 68, 1991, 193–231 (movement towards more complex religio-political organisation).
Fabietti, Ugo, 'The role played by the organization of the "Hums" in the evolution of political ideas in pre-Islamic Mecca', *PSAS* 18, 1988, 25–33 (as for Dostal in the previous entry).

Harding, G.L., 'The Safaitic tribes', *al-Abhath* 22, 1969, 3–25.

Henninger, Joseph, 'La Société bédouine ancienne', *ASB* 69–93.

—— *Arabica varia: Aufsätze zur kulturgeschichte Arabiens und seiner Randgebiete*, Freiburg (Universitätsverlag) and Göttingen (Vandenhoeck and Ruprecht), 1989.

Hufi, A.M. al-, *Al-ḥayât al-'arabiyya min al-shi'r al-jâhiliyy*, Cairo, Nahda, 1962.

Jacob, Georg, *Altarabisches Beduinenleben*, Hildesheim, Georg Olms, 1967 (repr. of 1897 edition).

Korotayev, Andrey, 'Sabaean cultural–political area: some general trends of evolution', *PSAS* 23, 1993, 49–62.

—— 'Internal structure of Middle Sabaean *bayt*', *AAE* 5, 1994, 174–83.

—— 'Middle Sabaean cultural–political area: problem of local taxation and temple tithe', *Le Muséon* 107, 1994, 15–22.

—— 'The political role of the *sha'b* of the first order', *Raydan* 6, 1994, 47–52.

—— 'The social sense of Middle Sabaean epithet names', *PSAS* 24, 1994, 157–64.

—— 'Some trends of evolution of the Sabaean cultural–political area: from clan titles to clan names?', *New Arabian Studies* 2, 1994, 153–64.

—— 'Was there any level of socio-political integration between *bayt* and *sha'b* of third order?', *Raydan* 6, 1994, 53–55 (i.e. between a lineage and the local territorial community; the reply is yes).

—— *Ancient Yemen: some general trends of evolution of the Sabaic language and Sabaean culture*, Oxford, OUP/JSS, 1995.

—— 'Middle Sabaean cultural–political area: *qayls* and their tribesmen, clients and *maqtawîs*', *Acta Orientalia* 56, 1995, 62–77.

—— 'How could royal power exist without royal taxation? (material sources of Middle Sabaean royal power)', *PSAS* 26, 1996, 75–78.

—— 'Middle Sabaean royal succession', *Annali dell'Istituto Orientale di Napoli* 56, 1996, 297–304.

—— 'Individual and collective concerns of the Sabaeans in 1st–4th c. AD', *PSAS* 28, 1998, 157–67.

Preissler, Holger, 'Das kulturelle Niveau von Abhängigen in mittelsabäischen Inschriften', *Südarabien* 133–41.

Robin, Christian, 'La Cité et l'organisation sociale à Ma'in: l'exemple de YTL (Baraqish)', *SHA* 2.157–64.

Salem, A.H., *et al.*, 'The genetics of traditional living: Y-chromosomal and mitochondrial lineages in the Sinai peninsula', *American Journal of Human Genetics* 59, 1996, 741–43.

Sartre, M., 'Palmyre: cité grecque', *Annales Archéologiques Arabes Syriennes* 42, 1996, 385–406.

Schlumberger, D., 'Les quatre tribus de Palmyre', *Syria* 48, 1971, 121–33 (civic bodies, not kinship groups).

Serjeant, R.B., 'The Da'if and the Mustad'af and the status accorded them in the Qur'an', *Journal for Islamic Studies* 7 (Johannesburg), 1987, 32–47 (re: socially inferior, non-arms-bearing people).

Sima, Alexander, 'Notes on '*shr* in Sabaean inscriptions', *PSAS* 29, 1999, 159–66 (re: tithes).

Law and legislation

Beeston, A.F.L., 'A Sabaean penal law', *Le Muséon* 64, 1951, 305–15.

—— 'A Sabaean trader's misfortunes', *JSS* 14, 1969, 227–30 (re: Ja 750).

—— 'Miscellaneous epigraphic notes II', *Raydan* 5, 1988, 5–32 (re: Doe 7 and RES 3910).

Cussini, Eleonora, 'Transfer of property at Palmyra', *Aram* 7, 1995, 233–50.

Dareste, R., 'Lois des Homérites', *Nouvelle Revue Historique de Droit Français et Etranger* 59, 1905, 157–70.

Healey, John F., 'Sources for the study of Nabataean law', *New Arabian Studies* 1, 1993, 203–14.

Irvine, A.K., 'Homicide in pre-Islamic south Arabia', *BSOAS* 30, 1967, 277–92.

Korotayev, Andrey, 'A socio-political conflict in the Qatabanian kingdom?', *PSAS* 27, 1997, 141–58.

Loundine, A.G., 'Les Inscriptions du Jabal al-'Amud et le conseil des anciens de Saba', *PSAS* 19, 1989, 93–96.

Procksch, Otto, *Uber die Blutrache bei den vorislamischen Arabern*, Leipzig, Teubner, 1899.

Reinert, Werner, *Das Recht in der altarabischen Poesie*, Cologne, University of Cologne, 1963.

Robin, Christian, 'L'Offrande d'une main en Arabie préislamique', in *id.*, ed., *Mélanges linguistiques offerts à M. Rodinson*, Paris, Geuthner, 1985, 307–20 (argues that such offerings were made in expiation and served as a substitute for the offender's own hand).

—— 'A propos d'une nouvelle inscription du règne de Sha'r Awtar: un réexamen de l'éponymat sabéen', *AF* 230–49 (re: the term in office of the tribal elders who sat on the supreme council).

Segal, J.B., 'Aramaic legal texts from Hatra', *Journal of Jewish Studies* 33, 1982, 109–17.

Wolff, H.J., 'Römisches Provinzialrecht in der Provinz Arabia', *Aufstieg und Niedergang der römischen Welt* 1970, 763–806.

Marriage and the role of women

Abbott, Nabia, 'Pre-Islamic Arab queens', *American Journal of Semitic Languages* 58, 1941, 1–22.

—— 'Women and the state on the eve of Islam', *American Journal of Semitic Languages* 58, 1941, 259–84.

Amaldi, Daniela, 'Women in pre-Islamic poetry', in F. de Jong, ed., *Verse and the fair sex*, Utrecht, Houtsma Stichting, 1993, 77–84.

Avanzini, A., 'Remarques sur le "matriarchat" en Arabie du sud', *AAKM* 157–61.

Beeston, A.F.L., 'The so-called harlots of Hadramawt', *Oriens* 5, 1952, 16–22 (priestesses inciting revolt upon death of Muhammad).

—— 'The position of women in pre-Islamic south Arabia', *Proceedings of the 22nd Congress of Orientalists 1951*, Leiden, Brill, 1957, 101–106.

—— 'Temporary marriage in pre-Islamic south Arabia', *Arabian Studies* 4, 1978, 21–25.

—— 'Miscellaneous epigraphic notes', *Raydan* 4, 1981, 9–28 (re: Qutra 1).

—— 'Women in Saba', in R. Bidwell and G.R. Smith, eds, *Arabian and Islamic studies: articles presented to R.B. Serjeant*, London, Longman, 1983, 7–13.

—— 'YMN 19: a Sabaean divorce case?', *Südarabien* 1–4.

Chelhod, Joseph, 'Du nouveau à propos du "matriarchat" arabe', *Arabica* 28, 1981, 76–106.

Dostal, Walter, '"Sexual hospitality" and the problem of matrilinearity in southern Arabia', *PSAS* 20, 1990, 17–30.

Frantsouzoff, S.A., 'Die Frau im antiken Südarabien', in *Im Land der Königin von Saba*, Staatliches Museum für Völkerkunde, Munich, 1999, 151–69.

Korotayev, Andrey, 'Were there any truly matrilineal lineages in the Arabian peninsula?', *PSAS* 25, 1995, 83–98.

Lichtenstadter, I., *Women in the aïyâm al-'arab: a study of female life during warfare in pre-Islamic Arabia*, London, Royal Asiatic Society, 1935.

Müller, Walter, 'Sabaeische Texte zur Polyandrie', *NESE* 2.125–44 (but see Ryckmans, 'A three generations' . . . ', 413).

Perron, A., *Femmes arabes avant et depuis l'Islamisme*, Paris, Librairie Nouvelle, 1858 (mostly descriptive and uncritical).

Preissler, Holger, 'Kinder in mittelsabäischen Inschriften', *AF* 223–29.

Robertson Smith, W., *Kinship and marriage in early Arabia*, London, Adam and Charles Black, 1903.

Robin, Christian, 'Two inscriptions from Qaryat al-Faw mentioning women', *ATB* 168–75.

Ryckmans, Jacques, 'A three generations' matrilineal genealogy in a Hasaean inscription', *BAA* 407–17.

Feasting and revelling

Alavoine, V., 'Le *mrzh*: est-il un banquet funéraire? Etude des sources épigraphiques et bibliques', *Le Muséon* 113, 2000, 1–23 (no, not necessarily).

Ingholt, Harald, 'Un nouveau thiase à Palmyre', *Syria* 7, 1926, 128–41.

Loundine, A.G., 'Le Banquet rituel dans l'état de Saba', *PSAS* 20, 1990, 95–100.

Maraqten, Mohammed, 'Wine drinking and wine prohibition in Arabia before Islam', *PSAS* 23, 1993, 95–115.

Nanah, Mouhamed Fouaed, *Freigebigkeit und Geiz in der Vorstellungswelt der vorislamischen arabischen Dichter*, Erlangen, Friedrich-Alexander Universität, 1987.

Ryckmans, Jacques, 'Le Repas rituel dans la religion sud-arabe', in M.A. Beek *et al.*, eds, *Symbolae biblicae et mesopotamicae F.M. Theodoro dedicatae*, Leiden, Brill, 1973, 327–34.

—— 'Ritual meals in the ancient south Arabian religion', *PSAS* 3, 1973, 36–39.

Tarrier, Dominique, 'Banquets rituels en Palmyrène et en Nabatène', *Aram* 7, 1995, 165–82.

Will, E., 'Les Salles de banquet de Palmyre et d'autres lieux', *Topoi* 7, 1997, 873–87.

Zayadine, F., 'A Nabataean inscription from Beida', *ADAJ* 21, 1976, 139–42 (mentions a *rb mrzh*'/symposiarch).

6 Religion

Polytheism

Ababneh, Mohammed I., *Ba'alshamîn 'inda l-Sâmiyyîn*, Amman, Yarmouk University, 1994.

Ali, Jawad, 'Adyân al-'arab qabl al-islâm', *SHA* 2.107–16.

Beeston, A.F.L., *The Labakh texts* (Qahtan 2), London, Luzac, 1971.

—— 'Theocracy in the Sayhad culture', *PSAS* 7, 1977, 5–10.

—— 'The religions of pre-Islamic Yemen', in Chelhod, J., ed., *L'Arabie du sud I*, Paris, Maisonneuve et Larose, 1984, 259–69.

—— 'Sayhadic divine designations', *PSAS* 21, 1991, 1–5.

Dalley, Stephanie, 'Bel at Palmyra and elsewhere in the Parthian period', *Aram* 7, 1995, 137–51.

Drijvers, H.J.W., *The religion of Palmyra*, Leiden, Brill, 1976.

EI, *s.v.* 'al-'Uzza' (M.C.A. Macdonald and L. Nehmé).

Fahd, Toufic, *Le Panthéon de l'Arabie centrale à la veille de l'hégire*, Paris, Geuthner, 1968.

296

Figueras, Pau, 'The Roman worship of Athena–Allat in the Decapolis and the Negev', *Aram* 4, 1992, 173–83.

Gawlikowski, M., 'Les Dieux des Nabatéens', *Aufstieg und Niedergang der römischen Welt* 1990, 2659–77.

—— 'Les Dieux de Palmyre', *Aufstieg und Niedergang der römischen Welt* 1990, 2605–58.

Grimme, Hubert, *Texte und Untersuchungen zur safatenisch–arabischen Religion*, Paderborn, Ferdinand Schöning, 1929.

Henninger, Joseph, 'La Religion bédouine préislamique', *ASB* 115–40; English tr. ('Pre-Islamic bedouin religion') in AAEI 109–28.

—— 'Geisterglaube bei den vorislamischen Arabern', in *Festschrift Paul Schebesta*, Vienna, St Gabriel, 1963, 279–316.

—— *Arabica sacra: Aufsätze zur religionsgeschichte Arabiens und seiner Randgebiete*, Freiburg (Universitätsverlag) and Göttingen (Vandenhoeck and Ruprecht), 1981.

Kaizer, T., 'De dea syria et aliis diis deabusque: a study of the variety of appearances of *Gad* in Aramaic inscriptions', *Orientalia Louvaniensa Periodica* 28, 1997, 147–66; 29, 1998, 33–62.

—— *A study of the social patterns of worship at Palmyra in the Roman period*, Oxford, University of Oxford, 2000.

Knauf, E.A., 'Dushara and Shai al-Qaum', *Aram* 2, 1990, 175–83.

Korotayev, A.: many of his articles cited above (ch. 5: tribes) are relevant to the social aspects of south Arabian religion.

Krone, Susanne, *Die altarabische Gottheit al-Lat*, Frankfurt-am-Main, Peter Lang, 1992.

Lecker, M., 'Idol worship in pre-Islamic Medina', *Le Muséon* 106, 1993, 331–46.

Lundin, A.G., 'Die arabischen Göttinnen Ruda und al-'Uzza', *Hudhud* 211–18.

Muhyi l-din, A., "Ibâdat al-arwâḥ fî l-mujtama' al-'arabiyy al-jâhiliyy', *SHA* 2.153–64.

Nashef, Khaled al-, 'The deities of Dilmun', *BAA* 340–66.

Naveh, Joseph, 'The inscriptions from Failaka and the lapidary Aramaic script', *BASOR* 297, 1995, 1–4 (invocation of Bel, Nabu, Poseidon and Artemis).

Pirenne, Jacqueline, 'Une législation hydrologique en Arabie du sud antique', in *Hommages à A. Dupont-Sommer*, Paris, Maisonneuve, 1971, 117–35 (re: Ry 478; see also Beeston, 'Kingship', 262).

Roche, M.J., 'Remarques sur les Nabatéens en Méditerranée', *Semitica* 45, 1996, 73–99 (dedications of Nabataeans abroad).

Ryckmans, G., *Les Religions arabes préislamiques*, Louvain, Bibliothèque du Muséon, 1951 (useful survey).

Ryckmans, Jacques, 'Le Panthéon de l'Arabie du sud préislamique', *Revue de l'Histoire des Religions* 206, 1989, 151–69.

Tarrier, Dominique, 'Baalshamin dans le monde Nabatéen', *Aram* 2, 1990, 197–203.

Teixidor, J., *The pantheon of Palmyra*, Leiden, Brill, 1979.

—— 'Une inscription araméenne provenant de l'émirat de Sharjah', *CRAIBL* 1992, 695–707 (Kahl and Manat in a funerary text on a bronze plaque, *c.*2nd c. AD).

Watt, W. Montgomery, 'Belief in a "high god" in pre-Islamic Mecca', *JSS* 16, 1971, 35–40.

Wellhausen, J., *Reste arabischen Heidentums*, Berlin, Walter de Gruyter, 1927 (uses chiefly Muslim sources, but still a fundamental study).

Zayadine, F., 'The pantheon of the Nabataean inscriptions in Egypt and Sinai', *Aram* 2, 1990, 151–74.

Monotheism

AAW, 'Christliche Mission in Südarabien', 4.306–18.

Baron, S.W., *A social and religious history of the Jews III*, New York, Columbia University, 1957, esp. 60–74 and notes 75–87 thereto.

Beeston, A.F.L., 'Himyarite monotheism', *SHA* 2.149–54.

—— 'Judaism and Christianity in pre-Islamic Yemen', in Chelhod, J., ed., *L'Arabie du sud I*, Paris, Maisonneuve et Larose, 1984, 271–78.

Degen, Rainer, 'Die hebräische Inschrift DJE23 aus Jemen', *NESE* 2.111–16.

Frantsouzoff, S.A., 'A *Gezerah*-decree from ancient southern Arabia', *Aram* 8, 1996, 299–306 (re: the Jewish Sabaic inscription Hasi1).

Gil, M., 'The origin of the Jews of Yathrib', *Jerusalem Studies in Arabic and Islam* 4, 1984, 203–24 (repr. in AAEI 145–66).

Korotayev, Andrey, '"Aramaeans" in a late Sabaic inscription', *Aram* 8, 1996, 293–98 (re: the Jewish Sabaic inscription Hasi1).

Müller, Walter, 'Eine hebräisch–sabäische Bilinguis aus Bait al-Ašwal', *NESE* 2.117–24.

Nau, François, *Les Arabes chrétiens de Mésopotamie et de Syrie*, Paris, Imprimerie Nationale, 1933.

Rippin, Andrew, 'Rahman and the Hanifs', in W. Hallaq and D.P. Little, eds, *Islamic studies presented to C.J. Adams*, Leiden, Brill, 1991, 153–68.

Robin, Christian, 'Judaïsme et Christianisme en Arabie du sud', *PSAS* 10, 1980, 85–96.

—— and Beaucamp, Joelle, 'Le Christianisme dans la péninsule arabique d'après l'épigraphie et l'archéologie', *Travaux et Mémoires* 8, 1981, 45–61.

Trimingham, J.S., *Christianity among the Arabs in pre-Islamic times*, London, Longman, 1979.

Magic and medicine

Lecker, M., 'The bewitching of the Prophet Muhammad by the Jews', *al-Qantara* 13, 1992, 561–69.

Maraqten, Mohammed, 'An inscribed amulet from Shabwa', *AAE* 7, 1996, 88–94.

Ryckmans, Jacques, 'Un rite d'istisqa' au temple sabéen de Marib', *Annuaire de l'Institut de Philologie et d'Histoire Orientales et Slaves* 20, 1973, 379–88 (re: Ja 735).

—— ''Uzza et Lat dans les inscriptions sud-arabes à propos de deux amulettes méconnues', *JSS* 25, 1980, 193–204.

Divination

Beeston, A.F.L., 'The oracle sanctuary of Jar al-Labba', *Le Muséon* 62, 1949, 207–28.

Crone, Patricia, 'Tribes without saints', paper given at Mellon Seminar, Princeton University, 1991 (re: diviners).

Drijvers, H.J.W., 'Inscriptions from Allat's sanctuary', *Aram* 7, 1995, 109–19.

Fahd, Toufic, *La Divination arabe*, Leiden, Brill, 1966.

Miller, E. 'Fragment inédit d'Appien' (*peri Arabôn manteias*), *Revue Archéologique* 1, 1869, 101–10.

Ryckmans, Jacques, 'La Mancie par HRB en Arabie du sud ancienne', in Erwin Graf, ed., *Festschrift Werner Caskel*, Leiden, Brill, 1968, 261–73.

Sacred offices, places, times

Beeston, A.F.L., 'Notes on old south Arabian lexicography IV', *Le Muséon* 65, 1952, 139–47 (re: Nami 74).

—— 'The "Ta'lab lord of pastures" texts', *BSOAS* 17, 1955, 154–56 (re: RES 4176).

—— 'The Hasaean tombstone J1052', *Journal of Ancient Near Eastern Studies* (Columbia University) 11, 1979, 17–18 (re: priest of Yabish).

—— 'The constructions at Itwat', *PSAS* 14, 1984, 40–41.

—— 'The Qatabanic text VL1', *PSAS* 16, 1986, 7–11 (re: *rshw*).

Frantsouzoff, S.A., 'Regulation of conjugal relations in ancient Raybun', *PSAS* 27, 1997, 113–27.

Gawlikowski, M., *Palmyre VI: le temple palmyrénien*, Warsaw, PWN, 1973 (re: relationship between tribes/priests/temples).

—— 'Sacred space in ancient Arab religions', SHAJ 1, 1982, 301–303.

Ghul, M.A., 'The pilgrimage at Itwat (revised by A.F.L. Beeston)', *PSAS* 14, 1984, 33–39 (re: RES 4176).

Lammens, Henri, 'Les Sanctuaires préislamites dans l'Arabie occidentale', *Mélanges de l'Université Saint Joseph* 11, 1926, 39–173.

Müller, Walter, 'Zwei sabäische Votivinschriften an die Sonnengöttin NAMI 74 und Yemen Museum 1965', *Sayhadica* 57–73.

—— 'Das Statut des Gottes Ta'lab von Riyam für seinen Stamm Sum'ay', *Südarabien* 89–110 (re: RES 4176).

Noja, Sergio, 'Une hypothèse sur l'origine du vêtement du *muḥrim*', *Annali dell'Istituto Orientale di Napoli* 45, 1985, 405–409 (re: similarity of Muslim pilgrim garb to attire of a south Arabian statuette).

Pirenne, Jacqueline, 'Le Site préislamique de al-Jaw, la Bible, le Coran et le Midrash', *Revue Biblique* 82, 1975, 34–69.

Robin, Christian, 'Les Montagnes dans la religion sudarabique', *Hudhud* 263–81.

Serjeant, R.B., 'Haram and Hawtah, the sacred enclave in Arabia', in *Mélanges Taha Husain*, Cairo, Dar al-Ma'arif, 1962, 41–58 (repr. in AAEI 167–84).

Offerings to the gods

Beeston, A.F.L., 'Miscellaneous epigraphic notes II', *Raydan* 5, 1988, 5–32 (pp. 11–14 deal with the Mi'sal and Gidma texts relating to human sacrifice).

Christides, Vassilios, 'Once again the "Narrations" of Nilus Sinaiticus', *Byzantion* 43, 1973, 39–50.

Henninger, Joseph, 'Das Opfer in den altsüdarabischen Hochkulturen', *Anthropos* 37–40, 1946–47, 779–810.

—— 'Le Sacrifice chez les Arabes', *Ethnos* 13, 1948, 1–16.

—— 'Die unblutige Tierweihe der vorislamischen Araber in ethnologischer Sicht', *Paideuma* 4, 1950, 179–90.

—— 'Neuere Untersuchungen über Menschenopfer bei semitischen Volkern', *Hudhud* 65–78.

Maraqten, Mohammed, 'New evidence of infanticide in ancient Yemen', *PSAS* forthcoming (re: MSS 74, a text on palm-stalk regarding 'those who kill their children' for cultic reasons).

Mayerson, Philip, 'Observations on the "Nilus" *Narrationes*', *Journal of the American Research Centre in Egypt* 12, 1975, 51–74.

Milik, J.T., *Dédicaces faites par les dieux (Palmyre, Hatra, Tyr)*, Paris, Geuthner, 1972 (re: what one can learn from dedications, such as professions, banqueting, etc.).

Müller, Walter, 'Die angeblichen "Töchter Gottes" im Licht einer neuen qatabanischen Inschrift', *NESE* 2.145–48 (re: symbolic dedication of a person to a deity).

—— 'Notes on the use of frankincense in south Arabia', *PSAS* 6, 1976, 124–36.

Pirenne, Jacqueline, 'RShW, RShWT, FDY, FDYT and the priesthood in ancient south Arabia', *PSAS* 6, 1976, 137–43 (argues that the terms refer to sacrifice, not to priesthood).

Ryckmans, G., 'Le Sacrifice DBH dans les inscriptions Safaîtiques', *Hebrew Union College Annual* 23, 1950–51, 431–38.

Ryckmans, Jacques, 'Les Confessions publiques sabéennes: le code sud-arabe de pureté rituelle', *Annali dell'Istituto Orientale di Napoli* 32, 1972, 1–15.

—— 'Sacrifices, offrandes et rites connexes en Arabie du Sud pré-Islamique', in J. Quaegebeur, ed., *Ritual and sacrifice in the ancient Near East*, Louvain, Peeters, 1993, 355–80.

7 Art, architecture and artefacts

Since we have no literary texts from pre-Islamic Arabia, it is on the material culture that scholars have had to concentrate, and consequently the secondary literature for this topic is vast. Here I will only cite the works directly relevant to what I have said in this chapter and a few useful monographs. The only survey of Arabian art is that by D.T. Potts in J. Turner, ed., *The dictionary of art*, New York, Grove, 1996, 2.246–75. After that one can either turn to the appropriate section in the survey works listed for chapters 1–3 or else delve into journals such as *AAE, ABADY, ADAJ, BASOR, Atlal, PSAS* and *Syria*. For east Arabia see also the bibliography compiled by E. Haerinck and K.G. Stevens, *Preislamic archaeology of Kuwait, northeastern Arabia, Bahrain, Qatar, United Arab Emirates and Oman* (Louvain, Peeters, 1985); *First supplement (1985–95)*, Louvain, Peeters, 1996.

Arabian material culture?

AAW, 'Mšatta und der Beginn der arabischen Kunst', 1.592–607.

Audouin, Rémy, 'Etude du décor des temples des Banat 'Ad', *AA* 121–42.

Badawy, A., 'The contribution of the Arabs to Islamic Art', *Rivista degli Studi Orientali* 39, 1964, 261–85.

Boucharlat, R., 'Archaeology and artifacts of the Arabian peninsula', *CANE* 2.1335–53.

Breton, J.F., 'Arabie méridionale et Orient hellénisé', *AMB* 191–99.

Buffa, Vittoria, 'Note per una tipologia delle techniche costruttive del periodo sudarabico antico', *AA* 165–77.

Colledge, Malcolm, *The art of Palmyra*, London, Thames and Hudson, 1976.

Creswell, K.A.C., *A short account of early Muslim architecture*, Harmondsworth, Penguin, 1958; revised and supplemented by James W. Allan, Aldershot, Scolar, 1989.

Ettinghausen, R., and Grabar, Oleg, *The art and architecture of Islam 650–1250*, Harmondsworth, Penguin, 1987.

Frantsouzoff, S.A., 'A parallel to the Second Commandment in the inscriptions of Raybun', *PSAS* 28, 1998, 61–67 (re: prohibition of graven images in Hadramawt).

Hillenbrand, Robert, *Islamic art and architecture*, London, Thames and Hudson, 1999.

McKenzie, Judith, 'The development of Nabataean sculpture at Petra and Khirbet Tannur', *Palestine Exploration Quarterly* 120, 1988, 81–107.

Maigret, Alessandro de, 'Alcune considerazioni sulle origini e lo sviluppo dell'arte sudarabica', *AF* 142–59.

Parlasca, Ingemarie, 'Probleme Nabatäischer Koroplastik: aspekte der auswärtigen Kulturbeziehungen Petras', in A. Invernizzi and J.F. Salles, eds, *Arabia Antiqua*, Rome, IsMEO, 1993, 55–79.

Parlasca, Klaus, 'Bemerkungen zu den archäologischen Beziehungen zwischen Südarabien und dem griechisch–römischen Kulturkreis', *PA* 281–88.

—— 'Some problems of Palmyrene plastic art', *Aram* 7, 1995, 59–71 (re: funerary sculpture).

Parr, P.J., 'Pottery, people and politics', in *id.* and Roger Moorey, eds, *Archaeology in the Levant: essays for Kathleen Kenyon*, Warminster, Aris and Phillips, 1978, 203–209.

—— 'The present state of archaeological research in the Arabian peninsula', *SHA* 2.43–54.

Potts, D.T., 'Tayma and the Assyrian empire', *AAE* 2, 1991, 10–23 (re: Assyrian influence on Tayma relief).

Roche, M.J., 'Khirbet et-Tannur et les contacts entre Edomites et Nabatéens', *Transeuphratène* 18, 1999, 59–69 (re: persistence of Edomite cult features in Nabataea).

Schmidt-Colinet, A., 'Aspects of Romanization: the tomb architecture at Palmyra and its decoration', in Susan Alcock, ed., *The early Roman empire in the east*, Oxford, Oxbow, 1997, 157–77.

Talgam, Rina, *The stylistic origins of Umayyad sculpture as shown in Khirbat al-Mafjar, Mshatta, and Qaṣr al-Hayr west*, forthcoming.

Vycichl, Werner, 'Studies on Nabataean archaeology and religion', in F. Zayadine ed., *Petra and the caravan cities,* 1990, 147–51.

Will, Ernest, 'De la Syrie au Yémen: problèmes des relations dans le domaine de l'art', *AP* 271–80.

—— 'Architecture locale et architecture impériale à Palmyre', *Aram* 7, 1995, 29–35.

Settlements

(Recently many studies on individual sites have been published and these will also contain information on funerary structures, public buildings, etc.)

Abu-Duruk, H.I., *Introduction to the archaeology of Tayma*, Riyad, Dept of Antiquities and Museums, 1986.

Ansary, A.R., *Qaryat al-Fau: a portrait of pre-Islamic civilisation in Saudi Arabia*, Riyad, University of Riyad, 1982.

Beeston, A.F.L., 'Functional significance of the old South Arabian town', *PSAS* 1, 1971, 26–28.

—— 'Pre-Islamic San'a', in R.B. Serjeant and R. Lewcock, eds, *San'a: an Arabian Islamic city*, London, World of Islam Festival Trust, 1983, 36–38.

Breton, J.F., ed., *Fouilles de Shabwa II*, Paris, Geuthner, 1992 (reprinted from *Syria* 68, 1991).

Doe, Brian, *Monuments of south Arabia*, Naples and Cambridge, Falcon–Oleander, 1983.

Failaka/Dilmun: the second millennium settlements, 2 vols, Moesgaard, Jutland Archaeological Society, 1983–87 (seals, pottery).

Frifelt, Karen, *The island of Umm an-Nar*, 2 vols, Moesgaard, Jutland Archaeological Society, 1991.

Hojlund, Flemming, and Andersen, H.H., *Qala'at al-Bahrain*, 2 vols, Moesgaard, Jutland Archaeological Society, 1994–97.

Ikaros: the Hellenistic settlements, 3 vols, Moesgaard, Jutland Archaeological Society, 1982–89 (figurines, pottery, sacred enclosure).

Kennet, Derek, *et al.*, 'Ra's al-Khaimah tower survey 1991–2', *PSAS* 23, 1993, 9–47.

Lindner, Manfred, ed., *Petra und das Königreich der Nabatäer*, Munich, Delp, 1989.

McKenzie, Judith, *The architecture of Petra*, Oxford, OUP, 1990.

Michalowski, K., and Gawlikowski, M., *Palmyre I–IX*, Warsaw, PWN, 1960–84.

Mouton, M., *Mleiha I: environnement, stratégies de subsistance et artisanats*, Lyons, Maison de l'Orient, 1999.

Nehmé, Laila, and Villeneuve, F., *Pétra: métropole de l'Arabie antique*, Paris, Seuil, 1999.

Palmyre: Bilan et perspectives, Colloque de Strasbourg 1973, Strasbourg, AECR, 1976 (aspects of material culture of Palmyra).

Potts, D.T., *Ancient Magan: the secrets of Tell Abraq*, London, Trident, 2000.

Ryckmans, Jacques, 'Al-Ukhdud: the Philby–Ryckmans–Lippens expedition of 1951', *PSAS* 11, 1981, 55–63 (re: Najran).

—— 'Villes fortifiées du Yémen antique', *Bulletin de la classe des lettres et des sciences morales et politiques* (Académie Royale de Belgique) 67, 1981–85, 253–66.

Salles, J.F., *et al.*, *Failaka: fouilles françaises*, 3 vols, Lyons, Maison de l'Orient, 1984–90.

Saud, A.S. al-, *Central Arabia during the early Hellenistic period*, Riyad, King Fahd National Library, 1997 (re: the site of al-'Ayun in the area of al-Aflaj).

Schmidt, Jürgen, *et al.*, 'Marib und Umgebung', *ABADY* 1, 1982, 5–89; 2, 1983; 3, 1986, 1–95; 4, 1987, 63–142.

Schreiber, Jürgen, *Die Siedlungsarchitektur auf der Halbinsel Oman vom 3. bis zur Mitte des 1. Jahrtausends v. Chr.*, Münster, Ugarit-Verlag, 1998.

Semitica 43–44, 1995: *La ville de 1200 avant JC à l'hégire* (contains articles on Petra, Palmyra and cities of south Arabia).

Stucky, Rolf, 'Das nabataeische Wohnhaus und das urbanistische System der Wohnquartiere in Petra', in A. Invernizzi and J.F. Salles, eds, *Arabia antiqua*, Rome, IsMEO, 1993, 37–53.

Sudairi, A.A. al-, *The desert frontier of Arabia: al-Jawf through the ages*, London, Stacey International, 1995.

Weber, Thomas, and Wenning, Robert, eds, *Petra: antike Felsstadt zwischen arabischer Tradition und griechischer Norm*, Mainz-am-Rhein, Zabern, 1997.

Funerary structures and objects

Cleveland, Ray L., *An ancient south Arabian necropolis*, Baltimore, Johns Hopkins, 1965.

Gawlikowski, M., *Monuments funéraires de Palmyre*, Warsaw, PWN, 1970.

Harding, G. Lankester, 'The cairn of Hani'', *ADAJ* 2, 1953, 8–55.

—— 'The cairn of Sa'd', in P.J. Parr and Roger Moorey, eds, *Archaeology in the Levant: essays for Kathleen Kenyon*, Warminster, Aris and Phillips, 1978, 243–49.

Jasim, S.A., 'The excavation of a camel cemetery at Mleiha, Sharjah', *AAE* 10, 1999, 69–101.

Kirkbride, Diana, 'Ancient Arabian ancestor idols', *Archaeology* 22, 1969, 116–21, 188–95 (examples of gravemarkers carved with human outlines).

Mouton, M., 'Les Tours funéraires d'Arabie, *nefesh* monumentales', *Syria* 74, 1997, 81–99.

Salles, J.F., and Lombard, P., *La Nécropole de Janussan (Bahrain)*, Lyons, Maison de l'Orient, 1984.

Schmidt-Colinet, A., *Das Tempelgrab nr. 36 in Palmyra: Studien zur palmyrenische Grabarchitektur und ihrer Ausstattung*, Mainz-am-Rhein, P. von Zabern, 1992.

Vogt, Burkhard, *Zur Chronologie und Entwicklung der Gräber des späten 4.–2. Jtsd. v. Chr. auf der Halbinsel Oman*, Göttingen, Georg-August-Universität, 1985.

—— 'Death, resurrection and the camel', *AF* 279–90.

Palaces and temples

Breton, J.F., 'Religious architecture in ancient Hadramawt', *PSAS* 10, 1980, 5–16.

—— 'Le Château royal de Shabwa', *Syria* 68, 1991, 209–28.

—— 'Le Sanctuaire de 'Athtar Dhu Risaf d'as-Sawda' (Yémen)', *CRAIBL* 1992, 429–53.

—— 'Les Temples de Ma'in et du Jawf (Yémen): état de la question', *Syria* 75, 1998, 61–80.

—— and Robin, Christian, 'Le Sanctuaire préislamique du Ğabal al-Lawd (nord-Yémen)', *CRAIBL* 1982, 590–629.

Crawford, Harriet, *et al.*, eds, *The Dilmun temple at Saar*, London, Kegan Paul, 1997.

Hammond, Philip, *The temple of the Winged Lions, Petra*, Fountain Hills (Arizona), Petra Publishing, 1996.

Maigret, Alessandro de, 'The excavations of the temple of Nakrah at Baraqish', *PSAS* 21, 1991, 159–72.

Nehmé, Leila, 'L'Espace cultuel à l'époque Nabatéenne', *Topoi* 7, 1997, 1023—67.

—— and Robin, Christian, 'Le Temple de Nakrah à Yathill (Baraqish)', *CRAIBL* 1993, 427–96.

Schmidt, Jürgen, 'Zur altsüdarabischen Tempelarchitektur', *ABADY* 1, 1982, 161–69.

Sedov, A.V., and Batayi', Ahmad, 'Temples of ancient Hadramawt', *PSAS* 24, 1994, 183–96.

Tholbecq, L., 'Les Sanctuaires des Nabatéens', *Topoi* 7, 1997, 1069–95.

Cultic objects

Avner, Uzi, 'Nabataean standing stones and their interpretation', *Aram*, forthcoming.

Connelly, J.B., 'Votive offerings from Hellenistic Failaka', *AP* 145–58.

Lammens, H., 'Le Culte des bétyles et les processions religieuses chez les arabes préislamites', in *id.*, *L'Arabie occidentale avant l'hégire*, Beirut, Imprimerie Catholique, 1928, 101–79.

Maraqten, Mohammed, 'Typen altsüdarabische Altäre', *AF* 160–77.

Patrich, Joseph, *The formation of Nabataean art: prohibition of a graven image among the Nabataeans*, Jerusalem, Magnes Press, 1990.

Pirenne, Jacqueline, 'La Religion des arabes préislamiques d'après trois sites rupestres et leurs inscriptions', in *Al-Bahit: Festschrift Joseph Henninger*, Bonn, Anthropos-Institut, 1976, 177–217.

—— 'Sud-Arabe: Qyf-Qf/Mqf. De la lexicographie à la spiritualité des idolatres', *Semitica* 30, 1980, 93–124.

Ryckmans, G., 'Sud-arabe mdhbht = Hébreu mzbḥ: et termes apparentés', in Erwin Graf, ed., *Festschrift Werner Caskel*, Leiden, Brill, 1968, 253–60.

Tawil, H.M. al-, *Early Arab icons: literary and archaeological evidence for the cult of religious images in pre-Islamic Arabia*, Iowa, University of Iowa, 1993 (mostly uses Muslim sources).

Toorn, Karel van der, 'Worshipping stones: on the definition of cult symbols', *Journal of Northwest Semitic Languages* 23, 1997, 1–14 (argues that cult-stones were perceived as manifestations of deities).

Wenning, Robert, 'Hegra and Petra: some differences', *Aram* 8, 1996, 253–67 (esp. niches and betyls).

Zayadine, Fawzi, ed., *Petra and the caravan cities*, Amman, Department of Antiquities, 1990 (contains articles on representation of Nabataean deities and use of figurines).

Weaponry and warfare

Beeston, A.F.L., *Warfare in ancient south Arabia (2nd–3rd c. AD)*, London, Luzac, 1976 (Qahtan 3).

Graf, David, 'The Nabataean army and the cohortes Ulpiae Petraeorum', in E. Dabrowa, ed., *The Roman and Byzantine army in the east*, Krakow, Uniwersytet Jagiellonski, 1994, 265–311.

Macdonald, M.C.A., 'Camel hunting or camel raiding?', *AAE* 1, 1990, 24–28.

—— 'Hunting, fighting and raiding: the horse in pre-Islamic Arabia', in David Alexander, ed., *Furusiyya: the horse in the art of the Near East*, Riyad, King Abdulaziz Public Library, 1996, 73–83.

Mouton, M., 'Les Pointes de flèches en fer des sites préislamiques de Mleiha et ed-Dur, E.A.U.', *AAE* 1, 1990, 88–103.

Potts, D.T., 'Late Sasanian armament from southern Arabia', *Electrum* 1, 1997, 127–37.

—— 'Some issues in the study of the pre-Islamic weaponry of southeastern Arabia', *AAE* 9, 1998, 182–208.

Schwarzlose, F.W., *Die Waffen der alten Araber aus ihren Dichtern dargestellt*, Leipzig, Hinrichs, 1886.

Rock art

Anati, E., *Rock art in central Arabia*, 4 vols, Louvain, Institut Orientaliste, 1968–74.

Betts, A.V.G., 'The hunter's perspective: 7th millennium BC rock carvings from eastern Jordan', *World Archaeology* 19, 1987, 214–25.

Jung, M., *Research on rock art in north Yemen*, Naples, AION supplement, 1991.

Khan, Majeed, *et al.*, 'Rock art and epigraphic survey of northern Saudi Arabia', *Atlal* 9, 1985, 128–44; 10, 1986, 82–93; 11, 1988, 61–76; 12, 1989, 41–52; 13, 1990, 35–40; 14, 1996, 55–72.

—— 'Schematisation and form in the rock art of northern Saudi Arabia', *Atlal* 11, 1988, 95–100.

—— 'Sacred images of the metaphysical world', *Atlal* 12, 1989, 55–58.

Ziolkowski, M.C., 'A study of the petroglyphs from Wadi al-Hayl, Fujairah', *AAE* 9, 1998, 13–89.

Coins and seals

Meshorer, Yaakov, *Nabataean coins*, Jerusalem, Hebrew University (Qedem 3), 1975.

Munro-Hay, S.C.H., 'The coinage of Shabwa and other ancient south Arabian coinage in the National Museum, Aden', *Syria* 68, 1991, 393–418.

—— 'Coins of ancient south Arabia', *Numismatic Chronicle* 1994, 191–203; 1996, 33–47.

Pickworth, Diana, 'Die Glyptik Südarabiens', in *Im Land der Königin von Saba*, Munich, Staatliches Museum für Völkerkunde, 1999, 144–47.

Potts, D.T., *The pre-Islamic coinage of eastern Arabia*, Copenhagen, Carsten Niebuhr Institute, 1991; *Supplement*, 1994.

Robin, Christian, 'Monnaies provenant de l'Arabie du nord-est', *Semitica* 24, 1974, 83–125.

Sindi, Khalid Mohammed al-, *Dilmun seals*, Bahrain, Bahrain National Museum, 1999.

Artisans and crafts

Khan, Ahmad, 'The tanning cottage industry in pre-Islamic Arabia', *Journal of the Pakistan Historical Society* 19, 1971, 85–100.

Schmidt-Colinet, A., 'A Nabataean family of sculptors at Hegra', *Berytus* 31, 1983, 95–102.

Schmitt-Korte, K., 'Nabataean pottery: a typological and chronological framework', *SHA* 2.7–40.

Stauffer, A., and Asad, K., *Die Textilien aus Palmyra*, Mainz-am-Rhein, P. von Zabern, 2000.

8 Language and literature

Scripts

AAW, 'Anfänge der arabischen Schriftsprache', 2.357–69, 4.1–13.

Beeston, A.F.L., 'Mahmoud Ali Ghul and the Sabaean cursive script', *ASMG* 15–19.

Bordreuil, Pierre, and Pardee, Dennis, 'Un Abécédaire du type sud-sémitique découvert en 1988 dans les fouilles de Ras Shamra-Ougarit', *CRAIBL* 1995, 855–60.

Bron, F., 'Vestiges de l'écriture sud-sémitique dans le Croissant Fertile', *PA* 81–91.

Dietrich, M., and Loretz, O., *Die Keilalphabete: die phönizisch-kanaanäischen und altarabischen Alphabete in Ugarit*, Münster, Ugarit-Verlag, 1988.

Gruendler, B., *The development of the Arabic scripts from the Nabatean era to the first Islamic century*, Atlanta (Ga.), Scholars, 1993.

Healey, John F., 'The Nabataean contribution to the development of the Arabic script', *Aram* 2, 1990, 93–98.

Khan, M., 'Recent rock art and epigraphic investigations in Saudi Arabia', *PSAS* 21, 1991, 113–22.

Knauf, E.A., 'The migration of the script and the formation of the state in south Arabia', *PSAS* 19, 1989, 79–91.

Macdonald, M.C.A., 'ABCs and letter order in ancient north Arabian', *PSAS* 16, 1986, 101–68.

—— 'Cursive Safaitic inscriptions? A preliminary investigation', *ASMG* 62–81.

Naveh, Joseph, 'The inscriptions from Failaka and the lapidary Aramaic script', *BASOR* 297, 1995, 1–4.

Robin, Christian, 'Les Ecritures de l'Arabie avant l'Islam', *AAKM* 127–37.

Ryckmans, Jacques, 'Alphabets, scripts and languages in pre-Islamic Arabian epigraphical evidence', *SHA* 2.73–86.

—— 'L'Ordre alphabétique sud-sémitique et ses origines', in Christian Robin, ed., *Mélanges linguistiques offerts à M. Rodinson*, Paris, Geuthner, 1985, 343–59.

—— 'Pétioles de palmes et bâtonnets sud-arabes inscrits', *AF* 250–59.

Shahri, A.A.M al-, 'Recent epigraphic discoveries in Dhofar', *PSAS* 21, 1991, 173–91.

Languages

Beeston, A.F.L., 'The inscription Jaussen–Savignac 71', *PSAS* 3, 1973, 69–72.

—— 'Nemara and Faw', *BSOAS* 42, 1979, 1–6 (tr. of 'Igl text).

—— 'Languages of pre-Islamic Arabia', *Arabica* 28, 1981, 178–86.

—— 'Languages: pre-Islamic south Arabian', *The Anchor Bible dictionary*, New York, Doubleday, 1992, 4.223–26.

Bellamy, James, 'Two pre-Islamic Arabic inscriptions revised: Jabal Ramm and Umm al-Jimal', *Journal of the American Oriental Society* 108, 1988, 369–78 (both undated).

Cantineau, J., *Le Nabatéen*, Paris, Ernest Leroux, 1930–32.

Corriente, F., 'From old Arabic to classical Arabic through the pre-Islamic koine: some notes on the native grammarians' sources, attitudes and goals', *JSS* 21, 1976, 62–98.

Costa, P., 'Further comments on the bilingual inscription from Baraqish', *PSAS* 16, 1986, 33–36 (a short Greek/Latin text; see also C. Marek, 'Der römische Inschriftenstein von Baraqis', *AF* 178–90).

Diem, W., 'Some glimpses of the rise and early development of Arabic orthography', *Orientalia* 45, 1976, 251–61.

Drewes, A.J., 'The phonemes of Lihyanite', in Christian Robin, ed., *Mélanges linguistiques offerts à M. Rodinson*, Paris, Geuthner, 1985, 165–73.

Healey, John, and Smith, G. Rex, 'Jaussen–Savignac 17: the earliest dated Arabic document', *Atlal* 12, 1989, 77–84 (a funerary text dated AD 287 in Arabic with some Nabataean features).

Kropp, Manfred, 'The inscription Ghoneim AFO 27. 1980. ABB. 10', *PSAS* 22, 1992, 55–67.

Livingstone, Alasdair, 'A linguistic, tribal and onomastical study of the Hasaean inscriptions', *Atlal* 8, 1984, 86–108.

—— 'An early attestation of the Arabic definite article', *JSS* 42, 1997, 259–61.

Macdonald, M.C.A., 'Reflections on the linguistic map of pre-Islamic Arabia', *AAE* 11, 2000, 28–79.

—— 'The form of the definite article in classical Arabic: some light from the Jahiliyya', *JSS*, forthcoming.

Maraqten, Mohammed, 'The Arabic words in Palmyrene inscriptions', *Aram* 7, 1995, 89–108.

Müller, Walter, 'Das Altarabische und das klassische Arabisch', in W. Fischer, ed., *Grundriss der arabischen Philologie I*, Wiesbaden, Reichert, 1982, 17–36.

O'Connor, M., 'The Arabic loanwords in Nabataean Aramaic', *Journal of Near Eastern Studies* 45, 1986, 213–29.

Rabin, Chaim, *Ancient west-Arabian*, London, Taylor's Foreign Press, 1951.
Robin, Christian, 'Les Langues de la péninsule Arabique', *AAKM* 89–111.
—— 'Les Plus Anciens Monuments de la langue arabe', *AAKM* 113–25.
Said, Salah Ahmad, *Das Arabische in vorislamischer Zeit*, Erlangen, Friedrich-Alexander Universität, 1994 (re: Safaitic and Dedanitic).
Seray, Hamad bin, and Healey, John, 'Aramaic in the Gulf: towards a corpus', *Aram*, forthcoming.

Documents

Abdallah, Y.M., 'Ein altsüdarabischer Vertragstext von den neuentdeckten Inschriften auf Holz', *AF* 1–12.
André-Salvini, B., and Lombard, P., 'La Découverte épigraphique de 1995 à Qal'at al-Bahrein', *PSAS* 27, 1997, 165–70 (a new find of cuneiform tablets, mostly brief economic texts).
Cotton, H.M., *et al.*, 'The papyrology of the Roman Near East: a survey', *Journal of Roman Studies* 85, 1995, 214–35 (pp. 223–25: Arabia).
Frantsouzoff, S.A., 'Hadramitic documents written on palm-leaf stalks', *PSAS* 29, 1999, 55–66.
Ghul, Omal al-, 'The names of the buildings in the Greek papyrus no. 10 from Petra', *PSAS* 29, 1999, 67–71 (one of a number of papyri concerning acquisition/cession of property in Petra).
Maraqten, Mohammed, 'Writing materials in pre-Islamic Arabia', *JSS* 43, 1998, 287–310.
Puech, E., 'Présence arabe dans les manuscrits de "La grotte aux lettres" du Wadi Khabra', *PA* 37–46 (four legal papyri from AD 90s).
Ryckmans, Jacques, 'Inscribed old south Arabian sticks and palm-leaf stalks', *PSAS* 23, 1993, 127–40.
—— and Loundine, A.G., 'Un Pétiole de palme inscrit en minéen', *Südarabien* 171–80.
—— *et al.*, *Textes du Yémen antique inscrits sur bois,* Louvain, Institut Orientaliste, 1994.

Inscriptions

(For further examples of juridical texts see chapter 5 above re: law.)
AAW, 'Neue lihyanische Inschriften mit einem Beitrag G. Ryckmans', 5.1.24–33.
Avanzini, A., 'For a study on the formulary of construction inscriptions', *Sayhadica* 11–20.
Beeston, A.F.L., *The mercantile code of Qataban* (Qahtan 1), London, Luzac, 1959.

—— 'A Minaean market code', *BSOAS* 41, 1978, 142–45 (re: M 356, a Dedanite–Minaean inscription).

Branden, A. van den, *Les Inscriptions Thamoudéennes*, Louvain, Bibliothèque du Muséon, 1950.

—— *Les Textes Thamoudéens de Philby*, 2 vols, Louvain, Bibliothèque du Muséon, 1956.

—— *Les Inscriptions dédanites*, Beirut, l'Université Libanaise, 1962.

EI, *s.v.* 'Safaitic', 'Thamudic'.

Gawlikowski, M., and As'ad, K., 'Le Péage à Palmyre en 11 après J.C.', *Semitica* 41–42, 1991–92, 163–72 (re: inscription concerning a camel tax).

Gruntfest, Y., 'Language and style of the South Arabian inscriptions: votive inscriptions from Marib', *Jerusalem Studies in Arabic and Islam* 7, 1986, 1–34.

King, Geraldine, 'The Basalt Desert Rescue Survey and some preliminary remarks on the Safaitic inscriptions and rock drawings', *PSAS* 20, 1990, 55–78.

Kropp, Manfred, 'Individual public confession or stylised document of lawsuit?', *PSAS*, forthcoming (argues that south Arabian expiation texts illustrate judicial process, not personal piety).

Lundin, A.G., 'Die Inschriften des antiken Raybun', *Mare Erythraeum* (Munich) 1, 1997, 19–26.

Macdonald, M.C.A., 'The seasons and transhumance in the Safaitic inscriptions', *Journal of the Royal Asiatic Society* 3.2, 1992, 1–11.

—— *et al.*, 'Les Inscriptions safaïtiques de Syrie cent quarante ans après leur découverte', *CRAIBL* 1996, 435–94.

—— 'Some reflections on epigraphy and ethnicity in the Roman Near East', *Mediterranean Archaeology* 11, 1998, 177–90.

Maraqten, Mohammed, 'Curse formulae in South Arabian inscriptions and some of their Semitic parallels', *PSAS* 28, 1998, 189–99.

Matthews, J.F., 'The tax law of Palmyra', *Journal of Roman Studies* 74, 1984, 157–80.

Müller, Walter, 'Some remarks on the Safaitic inscriptions', *PSAS* 10, 1980, 67–74.

Nehmé, Laila, 'La Géographie des inscriptions de Pétra', *Antiquités Sémitiques* 2, 1997, 125–43.

Puech, E., 'Inscriptions araméennes du Golfe: Failaka, Qala'at al-Bahrein et Mulayha', *Transeuphratène* 16, 1998, 31–55.

Robin, Christian, 'L'Epigraphie de l'Arabie avant l'Islam: intérêt et limites', *AAKM* 13–24.

Ryckmans, Jacques, 'Les Inscriptions anciennes de l'Arabie du sud', *Oosters Genootschap in Nederland* (Leiden, Brill) 4, 1973, 79–110.

—— 'Formal inertia in the South Arabian inscriptions', *PSAS* 4, 1974, 131–39.

Scagliarini, Fiorella, 'The Dedanitic inscriptions from Ǧabal 'Ikma in northwestern Hejaz', *PSAS* 29, 1999, 143–50.

Sima, Alexander, *Die lihyanischen Inschriften von al-'Udhayb*, Rahden, Marie Leidorf, 1999.

—— 'Die sabäische Buss- und Sühneinschrift YM 10.703', *Le Muséon* 113, 2000, 185–204.

Theeb, S.A. al-, *Aramaic and Nabataean inscriptions from north-west Saudi Arabia*, Riyad, King Fahd National Library, 1993.

—— *Dirâsa taḥlîliyya li-nuqûsh nabaṭiyya qadîma min shimâl gharb al-mamlakat al-'arabiyya*, Riyad, King Fahd National Library, 1995.

—— *Nuqûsh al-Ḥijr al-nabaṭiyya*, Riyad, King Fahd National Library, 1998.

Winnett, F.V., 'Some Thamudic religious texts in the light of the Ha'il inscriptions', *Berytus* 22, 1973, 95–100.

Poetry

Abdallah, Y.M., 'Naqsh al-qaṣîda al-Ḥimyariyya aw tarnîmat al-Shams', *Raydan* 5, 1988, 81–100.

Beeston, A.F.L., *et al.*, eds, *Arabic literature to the end of the Umayyad period*, Cambridge, CUP, 1983 (has useful sections on 'pre-Islamic poetry', 'Early Arabic prose' and 'The Qur'an').

—— 'Antecedents of classical Arabic verse?', in *Festschrift Ewald Wagner*, Beirut, Franz Steiner, 1994, 1.234–43.

Bellamy, James, 'Arabic verses from the first/second century: the inscription of 'En 'Avdat', *JSS* 35, 1990, 73–79.

Caskel, Werner, *Das Schicksal in der altarabischen Poesie*, Leipzig, Eduard Pfeiffer, 1926.

Fares, Bichr, *L'Honneur chez les Arabes avant l'Islam*, Paris, Librairie d'Amérique et d'Orient, 1932.

Frolov, Dmitry, *Classical Arabic verse: history and theory of 'Arud*, Leiden, Brill, 2000.

Gabrieli, Francesco, 'La letteratura beduina preislamica', *ASB* 95–114.

Gamal, Adel S., 'The beginnings of classical Arabic poetry', in M. Mir, ed., *Literary heritage of classical Islam*, Princeton, Darwin, 1993, 41–67.

Goldziher, Ignaz, 'Muruwwa and Din', in *id.*, *Muslim studies 1*, Chicago, Aldine, 1967, 11–44 (original German: Max Niemeyer/Halle 1889; classic exposition of pagan Arab honour and its conflict with Islam).

Jones, Alan, *Early Arabic poetry*, 2 vols, Oxford, Ithaca, 1992–96.

Kennedy, P.F., *The wine song in classical Arabic poetry*, Oxford, Clarendon, 1997 (tr. of 'Adi ibn Zayd).

Kropp, Manfred, 'A Puzzle of Old Arabic tenses and syntax: the inscription of 'En 'Avdat', *PSAS* 24, 1994, 165–74.

Negev, Avraham, 'Obodas the God', *Israel Exploration Journal* 36, 1986, 56–60 (re: 'En 'Avdat inscription).

Noja, Sergio, 'Uber die älteste arabische Inschrift', in *Studia semitica necnon iranica R. Macuch dedicata*, Wiesbaden, Harrassowitz, 1989, 187–94 (re: 'En 'Avdat inscription).

Shahid, Irfan, 'The composition of Arabic poetry in the fourth century', *SHA* 2.87–93.

Prose

Abu 'Ubayda Mu'ammar ibn al-Muthanna, *Ayyâm al-'arab qabl al-Islâm*, ed. A.J. al-Bayyati, Beirut, 'Alam al-Kutub, 1987.

Beeston, A.F.L., *Warfare in ancient south Arabia (2nd–3rd c. AD)*, London, Luzac, 1976 (tr. of Ja 643).

Caskel, Werner, 'Aijam al-'Arab: studien zur altarabischen Epik', *Islamica* 3, 1930, 1–99.

EI, *s.v.* 'Ayyam', 'Khatib', 'Mathal', 'Sadj''.

Jones, Alan, 'The prose literature of pre-Islamic Arabia', in J.R. Smart, ed., *Tradition and modernity in Arabic language and literature*, Richmond (Surrey), Curzon, 1996, 229–41.

—— 'The Qur'an in the light of earlier Arabic prose', *University lectures in Islamic studies* (ed. A. Jones) 1, 1997, 67–83.

Khuza'i, Da'bul ibn 'Ali (d. 246/860), *Waṣâyâ al-mulûk wa-anbâ' al-mulûk min walad Qaḥtân ibn Hûd*, ed. Nizar Abazir, Beirut, Dar Sader, 1997.

Meyer, Egbert, *Der historische Gehalt der Aiyam al-'Arab*, Wiesbaden, Harrassowitz, 1970.

Qatamish, A. al-, *Al-amthâl al-'arabiyya: dirâsa ta'rîkhiyya wa-taḥlîliyya*, Damascus, Dar al-Fikr, 1988.

Sellheim, R., *Die klassisch-arabischen Sprichwörtersammlungen insbesondere die des Abu 'Ubaid*, The Hague, Mouton, 1954.

Stetkevych, Jaroslav, *Muhammad and the golden bough: reconstructing Arabian myth*, Bloomington, Indiana University, 1996.

9 Arabhood and Arabisation

There is no work devoted to this subject. See the relevant references given in ch. 3 (esp. Byzantine/Sasanian period), ch. 4 (esp. nomad–sedentary relations), ch. 8 (language and poetry). Also useful are the following works:

Bashear, Suliman, *Arabs and others in early Islam*, Princeton, Darwin, 1997.

Dagorn, René, *La Geste d'Ismaël d'après l'onomastique et la tradition arabes*, Geneva, Librairie Droz, 1981 (argues from onomastic evidence that Ishmael was unimportant to pre-Islamic Arabs).

Drory, Rina, 'The Abbasid construction of the Jahiliyya: cultural authority in the making', *Studia Islamica* 83, 1996, 33–49.

Geary, P.J., *Before France and Germany: the creation and transformation of the Merovingian world*, Oxford, OUP, 1988 (provides interesting parallels, though the east is very different from the west: more ancient, more urbanised, more ecologically fragile, etc.).

Grunebaum, G.E. von, 'The nature of Arab unity before Islam', *Arabica* 10, 1963, 4–23 (repr. in AAEI 1–20).

Kister, M.J., 'Mecca and Tamim', 'Some reports concerning Mecca' and 'Al-Hira: some notes on its relations with Arabia', in *id.*, *Studies on Jahiliyya and early Islam*, Aldershot, Variorum, 1980, I–III.

——— 'Mecca and the tribes of Arabia', in *id.*, *Society and religion from Jahiliyya to Islam*, Aldershot, Variorum, 1990, II (illustrates how 'the period of the sixth and the beginning of the seventh century was characterised by intertribal conflicts and by the pressure of the Byzantine and Persian empires, through their vassal states, on the tribal divisions aimed at widening their control over the Arabian peninsula', p. 37).

Korotaev, A., *et al.*, 'Origins of Islam: political–anthropological and environmental context', *Acta Orientalia* (Hungary) 52, 1999, 243–76 (effects of climate change on 6th-century Arabia).

Mayerson, Philip, 'The use of the term *phyarchos* in the Roman–Byzantine east', *Zeitschrift für Papyrologie und Epigraphik* 88, 1991, 291–95 (tribal chief, not an administrative office).

Millar, Fergus, 'Empire, community and culture in the Roman Near East: Greeks, Syrians, Jews and Arabs', *Journal of Jewish Studies* 38, 1987, 143–64 (examines vitality of local identities).

Müller, Walter, 'Sabäische Felsinschriften von der Jemenitischen Grenze zur Rub' al-Khali', *NESE* 3.113–35 (though Sabaic texts, they have many correspondences with north Arabian).

Robin, Christian, 'La Pénétration des arabes nomades au Yémen', *AAKM* 71–88.

Ryckmans, Jacques, 'Aspects nouveaux du problème Thamoudéen', *Studia Islamica* 5, 1956, 5–17 (points out differences between Thamudic inscriptions of north Arabia and those of south; moderated by A. van den Branden, 'L'Unité de l'alphabet Thamoudéen', *Studia Islamica* 7, 1957, 5–27).

——— 'Les Inscriptions sud-arabes anciennes et les études arabes', *Annali dell'Istituto Orientale di Napoli* 35, 1975, 443–63.

And for the boom in the Near Eastern countryside see:

Di Segni, Leah, 'Epigraphic documentation on building in the provinces of Palaestina and Arabia 4–7th c.', *Journal of Roman Archaeology* suppl. 31, 1999, 149–65.

Foss, Clive, 'The Near Eastern countryside in late antiquity: a review article', *Journal of Roman Archaeology* suppl. 14, 1995, 213–34.

Mayerson, Philip, 'Urbanization in Palaestina Tertia: pilgrims and paradoxes', in *id.*, *Monks, martyrs, soldiers and Saracens*, Jerusalem, IEJ, 1994, 232–45.

Tate, Georges, 'The Syrian countryside during the Roman era', in Susan Alcock, ed., *The early Roman empire in the East*, Oxford, Oxbow, 1997, 55–71.

Vries, Bert de, *Umm el-Jimal: a frontier town and its landscape in northern Jordan*, Portsmouth (RI), Journal of Roman Archaeology, 1998.

INDEX